# Demonology and Devil-lore

Volume 2

Demonology and Devil-lore 2
Author: Moncure Daniel Conway


Cover image: *Belzebub appears in Mandragora smoke,* "Compendium rarissimum totius Artis
Magicae sistematisatae per celeberrimos Artis hujus Magistros" - Germany 1775
Lay-out: www.burokd.nl


ISBN 978-94-92355-16-4

VAMzzz Publishing
P.O. Box 3340
1001 AC Amsterdam
The Netherlands
www.vamzzz.com
contactvamzzz@gmail.com

# DEMONOLOGY
### and DEVIL-LORE 2

Moncure Daniel Conway

VAMzzz PUBLISHING

Moncure Daniel Conway
Stafford County, March 17, 1832 – Paris, November 15, 1907

# contents

## Part IV The Devil

5

A Hebrew Renaissance — Spells — Shelley at Oxford — Book-burning — Japanese ink-devil — Book of Cyprianus — Devil's Bible — Red letters — Dread of Science — Roger Bacon — Luther's Devil — Lutherans and Science

## Chapter XXIV Witchcraft

Minor gods — Saint and Satyr — Tutelaries — Spells — Early Christianity and the poor — Its doctrine as to pagan deities — Mediæval Devils — Devils on the stage — An Abbot's revelations — The fairer deities — Oriental dreams and spirits — Calls for Nemesis — Lilith and her children — Neoplatonicism — Astrology and Alchemy — Devil's College — Shem-hammphorásch — Apollonius of Tyana — Faustus — Black Art Schools — Compacts with the Devil — Blood-covenant — Spirit-seances in old times — The Fairfax delusion — Origin of its devil — Witch, goat, and cat — Confessions of Witches — Witchcraft in New England — Witch trials — Salem demonology — Testing witches — Witch trials in Sweden — Witch Sabbath — Mythological elements — Carriers — Scotch Witches — The cauldron — Vervain — Rue — Invocation of Hecaté — Factors of Witch persecution — Three centuries of massacre — Würzburg horrors — Last victims — Modern Spiritualism

## Chapter XXV Faust and Mephistopheles

Mephisto and Mephitis — The Raven Book — Papal sorcery — Magic seals — Mephistopheles as dog — George Sabellicus *alias* Faustus — The Faust myth — Marlowe's Faust — Good and evil angels — El Magico Prodigioso — Cyprian and Justina — Klinger's Faust — Satan's sermon — Goethe's Mephistopheles — His German characters — Moral scepticism — Devil's gifts — Helena — Redemption through Art — Defeat of Mephistopheles

## Chapter XXVI The Wild Huntsman

The Wild Hunt — Euphemisms — Schimmelreiter — Odinwald — Pied Piper — Lyeshy — Waldemar's Hunt — Palne Hunter — King Abel's Hunt — Lords of Glorup — Le Grand Veneur — Robert le Diable — Arthur — Hugo — Herne — Tregeagle — Der Freischütz — Elijah's chariot — Mahan Bali — Déhak — Nimrod — Nimrod's defiance of Jehovah — His Tower — Robber Knights — The Devil in Leipzig — Olaf hunting pagans — Hunting-horns — Raven — Boar — Hounds — Horse — Dapplegrimm — Sleipnir — Horseflesh — The mare Chetiya — Stags — St. Hubert — The White Lady — Myths of Mother Rose — Wodan hunting St. Walpurga — Friar Eckhardt

## Post Scriptum

Volume II

# Part IV
# The Devil

# Chapter I
## Diabolism

'WE ARE ALL nothing other than Wills,' says St. Augustine; and he adds that of the good and bad angels the nature is the same, the will different. In harmony with this John Beaumont says, 'A good desire of mind is a good God.' [1] To which all the mythology of Evil adds, a bad desire of mind is a Devil. Every personification of an evil Will looks beyond the outward phenomena of pain, and conceives a heart that loves evil, a spirit that makes for wickedness. At this point a new element altogether enters. The physical pain incidentally represented by the Demon, generalised and organised into a principle of harmfulness in the Dragon, begins now to pass under the shadow cast by the ascending light of man's moral nature. Man becomes conscious of moral and spiritual pains: they may be still imaginatively connected with bodily agonies, but these drop out of the immediate conception, disappear into a distant future, and are even replaced by the notion of an evil symbolised by pleasure.

The fundamental difference between either a Demon or Dragon and a Devil may be recognised in this: we never find the former voluntarily bestowing physical pleasure or happiness on man, whereas it is a chief part of the notion of a Devil that he often confers earthly favours in order to corrupt the moral nature.

There are, indeed, apparent exceptions to this theorem presented in the agatho-dragons which have already been considered in our chapter on the Basilisk; but the reader will observe that there is no intimation in such myths of any malign ulterior purpose in the good omens brought by those exceptional monsters, and that they are really forms of malevolent power whose afflictive intent is supposed to have been vanquished by the superior might of the heroes or saints to whose glory they are reluctantly compelled to become tributary.

Undoubtedly the Dragon attended this moral and religious development of man's inward nature very far, and still occupies, as at once prisoner and gaoler in the underworld, a subordinate relation to it. In the long process he has undergone certain transformations, and in particular his attribute of wings, if not derived from the notion of his struggle against holier beings, seems to have been largely enhanced thereby. The exceptional wings given to serpents in Greek art, those, for instance, which draw Demeter and Persephone in their chariot, are trifling as compared with the fully-developed wings of our conventional Dragon of the christian era. Such wings might have been developed occasionally to denote the flying cloud, the fire-breathing storm, or explain how some Ráhu was enabled to pursue the sun and moon and swallow them temporarily in the phenomena of eclipse. But these wings grew to more important dimensions when they were caught up into the Semitic conception of winged genii and destroying angels, and associated with an ambitious assault on heaven and its divine or angelic occupants.

'There was war in Heaven,' says the Apocalypse. The traditional descriptions of this war follow pretty closely, in dramatic details, other and more ancient struggles which reflect man's encounters with the hardships of nature. In those encounters man imagined the gods descending earthward to mingle in the fray; but even where the struggle mounted highest the scenery is mainly terrestrial and the issues those of place and power, the dominion of visible Light established above Darkness, or of a comparatively civilised over a savage race. The wars between the Devas and Asuras in India, the Devs and Ahuras in Persia, Buddha and the Nagas in Ceylon, Garúra and the Serpent-men in the north of India, gods and Frost-giants in Scandinavia, still concern man's relation to the fruits of the earth, to heat and frost, to darkness or storm and sunshine.

But some of these at length find versions which reveal their tendency towards spiritualisation. The differences presented by one of these legends which has survived among us in nearly its ancient form from the same which remains in a partly mystical form will illustrate the transitional phase. Thus, Garúra expelling the serpents from his realm in India is not a saintly legend; this exterminator of serpents is said to have compelled the reptile race to send him one of their number daily that he might eat it, and the rationalised tradition interprets this as the prince's cannibalism. The expulsion of Nagas or serpents from Ceylon by Buddha, in order that he might consecrate that island to the holy law, marks the pious accentuation of the fable. The expulsion of snakes from Ireland by St. Patrick is a legend conceived in the spirit of the curse pronounced upon the serpent in Eden, but in this case the modern myth is the more primitive morally, and more nearly represents the exploit of Garúra. St. Patrick expels the snakes that he may make Ireland a paradise physically, and establish his reputation as an apostle by fulfilling the signs of one named by Christ;[2] and in this particular it slightly rises above the Hindu story. In the case of the serpent cursed in Eden a further moralisation of the conflict is shown. The serpent is not present in Eden, as in the realms of Garúra and St. Patrick, for purposes of physical devastation or pain, but to bestow a pleasure on man with a view to success in a further issue between himself and the deity. Yet in this Eden myth the ancient combat is not yet fairly spiritualised; for the issue still relates, as in that between the Devas and Asuras, to the possession of a magical fruit which by no means confers sanctity. In the apocalyptic legend of the war in heaven,[3] the legend has become fairly spiritualised. The issue is no longer terrestrial, it is no longer for mere power; the Dragon is arrayed against the woman and child, and against the spiritual 'salvation' of mankind, of whom he is 'accuser' and 'deceiver.'

Surely nobody could be 'deceived' by 'a great fiery-red Dragon, having seven heads and ten horns'! In this vision the Dragon is pressed as far as the form can go in the symbolisation of evil. To devour the child is its legitimate work, but as 'accuser of the brethren before God day and night' the monstrous shape were surely out of place by any mythologic analogy; and one could hardly imagine such a physiognomy capable of deceiving 'the whole world.' It is not wonderful, therefore, that the Dragon's presence in heaven is only mentioned in connection with his fall from it. It is significant that the wings are lost in this fall; for while his 'angelic' relationship suggests the previous wings, the woman is able to escape the fallen monster by the two wings given her.[4] Wingless now, 'the old serpent' once more, the monster's shape has no adaptation to the moral and religious struggle which is to ensue. For his shape is a method, and it means the perfection of brute force. That, indeed, also remains in the sequel of this magnificent myth. As in the legend of the Hydra two heads spring up in place of that which falls, so in this Christian legend out of the overthrown monster, henceforth himself concealed, two arise from his inspiration,—the seven-headed, ten-horned Beast who continues the work of wrath and pain; but also a lamb-like Beast, with only two horns (far less terrible), and able to deceive by his miracles, for he is even able to call down fire from heaven. The ancient Serpent-dragon, the expression of natural pain, thus goes to pieces. His older part remains to work mischief and hurt; and the cry is uttered, 'Be merry, ye heavens, and ye that tabernacle in them: woe to the earth and the sea! for the devil is come down unto you, having great wrath because he knows that he has a short time.'[5] But there is a lamb-like part of him too, and his relation to the Dragon is only known by his voice.

This subtle adaptation of the symbol of external pain to the representation of the moral struggle, wherein the hostile power may assume deceptive forms of beauty and pleasure, is only one impressive illustration of the transfer of human conceptions of evil from outward to inward nature. The transition is from a malevolent, fatal, principle of harmfulness to the body to a malevolent, fatal, principle of evil to the conscience. The Demon was natural; the Dragon was both physical and metaphysical; the Devil was and is theological. In the primitive Zoroastrian theology, where the Devil first appears in clear definition, he is the opponent of the Good Mind, and the combat between the two, Ormuzd and Ahriman, is the spiritualisation of the combat between Light and Darkness, Pain and Happiness, in the external world. As these visible antagonists were supposed to be exactly balanced against each other, so are their spiritual correlatives. The Two Minds are described as Twins.

'Those old Spirits, who are twins, made known what is good and what is evil in thoughts, words, and deeds. Those who are good distinguished between the two; not so those who are evil-doers.

'When these two Spirits came together they made first life and death, so that there should be at last the most wretched life for the bad, but for the good blessedness.

'Of these two Spirits the evil one chose the worst deeds; the kind Spirit, he whose garment is the immovable sky, chose what is right.'[6]

This metaphysical theory follows closely the primitive scientific observations on which it is based; it is the cold of the cold, the gloom of the darkness, the sting of death, translated into some order for the intellect which, having passed through the Dragon, we find appearing in this Persian Devil; and against his blackness the glory of the personality from whom all good things proceed shines out in a splendour no longer marred by association with the evil side of nature. Ormuzd is celebrated as 'father of the *pure* world,' who sustains 'the earth and the clouds that they do not fall,' and 'has made the *kindly* light and the darkness, the kindly sleep and the awaking;'[7]

at every step being suggested the father of the *impure* world, the *unkindly* light, darkness or sleep.

The ecstasy which attended man's first vision of an ideal life defied the contradictory facts of outward and inward nature. So soon as he had beheld a purer image of himself rising above his own animalism, he must not only regard that animalism as an instigation of a devil, but also the like of it in nature; and this conception will proceed *pari passu* with the creation of pure deities in the image of that higher self. There was as yet no philosophy demanding unity in the Cosmos, or forbidding man to hold as accursed so much of nature as did not obviously accord with his ideals.

Mr. Edward B. Tylor has traced the growth of Animism from man's shadow and his breathing; Sir John Lubbock has traced the influence of dreams in forming around him a ghostly world; Mr. Herbert Spencer has given an analysis of the probable processes by which this invisible environment was shaped for the mental conception in accordance with family and social conditions. But it is necessary that we should here recognise the shadow that walked by the moral nature, the breathings of religious aspiration, and the dreams which visited a man whose moral sense was so generally at variance with his animal desires. The code established for the common good, while necessarily having a relation to every individual conscience, is a restriction upon individual liberty. The conflict between selfishness and duty is thus inaugurated; it continues in the struggle between the 'law in the members and the law in the spirit,' which led Paul to beat his body (ὑπωπιαζομαί) to keep it in subjection; it passes from the Latin poet to the Englishman, who turns his experience to a rune—

I see the right, and I approve it too;
Condemn the wrong, and yet the wrong pursue.

As the light which cast it was intense, even so intense was the shadow it cast beneath all it could not penetrate. Passionate as was the saintliest man's love of good, even so passionate was his spiritual enemy's love of evil. High as was the azure vault that mingled with his dreams of purity, so deep was the abyss beneath his lower nature. The superficial equalities of phenomena, painful and pleasurable, to his animal nature had cast the mould into which his theories of the inward and the moral phenomena must be cast; and thus man—in an august moment—surrendered himself to the dreadful conception of a supreme Principle of Wickedness: wherever good was there stood its adversary; wherever truth, there its denier; no light shone without the dark presence that would quench it; innocence had its official accuser, virtue its accomplished tempter, peace its breaker, faith its disturber and mocker. Nay, to this impersonation was added the last feature of fiendishness, a nature which found its supreme satisfaction in ultimately torturing human beings for the sins insti-gated by himself.

It is open to question how far any average of mankind really conceived this theological dogma. Easy as it is to put into clear verbal statement; readily as the analogies of nature supply arguments for and illustrations of a balance between moral light and darkness, love and hatred; yet is man limited in subjective conceptions to his own possibilities, and it may almost be said that to genuinely believe in an absolute Fiend a man would have to be potentially one himself. But any human being, animated by causeless and purposeless desire to inflict pain on others, would be universally regarded as insane, much more one who would without motive corrupt as well as afflict.

Even theological statements of the personality of Evil, and what that implies, are rare. The following is brave enough to be put on record, apart from its suggestiveness.

'It cannot be denied that as there is an inspiration of holy love, so is there an inspiration of hatred, or frantic pleasure, with which men surrender themselves to the impulses of destructiveness; and when the popular language speaks of possessions of Satan, of incarnate devils, there lies at the bottom of this the grave truth that men, by continued sinning, may pass the ordinary limit between human and diabolic depravity, and lay open in themselves a deep abyss of hatred which, without any mixture of self-interest, finds its gratification in devastation and woe.'[8]

On this it may be said that the popular commentary on cases of the kind is contained in the very phrase alluded to, 'possession,'—the implication being that such disinterested depravity is nowise possible within the range of simple human experience,—and, in modern times, 'possessions' are treated in asylums. Morbid conditions, however, are of such varied degrees that it is probable many have imagined a Being in whom their worst impulses are unrestrained, and thus there have been sufficient popular approximations to an imaginative conception of a Devil to enable the theological dogma, which few can analyse, to survive.

It must not be supposed, however, that the moral and spiritual ideals, to which allusion has just been made, are normally represented in the various Devils which we have to consider. It is the characteristic of personifications, whether celestial or infernal, to supersede gradually the ideas out of which they spring. As in the fable of Agni, who is said to have devoured his parents when he was born, a metaphor of fire consuming the two sticks which produce it, religious history shows both deities and devils, by the flame of personal devotion or hatred they engender, burning up the ideas that originate them. When instead of unconscious forces and inanimate laws working to results called good and evil, men see great personal Wills engaged in personal conflict, the universe becomes a government of combat; the stars of heaven, the angels and the imps, men and women, the very plants and animals, are caught up in the battle, to be marshalled on one side or the other; and in the military spirit and fury of the struggle the spiritual ideals become as insignificant beneath the phantom-hosts they evoked as the violets and daisies which an army tramples in its march. There is little difference at last between the moral characteristics of the respective armies of Ormuzd and Ahriman, Michael and Satan; their strategy and ferocity are the same.[9] Wherever the conception is that of a universe divided into hostile camps, the appropriate passions are kindled, and in the thick of the field, where Cruelty and Gentleness met, is seen at last a horned Beast confronted by a horned Lamb.[10] On both sides is exaltation of the horn.

We need only look at the outcome of the gentle and lowly Jesus through the exigencies of the church militant to see how potent are such forces. Although lay Christians of ordinary education are accustomed to rationalise their dogmas as well as they can, and dwell on the loving and patient characteristics of Jesus, the horns which were attached to the brow of him who said, 'Love your enemies' by ages of Christian warfare remain still in the Christ of Theology, and they are still depended on to overawe the 'sinner.' In an orthodox family with which I have had some acquaintance, a little boy, who had used naughty expressions of resentment towards a playmate was admonished that he should be more like Christ, 'who never did any harm to his enemies.' 'No,' answered the wrathful child, 'but he's a-going to.'

As in Demonology we trace the struggles of man with external obstructions, and the phantasms in which these were reflected until they were understood or surmounted, we have now to consider the forms which report human progression on a higher plane,—that of social, moral, and religious evolution. Creations of a crude Theology, in its attempt to interpret the moral sentiment, the Devils to which we now turn our attention have multiplied as the various interests of mankind have come into relations with their conscience. Every degree of ascent of the moral nature has been marked by innumerable new shadows cast athwart the mind and the life of man. Every new heaven of ideas is followed by a new earth, but ere this conformity of things to thoughts can take place struggles must come and the old demons will be recalled for new service. As time goes on things new grow old; the fresh issues pass away, their battlefields grow cold; then the brood of superstition must flit away to the next field where carrion is found. Foul and repulsive as are these vultures of the mind—organisms of moral sewage—every one of them is a witness to the victories of mankind over the evils they shadow, and to the steady advance of a new earth which supplies them no habitat but the archæologist's page.

## NOTES

1 'Treatise of Spirits.' By John Beaumont, Gent. London, 1705.
2 Luke x. 19.
3 Rev. xii.
4 Rev. xii. cf. verses 4, 9 and 14.
5 Rev. xii. 12.
6 'Zendavesta,' Yaçna xxx.; Max Müller, 'Science of Religion,' p. 238.
7 Yaçna xliii.
8 'Die Christliche Lehre von der Sünde.' Von Julius Müller, Breslau, 1844, i. 193.
9 'Ormazd brought help to me; by the grace of Ormazd my troops entirely defeated the rebel army and took Sitratachmes, and brought him before me. Then I cut off his nose and his ears, and I scourged him. He was kept chained at my door. All the kingdom beheld him. Afterwards I crucified him at Arbela.' So says the tablet of Darius Hystaspes. But what could Darius have done 'by the grace of Ahriman'?
10 Cf. Rev. v. 6 and xii. 15.

# Chapter II
## The Second Best

Respect for the Devil — Primitive atheism — Idealisation — Birth of new gods —
New gods diabolised — Compromise between new gods and old —
Foreign deities degraded — Their utilisation

A LADY RESIDING in Hampshire, England, recently said to a friend of the present writer, both being mothers, 'Do you make your children bow their heads whenever they mention the Devil's name? I do,' she added solemnly,—'I think it's safer.'

This instance of reverence for the Devil's name, occurring in a respectable English family, may excite a smile; but if my reader has perused the third and fourth chapters (Part I.) of this work, in which it was necessary to state certain facts and principles which underlie the phenomena of degradation in both Demonology and Devil-lore, he will already know the high significance of nearly all the names which have invested the personifications of evil; and he will not be surprised to find their original sanctity, though lowered, sometimes, surviving in such imaginary forms after the battles in which they were vanquished have passed out of all contemporary interest. If, for example, instead of the Devil, whose name is uttered with respect in the Hampshire household, any theological bogey of our own time were there mentioned, such as 'Atheist,' it might hardly receive such considerate treatment.

The two chapters just referred to anticipate much that should

25

be considered at this point of our inquiry. It is only necessary here to supplement them with a brief statement, and to some extent a recapitulation, of the processes by which degraded deities are preserved to continue through a structural development and fulfil a necessary part in every theological scheme which includes the conception of an eternal difference between good and evil.

Every personification when it first appears expresses a higher and larger view. When deities representing the physical needs of mankind have failed, as they necessarily must, to meet those needs, atheism follows, though it cannot for a long time find philosophical expression. It is an atheism *ad hoc*, so to say, and works by degrading particular gods instead of by constructing antitheistic theories. Successive dynasties of deities arise and flourish in this way, each representing a less arbitrary relation to nature,—peril lying in that direction,—and a higher moral and spiritual ideal, this being the stronghold of deities. It is obvious that it is far easier to maintain the theory that prayers are heard and answered by a deity if those prayers are limited to spiritual requests, than when they are petitions for outward benefits. By giving over the cruel and remorseless forces of nature to the Devil,—*i.e.*, to this or that personification of them who, as gods, had been appealed to in vain to soften such forces,—the more spiritual god that follows gains in security as well as beauty what he surrenders of empire and omnipotence. This law, illustrated in our chapter on Fate, operates with tremendous effect upon the conditions under which the old combat is spiritualised.

An eloquent preacher has said:—'Hawthorne's fine fancy of the youth who ascribed heroic qualities to the stone face on the brow of a cliff, thus converting the rocky profile into a man, and, by dint of meditating on it with admiring awe, actually transferred to himself the moral elements he worshipped, has been made fact a thousand times, is made fact every day, by earnest spirits who by faithful longing turn their visions into verities, and obtain live answers to their petitions to shadows."[1]

However imaginary may be the benedictions so derived by the worshipper from his image, they are most real as they redound to the glory and power of the image. The crudest personification, gathering up the sanctities of generations, associated with the holiest hopes, the best emotions, the profoundest aspirations of human nature, may be at length so identified with these sentiments that they all seem absolutely dependent upon the image they invest. Every criticism of such a personification then seems like a blow aimed at the moral laws. If educated men are still found in Christendom discussing whether morality can survive the overthrow of such personifications, and whether life were worth living without them, we may readily understand how in times when the social, ethical, and psychological sciences did not exist at all, all that human beings valued seemed destined to stand or fall with the Person supposed to be their only keystone.

But no Personage, however highly throned, can arrest the sun and moon, or the mind and life of humanity. With every advance in physical or social conditions moral elements must be influenced; every new combination involves a recast of experiences, and presently of convictions. Henceforth the deified image can only remain as a tyrant over the heart and brain which have created it,—

Creatura a un tempo
E tiranno de l'uom, da cui soltanto
Ebbe nomi ed aspetti e regno e altari.[2]

This personification, thus 'at once man's creature and his tyrant,' is objectively a name. But as it has been invested with all that
has been most sacred, it is inevitable that any name raised against
it shall be equally associated with all that has been considered bas-
est. This also must be personified, for the same reason that the
good is personified; and as names are chiefly hereditary, it pretty
generally happens that the title of some fallen and discredited deity
is advanced to receive the new anathema. But what else does he receive? The new ideas; the growing ideals and the fresh enthusiasms
are associated with some fantastic shape with anathematised name
evoked from the past, and thus a portentous situation is reached.
The worshippers of the new image will not accept the bad name and
its base associations; they even grow strong enough to claim the
name and altars of the existing order, and give battle for the same.
Then occurs the demoralisation, literally speaking, of the older theology. The personification reduced to struggle for its existence can
no longer lay emphasis upon the moral principles it had embodied,
these being equally possessed by their opponents; nay, its parti-
sans manage to associate with their holy Name so much bigotry
and cruelty that the innovators are at length willing to resign it. The
personal loyalty, which is found to continue after loyalty to principles has ceased, proceeds to degrade the virtues once reverenced
when they are found connected with a rival name. 'He casteth out
devils through Beelzebub' is a very ancient cry. It was heard again

when Tertullian said, 'Satan is God's ape.' St. Augustine recognises the similarity between the observances of Christians and pagans as proving the subtle imitativeness of the Devil; the phenomena referred to are considered elsewhere, but, in the present connection, it may be remarked that this readiness to regard the same sacrament as supremely holy or supremely diabolical as it is celebrated in honour of one name or another, accords closely with the reverence or detestation of things more important than sacraments, as they are, or are not, consecrated by what each theology deems official sanction. When sects talk of 'mere morality' we may recognise in the phrase the last faint war-cry of a god from whom the spiritual ideal has passed away, and whose name even can survive only through alliance with the new claimant of his altars. While the new gods were being called devils the old ones were becoming such.

The victory of the new ideal turns the old one to an idol. But we are considering a phase of the world when superstition must invest the new as well as the old, though in a weaker degree. A new religious system prevails chiefly through its moral superiority to that it supersedes; but when it has succeeded to the temples and altars consecrated to previous divinities, when the ardour of battle is over and conciliation becomes a policy as well as a virtue, the old idol is likely to be treated with respect, and may not impossibly be brought into friendly relation with its victorious adversary. He may take his place as 'the second best,' to borrow Goethe's phrase, and be assigned some function in the new theologic régime. Thus, behind the simplicity of the Hampshire lady instructing her children to bow at mention of the Devil's name, stretch the centuries in which

Christian divines have as warmly defended the existence of Satan as that of God himself. With sufficient reason: that infernal being, some time God's 'ape' and rival, was necessarily developed into his present position and office of agent and executioner under the divine government. He is the great Second Best; and it is a strange hallucination to fancy that, in an age of peaceful inquiry, any divine personification can be maintained without this patient Goat, who bears blame for all the faults of nature, and who relieves divine Love from the odium of supplying that fear which is the mother of devotion,—at least in the many millions of illogical eyes into which priests can still look without laughing.

Such, in brief outline, has been the interaction of moral and intellectual forces operating within the limits of established systems, and of the nations governed by them. But there are added factors, intensifying the forces on each side, when alien are brought into rivalry and collision with national deities. In such a contest, besides the moral and spiritual sentiments and the household sanctities, which have become intertwined with the internal deities, national pride is also enlisted, and patriotism. But on the other side is enlisted the charm of novelty, and the consciousness of fault and failure in the home system. Every system imported to a foreign land leaves behind its practical shortcomings, puts its best foot forward—namely, its theoretical foot—and has the advantage of suggesting a way of escape from the existing routine which has become oppressive. Napoleon I. said that no people profoundly attached to the institutions of their country can be conquered; but what people are attached to the priestly system over them? That internal dissatisfaction which, in secular government, gives welcome to a dashing Corsican or a Prince of Orange, has been the means of introducing many an alien religion, and giving to many a prophet the honour denied him in his own country. Buddha was a Hindu, but the triumph of his religion is not in India; Zoroaster was a Persian, but there are no Parsees in Persia; Christianity is hardly a colonist even in the native land of Christ.

These combinations and changes were not effected without fierce controversies, ferocious wars, or persecutions, and the formation of many devils. Nothing is more normal in ancient systems than the belief that the gods of other nations are devils. The slaughter of the priests of Baal corresponds with the development of their god into Beelzebub. In proportion to the success of Olaf in crushing the worshippers of Odin, their deity is steadily transformed to a diabolical Wild Huntsman. But here also the forces of partial recovery, which we have seen operating in the outcome of internal reform, manifest themselves; the vanquished, and for a time outlawed deity, is, in many cases, subsequently conciliated and given an inferior, and, though hateful, a useful office in the new order. Sometimes, indeed, as in the case of the Hindu destroyer Siva, it is found necessary to assign a god, anathematised beyond all power of whitewash, to an equal rank with the most virtuous deity. Political forces and the exigencies of propagandism work many marvels of this kind, which will meet us in the further stages of our investigation.

Every superseded god who survives in subordination to another is pretty sure to be developed into a Devil. Euphemism may tell pleasant fables about him, priestcraft may find it useful to perpetuate belief in his existence, but all the evils of the universe, which it is inconvenient to explain, are gradually laid upon him, and sink him down, until nothing is left of his former glory but a shining name.

NOTES
1 'Prayer and Work.' By Octavius B. Frothingham. New York, 1877.
2 'Lucifero, Poema di Mario Rapisardi.' Milano, 1877.

## Chapter III
# Ahriman: The Divine Devil

Mr. Irving's impersonation of Superstition — Revolution against pious privilege — Doctrine of 'merits' — Saintly immorality in India — A Pantheon turned Inferno — Zendavesta on Good and Evil — Parsî Mythology — The Combat of Ahriman with Ormuzd — Optimism — Parsî Eschatology — Final Restoration of Ahriman

ANY ONE WHO has witnessed Mr. Henry Irving's scholarly and masterly impersonation of the character of Louis XI. has had an opportunity of recognising a phase of superstition which happily it were now difficult to find off the stage. Nothing could exceed the fine realism with which that artist brought before the spectator the perfected type of a pretended religion from which all moral features have been eliminated by such slow processes that the final success is unconsciously reached, and the horrible result appears unchecked by even any affectation of actual virtue. We see the king at sound of a bell pausing in his instructions for a treacherous assassination to mumble his prayers, and then instantly reverting to the villany over whose prospective success he gloats. In the secrecy of his chamber no mask falls, for there is no mask; the face of superstition and vice on which we look is the real face which the ages of fanaticism have transmitted to him.

Such a face has oftener been that of a nation than that of an individual, for the healthy forces of life work amid the homes and hearts of mankind long before their theories are reached and influenced. Such a face it was against which the moral insurrection which bears the name of Zoroaster arose, seeing it as physiognomy of the Evil Mind, naming it Ahriman, and, in the name of the conscience, aiming at it the blow which is still felt across the centuries.

Ingenious theorists have accounted for the Iranian philosophy of a universal war between Ormuzd (Ahuramazda) the Good, and Ahriman (Angromainyus) the Evil, by vast and terrible climatic changes, involving extremes of heat and cold, of which geologists find traces about Old Iran, from which a colony of Aryans migrated to New Iran, or Persia. But although physical conditions of this character may have supplied many of the metaphors in which the conflict between Good and Evil is described in the Avesta, there are other characteristics of that ancient scripture which render it more probable that the early colonisation of Persia was, like that of New England, the result of a religious struggle. Some of the gods most adored in India reappear as execrated demons in the religion of Zoroaster; the Hindu word for god is the Parsî word for devil. These antagonisms are not merely verbal; they are accompanied in the Avesta with the most furious denunciations of theological opponents, whom it is not difficult to identify with the priests and adherents of the Brahman religion.

The spirit of the early scriptures of India leaves no room for doubt as to the point at which this revolution began. It was against pious Privilege. The saintly hierarchy of India were a caste quite irresponsible to moral laws. The ancient gods, vague names for the powers of nature, were strictly limited in their dispensations to those of their priests;[1] and as to these priests the chief necessities were ample offerings, sacrifices, and fulfilment of the ceremonial ordinances in which their authority was organised, these were the performances rewarded by a reciprocal recognition of authority. To the image of this political régime, theology, always facile, accommodated the regulations of the gods. The moral law can only live by being supreme; and as it was not supreme in the Hindu pantheon, it died out of it. The doctrine of 'merits,' invented by priests purely for their own power, included nothing meritorious, humanly considered; the merits consisted of costly sacrifices, rich offerings to temples, tremendous penances for fictitious sins, ingeniously devised to aggrandise the penances which disguised power, and prolonged austerities that might be comfortably commuted by the wealthy. When this doctrine had obtained general adherence, and was represented by a terrestrial government corresponding to it, the gods were necessarily subject to it. That were only to say that the powers of nature were obedient to the 'merits' of privileged saints; and from this it is an obvious inference that they are relieved from moral laws binding on the vulgar.

The legends which represent this phase of priestly dominion are curiously mixed. It would appear that under the doctrine of 'merits' the old gods declined. Such appears to be the intimation of the stories which report the distress of the gods through the power of human saints. The Rajah Ravana acquired such power that he was said to have arrested the sun and moon, and so oppressed the gods that they temporarily transformed themselves to monkeys in order to destroy him. Though Viswámitra murders a saint, his merits are such that the gods are in great alarm lest they become his menials; and the completeness, with which moral considerations are left out of the struggle on both sides is disclosed in the item that the gods commissioned a nymph to seduce the saintly murderer, and so reduce a little the force of his austerities. It will be remembered that the ancient struggle of the Devas and Asuras was not owing to any moral differences, but to an alleged unfair distribution of the ambrosia produced by their joint labours in churning the ocean. The fact that the gods cheated the demons on that occasion was never supposed to affect the supremacy they acquired by the treachery; and it could, therefore, cause no scandal when later legends reported that the demons were occasionally able to take gods captive by the practice of these wonderful 'merits' which were so independent of morals. One Asura is said to have gained such power in this way that he subjugated the gods, and so punished them that Siva, who had originally endowed that demon, called into being Scanda, a war-god, to defend the tortured deities. The most ludicrous part of all is that the gods themselves were gradually reduced to the necessity of competing like others for these tremendous powers; thus the Bhagavat Purana states that Brahma was enabled to create the universe by previously undergoing penance for sixteen thousand years.

The legends just referred to are puranic, and consequently of much later date than the revolution traceable in the Iranian religion; but these later legends are normal growths from vedic roots. These were the principles of ancient theology, and the foundation of priestly government. In view of them we need not wonder that Hindu theology devised no special devil; almost any of its gods might answer the purposes of one. Nor need we be surprised that it had no particular hell; any society organised by the sanctions of religion, but irresponsible to its moral laws, would render it unnecessary to look far for a hell.

From this cosmological chaos the more intelligent Hindus were of course liberated; but the degree to which the fearful training had corrupted the moral tissues of those who had been subjected to it was revealed in the bald principle of their philosophers, that the superstition must continue to be imposed on the vulgar, whilst the learned might turn all the gods into a scientific terminology.

The first clear and truthful eye that touched that system would transform it from a Heaven to an Inferno. So was it changed under the eye of Zoroaster. That ancient pantheon which had become a refuge for all the lies of the known world; whose gods were liars and their supporters liars; was now turned into a realm of organised disorder, of systematised wrong; a vast creation of wickedness, at whose centre sat its creator and inspirer, the immoral god, the divine devil—Ahriman.

It is indeed impossible to ascertain how far the revolt against the old Brahmanic system was political. It is, of course, highly improbable that any merely speculative system would excite a revolution; but at the same time it must be remembered that, in early days, an importance was generally attached to even abstract opinions such as we still find among the superstitious who regard an atheistic sentiment as worse than a theft. However this may have been, the Avesta does not leave us in any doubt as to the main fact,—namely, that at a certain time and place man came to a point where he had to confront antagonism to fundamental moral principles, and that he found the so-called gods against him. In the establishment of those principles priests recognised their own disestablishment. What those moral laws that had become necessary to society were is also made clear. 'We worship the Pure, the Lord of Purity!' 'We honour the good spirit, the good kingdom, the good law,—all that is good.' 'Evil doctrine shall not again destroy the world.' 'Good is the thought, good the word, good the deed, of the pure Zarathustra.' 'In the beginning the two heavenly Ones spoke—the Good to the Evil—thus: Our souls, doctrines, words, works, do not unite together.' These sentences are from the oldest Gâthâs of the Avesta.

The following is a very ancient Gâthâ:—'All your Devas (Hindu 'gods') are only manifold children of the Evil Mind, and the great One who worships the Saoma of lies and deceits; besides the treacherous acts for which you are notorious in the Seven Regions of the earth. You have invented all the evil that men speak and do, which is indeed pleasant to the Devas, and is devoid of all goodness, and therefore perishes before the insight of the truth of the wise. Thus you defraud men of their good minds and of their immortality by your evil minds—as well by those of the Devas as through that of the Evil Spirit—through evil deeds and evil words, whereby the power of liars grows.

> '1. Come near, and listen to the wise sayings of the omniscient, the songs in praise of the Living One, and the prayers of the Good Spirit, the glorious truths whose origin is seen in the flames.
> '2. Listen, therefore, to the Earth spirit—Look at the flames with reverent mind. Every one, man and woman, is to be distinguished according to his belief. Ye ancient Powers, watch and be with us!

'3. From the beginning there were two Spirits, each active in itself. They are the good and the bad in thought, word, and deed. Choose ye between them: do good, not evil!

'4. And these two Spirits meet and create the first existence, the earthy, that which is and that which is not, and the last, the spiritual. The worst existence is for the liars, the best for the truthful.

'5. Of these two spirits choose ye one, either the lying, the worker of Evil, or the true holiest spirit. Whoso chooses the first chooses the hardest fate; whoso the last, honours Ahuramazda in faith and in truth by his deeds.

'6. Ye cannot serve both of these two. An evil spirit whom we will destroy surprises those who deliberate, saying, Choose the Evil Mind! Then do those spirits gather in troops to attack the two lives of which the prophets prophesy.

'7. And to this earthly life came Armaiti with earthly power to help the truth, and the good disposition: she, the Eternal, created the material world, but the Spirit is with thee, O Wise One! the first of creations in time.

'8. When any evil falls upon the spirit, thou, O Wise One, givest temporal possessions and a good disposition; but him whose promises are lies, and not truth, thou punishest.'

Around the hymns of the Avesta gradually grew a theology and a mythology which were destined to exert a powerful influence on the world. These are contained in the Bundehesch.[2] Anterior to all things and all beings was Zeruane-Akrene ('Boundless Time'), so exalted that he can only be worshipped in silence. From him emanated two Ferouers, spiritual types, which took form in two beings, Ormuzd and Ahriman. These were equally pure; but Ahriman became jealous of his first-born brother, Ormuzd. To punish Ahriman for his evil feeling, the Supreme Being condemned him to 12,000 years' imprisonment in an empire of rayless Darkness. During that period must rage the conflict between Light and Darkness, Good and Evil.

As Ormuzd had his pre-existing type or Ferouer, so by a similar power—much the same as the Platonic Logos or Word—he created the pure or spiritual world, by means of which the empire of Ahriman should be overthrown. On the earth (still spiritual) he raised the exceeding high mountain Albordj, Elburz (snow mountain),[3] on whose summit he fixed his throne; whence he stretched the bridge Chinevat, which, passing directly over Duzhak, the abyss of Ahriman (or hell), reaches to the portal of Gorodman, or heaven. All this was but a Ferouer world—a prototype of the material world. In anticipation of its incorporation in a material creation, Ormuzd (by emanations) created in his own image six Amshaspands, or agents, of both sexes, to be models of perfection to lower spirits—and to mankind, when they should be created—and offer up their prayers to himself. The second series of emanations were the Izeds, benevolent genii and guardians of the world, twenty-eight in number, of whom the chief is Mithras, the Mediator. The third series of emanations were the innumerable Ferouers of things and men—for each must have its *soul*, which shall purify them in the day of resurrection. In antagonism to all these, Ahriman produced an exactly similar host of dark and evil powers. These Devas rise, rank on rank, to their Arch-Devs—each of whom is chained to his planet—and their head is Ash-Mogh, the 'two-footed serpent of lies,' who seems to correspond to Mithras, the divine Mediator.

After a reign of 3000 years Ormuzd entered on the work of realising his spiritual emanations in a material universe. He formed the sun as commander-in-chief, the moon as his lieutenant, the planets as captains of a great host—the stars—who were soldiers in his war against Ahriman. The dog Sirius he set to watch at the bridge Chinevat (the Milky Way), lest thereby Ahriman should scale the heavens. Ormuzd then created earth and water, which Ahriman did not try to prevent, knowing that darkness was inherent in these. But he struck a blow when life was produced. This was in form of a Bull, and Ahriman entered it and it perished; but on its destruction there came out of its left shoulder the seed of all clean and gentle animals, and, out of its right shoulder—Man.

Ahriman had matched every creation thus far; but to make man was beyond his power, and he had no recourse but to destroy him. However, when the original man was destroyed, there sprang from his body a tree which bore the first human pair, whom Ahriman, however, corrupted in the manner elsewhere described.

It is a very notable characteristic of this Iranian theology, that although the forces of good and evil are co-extensive and formally balanced, in potency they are not quite equal. The balance of force is just a little on the side of the Good Spirit. And this advantage appears in man. Zoroaster said, 'No earthly man with a hundredfold strength does so much evil as Mithra with heavenly strength does good;' and this thought reappears in the Parsî belief that the one part of paradisiac purity, which man retained after his fall, balances the ninety-nine parts won by Ahriman, and in the end will redeem him. For this one divine ray preserved enables him to receive and obey the Avesta, and to climb to heaven by the stairway of three vast steps—pure thought, pure word, pure deed. The optimistic essence of the mythology is further shown in the belief that every destructive effort of Ahriman resulted in a larger benefit than Ormuzd had created. The Bull (Life) destroyed, man and animal sprang into being; the man destroyed, man and woman appeared. And so on to the end. In the last quarter of the 12,000 years for which Ahriman was condemned, he rises to greater power even than Ormuzd, and finally he will, by a fiery comet, set the visible universe in conflagration; but while this scheme is waxing to consummation Ormuzd will send his holy Prophet Sosioch, who will convert mankind to the true law,[4] so that when Ahriman's comet consumes the earth he will really be purifying it. Through the vast stream of melted metals and minerals the righteous shall pass, and to them it will be as a bath of warm milk: the wicked in attempting to pass shall be swept into the abyss of Duzhak; having then suffered three days and nights, they shall be raised by Ormuzd refined and purified. Duzhak itself shall be purified by this fire, and last of all Ahriman himself shall ascend to his original purity and happiness. Then from the ashes of the former world shall bloom a paradise that shall remain for ever.

In this system it is notable that we find the monster serpent of vedic mythology, Ahi, transformed into an infernal region, Duzhak. The dragon, being a type of physical suffering, passes away in Iranian as in the later Semitic mythology before the new form, which represents the stings of conscience though it may be beneath external pleasure. In this respect, therefore, Ahriman fulfils the definition of a devil already given. In the Avesta he fulfils also another condition essential to a devil, the love of evil in and for itself. But in the later theology it will be observed that evil in Ahriman is not organic. The war being over and its fury past, the hostile chief is seen not so black as he had been painted; the belief obtains that he does not actually love darkness and evil. He was thrust into them as a punishment for his jealousy, pride, and destructive ambition. And because that dark kingdom was a punishment—therefore not congenial—it was at length (the danger past) held to be disciplinary. Growing faith in the real supremacy of Good discovers the immoral god to be an exaggerated anthropomorphic egoist; this divine devil is a self-centred potentate who had attempted to subordinate moral law and human welfare to his personal ascendancy. His fate having sealed the sentence on all ambitions of that character, humanity is able to pardon the individual offender, and find a hope that Ahriman, having learned that no real satisfaction for a divine nature can be found in mere power detached from rectitude, will join in the harmony of love and loyalty at last.

---

NOTES

1   E quanto ebbe e mantiene a l'uom soltanto
    Il deve, a l'uom che d'oqui sue destino
    O prospero, o maligno, arbitro e solo.
    'Whatever he (God) had, he owed to man alone, to man who, for good or ill, is sole arbiter of his own fate.'—Rapisardi's Lucifero.
2   The following abridgment mainly follows that of James Freeman Clarke in his 'Ten Great Religions.'
3   White or Snowy Mountain. Cf. Alp, Elf, &c.
4   'Elias shall first come and restore all things.'

# Chapter IV
## Viswámitra: The Theocratic Devil

Priestcraft and Pessimism — An Aryan Tetzel and his Luther — Brahman Frogs
— Evolution of the sacerdotal Saint — Viswámitra the Accuser of Virtue —
The Tamil Passion-play 'Hariśchandra' — Ordeal of Goblins — The Martyr of
Truth — Virtue triumphant over ceremonial 'merits' — Hariśchandra and Job

**PRIESTCRAFT IN GOVERNMENT** means pessimism in the creed and despair in the heart. Under sacerdotal rule in India it seemed paradise enough to leave the world, and the only hell dreaded was a return to it. 'The twice-born man,' says Manu, 'who shall without intermission have passed the time of his studentship, shall ascend after death to the most exalted of regions, and no more spring to birth again in this lower world.' Some clause was necessary to keep the twice-born man from suicide. Buddha invented a plan of suicide-in-life combined with annihilation of the gods, which was driven out of India because it put into the minds of the people the philosophy of the schools. Thought could only be trusted among classes interested to conceal it.

The power and authority of a priesthood can only be maintained on the doctrine that man is 'saved' by the deeds of a ceremonial law; any general belief that morality is more acceptable to gods than ceremonies must be fatal to those occult and fictitious virtues which hedge about every pious impostor. Sacerdotal power in India depended on superstitions carefully fostered concerning the mystical properties of a stimulating juice (soma), litanies, invocations, and benedictions by priests; upon sacrifices to the gods, including their priests, austerities, penances, pilgrimages, and the like; one characteristic running through all the performances—their utter worthlessness to any being in the universe except the priest. An artificial system of this kind has to create its own materials, and evoke forces of evolution from many regions of nature. It is a process requiring much more than the wisdom of the serpent and more than its harmfulness; and there is a bit of nature's irony in the fact that when the Brahman Rishi gained supremacy, the Cobra was also worshipped as belonging to precisely the same caste and sanctity.

There are traces of long and fierce struggles preceding this consummation. Even in the Vedic age—in the very dawn of religious history—Tetzel appears with his indulgences and Luther confronts him. The names they bore in ancient India were Viswámitra and Vasishtha. Both of these were among the seven powerful Rishis who made the hierarchy of India in the earliest age known to us. Both were composers of some of the chief hymns of the Vedas, and their respective hymns bear the stamp of the sacerdotal and the anti-sacerdotal parties which contended before the priestly sway had reached its complete triumph. Viswámitra was champion of the high priestly party and its political pretensions. In the Rig-Veda there are forty hymns ascribed to him and his family, nearly all of which celebrate the divine virtues of Soma-juice and the Soma-sacrifice. As the exaltation of the priestly caste in Israel was connected with a miracle, in which the Jordan stopped flowing till the ark had been carried over, so the rivers Sutledge and Reyah were said to have rested from their course when Viswámitra wished to cross them in seeking the Soma. This Rishi became identified in the Hindu mind for all time with political priestcraft. On the other hand, Vasishtha became equally famous for his hostility to that power, as well as for his profoundly religious character,—the finest hymns of the Vedas, as to moral feeling, being those that bear his name. The anti-sacerdotal spirit of Vasishtha is especially revealed in a strange satirical hymn in which he ridicules the ceremonial Bráhmans under the guise of a panegyric on frogs. In this composition occur such verses as these:—

'Like Bráhmans at the Soma-sacrifice of Atirâtra, sitting round a full pond and talking, you, O frogs, celebrate this day of the year when the rainy season begins.
'These Bráhmans, with their Soma, have had their say, performing the annual rite. These Adhwaryus, sweating while they carry the hot pots, pop out like hermits.
'They have always observed the order of the gods as they are to be worshipped in the twelvemonth; these men do not neglect their season....
'Cow-noise gave, Goat-noise gave, the Brown gave, and the Green gave us treasures. The frogs, who give us hundreds of cows, lengthened our life in the rich autumn.' [1]

Viswámitra and Vasishtha appear to have been powerful rivals in seeking the confidence of King Sudás, and from their varying fortunes came the tremendous feud between them which plays so large a part in the traditions of India. The men were both priests, as are both ritualists and broad-churchmen in the present day. They were borne on the stream of mythologic evolution to representative regions very different from any they could have contemplated. Vasishtha, ennobled by the moral sentiment of ages, appears as the genius of truth and justice, maintaining these as of more 'merit' than any ceremonial perfections. The Bráhmans, whom he once ridiculed, were glad enough in the end to make him their patron saint, though they did not equally honour his principles. On the other hand, Viswámitra became the type of that immoral divinity which received its Iranian anathema in Ahriman. The murder he commits is nothing in a personage whose Soma-celebrations have raised him so high above the trivialities of morality.

It is easy to see what must be the further development of such a type as Viswámitra when he shall have passed from the guarded pages of puranic tradition to the terrible simplicities of folklore. The saint whose majesty is built on 'merits,' which have no relation to what the humble deem virtues, naturally holds such virtues in cynical contempt; naturally also he is indignant if any one dares to suggest that the height he has reached by costly and prolonged observances may be attained by poor and common people through the practice of virtue. The next step is equally necessary. Since it is hard to argue down the facts of human nature, Vasishtha is pretty sure to have a strong, if sometimes silent, support for his heretical theory of a priesthood representing virtue; consequently Viswámitra will be reduced at length to deny the existence of virtue, and will become the Accuser of those to whom virtues are attributed. Finally, from the Accuser to the Tempter the transition is inevitable. The public Accuser must try and make good his case, and if the facts do not support it, he must create other facts which will, or else bear the last brand of his tribe—Slanderer.

Leaving out of sight all historical or probable facts concerning Viswámitra and Vasishtha, but remembering the spirit of them, let us read the great Passion-play of the East, in which their respective parts are performed again as intervening ages have interpreted them. The hero of this drama is an ancient king named Hariśchandra, who, being childless, and consequently unable to gain immortality, promised the god Varuna to sacrifice to him a son if one were granted him. The son having been born, the father beseeches Varuna for respite, which is granted again and again, but stands firmly by his promise, although it is finally commuted. The repulsive features of the ancient legend are eliminated in the drama, the promise now being for a vast sum of money which the king cannot pay, but which Viswámitra would tempt him to escape by a technical fiction. Sir Mutu Cumára Swámy, whose translation I follow, presents many evidences of the near relation in which this drama stands to the religious faith of the people in Southern India and parts of Ceylon, where its representation never fails to draw vast crowds from every part of the district in which it may occur, the impression made by it being most profound.[2]

We are first introduced to Hariśchandra, King of Ayòdiah (Oude), in his palace, surrounded by every splendour, and by the devotion of his prosperous people. His first word is an ascription to the 'God of gods.' His ministers come forward and recount the wealth and welfare of the nation. The first Act witnesses the marriage of Hariśchandra with the beautiful princess Chandravatí, and it closes with the birth of a son.

The second Act brings us into the presence of Indra in the Abode of the Gods. The Chief enters the Audience Hall of his palace, where an assembly of deities and sages has awaited him. These sages are holy men who have acquired supernatural power by their tremendous austerities; and of these the most august is Viswámitra. By the magnitude and extent of his austerities he has gained a power beyond even that of the Triad, and can reduce the worlds to cinders. All the gods court his favour. As the Council proceeds, Indra addresses the sages—'Holy men! as gifted with supernatural attributes, you roam the universe with marvellous speed, there is no place unknown to you. I am curious to learn who, in the present times, is the most virtuous sovereign on the earth below. What chief of mortals is there who has never told a lie—who has never swerved from the course of justice?' Vasishtha, a powerful sage and family-priest of Hariśchandra, declares that his royal disciple is such a man. But the more powerful Viswámitra denounces Hariśchandra as cruel and a liar. The quarrel between the two Rishis waxes fierce, until Indra puts a stop to it by deciding that an experiment shall be made on Hariśchandra. Vasishtha agrees that if his disciple can be shown to have told a lie, or can be made to tell one, the fruit of his life-long austerities, and all the power so gained, shall be added to Viswámitra; while the latter must present his opponent with half of his 'merits' if Hariśchandra be not made to swerve from the truth. Viswámitra is to employ any means whatever, neither Indra or any other interfering.

Viswámitra sets about his task of trying and tempting Hariśchandra by informing that king that, in order to perform a sacrifice of special importance, he has need of a mound of gold as high as a missile slung by a man standing on an elephant's back. With the demand of so sacred a being Hariśchandra has no hesitation in complying, and is about to deliver the gold when Viswámitra requests him to be custodian of the money for a time, but perform the customary ceremony of transfer. Holding Hariśchandra's written promise to deliver the gold whensoever demanded, Viswámitra retires with compliments. Then wild beasts ravage Hariśchandra's territory; these being expelled, a demon boar is sent, but is vanquished by the monarch. Viswámitra then sends unchaste dancing-girls to tempt Hariśchandra; and when he has ordered their removal, Viswámitra returns with them, and, feigning rage, accuses him of slaying innocent beasts and of cruelty to the girls. He declares that unless Hariśchandra yields to the Pariah damsels, he himself shall be reduced to a Pariah slave. Hariśchandra offers all his kingdom and possessions if the demand is withdrawn, absolutely refusing to swerve from his virtue. This Viswámitra accepts, is proclaimed sovereign of Ayòdiah, and the king goes forth a beggar with his wife and child. But now, as these are departing, Viswámitra demands that mound of gold which was to be paid when called for. In vain Hariśchandra pleads that he has already delivered up all he possesses, the gold included; the last concession is declared to have nothing to do with the first. Yet Viswámitra says he will be charitable; if Hariśchandra will simply declare that he never pledged the gold, or, having done so, does not feel bound to pay it, he will cancel that debt. 'Such a declaration I can never make,' replies Hariśchandra. 'I owe thee the gold, and pay it I shall. Let a messenger accompany me and leave me not till I have given him thy due.'

From this time the efforts of Viswámitra are directed to induce

Hariśchandra to declare the money not due. Amid his heartbroken people—who cry, 'Where are the gods? Can they tolerate this?'—he who was just now the greatest and happiest monarch in the world goes forth on the highway a wanderer with his Chandravatí and their son Devaráta dressed in coarsest garments. His last royal deed is to set the crown on his tempter's head. The people and officers follow, and beg his permission to slay Viswámitra, but he rebukes them, and counsels submission. Viswámitra orders a messenger, Nakshatra, to accompany the three wretched ones, and inflict the severest sufferings on them until the gold is paid, and amid each ordeal to offer Hariśchandra all his former wealth and happiness if he will utter a falsehood.

They come to a desert whose sands are so hot that the wife faints. Hariśchandra bears his son in his arms, but in addition is compelled to bear Nakshatra (the Bráhman and tormentor) on his shoulders. They so pass amid snakes and scorpions, and receive terrible stings; they pass through storm and flood, and yet vainly does Nakshatra suggest the desired falsehood.

Then follows the ordeal of Demons, which gives an interesting insight into Tamil Demonology. One of the company exclaims—'How frightful they look! Who can face them? They come in battalions, young and old, small and great—all welcome us. They disport themselves with a wild dance; flames shoot from their mouths; their feet touch not the earth; they move in the air. Observe you the bleeding corpses of human beings in their hands. They crunch them and feed on the flesh. The place is one mass of gore and filth. Wolves and hyænas bark at them; jackals and dogs follow them. They are near. May Siva protect us!'

NAKSHATRA. How dreadful! Hariśchandra, what is this? Look! evil demons stare at me—I tremble for my life. Protect me now, and I ask you no more for the gold.

HARIŚCHANDRA. Have no fear, Nakshatra. Come, place thyself in the midst of us.

CHIEF OF THE GOBLINS. Men! little men! human vermin! intrude ye thus into my presence? Know that, save only the Bráhman standing in the midst of you, you are all my prey to-night.

HARIŚCHANDRA. Goblin! certainly thou art not an evil-doer, for thou hast excepted this holy Bráhman. As for ourselves, we know that the bodies which begin to exist upon earth must also cease to exist on it. What matters it when death comes? If he spares us now he reserves us only for another season. Good, kind demon! destroy us then together; here we await our doom.

NAKSHATRA. Hariśchandra! before you thus desert me, make the goblin promise you that he will not hurt me.

HARIŚCHANDRA. Thou hast no cause for alarm; thou art safe.

CHIEF OF THE GOBLINS. Listen! I find that all four of you are very thin; it is not worth my while to kill you. On examining closely, I perceive that the young Bráhman is plump and fat as a wild boar. Give him up to me—I want not the rest.

NAKSHATRA. O Gods! O Hariśchandra! you are a great monarch! Have mercy on me! Save me, save me! I will never trouble you for the gold, but treat you considerately hereafter.

HARIŚCHANDRA. Sir, thy life is safe, stand still.

NAKSHATRA. Allow me, sirs, to come closer to you, and to hold you by the hand (*He grasps their hands.*)

HARIŚCHANDRA. King of the Goblins! I address thee in all sincerity; thou wilt confer on us a great favour indeed by despatching us

speedily to the Judgment Hall of the God of Death. The Bráhman must not be touched; devour us.

THE GOBLIN (*grinding his teeth in great fury*). What! dare you disobey me? Will you not deliver the Bráhman?

HARIŚCHANDRA. No, we cannot. We alone are thy victims.
[*Day breaks, and the goblins disappear.*]

Having thus withstood all temptation to harm his enemy, or to break a promise he had given to treat him kindly, Hariśchandra is again pressed for the gold or the lie, and, still holding out, an ordeal of fire follows. Trusting the God of Fire will cease to afflict if one is sacrificed, Hariśchandra prepares to enter the conflagration first, and a pathetic contention occurs between him and his wife and son as to which shall be sacrificed. In the end Hariśchandra rushes in, but does not perish.

Hariśchandra is hoping to reach the temple of Vis Wanàth [3] at Kasi and invoke his aid to pay the gold. To the temple he comes only to plead in vain, and Nakshatra tortures him with instruments. Finally Hariśchandra, his wife and child, are sold as slaves to pay the debt. But Viswámitra, invisibly present, only redoubles his persecutions. Hariśchandra is subjected to the peculiar degradation of having to burn dead bodies in a cemetery. Chandravatí and her son are subjected to cruelties. The boy is one day sent to the forest, is bitten by a snake, and dies. Chandravatí goes out in the night to find the body. She repairs with it to the cemetery. In the darkness she does not recognise her husband, the burner of the bodies, nor he his wife. He has strictly promised his master that every fee shall be paid, and reproaches the woman for coming in the darkness to avoid payment. Chandravatí offers in payment a sacred chain which Siva had thrown round her neck at birth, invisible to all but a perfect man. Hariśchandra alone has ever seen it, and now recognises his wife. But even now he will not perform the last rites over his dead child unless the fee can be obtained as promised. Chandravatí goes out into the city to beg the money, leaving Hariśchandra seated beside the dead body of Devaráta. In the street she stumbles over the corpse of another child, and takes it up; it proves to be the infant Prince, who has been murdered. Chandravatí—arrested and dragged before the king—in a state of frenzy declares she has killed the child. She is condemned to death, and her husband must be her executioner. But the last scene must be quoted nearly in full.

> VERAKVOO (*Hariśchandra's master, leading on Chandravatí*). Slave! this woman has been sentenced by our king to be executed without delay. Draw your sword and cut her head off. (*Exit.*)

> HARIŚCHANDRA. I obey, master. (*Draws the sword and approaches her.*)

> CHANDRAVATÍ (*coming to consciousness again*). My husband! What! do I see thee again? I applaud thy resolution, my lord. Yes; let me die by thy sword. Be not unnerved, but be prompt, and perform thy duty unflinchingly.

> HARIŚCHANDRA. My beloved wife! the days allotted to you in this world are numbered; you have run through the span of your existence. Convicted as you are of this crime, there is no hope for

your life; I must presently fulfil my instructions. I can only allow
you a few seconds; pray to your tutelary deities, prepare yourself
to meet your doom.

Viswámitra (*who has suddenly appeared*). Hariśchandra! what, are
you going to slaughter this poor woman? Wicked man, spare her!
Tell a lie even now and be restored to your former state!

Hariśchandra. I pray, my lord, attempt not to beguile me from the
path of rectitude. Nothing shall shake my resolution; even though
thou didst offer to me the throne of Indra I would not tell a lie.
Pollute not thy sacred person by entering such unholy grounds.
Depart! I dread not thy wrath; I no longer court thy favour.
Depart. (Viswámitra *disappears*.)

My love! lo I am thy executioner; come, lay thy head gently on this
block with thy sweet face turned towards the east. Chandravatí,
my wife, be firm, be happy! The last moment of our sufferings has
at length come; for to sufferings too there is happily an end. Here
cease our woes, our griefs, our pleasures. Mark! yet awhile, and
thou wilt be as free as the vultures that now soar in the skies.

This keen sabre will do its duty. Thou dead, thy husband dies
too—this self-same sword shall pierce my breast. First the child—
then the wife—last the husband—all victims of a sage's wrath. I
the martyr of Truth—thou and thy son martyrs for me, the martyr
of Truth. Yes; let us die cheerfully and bear our ills meekly. Yes;
let all men perish, let all gods cease to exist, let the stars that
shine above grow dim, let all seas be dried up, let all mountains
be levelled to the ground, let wars rage, blood flow in streams, let
millions of millions of Hariśchandras be thus persecuted; yet let
Truth be maintained—let Truth ride victorious over all—let Truth
be the light—Truth the guide—Truth alone the lasting solace of
mortals and immortals. Die, then, O goddess of Chastity! Die, at
this the shrine of thy sister goddess of Truth!

[*Strikes the neck of* Chandravatí *with great force; the sword,
instead of harming her, is transformed into a string of superb*

*pearls, which winds itself around her: the gods of heaven, all
sages, and all kings appear suddenly to the view of* HARIŚCHANDRA.]

SIVA (*the first of the gods*). Hariśchandra, be ever blessed! You
have borne your severe trials most heroically, and have proved

to all men that virtue is of greater worth than all the vanities of a
fleeting world. Be you the model of mortals. Return to your land,
resume your authority, and rule your state. Devaráta, victim of
Viswámitra's wrath, rise! (*He is restored to life.*)
Rise you, also, son of the King of Kasi, with whose murder
you, Chandravatí, were charged through the machinations of
Viswámitra. (*He comes to life also.*)

HARIŚCHANDRA. All my misfortunes are of little consequence, since
thou, O God of gods, hast deigned to favour me with thy divine
presence. No longer care I for kingdom, or power, or glory. I
value not children, or wives, or relations. To thy service, to thy
worship, to the redemption of my erring soul, I devote myself
uninterruptedly hereafter. Let me not become the sport of men.
The slave of a Pariah cannot become a king; the slave-girl of a
Bráhman cannot become a queen. When once the milk has been
drawn from the udder of a cow nothing can restore the self-same
milk to it. Our degradation, O God, is now beyond redemption.

VISWÁMITRA. I pray, O Siva, that thou wouldst pardon my folly.
Anxious to gain the wager laid by me before the gods, I have
most mercilessly tormented this virtuous king; yet he has proved
himself the most truthful of all earthly sovereigns, triumphing
victoriously over me and my efforts to divert him from his
constancy. Hariśchandra, king of kings! I crave your forgiveness.

VERAKVOO (*throwing off his disguise*). King Hariśchandra, think not
that I am a Pariah, for you behold in me even Yáma, the God of
Death.

KALAKANDA (*Chandravati's cruel master, throwing off his disguise*).
Queen! rest not in the belief that you were the slave of a Bráhman.
He to whom you devoted yourself am even I—the God of Fire, Agni.

Vasishtha. Hariśchandra, no disgrace attaches to thee nor to the Solar race, of which thou art the incomparable gem. Even this cemetery is in reality no cemetery: see! the illusion lasts not, and thou beholdest here a holy grove the abode of hermits and ascetics. Like the gold which has passed through successive crucibles, devoid of all impurities, thou, O King of Ayòdiah, shinest in greater splendour than even yon god of light now rising to our view on the orient hills. (*It is morning.*)

Siva. Hariśchandra, let not the world learn that Virtue is vanquished, and that its enemy, Vice, has become the victor. Go, mount yon throne again—proclaim to all that we, the gods, are the guardians of the good and the true. Indra! chief of the gods, accompany this sovereign with all your retinue, and recrown him emperor of Ayòdiah. May his reign be long—may all bliss await him in the other world!

---

The plot of this drama has probably done as much and as various duty as any in the world. It has spread like a spiritual banyan, whose branches, taking root, have swelled to such size that it is difficult now to say which is the original trunk. It may even be that the only root they all had in common is an invisible one in the human heart, developed in its necessary struggles amid nature after the pure and perfect life.

But neither in the Book of Job, which we are yet to consider, nor in any other variation of the theme, does it rise so high as in this drama of Hariśchandra. In Job it represents man loyal to his deity amid the terrible afflictions which that deity permits; but in Hariśchandra it shows man loyal to a moral principle even against divine orders to the contrary. Despite the hand of the licenser, and the priestly manipulations, visible here and there in it—especially towards the close—sacerdotalism stands confronted by its reaction at last, and receives its sentence in the joy with which the Hindu sees the potent Rishis with all their pretentious 'merits,' and the gods themselves, kneeling at the feet of the man who stands by Truth.

It is amusing to find the wincings of the priests through many centuries embodied in a legend about Hariśchandra after he went to heaven. It is related that he was induced by Nárada to relate his actions with such unbecoming pride that he was lowered from Svarga (heaven) one stage after each sentence; but having stopped in time, and paid homage to the gods, he was placed with his capital in mid-air, where eyes sacerdotally actinised may still see the aerial city at certain times. The doctrine of 'merits' will no doubt be able for some time yet to charge 'good deeds' with their own sin—pride; but, after all, the priest must follow the people far enough to confess that one must look upward to find the martyr of Truth. In what direction one must look to find his accuser requires no further intimation than the popular legend of Viswámitra.

---

NOTES

1   That this satirical hymn was admitted into the Rig-Veda shows that these hymns were collected whilst they were still in the hands of the ancient Hindu families as common-property, and were not yet the exclusive property of Bráhmans as a caste or association. Further evidence of the same kind is given by a hymn in which the expression occurs—'Do not be as lazy as a Bráhman.'—Mrs. Manning's Ancient and Mediæval India, i. 77. In the same work some particulars are given of the persons mentioned in this chapter. The Frog-satire is translated by Max Müller, A. S. L., p. 494.

2   'Arichandra, the Martyr of Truth: A Tamil Drama translated into English by Mutu Coomâra Swâmy, Mudliar, Member of Her Majesty's Legislative Council of Ceylon,' &c. London: Smith, Elder, & Co. 1863. This drama, it must be constantly borne in mind, in nowise represents the Vedic legend, told in the Aitereya-Bráhmana, vii. 13–18; nor the puranic legend, told in the Merkandeya-Purána. I have altered the spelling of the names to the Sanskrit forms, but otherwise follow Sir M. C. S.'s translation.

3   Siva; the 'lord of the world,' and of wealth. Cf. Pluto, Dis, Dives.

# Chapter V
## Elohim and Jehovah

Deified power — Giants and Jehovah — Jehovah's manifesto —
The various Elohim — Two Jehovahs and two Tables — Contradictions —
Detachment of the Elohim from Jehovah

**THE SACRED BOOKS** of the Hebrews bring us into the presence of the gods (Elohim) supposed to have created all things out of nothing—nature-gods—just as they are in transition to the conception of a single Will and Personality. Though the plural is used ('gods') a singular verb follows: the tendency is already to that concentration which resulted in the enthronement of one supreme sovereign—Jehovah. The long process of evolution which must have preceded this conception is but slightly traceable in the Bible. It is, however, written on the face of the whole world, and the same process is going on now in its every phase. Whether with Gesenius [1] we take the sense of the word Elohim to be 'the revered,' or, with Fürst,[2] 'the mighty,' makes little difference; the fact remains that the word is applied elsewhere to gods in general, including such as were afterwards deemed false gods by the Jews; and it is more important still that the actions ascribed to the Elohim, who created the heavens and the earth, generally reflect the powerful and un-moral forces of nature. The work of creation in Genesis (i. and ii. 1–3) is that of giants without any moral quality whatever. Whether or not we take in their obvious sense the words, 'Elohim created man in his own image, ... male and female created he them,' there can be no question of the meaning of Gen. vi. 1, 2: 'The sons of Elohim saw the daughters of men that they were beautiful, and they took to themselves for wives whomsoever they chose.' When good and evil come to be spoken of, the name Jehovah [3] at once appears. The Elohim appear again in the Flood, the wind that assuaged it, the injunction to be fruitful and multiply, the cloud and rainbow; and gradually the germs of a moral government begin to appear in their assigning the violence of mankind as reason for the deluge, and in the covenant with Noah. But even after the name Jehovah had generally blended with, or even superseded, the other, we find Elohim often used where strength and wonder-working are thought of—*e.g.*, 'Thou art the god that doest wonders' (Ps. lxxvii.). 'Thy way is in the sea, and thy path in the great waters, and thy footsteps are not known.'

Against the primitive nature-deities the personality and jealous supremacy of Jehovah was defined. The golden calf built by Aaron was called Elohim (plural, though there was but one calf). Solomon was denounced for building altars to the same; and when Jeroboam built altars to two calves, they are still so called. Other rivals—Dagon (Judges xvi.), Astaroth, Chemosh, Milcom (1 Kings xi.)—are called by the once-honoured name. The English Bible translates Elohim, God; Jehovah, the LORD; Jehovah Elohim, the LORD God; and the critical reader will find much that is significant in the varied use of these names. Thus (Gen. xxii.) it is Elohim that demands the sacrifice of Isaac, Jehovah that interferes to save him. At the same time, in editing the story, it is plainly felt to be inadmissible that Abraham should be supposed loyal to any other god than Jehovah; so Jehovah adopts the sacrifice as meant for himself, and the place where the ram was provided in place of Isaac is called Jehovah-Jireh. However, when we can no longer distinguish the two antagonistic conceptions by different names their actual incongruity is even more salient, and, as we shall see, develops a surprising result.

Jehovah inaugurates his reign by a manifesto against these giants, the Elohim, for whom the special claim—clamorously asserted when Aaron built the Golden Calf, and continued as the plea for the same deity—was that *they* (Elohim) had brought Israel out of Egypt. 'I,' cries Jehovah, 'am the Lord thy God, which have brought thee out of the land of Egypt, out of the house of bondage: thou shalt have no other gods but me;' and the first four commandments of the law are devoted entirely to a declaration of his majesty, his power (claiming credit for the creation), his jealous determination to punish his opponents and reward his friends, to vindicate the slightest disrespect to his name. The narrative of the Golden Calf was plainly connected with Sinai in order to illustrate the first commandment. The punishment of the believers in another divine emancipator, even though they had not yet received the proclamation, must be signal. Jehovah is so enraged that by his order human victims are offered up to the number of three thousand, and even after that, it is said, Jehovah plagued Israel on account of their Elohim-worship. In the same direction is the command to keep holy the Sabbath day, because on it he rested from the work of creation (Gen. xx.), or because on that day he delivered Israel from Egypt (Deut. v.), the editors do not seem to remember exactly which, but it is well enough to say both, for it is taking the two picked laurels from the brow of Elohim and laying them on that of Jehovah. In all of which it is observable that there is no moral quality whatever. Nero might equally command the Romans to have no other gods before himself, to speak his name with awe, to rest when he stopped working. In the fifth commandment, arbitrarily ascribed to the First Table, we have a transition to the moral code; though even there the honour of parents is jealously associated with Jehovah's greatness ('that thy days may be long in the land which Jehovah Elohim giveth thee'). The nature-gods were equal to that; for the Elohim had begotten the giants who were 'in the earth in those days.'

'Elohim spake unto Moses, and said unto him, I am Jehovah; and I appeared unto Abraham, unto Isaac, and unto Jacob by (the name of) God Almighty (*El-Shaddai*), but by my name JEHOVAH was I not known to them' (Exod. vi. 2, 3).

The ancient gods—the Elohim—were, in the process of absorption into the one great form, the repository of their several powers, distinguishable; and though, for the most part, they bear names related to the forces of nature, now and then they reflect the tendencies to humanisation. Thus we have 'the most high god' (*El-elyon—e.g.*, Gen. xiv. 18); 'the everlasting-god' (*El-elim*, Gen. xxi. 33); 'the jealous god' (*El-kana*, Exod. xx. 5); 'the mighty god, and terrible' (*El-gadol* and *nora*, Deut. vii. 21); 'the living god' (*El-chi*, Josh. iii. 10); 'the god of heaven' (*El-shemim*, Ps. cxxxvi. 26); the 'god almighty' (*El-shaddai*,[4] Exod. vi. 2). These Elohim, with each of whose names I have referred to an instance of its characteristic use, became epithets, as the powers they represented were more and more absorbed by the growing personality of Jehovah; but these epithets were also characters, and their historic expressions had also to undergo a process of slow and difficult digestion. The all-devouring grandeur of Jehovah showed what it had fed on. Not only all the honours, but many of the dishonours, of the primitive deities adhered to the sovereign whose rule was no doubt inaugurated by their disgrace and their barbarism. The costliness of the glory of divine absolutism is again illustrated in the evolution of the premature monotheism, which had for its figure-head the dread Jehovah, who, as heir of the nature-gods, became responsible for the monstrosities of a tribal demonolatry, thus being compelled to fill simultaneously the *rôles* of the demon and the lawgiver.[5]

The two tables of the law—one written by Jehovistic theology, the other by the moral sense of mankind—ascribed to this dual deity, for whom unity was so fiercely insisted on, may be read in their outcome throughout the Bible. They are here briefly, in a few examples, set forth side by side.

| Table of Jehovah I. | Table of Jehovah II. |
| --- | --- |
| Exod. xxxiii. 27. 'Slay every man his brother, every man his companion, and every man his neighbour.' | Exod. xx. 13. 'Thou shalt not kill.' |
| Num. xv. 32. 'While the children of Israel were in the wilderness, they found a man that gathered sticks upon the Sabbath Day.... And they put him in ward, because it was not declared what should be done to him. And the Lord said unto Moses, The man shall be surely put to death: all the congregation shall stone him with stones without the camp.' Neither this nor the similar punishment for blasphemy (Lev. xxiv.), were executions of existing law. For a fearful instance of murder inflicted on the innocent, and accepted as a human sacrifice by Jehovah, see 2 Sam. xxi.; and for the brutal murder of Shimei, who denounced and resented the crime which hung the seven sons of Saul 'before the Lord,' see 1 Kings ii. But the examples are many. | |
| In the story of Abraham, Sarai, and Hagar (Gen. xvi.), Lot and his daughters (xix.), Abraham's presentation of his wife to Abimilech (xx.), the same done by Isaac (xxvi.), Judah, Tamar (xxxviii.), and other cases where the grossest violations of the seventh commandment go unrebuked by Jehovah, while in constant communication with the guilty parties, we see how little the second table was supported by the first. | Exod. xx. 14. 'Thou shalt not commit adultery.' |

| TABLE OF JEHOVAH I. | TABLE OF JEHOVAH II. |
|---|---|
| The extortions, frauds, and thefts of Jacob (Gen. xxv., xxvii., xxx.), which brought upon him the unparalleled blessings of Jehovah; the plundering of Nabal's property by David and his fellow-bandits; the smiting of the robbed farmer by Jehovah and the taking of his treacherous wife by David (1 Sam. xxv.), are narratives befitting a Bible of footpads. | Exod. xx. 15. 'Thou shalt not steal.' |
| Jehovah said, 'Who shall deceive Ahab?... And there came forth a spirit, and stood before Jehovah, and said, I will deceive him. And Jehovah said, Wherewith? And he said, I will go forth and be a lying spirit in the mouth of all these thy prophets. And he said, Thou shalt deceive him, and prevail also: go forth and do so. Now, therefore, Jehovah hath put a lying spirit in the mouth of all these thy prophets, and Jehovah hath spoken evil concerning thee' (1 Kings xxii.). See Ezek. xx. 25. | Exod. xx. 16. 'Thou shalt not bear false witness against thy neighbour.' |
| Deut xx. 10–18, is a complete instruction for invasion, murder, rapine, eating the spoil of the invaded, taking their wives, their cattle, &c., all such as might have been proclaimed by a Supreme Bashi-Bazouk. | Exod. xx. 17. 'Thou shalt not covet they neighbour's wife, thou shalt not covet thy neighbour's wife, nor his man-servant, nor his maid-servant, nor his ox, nor his ass, nor anything that is thy neighbour's.' |

Instances of this discrepancy might be largely multiplied. Any one who cares to pursue the subject can trace the building upon the powerful personal Jehovah of a religion of human sacrifices, anathemas, and priestly despotism; while around the moral ruler and judge of the same name, whose personality is more and more dispersed in pantheistic ascriptions, there grows the common law, and then the more moral law of equity, and the corresponding sentiments which gradually evolve the idea of a parental deity.

It is obvious that the more this second idea of the deity prevails, the more he is regarded as 'merciful,' 'long-suffering,' 'a God of truth and without iniquity, just and right,' 'delighting not in sacrifice but mercifulness,' 'good to all,' and whose 'tender mercies are over all his works,' and having 'no pleasure in the death of him that dieth;' the less will it be possible to see in the very same being the 'man of war,' 'god of battles,' the 'jealous,' 'angry,' 'fire-breathing' one, who 'visits the sins of the fathers upon the children,' who laughs at the calamities of men and mocks when their fear cometh. It is a structural necessity of the human mind that these two shall be gradually detached the one from the other. From one of the Jehovahs represented in parallel columns came the 'Father' whom Christ adored: from the other came the Devil he abhorred.

---

**NOTES**

1  Thes. Heb., p. 94.

2  Heb. Handw., p. 90.

3  Or Jahveh. I prefer to use the best known term in a case where the more exact spelling adds no significance.

4  This, the grandest of all the elohistic names, became the nearest Hebrew word for devils—shedim.

5  Even his jealous command against rivals, i.e., 'graven images,' had to be taken along with the story of Laban's images (Gen. xxxi.), when, though 'God came to Laban,' the idolatry was not rebuked.

# Chapter VI
## The Consuming Fire

The Shekinah — Jewish idols — Attributes of the fiery and cruel Elohim
compared with those of the Devil — The powers of evil combined under a head
— Continuity — The consuming fire spiritualised

THAT ABRAHAM WAS a Fire-worshipper might be suspected from the immemorial efforts of all Semitic authorities to relieve him of traditional connection with that particular idolatry. When the good and evil powers were being distinguished, we find the burning and the bright aspects of Fire severally regarded. The sign of Jehovah's covenant with Abram included both. 'It came to pass that when the sun went down, and it was dark, behold a smoking furnace and a burning lamp that passed between those pieces' (of the sacrifice). In the legend of Moses we have the glory resting on Sinai and the burning bush, the bush which, it is specially remarked, was 'not consumed,' an exceptional circumstance in honour of Moses. To these corresponded the Urim and Thummim, marking the priest as source of light and of judgment. In his favourable and adorable aspect Jehovah was the Brightness of Fire. This was the Shekinah. In the Targum, Jonathan Ben Uzziel to the Prophets, it is said: 'The mountains trembled before the Lord; the mountains Tabor, Hermon, Carmel said one to the other: Upon me the Shekinah will rest, and to me will it come. But the Shekinah rested upon Mount Sinai, weakest and smallest of all the mountains. This Sinai trembled and shook, and its smoke went up as the smoke of an oven, because of the glory of the God of Israel which had manifested itself upon it.' The Brightness [1] passed on to illumine every event associated with the divine presence in Semitic mythology; it was 'the glory of the Lord' shining from the Star of Bethlehem, and the figure of the Transfiguration.

The Consuming Fire also had its development. Among the spiritual it was spiritualised. 'Who among us shall dwell with the Devouring Fire?' cries Isaiah. 'Who among us shall dwell with the Everlasting Burnings? He that walketh righteously and speaketh uprightly; he that despiseth the gain of oppressions, that shaketh his hands from holding of bribes, that stoppeth his ears from hearing of blood, and shutteth his eyes from seeing evil.' It was by a prosaic route that the Devouring Fire became the residence of the wicked.

After Jeroboam (1 Kings xiii.) had built altars to the Elohim, under form of Calves, a prophet came out of Judah to denounce the idolatry. 'And he cried against the altar in the word of Jehovah, and said, O altar, altar! thus saith Jehovah, Behold, a child shall be born unto the house of David, Josiah by name; and upon thee shall he offer the priests of the high places that burn incense upon thee, and men's bones shall be burnt upon thee.' It was deemed so important that this prophecy should be fulfilled in the letter, when it could no longer be fulfilled in reality, that some centuries later Josiah dug up the bones of the Elohistic priests and burned them upon their long-ruined altars (2 Kings xxiii.).

The incident is significant, both on account of the prophet's personification of the altar, and the institution of a sort of Gehenna in connection with it. The personification and the Gehenna became much more complete as time went on. The Jews originally had no Devil, as indeed had no races at first; and this for the obvious reason that their so-called gods were quite equal to any moral evils that were to be accounted for, as we have already seen they were adequate to explain all physical evils. But the antagonists of the moral Jehovah were recognised and personified with increasing clearness, and were quite prepared for connection with any General who might be theoretically proposed for their leadership. When the Jews came under the influence of Persian theology the archfiend was elected, and all the Elohim—Moloch, Dagon, Astarte, Chemosh, and the rest—took their place under his rebellious ensign.

The descriptions of the Devil in the Bible are mainly borrowed from the early descriptions of the Elohim, and of Jehovah in his Elohistic character.[2] In the subjoined parallels I follow the received English version.

| | |
|---|---|
| Gen. xxii. 1. 'God tempted Abraham.' | Matt. iv. 1. 'Then was Jesus led up into the wilderness to be tempted of the devil.' See also 1 Cor. vii. 5, 1 Thes. iii. 5, James 1.13. |
| Exod. v. 3. 'I (Jehovah) will harden Pharaoh's heart;' v. 13, 'He hardened Pharaoh's heart.' | John xiii. 2. 'The devil having now put into the heart Judas Iscariot, Simon's son, to betray him.' |
| 1 Kings xxii. 23. 'Behold the Lord hath put a lying spirit in the mouth of all these thy prophets, and the Lord hath spoken evil concerning them.' Ezek. xiv. 9. 'If the prophet be deceived when he hath spoken a thing, I the Lord have deceived that prophet, and I will stretch out my hand upon him, and will destroy him from the midst of my people.' | John viii. 44. 'He (the devil) is a liar' ('and so is his father,' continues the sentence by right of translation). 1 Tim. iii. 2, 'slanderers' (diabolous). 2 Tim. iii. 3, 'false accusers' (diabolo). Also Titus ii. 3, Von Tischendorf translates 'calumniators.' |
| Isa. xlv. 7. 'I make peace and create evil. I the Lord do all these things.' Amos iii. 6. 'Shall there be evil in a city and the Lord hath not done it?' 1 Sam. xvi. 14. 'An evil spirit from the Lord troubled him' (Saul). | Matt. xiii. 38. 'The tares are the children of the wickied one.' 1 John iii. 8. 'He that committeth sin is of the devil; for the devil sinneth from the beginning.' |
| Exod. xii. 29. 'At midnight the Lord smote all the firstborn of Egypt.' Ver. 30. 'There was a great cry in Egypt; for there was not a house where there was not one dead.' Exod. xxxiii. 27. 'Thus saith the Lord God of Israel, Put every man his sword by his side, and go in and out from gate to gate throughout the camp, and slay every man his brother, and every man his companion, and every man his neighbour.' | John viii. 44. 'He (the devil) was a murderer from the beginning.' |

| | |
|---|---|
| Exod. vi. 9. 'Take thy rod and cast it before Pharaoh and it shall become a serpent.' Ver. 12. 'Aaron's rod swallowed up their rods.' Num. xxi. 6. 'Jehovah sent fiery serpents (Seraphim) among the people.' Ver. 8. 'And the Lord said unto Moses, Make thee a fiery serpent, and set it upon a pole: and it shall come to pass, that every one that is bitten, when he looketh upon it, shall live.' (This serpent was worshipped until destroyed by Hezekiah, 2 Kings xviii.) Compare Jer. viii. 17, Ps. cxlviii., 'Praise ye the Lord from the earth, ye dragons.' | Rev. xii. 7, &c. 'There was war in heaven: Michael and his angels fought against the dragon.... And the great dragon was cast out, that old serpent, called the Devil, and Satan, which deceiveth the whole world.... Woe to the inhabiters of the earth and of the sea! for the devil has come down to you, having great wrath.' |
| Gen. xix. 24. 'The Lord rained upon Sodom and Gomorrah brimstone and fire from the Lord out of heaven.' Deut. iv. 24. 'The Lord thy God is a consuming fire.' Ps. xi. 6. 'Upon the wicked he shall rain snares, fire and brimstone.' Ps. xviii. 8. 'There went up a smoke out of his nostrils.' Ps. xcvii. 3. 'A fire goeth before him, and burneth up his enemies round about.' Ezek. xxxviii. 19, &c. 'For in my jealousy, and in the fire of my wrath, have I spoken.... I will plead against him with pestilence and with blood, and I will rain upon him ... fire and brimstone.' Isa. xxx. 33. 'Tophet is ordained of old; yea, for the king is it prepared: he hath made it deep and wide; the pile thereof is fire and much wood; the breath of the Lord, like a stream of brimstone, doth kindle it.' | Matt. xxv. 41. 'Depart from me, ye cursed, into everlasting fire, prepared for the devil and his angels.' Mark ix. 44. 'Where their worm dieth not, and the fire is not quenched.' Rev. xx. 10. 'And the devil that deceiveth them was cast into the lake of fire and brimstone.' In Rev. ix. Abaddon, or Apollyon, is represented as the king of the scorpion tormentors; and the diabolical horses, with stinging serpent tails, are described as killing with the smoke and brimstone from their mouths. |

In addition to the above passages may be cited a notable passage from Paul's Epistle to the Thessalonians (ii. 3). 'Let no man deceive you by any means: for that day (of Christ) shall not come, except there come a falling away first, and that man of sin be revealed, the son of perdition; who opposeth and exalteth himself above all that is called God, or that is worshipped; so that he, as God, sitteth in the temple of God, showing himself that he is God. Remember ye not that, when I was yet with you, I told you these things? And now ye know what withholdeth that he might be revealed in his time. For the mystery of iniquity doth already work: only he who now letteth will let, until he be taken out of the way: and then shall that Wicked be revealed, whom the Lord shall consume with the spirit of his mouth, and shall destroy with the brightness of his coming: even him whose coming is after the working of Satan, with all power, and signs, and lying wonders, and with all the deceivableness of unrighteousness in them that perish; because they received not the love of the truth, that they might be saved. And for this cause God shall send them strong delusion, that they should believe a lie; that they all might be damned who believed not the truth, but had pleasure in unrighteousness.'

This remarkable utterance shows how potent was the survival in the mind of Paul of the old Elohist belief. Although the ancient deity, who deceived prophets to their destruction, and sent forth lying spirits with their strong delusions, was dethroned and outlawed, he was still a powerful claimant of empire, haunting the temple, and setting himself up therein as God. He will be consumed by Christ's breath when the day of triumph comes; but meanwhile he is not only allowed great power in the earth, but utilised by the true God, who even so far cooperates with the false as to send on some men 'strong delusions' ('a working of error,' Von Tischendorf translates), in order that they may believe the lie and be damned. Paul speaks of the 'mystery of iniquity;' but it is not so very mysterious when we consider the antecedents of his idea. The dark problem of the origin of evil, and its continuance in the universe under the rule of a moral governor, still threw its impenetrable shadow across the human mind. It was a terrible reality, visible in the indifference or hostility with which the new gospel was met on the part of the cultured and powerful; and it could only then be explained as a mysterious provisional arrangement connected with some divine purpose far away in the depths of the universe. But the passage quoted from Thessalonians shows plainly that all those early traditions about the divinely deceived prophets and lying spirits, sent forth from Jehovah Elohim, had finally, in Paul's time, become marshalled under a leader, a personal Man of Sin; but this leader, while opposing Christ's kingdom, is in some mysterious way a commissioner of God.

We may remark here the beautiful continuity by which, through all these shadows of terror and vapours of speculation, 'clouding the glow of heaven,'[3] the unquenchable ideal from first to last is steadily ascending.

'One or three things,' says the Talmud, 'were before this world—Water, Fire, and Wind. Water begat the Darkness, Fire begat Light, and Wind begat the Spirit of Wisdom.' This had become the rationalistic translation by a crude science of the primitive demons, once believed to have created the heavens and the earth. In the process we find the forces outlawed in their wild action, but becoming the choir of God in their quiet action:—

1 Kings xix. 11–13. 'And he said, Go forth, and stand upon the mount before the Lord. And, behold, the Lord passed by, and a great and strong wind rent the mountains, and brake in pieces the rocks before the Lord; but the Lord was not in the wind: and after the wind an earthquake; but the Lord was not in the earthquake: and after the earthquake a fire; but the Lord was not in the fire: and after the fire a still small voice. And it was so, when Elijah heard it, that he wrapped his face in his mantle.'

But man must have a philosophical as well as a moral development: the human mind could not long endure this elemental anarchy. It asked, If the Lord be not in the hurricane, the earthquake, the volcanic flame, who *is* therein? This is the answer of the Targum:[4]

'And he said, Arise and stand on the mountain before the Lord. And God revealed himself: and before him a host of angels of the wind, cleaving the mountain and breaking the rocks before the Lord; but not in the host of angels was the Shechinah. And after the host of the angels of the wind came a host of angels of commotion; but not in the host of the angels of commotion was the Shechinah of the Lord. And after the angels of commotion came a host of angels of fire; but not in the host of angels of fire was the Shechinah of the Lord. But after the host of the angels of the fire came voices singing in silence. And it was when Elijah heard this he hid his face in his mantle.'

The moral sentiment takes another step in advance with the unknown but artistic writer of the Epistle to the Hebrews. Moses had described God as a 'consuming fire;' and 'the sight of the glory of the Lord was like devouring fire on the top of the mount in the eyes of the children of Israel' (Exod. xxiv. 17). When next we meet this phrase it is with this writer, who seeks to supersede what Moses (traditionally) built up. 'Whose voice,' he says, 'then shook the earth; but now he hath promised, saying, Yet once more I shake not the earth only, but also heaven. And this word, 'yet once more,' signifieth the removing of those things that are shaken, as of things that are made, that those which cannot be shaken may remain.... For our God is a consuming fire.'

'*Our* God also!' cries each great revolution that advances. His consuming wrath is not now directed against man, but the errors which are man's only enemies: the lightnings of the new Sinai, while they enlighten the earth, smite the old heaven of human faith and imagination, shrivelling it like a burnt scroll!

In this nineteenth century, when the old heaven, amid which this fiery pillar glowed, is again shaken, the ancient phrase has still its meaning. The Russian Tourgenieff represents two friends who had studied together in early life, then parted, accidentally meeting once more for a single night. They compare notes as to what the long intervening years have taught them; and one sums his experience in the words—'I have burned what I used to worship, and worship what I used to burn.' The novelist artfully reproduces for this age a sentence associated with a crisis in the religious history of Europe. Clovis, King of the Franks, invoked the God of his wife Clotilda to aid him against the Germans, vowing to become a Christian if successful; and when, after his victory, he was baptized at Rheims, St. Remy said to him—'Bow thy head meekly, Sicambrian; burn what thou hast worshipped, and worship what thou hast burned!' Clovis followed the Bishop's advice in literal fashion, carrying fire and sword amid his old friends the 'Pagans' right zealously. But the era has come in which that which Clovis' sword and St. Remy's theology set up for worship is being consumed in its turn. Tourgenieff's youths are consuming the altar on which their forerunners were consumed. And in this rekindled flame the world now sees shrivelling the heavens once fresh, but now reflecting the aggregate selfishness of mankind, the hells representing their aggregate cowardice, and feeds its nobler faith with this vision of the eternal fire which evermore consumes the false and refines the world.

---

**NOTES**

1  It is not certain, indeed, whether this Brightness may not have been separately personified in the 'Eduth' (translated 'testimony' in the English version, Exod. xvi. 34), before which the pot of manna was laid. The word means 'brightness,' and Dr. Willis supposes it may be connected with Adod, the Phœnician Sun-god (Pentateuch, p. 186).

2  It is important not to confuse Satan with the Devil, so far as the Bible is concerned. Satan, as will be seen when we come to the special treatment of him required, is by no means invariably diabolical. In the Book of Job, for example, he appears in a character far removed from hostility to Jehovah or goodness.

3  Name ist Schall und Rauch,
   Umnebelnd Himmelsgluth.—Goethe.

4  'Targum to the Prophets,' Jonathan Ben Uzziel. See Deutsch's 'Literary Remains,' p. 379.

# Chapter VII
## Paradise and the Serpent

Herakles and Athena in a holy picture — Human significance of Eden —
The legend in Genesis puzzling — Silence of later books concerning it —
Its Vedic elements — Its explanation — Episode of the Mahábhárata —
Scandinavian variant — The name of Adam — The story re-read —
Rabbinical interpretations

MONTFAUCON HAS AMONG his plates one (XX.) representing an antique agate which he supposes to represent Zeus and Athena, but which probably relates to the myth of Herakles and Athena in the garden of Hesperides. The hero having penetrated this garden, slays the dragon which guards its immortalising fruit, but when he has gathered this fruit Athena takes it from him, lest man shall eat it and share the immortality of the gods. In this design the two stand on either side of the tree, around which a serpent is twined from root to branches. The history which Montfaucon gives of the agate is of equal interest with the design itself. It was found in an old French cathedral, where it had long been preserved and shown as a holy picture of the Temptation. It would appear also to have previously deceived some rabbins, for on the border is written in Hebrew characters, much more modern than the central figures, 'The woman saw that the tree was good for food, and that it was pleasant to the eyes, and a tree to be desired to make one wise.'

This mystification about a design, concerning whose origin and design there is now no doubt, is significant. The fable of Paradise and the Serpent is itself more difficult to trace, so many have been the races and religions which have framed it with their holy texts and preserved it in their sacred precincts. In its essence, no doubt, the story grows from a universal experience; in that aspect it is a mystical rose that speaks all languages. When man first appears his counterpart is a garden. The moral nature means order. The wild forces of nature—the Elohim—build no fence, forbid no fruit. They say to man as the supreme animal, Subdue the earth; every tree and herb shall be your meat; every animal your slave; be fruitful and multiply. But from the conflict the more real man emerges, and his sign is a garden hedged in from the wilderness, and a separation between good and evil.

The form in which the legend appears in the Book of Genesis presents one side in which it is simple and natural. This has already been suggested (vol. i. p. 330). But the legend of man defending his refuge from wild beasts against the most subtle of them is here overlaid by a myth in which it plays the least part. The mind which reads it by such light as may be obtained only from biblical sources can hardly fail to be newly puzzled at every step. So much, indeed, is confessed in the endless and diverse theological theories which the story has elicited. What is the meaning of the curse on the Serpent that it should for ever crawl thereafter? Had it not crawled previously? Why was the Tree of the knowledge of Good and Evil forbidden? Why, when its fruit was tasted, should the Tree of Life have been for the first time forbidden and jealously guarded? These riddles are nowhere solved in the Bible, and have been left to the fanciful inventions of theologians and the ingenuity of rabbins. Dr.

Adam Clarke thought the Serpent was an ape before his sin, and many rabbins concluded he was camel-shaped; but the remaining enigmas have been fairly given up.

The ancient Jews, they who wrote and compiled the Old Testament, more candid than their modern descendants and our omniscient christians, silently confessed their inability to make anything out of this snake-story. From the third chapter of Genesis to the last verse of Malachi the story is not once alluded to! Such a phenomenon would have been impossible had this legend been indigenous with the Hebrew race. It was clearly as a boulder among them which had floated from regions little known to their earlier writers; after lying naked through many ages, it became overgrown with rabbinical lichen and moss, and, at the Christian era, while it seemed part of the Hebrew landscape, it was exceptional enough to receive special reverence as a holy stone. That it was made the corner-stone of Christian theology may be to some extent explained by the principle of *omne ignotum pro mirifico*. But the boulder itself can only be explained by tracing it to the mythologic formation from which it crumbled.

How would a Parsi explain the curse on a snake which condemned it to crawl? He would easily give us evidence that at the time when most of those Hebrew Scriptures were written, without allusion to such a Serpent, the ancient Persians believed that Ahriman had tempted the first man and woman through his evil mediator, his anointed son, Ash-Mogh, 'the two-footed Serpent.'

But let us pass beyond the Persian legend, carrying that and the biblical story together, for submission to the criticism of a Bráhman. He will tell us that this Ash-Mogh of the Parsi is merely the ancient Aèshma-daéva of the Avesta, which in turn is Ahi, the great Vedic Serpent-monster whom Indra 'prostrated beneath the feet' of the stream he had obstructed—every stream having its deity. He would remind us that the Vedas describe the earliest dragon-slayer, Indra, as 'crushing the head' of his enemy, and that this figure of the god with his heel on a Serpent's head has been familiar to his race from time immemorial. And he would then tell us to read the Rig-Veda, v. 32, and the Mahábhárata, and we would find all the elements of the story told in Genesis.

In the hymn referred to we find a graphic account of how, when Ahi was sleeping on the waters he obstructed, Indra hurled at him his thunderbolt. It says that when Indra had 'annihilated the weapon of that mighty beast from him (Ahi), another, more powerful, conceiving himself one and unmatched, was generated.' This 'wrath-born son,' 'a walker in darkness,' had managed to get hold of the sacred Soma, the plant monopolised by the gods, and having drunk this juice, he lay slumbering and 'enveloping the world,' and then 'fierce Indra seized upon him,' and having previously discovered 'the vital part of him who thought, himself invulnerable,' struck that incarnation of many-formed Ahi, and he was *made the lowest of all creatures*.

But one who has perused the philological biography of Ahi already given, vol. i. p. 357, will not suppose that this was the end of him. We must now consider in further detail the great episode of the Mahábhárata, to which reference has been made in other connections.[1] During the Deluge the most precious treasure of the gods, the Amrita, the ambrosia that rendered them immortal, was lost, and the poem relates how the Devas and Asuras, otherwise gods and serpents, together churned the ocean for it. There were two great mountains,—Meru the golden and beautiful, adorned with healing plants, pleasant streams and trees, unapproachable by the sinful, guarded by serpents; Mandar, rocky, covered with rank vegetation, infested by savage beasts. The first is the abode of the gods, the last of demons. To find the submerged Amrita it was necessary to uproot Mandar and use it to churn the ocean. This was done by calling on the King Serpent Ananta, who called in the aid of another great serpent, Vásuki, the latter being used as a rope coiling and uncoiling to whirl the mountain. At last the Amrita appeared. But there also streamed forth from the ocean bed a terrible stench and venom, which was spreading through the universe when Siva swallowed it to save mankind,—the drug having stained his throat blue, whence his epithet 'Blue Neck.'

When the Asuras saw the Amrita, they claimed it; but one of the Devas, Narya, assumed the form of a beautiful woman, and so fascinated them that they forgot the Amrita for the moment, which the gods drank. One of the Asuras, however, Ráhu, assumed the form of a god or Deva, and began to drink. The immortalising nectar had not gone farther than his throat when the sun and moon saw the deceit and discovered it to Naraya, who cut off Ráhu's head. The head of Ráhu, being immortal, bounded to the sky, where its efforts to devour the sun and moon, which betrayed him, causes their eclipses. The tail (Ketu) also enjoys immortality in a lower plane, and is the fatal planet which sends diseases on mankind. A furious war between the gods and the Asuras has been waged ever since. And since the Devas are the strongest, it is not wonderful that it should have passed into the folklore of the whole Aryan world that the evil host are for ever seeking to recover by cunning the Amrita. The Serpents guarding the paradise of the Devas have more than once, in a mythologic sense, been induced to betray their trust and glide into the divine precincts to steal the coveted draught. This is the Kvásir[2] of the Scandinavian Mythology, which is the source of that poetic inspiration whose songs have magical potency. The sacramental symbol of the Amrita in Hindu Theology is the Soma juice, and this plant Indra is declared in the Rig-Veda (i. 130) to have discovered "hidden, like the nestlings of a bird, amidst a pile of rocks enclosed by bushes," where the dragon Drought had concealed it. Indra, in the shape of a hawk, flew away with it. In the Prose Edda the Frost Giant Suttung has concealed the sacred juice, and it is kept by the maid Gunlauth in a cavern overgrown with bushes. Bragi bored a hole through the rock. Odin in the shape of a worm crept through the crevice; then resuming his godlike shape, charmed the maid into permitting him to drink one draught out of the three jars; and, having left no drop, in form of an eagle flew to Asgard, and discharged in the jars the wonder-working liquid. Hence poetry is called Odin's booty, and Odin's gift.

Those who attentively compare these myths with the legend in Genesis will not have any need to rest upon the doubtful etymology of 'Adam' [3] to establish the Ayran origin of the latter. The Tree of the knowledge of Good and Evil which made man 'as one of us' (the Elohim) is the Soma of India, the Haoma of Persia, the *kvásir* of

Scandinavia, to which are ascribed the intelligence and powers of the gods, and the ardent thoughts of their worshippers. The Tree of Immortality is the Amrita, the only monopoly of the gods. 'The Lord God said, Behold the man is become as one of us, to know good and evil: and now, lest he put forth his hand, and take also of the tree of life, and eat, and live for ever: Therefore the Lord God sent him forth the garden of Eden to till the ground whence he had been taken. So he drove out the man; and he placed on the east of the garden of Eden cherubim, and a flaming sword which turned every way, to guard the way of the tree of life.'

This flaming sword turning every way is independent of the cherub, and takes the place of the serpent which had previously guarded the Meru paradise, but is now an enemy no longer to be trusted.

If the reader will now re-read the story in Genesis with the old names restored, he will perceive that there is no puzzle at all in any part of it:—'Now Ráhu [because he had stolen and tasted Soma] was more subtle than any beast of the field which the Devas had made, and he said to Adea Suktee, the first woman, Have the Devas said you shall not eat of every tree in the garden? And she said unto Ráhu, We may eat of the fruit of the trees of the garden; but of the Soma-plant, which is in the middle of the garden, the Devas have said we shall not eat or touch it on pain of death. Then Ráhu said to Adea, You will not suffer death by tasting Soma [I have done so, and live]: the Devas know that on the day when you taste it your eyes shall be opened, and you will be equal to them in knowledge of good and evil ... [and you will be able at once to discover which tree it is that bears the fruit which renders you immortal—the Amrita].... Adea took of the Soma and did eat, and gave also unto Adima, her husband, and the eyes of them both were opened.... And Indra, chief of the Devas, said to Ráhu, Because you have done this, you are cursed above all cattle and above every beast of the field; [for they shall transmigrate, their souls ascend through higher forms to be absorbed in the Creative principle; but] upon thy belly shalt thou go [remaining transfixed in the form you have assumed to try and obtain the Amrita]; and [instead of the ambrosia you aimed at] you shall eat dirt through all your existence.... And Indra said, Adima and Adea Suktee have [tasted Soma, and] become as one of us Devas [so far as] to know good and evil; and now, lest man put forth his hand [on our precious Amrita], and take also of the tree of life, and eat, and live for ever [giving us another race of Asuras or Serpent-men to compete with].... Indra and the Devas drove Adima out of Meru, and placed watch-dogs at the east of the garden; and [a sinuous darting flame, precisely matched to the now unchangeable form of Ráhu], a flaming sword which turned every way, to keep the way of the Amrita from Adima and Asuras.'

While the gods and serpents were churning the ocean for the Amrita, all woes and troubles for mortals came up first. That ocean shrinks in one region to the box of Pandora, in another to the fruit eaten by Eve. How foreign such a notion is to the Hebrew theology is shown by the fact that even while the curses are falling from the fatal fruit on the earth and man, they are all said to have proceeded solely from Jehovah, who is thus made to supplement the serpent's work.

It will be seen that in the above version of the story in Genesis I have left out various passages. These are in part such as must be more fully treated in the succeeding chapter, and in part the Semitic mosses which have grown upon the Aryan boulder. But even after the slight treatment which is all I have space to devote to the comparative study of the myth in this aspect, it may be safely affirmed that the problems which we found insoluble by Hebrew correlatives no longer exist if an Aryan origin be assumed. We know why the fruit of knowledge was forbidden: because it endangered the further fruit of immortality. We know how the Serpent might be condemned to crawl for ever without absurdity: because he was of a serpent-race, able to assume higher forms, and capable of transmigration, and of final absorption. We know why the eating of the fruit brought so many woes: it was followed by the stream of poison from the churned ocean which accompanied the Amrita, and which would have destroyed the race of both gods and men, had not Siva drank it up. If anything were required to make the Aryan origin of the fable certain, it will be found in the fact which will appear as we go on,—namely, that the rabbins of our era, in explaining the legend which their fathers severely ignored, did so by borrowing conceptions foreign to the original ideas of their race,—notions about human transformation to animal shapes, and about the Serpent (which Moses honoured), and mainly of a kind travestying the Iranian folklore. Such contact with foreign races for the first time gave the Jews any key to the legend which their patriarchs and prophets were compelled to pass over in silence.

## NOTES

1 See pp. 46 and 255. The episode is in Mahábhárata, I. 15.

2 Related to the Slav Kvas, with which, in Russian folklore, the Devil tried to circumvent Noah and his wife, as related in chap. xxvii. part iv.

3 In Sanskrit Adima means 'the first;' in Hebrew Adam (given almost always with the article) means 'the red,' and it is generally derived from adamah, mould or soil. But Professor Max Müller (Science of Religion, p. 320) says if the name Adima (used, by the way, in India for the first man, as Adam is in England) is the same as Adam, 'we should be driven to admit that Adam was borrowed by the Jews from the Hindus.' But even that mild case of 'driving' is unnecessary, since the word, as Sale reminded the world, is used in the Persian legend. It is probable that the Hebrews imported this word not knowing its meaning, and as it resembled their word for mould, they added the gloss that the first man was made of the dust or mould of the ground. It is not contended that the Hebrews got their word directly from the Hindu or Persian myth. Mr. George Smith discovered that Admi or Adami was the name for the first men in Chaldean fragments. Sir Henry Rawlinson points out that the ancient Babylonians recognised two principle races,—the Adamu, or dark, and the Sarku, or light, race; probably a distinction, remembered in the phrase of Genesis, between the supposed sons of Adam and the sons of God. The dark race was the one that fell. Mr. Herbert Spencer (Principles of Sociology, Appendix) offers an ingenious suggestion that the prohibition of a certain sacred fruit may have been the provision of a light race against a dark one, as in Peru only the Yuca and his relatives were allowed to eat the stimulating cuca. If this be true in the present case, it would still only reflect an earlier tradition that the holy fruit was the rightful possession of the deities who had won in the struggle for it.

Nor is there wanting a survival from Indian tradition in the story of Eve. Adam said, 'This now is bone of my bone, and flesh of my flesh.' In the Manu Code (ix. 22) it is written: 'The bone of woman is united with the bone of man, and her flesh with his flesh.' The Indian Adam fell in twain, becoming male and female (Yama and Yami). Ewald (Hist. of Israel, i. 1) has put this matter of the relation between Hebrew and Hindu traditions, as it appears to me, beyond doubt. See also Goldziher's Heb. Mythol., p. 326; and Professor King's Gnostics, pp. 9, 10, where the historic conditions under which the importation would naturally have occurred are succinctly set forth. Professor King suggests that Parsî and Pharisee may be the same word.

# Chapter VIII
## Eve

The Fall of Man — Fall of gods — Giants — Prajápati and Ráhu — Woman and
Star-serpent in Persia — Meschia and Meschiane — Bráhman legends of the
creation of Man — The strength of Woman — Elohist and Jehovist creations of
Man — The Forbidden Fruit — Eve reappears as Sara — Abraham surrenders
his wife to Jehovah — The idea not sensual — Abraham's circumcision — The
evil name of Woman — Noah's wife — The temptation of Abraham — Rabbinical
legends concerning Eve — Pandora — Sentiment of the Myth of Eve

THE INSIGNIFICANCE OF the Serpent of Eden in the scheme and
teachings of the Hebrew Bible is the more remarkable when it is
considered that the pessimistic view of human nature is therein fully
represented. In the story of the Temptation itself, there is, indeed,
no such generalisation as we find in the modern dogma of the Fall
of Man; but the elements of it are present in the early assumption
that the thoughts of man's heart run to evil continually,—which must
be an obvious fact everywhere while goodness is identified with
fictitious merits. There are also expressions suggesting a theory of
heredity, of a highly superstitious character,—the inheritance being
by force of the ancestral word or act, and without reference to inherent qualities. Outward merits and demerits are transmitted for
reward and punishment to the third and fourth generation; but the
more common-sense view appears to have gradually superseded
this, as expressed in the proverb that the fathers ate sour grapes
and the children's teeth were on edge.

In accounting for this condition of human nature, popular
traditions among the Jews always pointed rather to a fall of the

gods than to any such catastrophe to man. 'The sons of the Elohim (gods) saw the daughters of men that they were beautiful, and they took to themselves for wives whomsoever they chose.' 'There were giants in the earth in those days; and also after that, when the sons of God came in unto the daughters of men, and they bare children to them, the same became mighty men, which were of old men of renown.'[1] These giants were to the Semitic mind what the Ahis, Vritras, Sushnas and other monsters were to the Aryan, or Titans to the Greek mind. They were not traced to the Serpent, but to the wild nature-gods, the Elohim, and when Jehovah appears it is to wage war against them. The strength of this belief is illustrated in the ample accounts given in the Old Testament of the Rephaim and their king Og, the Anakim and Goliath, the Emim, the Zamzummim, and others, all of which gained full representation in Hebrew folklore. The existence of these hostile beings was explained by their fall from angelic estate.

The Book of Enoch gives what was no doubt the popular understanding of the fall of the angels and its results. Two hundred angels took wives of the daughters of men, and their offspring were giants three thousand yards in height. These giants having consumed the food of mankind, began to devour men, whose cries were brought to the attention of Jehovah by his angels. One angel was sent to warn Noah of the Flood; another to bind Azazel in a dark place in the desert till the Judgment Day; Gabriel was despatched to set the giants to destroying one another; Michael was sent to bury the fallen angels under the hills for seventy generations, till the Day of Judgment, when they should be sent to the fiery abyss for ever. Then every evil work should come to an end, and the plant of righteousness spring up.[2]

Such exploits and successes on the part of the legal Deity against outlaws, though they may be pitched high in heroic romance, are found beside a theology based upon a reverse situation. Nothing is more fundamental in the ancient Jewish system than the recognition of an outside world given over to idolatry and wickedness, while Jews are a small colony of the children of Israel and chosen of Jehovah. Such a conception in primitive times is so natural, and possibly may have been so essential to the constitution of nations, that it is hardly useful to look for parallels. Though nearly all races see in their traditional dawn an Age of Gold, a Happy Garden, or some corresponding felicity, these are normally defined against anterior chaos or surrounding ferocity. Every Eden has had its guards.

When we come to legends which relate particularly to the way in which the early felicity was lost, many facts offer themselves for comparative study. And with regard to the myths of Eden and Eve, we may remark what appears to have been a curious interchange of legends between the Hebrews and Persians. The ancient doctrines of India and Persia concerning Origins are largely, if not altogether, astronomical. In the Genesis of India we see a golden egg floating on a shoreless ocean; it divides to make the heaven above and earth beneath; from it emerges Prajápati, who also falls in twain to make the mortal and immortal substances; the parts of him again divide to make men and women on earth, sun and moon in the sky. This is but one version out of many, but all the legends about Prajápati converge in making him a figure of Indian astronomy. In the Rig-Veda he is Orion, and for ever lies with the three arrows in his belt which Sirius shot at him because of his love for Aldebaran,—towards which constellation he stretches. Now, in a sort of antithesis to this, the evil Ráhu is also cut in twain, his upper and immortal part pursuing and trying to eclipse the sun and moon, his tail (Ketu) becoming the 9th planet, shedding evil influences on mankind.[3] This tail, Ketu, is quite an independent monster, and we meet with him in the Persian planisphere, where he rules the first of the six mansions of Ahriman, and is the 'crooked serpent' mentioned in the Book of Job. By referring to vol. i. p. 253, the reader will see that this Star-serpent must stand as close to the woman with her child and sheaf as September stands to October. But unquestionably the woman was put there for honour and not disgrace; with her child and sheaf she represented the fruitage of the year.

There is nothing in Persian Mythology going to show that the woman betrayed her mansion of fruitage—the golden year—to the Serpent near her feet. In the Bundehesch we have the original man, Kaiomarts, who is slain by Ahriman as Prajápati (Orion) was by Sirius; from his dead form came Meschia and Meschiane, the first human pair. Ahriman corrupts them by first giving them goats' milk, an evil influence from Capricorn. After they had thus injured themselves he tempted them with a fruit which robbed them of ninety-nine hundredths of their happiness. In all this there is no indication that the woman and man bore different relations to the calamity. But after a time we find a Parsî postscript to this effect: 'The woman was the first to sacrifice to the Devas.' This is the one item in the Parsî Mythology which shows bias against woman, and as it is unsupported by the narratives preceding it, we may suppose that it was derived from some foreign country.

That country could hardly have been India. There is a story in remote districts of India which relates that the first woman was born out of an expanding lotus on the Ganges, and was there received in his paradise by the first man (Adima, or Manu). Having partaken of the Soma, they were expelled, after first being granted their prayer to be allowed a last draught from the Ganges; the effect of the holy water being to prevent entire corruption, and secure immortality to their souls. But nowhere in Indian legend or folklore do we find any special dishonour put upon woman such as is described in the Hebrew story.

Rather we find the reverse. Early in the last century, a traveller, John Marshall, related stories of the creation which he says were told him by the Brahmins, and others 'by the Brahmins of Persia.'[4]

'Once on a time,' the Brahmins said, 'as (God) was set in eternity, it came into his mind to make something, and immediately no sooner had he thought the same, but that the same minute was a perfect beautiful woman present immediately before him, which he called Adea Suktee, that is, the first woman. Then this figure put into his mind the figure of a man; which he had no sooner conceived in his mind, but that he also started up, and represented himself before him; this he called Manapuise, that is, the first man; then, upon a reflection of these things, he resolved further to create several places for them to abide in, and accordingly, assuming a subtil body, he breathed in a minute the whole universe, and everything therein, from the least to the greatest.'

'The Brahmins of Persia tell certain long stories of a great Giant that was led into a most delicate garden, which, upon certain conditions, should be his own for ever. But one evening in a cool shade one of the wicked Devatas, or spirits, came to him, and tempted him with vast sums of gold, and all the most precious jewels that can be imagined; but he courageously withstood that temptation, as not knowing what value or use they were of: but at length this wicked Devata brought to him a fair woman, who so charmed him that for her sake he most willingly broke all his conditions, and thereupon was turned out.'

In the first of these two stories the names given to the man and woman are popular words derived from Sanskrit. In the second the Persian characters are present, as in the use of Devatas to denote wicked powers; but for the rest, this latter legend appears to me certainly borrowed from the Jews so far as the woman is concerned. It was they who first perceived any connection between Virgo in the sixth mansion of Ormuzd, and Python in the seventh, and returned the Persians their planisphere with a new gloss. Having adopted the Dragon's tail (Ketu) for a little preliminary performance, the Hebrew system dismisses that star-snake utterly; for it has already evolved a terrestrial devil from its own inner consciousness.

The name of that devil is—WOMAN. The diabolisation of woman in their theology and tradition is not to be regarded as any indication that the Hebrews anciently held women in dishonour; rather was it a tribute to her powers of fascination such as the young man wrote to be placed under the pillow of Darius—'Woman is strongest.' As Darius and his council agreed that, next to truth, woman is strongest—

stronger than wine or than kings, so do the Hebrew fables testify by interweaving her beauty and genius with every evil of the world.

Between the Elohist and Jahvist accounts of the creation of man, there are two differences of great importance. The Elohim are said to have *created* man in their own image, male and female,—the word for 'created' being *bará*, literally meaning to *carve* out. Jehovah Elohim is said to have *formed* man,—nothing being said about his own image, or about male and female,—the word *formed* being *yatsar'*. The sense of this word *yatsar* in this place (Gen. ii. 7) must be interpreted by what follows: Jehovah is said to have formed man out of the *aphar'*, which the English version translates dust, but the Septuagint more correctly *sperma*. The literal meaning is a finely volatilised substance, and in Numbers xxiii. 10, it is used to represent the seed of Jacob. In the Jehovistic creation it means that man was formed out of the seminal principle of the earth combined with the breath of Jehovah; and the legend closely resembles the account of the ancient Satapatha-Bráhmana, which shows the creative power in sexual union with the fluid world to produce the egg from which Prajápati was born, to be divided into man and woman.

These two accounts, therefore,—to wit, that in the first and that in the second chapter of Genesis,—must be regarded as being of different events, and not merely varying myths of the same event. The offspring of Jehovah were 'living souls,' an expression not used in connection with the created images of the giants or Elohim. The Elohist pair roam about the world freely eating all fruits and herbs, possessing nature generally, and, as male and female, encouraged to increase and multiply; but Jehovah carefully separates *his* two children from general nature, places them in a garden, forbids certain food, and does not say a word about sex even, much less encourage its functions.

Adam was formed simply to be the gardener of Eden; no other motive is assigned. In proposing the creation of a being to be his helper and companion, nothing is said about a new sex,—the word translated 'help-meet' (*ézer*) is masculine. Adam names the being made 'woman,' (Vulg. *Virago*) only because she has been made out of man, but sex is not even yet suggested. This is so marked that the compiler has filled up what he considered an omission with (verse 24) a little lecture on duty to wives.

It is plain that the jealously-guarded ambrosia of Aryan gods has here been adapted to signify the sexual relation. That is the fruit in the midst of the garden which is reserved. The eating of it is immediately associated with consciousness of nudity and shame. The curse upon Eve is appropriate. Having taken a human husband, she is to be his slave; she shall bring forth children in sorrow, and many of them (Gen. iii. 16). Adam is to lose his position in Jehovah's garden, and to toil in accursed ground, barren and thorny.

Cast out thus into the wilderness, the human progeny as it increased came in contact with the giant's progeny,—those created by the Elohim (Gen. i.). When these had intermarried, Jehovah said that the fact that the human side in such alliance had been originally vitalised by his breath could not now render it immortal, because 'he (man) also is flesh,' *i.e.*, like the creatures of the nature-gods. After two great struggles with these Titans, drowning most of them, hurling down their tower and scattering them, Jehovah resolved upon a scheme of vast importance, and one which casts a flood of light upon the narrative just given. Jehovah's great aim is shown in the Abrahamic covenant to be to found a family on earth, of which he can say, 'Thou art my son; I have begotten thee.' Eve was meant to be the mother of that family, but by yielding to her passion for the man meant only to be her companion she had thwarted the purpose of Jehovah. But she reappears again under the name of Sara; and from first to last the sense of these records, however overlaid by later beliefs, is the expansion, varying fortunes, and gradual spiritualisation of this aspiration of a deity for a family of his own in the earth.

Celsus said that the story of the Virgin Mary and the Holy Ghost is one in which Christians would find little 'mystery' if the names were Danaë and Jupiter. The same may be said of the story of Sara and Jehovah, of which that concerning Mary is a theological travesty. Sarai (as she was called before her transfer to Jehovah, who then forbade Abraham to call her '*My* Princess,' but only 'Princess') was chosen because she was childless. Abraham was paid a large recompense for her surrender, and provision was made that he should have a mistress, and by her a son. This natural son was to be renowned and have great possessions; nominally Abraham was to be represented by Sara's miraculously-conceived son, and to control his fortunes, but the blood of the new race was to be purely divine in its origin, so that every descendant of Isaac might be of Jehovah's family in Abraham's household.

Abraham twice gave over his wife to different kings who were jealously punished by Jehovah for sins they only came near committing unconsciously, while Abraham himself was not even rebuked for the sin he did commit. The forbidden fruit was not eaten this time; and the certificate and proof of the supernatural conception of Isaac were made clear in Sarah's words—'God hath made me to laugh: all that hear will laugh with me: who would have said unto Abraham that Sarah should have given children suck? for I have borne a son in his old age.'[5]

It was the passionate nature and beauty of Woman which had thus far made the difficulty. The forbidden fruit was 'pleasant to the eyes,' and Eve ate it; and it was her 'voice' to which Adam had hearkened rather than to that of Jehovah (Gen. iii. 17). And, again, it was the easy virtue and extreme beauty of Sara (Gen. xii. 11, 14) which endangered the new scheme. The rabbinical traditions are again on this point very emphatic. It is related that when Abram came to the border of Egypt he hid Sara in a chest, and was so taking her into that country. The collector of customs charged that the chest contained raiment, silks, gold, pearls, and Abram paid for all these; but this only increased the official's suspicions, and he compelled Abram to open the chest; when this was done and Sara rose up, the whole land of Egypt was illumined by her splendour.[6]

There is no reason for supposing that the ideas underlying the relation which Jehovah meant to establish with Eve, and succeeded in establishing with Sara, were of a merely sensual description. These myths belong to the mental region of ancestor-worship, and the fundamental conception is that of founding a family to reign over all other families. Jehovah's interest is in Isaac rather than Sara, who, after she has borne that patriarch, lapses out of the story almost as completely as Eve. The idea is not, indeed, so theological as it became in the Judaic-christian legend of the conception of Jesus by Mary as spouse of the Deity; it was probably, however, largely ethnical in the case of Eve, and national in that of Sara.

It being considered of the utmost importance that all who claimed the advantages in the Jewish commonwealth accruing only to the legal, though nominal, 'children of Abraham,' should really be of divine lineage, security must be had against Isaac having any full brother. It might be that in after time some natural son of Sara might claim to be the one born of divine parentage, might carry on the Jewish commonwealth, slay the children of Jehovah by Sara, and so end the divine lineage with the authority it carried. Careful precautions having been taken that Ishmael should be an 'irreconcilable,' there is reason to suspect that the position of Isaac as Jehovah's 'only-begotten son' was secured by means obscurely hinted in the circumcision first undergone by Abraham, and made the sign of the covenant. That circumcision, wheresoever it has survived, is the relic of a more horrible practice of barbarian asceticism, is hardly doubtful; that the original rite was believed to have been that by which Abraham fulfilled his contract with Jehovah, appears to me intimated in various passages of the narrative which have survived editorial arrangement in accordance with another view. For instance, the vast inducements offered Abraham, and the great horror that fell on the patriarch, appear hardly explicable on the theory that nothing was conceded on Abraham's side beyond the surrender of a wife whom he had freely consigned to earthly monarchs.

Though the suspicion just expressed as to the nature of Abraham's circumcision may be doubted, it is not questionable that the rite of circumcision bears a significance in rabbinical traditions and Jewish usages which renders its initiation by Abraham at least a symbol of marital renunciation. Thus, the custom of placing in a room where the rite of circumcision was performed a pot of dust, was explained by the rabbins to have reference to the dust which Jehovah declared should be the serpent's food.[7] That circumcision should have been traditionally associated with the temptation of Eve is a confirmation of the interpretation which regards her (Eve) as the prototype of Sara and the serpent as sexual desire.

Although, if the original sense of Abraham's circumcision were what has been suggested, it had been overlaid, when the Book of Genesis in its present form was compiled, by different traditions, and that patriarch is described as having married again and had other children, the superior sanctity of Sara's son was preserved. Indeed, there would seem to have continued for a long time a tradition that the Abrahamic line and covenant were to be carried out by 'the seed of the woman' alone, and the paternity of Jehovah. Like Sara, Rebekah is sterile, and after her Rachel; the birth of Jacob and Esau from one, and of Joseph and Benjamin from the other, being through the intervention of Jehovah.

The great power of woman for good or evil, and the fact that it has often been exercised with subtlety—the natural weapon of the weak in dealing with the strong—are remarkably illustrated in the legends of these female figures which appear in connection with the divine schemes in the Book of Genesis. But even more the perils of woman's beauty are illustrated, especially in Eve and Sara. There were particular and obvious reasons why these representative women could not be degraded or diabolised in their own names or history, even where their fascinations tended to countervail the plans of Jehovah. The readiness with which Sara promoted her husband's prostitution and consented to her own, the treachery of Rebekah to her son Esau, could yet not induce Jewish orthodoxy to give evil names to the Madonnas of their race; but the inference made was expressed under other forms and names. It became a settled super- stition that wherever evil was going on, Woman was at the bottom of it. Potiphar's wife, Jezebel, Vashti, and Delilah, were among the many she-scape-goats on whom were laid the offences of their august official predecessors who 'could do no wrong.' Even after Satan has come upon the scene, and is engaged in tempting Job, it seems to have been thought essential to the task that he should have an agent beside the troubled man in the wife who bade him 'curse God and die.'

It is impossible to say at just what period the rabbins made their ingenious discovery that the devil and Woman entered the world at the same time,—he coming out of the hole left by removal of the rib from Adam before it was closed. This they found disclosed in the fact that it is in Genesis iii. 21, describing the creation of Woman, that there appears for the first time *Samech*—the serpent-letter S (in *Vajisgor*).[8] But there were among them many legends of a similar kind that leave one no wonder concerning the existence of a thanks- giving taught boys that they have not been created women, however much one may be scandalised at its continuance in the present day. It was only in pursuance of this theory of Woman that there was developed at a later day a female assistant of the Devil in another design to foil the plans of Jehovah, from the Scriptural narrative of which the female rôle is omitted. In the Scriptural legend of Noah his wife is barely mentioned, and her name is not given, but from an early period vague rumours to her discredit floated about, and these gathered consistency in the Gnostic legend that it was through her that Satan managed to get on board the Ark, as is elsewhere related (Part IV. chap. xxvii.), and was so enabled to resuscitate antediluvial violence in the drunken curses of Noah. Satan did this by working upon both the curiosity and jealousy of Noraita, the name assigned Noah's wife.

It has been necessary to give at length the comparative view of the myth of Eden in order that the reader may estimate the grounds upon which rests a theory which has been submitted after much hesitation concerning its sense. The 'phallic' theory by which it has become the fashion to interpret so many of these old fables, appears to me to have been done to death; yet I cannot come to any other conclusion concerning the legend of Eve than that she represents that passional nature of Woman which, before it was brought under such rigid restraint, might easily be regarded as a weakness to any tribe desirous of keeping itself separate from other tribes. The oath exacted by Abraham of his servant that he should seek out a wife from among his own people, and not among Canaanitish women, is one example among many of this feeling, which, indeed, survives among Jews at the present day. Such a sentiment might underlie the stories of Eve and Sara—the one mingling the blood of the family of Jehovah with mere human flesh, the other nearly confusing it with aliens. As the idea of tribal sanctity and separateness became strengthened by the further development of theocratic government, such myths would take on forms representing Jehovah's jealousy in defending his family line against the evil powers which sought to confuse or destroy it. One such attempt appears to underlie the story of the proposed sacrifice of Isaac. Although the account we have of that proceeding in the Bible was written at a time when the Elohist and Jahvist parties had compromised their rivalries to some extent, and suggests the idea that Jehovah himself ordered the sacrifice in order to try the faith of Abraham, enough of the primitive tradition lingers in the narrative to make it probable that its original intent was to relate how one of the superseded Elohim endeavoured to tempt Abraham to sacrifice Sara's only son, and so subvert the aim of Jehovah to perpetuate his seed. The God who 'tempted Abraham' is throughout sharply distinguished from the Jehovah who sent his angel to prevent the sacrifice and substitute an animal victim for Isaac.

Although, as we have seen, Sara was spared degradation into a she-devil in subsequent myths, because her body was preserved intact despite her laxity of mind, such was not the case with Eve. The silence concerning her preserved throughout the Bible after her fall is told was broken by the ancient rabbins, and there arose multitudinous legends in which her intimacies with devils are circumstantially reported. Her first child, Cain, was generally believed to be the son of one of the devils (Samaël) that consorted with her, and the world was said to be peopled with gnomes and demons which she brought forth during that 130 years at the end of which it is stated that Adam begot a son in his own image and likeness, and called his name Seth (Gen. v. 3). The previous children were supposed to be not in purely human form, and not to have been of Adam's paternity. Adam had during that time refused to have any children, knowing that he would only rear inmates of hell.

The legend of Eden has gone round the world doing various duty, but nearly always associated with the introduction of moral evil into the world. In the Lateran Museum at Rome there is a remarkable bas-relief representing a nude man and woman offering sacrifice before a serpent coiled around a tree, while an angel overthrows the altar with his foot. This was probably designed as a fling at the Ophites, and is very interesting as a survival from the ancient Aryan meaning of the Serpent. But since the adaptation of the myth by the Semitic race, it has generally emphasised the Tree of the Knowledge of Good and Evil, instead of the Tree of Immortality (Amrita), which is the chief point of interest in the Aryan myth. There are indeed traces of a conflict with knowledge and scepticism in it which we shall have to consider hereafter. The main popular association with it, the introduction into the world of all the ills that flesh is heir to, is perfectly consistent with the sense which has been attributed to its early Hebrew form; for this includes the longing for maternity, its temptations and its pains, and the sorrows and sins which are obviously traceable to it.

Some years ago, when the spectacular drama of 'Paradise' was performed in Paris, the Temptation was effected by means of a mirror. Satan glided behind the tree as a serpent, and then came forth as a handsome man, and after uttering compliments that she could not understand, presented Eve with a small oval mirror which explained them all. Mlle. Abingdon as Eve displayed consummate art in her expression of awakening self-admiration, of the longing for admiration from the man before her, and the various stages of self-consciousness by which she is brought under the Tempter's power. This idea of the mirror was no doubt borrowed from the corresponding fable of Pandora. On a vase (Etruscan) in the Hamilton Collection there is an admirable representation of Pandora opening her box, from which all evils are escaping. She is seated beneath a tree, around which a serpent is coiled. Among the things which have come out of the box is this same small oval mirror. In this variant, Hope, coming out last corresponds with the prophecy that the seed of the woman shall bruise the serpent's head. The ancient Etruscan and the modern Parisian version are both by the mirror finely connected with the sexual sense of the legend.

The theological interpretation of the beautiful myth of Eden represents a sort of spiritual vivisection; yet even as a dogma the story preserves high testimony: when woman falls the human race falls with her; when man rises above his inward or outward degradations and recovers his Paradise, it is because his nature is refined by the purity of woman, and his home sweetened by her heart. There is a widespread superstition that every Serpent will single out a woman from any number of people for its attack. In such dim way is felt her gentle bruising of man's reptilian self. No wonder that woman is excluded from those regions of life where man's policy is still to crawl, eat dust, and bite the heel.

It is, I suppose, the old Mystery of the Creation which left Coventry its legend of a Good Eve (Godiva, whose name is written 'good Eve' in a Conventry verse, 1494), whose nakedness should bring benefit to man, as that of the first Eve brought him evil. The fig-leaf of Eve, gathered no doubt from the tree whose forbidden fruit she had eaten, has gradually grown so large as to cloak her mind and spirit as well as her form. Her work must still be chiefly that of a spirit veiled and ashamed. Her passions suppressed, her genius disbelieved, her influence forced to seek hidden and often illegitimate channels, Woman now outwardly represents a creation of man to suit his own convenience. But the Serpent has also changed a great deal since the days of Eve, and now, as Intelligence, has found out man in his fool's-paradise, where he stolidly maintains that, with few exceptions, it *is* good for man to be alone. But good women are remembering Godiva; and realising that, the charms which have sometimes lowered man or cost him dear may be made his salvation. It shall be so when Woman can face with clear-eyed purity all the facts of nature, can cast away the mental and moral swathing-clothes transmitted from Eden, and put forth all her powers for the welfare of mankind,—a Good Eva, whom Coventry Toms may call naked, but who is 'not ashamed' of the garb of Innocence and Truth.

## NOTES

1 Gen. vi. 1, 2, 4.

2 vi.–xi. pp. 3–6. See Drummond's 'Jewish Messiah,' p. 21.

3 See vol. i. p. 255.

4 Phil. Trans. Ab. from 1700–1720, Part iv. p. 173.

5 Gen. xxi. 6, 7. The English version has destroyed the sense by supplying 'him' after 'borne.' Cf. also verses 1, 2. The rabbins were fully aware of the importance of the statement that it was Jehovah who 'opened the womb of Sara,' and supplemented it with various traditions. It was related that when Isaac was born, the kings of the earth refused to believe such a prodigy concerning even a beauty of ninety years; whereupon the breasts of all their wives were miraculously dried up, and they all had to bring their children to Sara to be suckled.

6 Fortieth Parascha, fol. 37, col. 1. The solar—or more correctly, so far as Sara is concerned, lunar—aspects of the legend of Abraham, Sara, and Isaac, however important, do not affect the human nature with which they are associated; nor is the special service to which they are pressed in Jewish theology altered by the theory (should it prove true) which derives these personages from Aryan mythology. There seems to be some reason for supposing that Sara is a semiticised form of Saranyú. The two stand in somewhat the same typical position. Saranyú, daughter of Tvashtar ('the fashioner'), was mother of the first human pair, Yama and Yami. Sara is the first mother of those born in a new (covenanted) creation. Each is for a time concealed from mortals; each leaves her husband an illegitimate representative. Saranyú gives her lord Savarná ('substitute'), who by him brings forth Manu,—that is 'Man,' but not the original perfect Man. Sara substitutes Hagar ('the fleeting'), and Ishmael is born, but not within the covenant.

7 Gen. iii. 14. Zerov. Hummor, fol. 8, col. 3. Parascha Bereschith. It is said that, according to Prov. xxv. 21, if thy enemy hunger thou must feed him; and hence dust must be placed for the serpent when its power over man is weakened by circumcision.

8 Parascha Bereschith, fol. 12, col. 4. Eisenmenger, Entdeckes Judenthum, ii. 409.

# Chapter IX
## Lilith

Madonnas — Adam's first wife — Her flight and doom — Creation of devils —
Lilith marries Samaël — Tree of Life — Lilith's part in the Temptation —
Her locks — Lamia — Bodeima — Meschia and Meschiane — Amazons —
Maternity — Rib-theory of Woman — Káli and Durga — Captivity of Woman

**THE ATTEMPT OF** the compilers of the Book of Genesis to amalgamate the Elohist and Jehovist legends, ignoring the moral abyss that yawns between them, led to some sufficiently curious results. One of these it may be well enough to examine here, since, though later in form than some other legends which remain to be considered, it is closely connected in spirit with the ancient myth of Eden and illustrative of it.

The differences between the two creations of man and woman critically examined in the previous chapter were fully recognised by the ancient rabbins, and their speculations on the subject laid the basis for the further legend that the woman created (Gen. i.) at the same time with Adam, and therefore not possibly the woman formed from his rib, was a first wife who turned out badly.

To this first wife of Adam it was but natural to assign the name of one of the many ancient goddesses who had been degraded into demonesses. For the history of Mariolatry in the North of Europe has been many times anticipated: the mother's tenderness and self-devotion, the first smile of love upon social chaos, availed to give every race its Madonna, whose popularity drew around her the fatal favours of priestcraft, weighing her down at last to be a type of corruption. Even the Semitic tribes, with their hard masculine deities, seem to have once worshipped Alilat, whose name survives in Elohim and Allah. Among these degraded Madonnas was Lilith, whose name has been found in a Chaldean inscription, which says, when a country is at peace 'Lilith (Lilatu) is not before them.' The name is from Assyr. *lay'lâ*, Hebrew *Lil*(night), which already in Accadian meant 'sorcery.' It probably personified, at first, the darkness that soothed children to slumber; and though the word *Lullaby* has, with more ingenuity than accuracy, been derived from *Lilith Abi*, the theory may suggest the path by which the soft Southern night came to mean a nocturnal spectre.

The only place where the name of Lilith occurs in the Bible is Isa. xxxiv. 14, where the English version renders it 'screech-owl.' In the Vulgate it is translated 'Lamia,' and in Luther's Bible, 'Kobold;' Gesenius explains it as 'nocturna, night-spectre, ghost.'

The rabbinical myths concerning Lilith, often passed over as puerile fancies, appear to me pregnant with significance and beauty. Thus Abraham Ecchelensis, giving a poor Arabic version of the legend, says, 'This fable has been transmitted to the Arabs from Jewish sources by some converts of Mahomet from Cabbalism and Rabbinism, who have transferred all the Jewish fooleries to the Arabs.'[1] But the rabbinical legend grew very slowly, and relates to principles and facts of social evolution whose force and meaning are not yet exhausted.

Premising that the legend is here pieced together mainly from

Eisenmenger,[2] who at each mention of the subjec gives ample references to rabbinical authorities, I will relate it without further references of my own.

Lilith was said to have been created at the same time and in the same way as Adam; and when the two met they instantly quarrelled about the headship which both claimed. Adam began the first conversation by asserting that he was to be her master. Lilith replied that she had equal right to be chief. Adam insisting, Lilith uttered a certain spell called *Schem-hammphorasch*—afterwards confided by a fallen angel to one of 'the daughters of men' with whom he had an intrigue, and of famous potency in Jewish folklore—the result of which was that she obtained wings. Lilith then flew out of Eden and out of sight.[3] Adam then cried in distress—'Master of the world, the woman whom thou didst give me has flown away.' The Creator then sent three angels to find Lilith and persuade her to return to the garden; but she declared that it could be no paradise to her if she was to be the servant of man. She remained hovering over the Red Sea, where the angels had found her, while these returned with her inflexible resolution. And she would not yield even after the angels had been sent again to convey to her, as the alternative of not returning, the doom that she should bear many children but these should all die in infancy.

This penalty was so awful that Lilith was about to commit suicide by drowning herself in the sea, when the three angels, moved by her anguish, agreed that she should have the compensation of possessing full power over all children after birth up to their eighth day; on which she promised that she would never disturb any babes who were under their (the angels') protection. Hence the charm (Camea) against Lilith hung round the necks of Jewish children bore the names of these three angels—Senói, Sansenói, and Sammangelóf. Lilith has special power over all children born out of wedlock for whom she watches, dressed in finest raiment; and she has especial power on the first day of the month, and on the Sabbath evening. When a little child laughs in its sleep it was believed that Lilith was with it, and the babe must be struck on the nose three times, the words being thrice repeated—'Away, cursed Lilith! thou hast no place here!'

The divorce between Lilith and Adam being complete, the second Eve (*i.e.*, Mother) was now formed, and this time out of Adam's rib in order that there might be no question of her dependence, and that the embarrassing question of woman's rights might never be raised again.

But about this time the Devils were also created. These beings were the last of the six days' creation, but they were made so late in the day that there was no daylight by which to fashion bodies for them. The Creator was just putting them off with a promise that he would make them bodies next day, when lo! the Sabbath—which was for a long time personified—came and sat before him, to represent the many evils which might result from the precedent he would set by working even a little on the day whose sanctity had already been promulgated. Under these circumstances the Creator told the Devils that they must disperse and try to get bodies as they could find them. On this account they have been compelled ever since to seek carnal enjoyments by nestling in the hearts of human beings and availing themselves of human senses and passions.

These Devils as created were ethereal spirits; they had certain atmospheric forms, but felt that they had been badly treated in not having been provided with flesh and blood, and they were envious of the carnal pleasures which human beings could enjoy. So long as man and woman remained pure, the Devils could not take possession of their bodies and enjoy such pleasures, and it was therefore of great importance to them that the first human pair should be corrupted. At the head of these Devils stood now a fallen angel—Samaël. Of this archfiend more is said elsewhere; at this point it need only be said that he had been an ideal flaming Serpent, leader of the Seraphim. He was already burning with lust and envy, as he witnessed the pleasures of Adam and Eve in Eden, when he found beautiful Lilith lamenting her wrongs in loneliness.

She became his wife. The name of Samaël by one interpretation signifies 'the Left'; and we may suppose that Lilith found him radical on the question of female equality which she had raised in Eden. He gave her a splendid kingdom where she was attended by 480 troops; but all this could not compensate her for the loss of Eden,—she seems never to have regretted parting with Adam,—and for the loss of her children. She remained the Lady of Sorrow. Her great enemy was Machalath who presided over 478 troops, and who was for ever dancing, as Lilith was for ever sighing and weeping. It was long believed that at certain times the voice of Lilith's grief could be heard in the air.

Samaël found in Lilith a willing conspirator against Jehovah in his plans for man and woman. The corruption of these two meant, to the troops of Samaël, bringing their bodies down into a plane where they might be entered by themselves (the Devils), not to mention at present the manifold other motives by which they were actuated. It may be remarked also that in the rabbinical traditions, after their Aryan impregnation, there are traces of a desire of the Devils to reach the Tree of Life.

Truly a wondrous Tree! Around it, in its place at the east of Eden, sang six hundred thousand lovely angels with happy hymns, and it glorified the vast garden. It possessed five hundred thousand different flavours and odours, which were wafted to the four sides of the world by zephyrs from seven lustrous clouds that made its canopy. Beneath it sat the disciples of Wisdom on resplendent seats, screened from the blaze of sun, moon, and cloud-veiled from potency of the stars (there was no night); and within were the joys referred to in the verse (Prov. viii. 21), 'That I may cause those that love me to inherit substance; and I will fill their treasures.'

*Fig. 1.—Lilith and Eve (Mediæval missal)*

Had there been an order of female rabbins the story of Lilith might have borne obvious modifications, and she might have appeared as a heroine anxious to rescue her sex from slavery to man. As it is the immemorial prerogative of man to lay all blame upon woman, that being part of the hereditary following of Adam, it is not wonderful that Lilith was in due time made responsible for the temptation of Eve. She was supposed to have beguiled the Serpent on guard at the gate of Eden to lend her his form for a time, after which theory the curse on the serpent might mean the binding of Lilith for ever in that form. This would appear to have originated the notion mentioned in Comestor (Hist. Schol., 12th cent.), that while the serpent was yet erect it had a virgin's head. The accompanying example is from a very early missal in the possession of Sir Joseph Hooker, of which I could not discover the date or history, but the theory is traceable in the eighth century. In this picture we have an early example of those which have since become familiar in old Bibles. Pietro d'Orvieto painted this serpent-woman in his finest fresco, at Pisa. Perhaps in no other picture has the genius of Michæl Angelo been more felicitous than in that on the ceiling of the Sistine Chapel, in which Lilith is portrayed. In this picture (Fig. 2) the marvellous beauty of his first wife appears to have awakened the enthusiasm of Adam; and, indeed, it is quite in harmony with the earlier myth that Lilith should be of greater beauty than Eve.

*Fig. 2.—Temptation and Expulsion (Michæl Angelo, Sistine Chapel)*

An artist and poet of our own time (Rossetti) has by both of his arts celebrated the fatal beauty of Lilith. His Lilith, bringing 'soft sleep,' antedates, as I think, the fair devil of the Rabbins, but is also the mediæval witch against whose beautiful locks Mephistopheles warns Faust when she appears at the Walpurgis-night orgie.

> The rose and poppy are her flowers; for where
> Is he not found, O Lilith, whom shed scent
> And soft-shed kisses and soft sleep shall snare?
> Lo! as that youth's eyes burned at thine, so went
> Thy spell through him, and left his straight neck bent,
> And round his heart one strangling golden hair.

The potency of Lilith's tresses has probably its origin in the hairy nature ascribed by the Rabbins to all demons (*shedim*), and found fully represented in Esau. Perhaps the serpent-locks of Medusa had a similar origin. Nay, there is a suggestion in Dante that these tresses of Medusa may have once represented fascinating rather than horrible serpents. As she approaches, Virgil is alarmed for his brother-poet:

'Turn thyself back, and keep thy vision hid;
For, if the Gorgon show, and then behold,
'Twould all be o'er with e'er returning up.'
So did the master say; and he himself
Turned me, and to my own hands trusted not,
But that with his too he should cover me.
O you that have a sane intelligence,
Look ye unto the doctrine which herein
Conceals itself 'neath the strange verses' veil.[4]

If this means that the security against evil is to veil the eyes from it, Virgil's warning would be against a beautiful seducer, similar to the warning given by Mephistopheles to Faust against the fatal charms of Lilith. Since, however, even in the time of Homer, the Gorgon was a popular symbol of terrors, the possibility of a survival in Dante's mind of any more primitive association with Medusa is questionable. The Pauline doctrine, that the glory of a woman is her hair, no doubt had important antecedents: such glory might easily be degraded, and every hair turn to a fatal 'binder,' like the one golden thread of Lilith round the heart of her victim; or it might ensnare its owner. In Treves Cathedral there is a curious old picture of a woman carried to hell by her beautiful hair; one devil draws her by it, another is seated on her back and drives her by locks of it as a bridle.

In the later developments of the myth of Lilith she was, among the Arabs, transformed to a Ghoul, but in rabbinical legend she appears to have been influenced by the story of Lamia, whose name is substituted for Lilith in the Vulgate. Like Lilith, Lamia was robbed of her children, and was driven by despair to avenge herself on all children.[5] The name of Lamia was long used to frighten Italian children, as that of Lilith was by Hebrew nurses.

It is possible that the part assigned to Lilith in the temptation of Eve may have been suggested by ancient Egyptian sculptures, which represent the Tree of Life in Amenti (Paradise) guarded by the Serpent-goddess Nu. One of these in the British Museum represents the Osirian on his journey to heaven, and his soul in form of a human-headed bird, drinking the water of Life as poured out to them from a jar by the goddess who coils around the sacred sycamore, her woman's bust and face appearing amid the branches much like Lilith in our old pictures.

The Singhalese also have a kind of Lilith or Lamia whom they call Bodrima, though she is not so much dreaded for the sake of children as for her vindictive feelings towards men. She is the ghost of a woman who died in childbirth and in great agony. She may be heard wailing in the night, it is said, and if she meets any man will choke him to death. When her wailing is heard men are careful to stay within doors, but the women go forth with brooms in their hands and abuse Bodrima with epithets. She fears women, especially when they carry brooms. But the women have also some compassion for this poor ghost, and often leave a lamp and some betel leaves where she may get some warmth and comfort from them. If Bodrima be fired at, there may be found, perhaps, a dead lizard near the spot in the morning.

As protomartyr of female independence, Lilith suffered a fate not unlike that of her sisters and successors in our own time who have appealed from the legendary decision made in Eden: she became the prototype of the 'strong-minded' and 'cold-hearted' woman, and personification of the fatal fascination of the passionless. Her special relation to children was gradually expanded, and she was regarded as the perilous seducer of young men, each of her victims perishing of unrequited passion. She was ever young, and always dressed with great beauty. It would seem that the curse upon her for forsaking Adam—that her children should die in infancy—was escaped in the case of the children she had by Samaël. She was almost as prolific as Echidna. Through all the latter rabbinical lore it is repeated, 'Samaël is the fiery serpent, Lilith the crooked serpent,' and from their union came Leviathan, Asmodeus, and indeed most of the famous devils.

There is an ancient Persian legend of the first man and woman, Meschia and Meschiane, that they for a long time lived happily together: they hunted together, and discovered fire, and made an axe, and with it built them a hut. But no sooner had they thus set up housekeeping than they fought terribly, and, after wounding each other, parted. It is not said which remained ruler of the hut, but we learn that after fifty years of divorce they were reunited.

These legends show the question of equality of the sexes to have been a very serious one in early times. The story of Meschia and Meschiane fairly represents primitive man living by the hunt; that of Eden shows man entering on the work of agriculture. In neither of these occupations would there be any reason why woman should be so unequal as to set in motion the forces which have diminished her physical stature and degraded her position. Women can still hunt and fish, and they are quite man's equal in tilling the soil.[6]

In all sex-mythology there are intimations that women were taken captive. The proclamation of female subordination is made not only in the legend of Eve's creation out of the man's rib, but in the emphasis with which her name is declared to have been given her because she was the Mother of all living. In the variously significant legends of the Amazons they are said to have burned away their breasts that they might use the bow: in the history of contemporary Amazons—such as the female Areoi of Polynesia—the legend is interpreted in the systematic slaughter of their children. In the hunt, Meschia might be aided by Meschiane in many ways; in dressing the garden Adam might find Lilith or Eve a 'help meet' for the work; but in the brutal régime of war the child disables woman, and the affections of maternity render her man's inferior in the work of butchery. Herakles wins great glory by slaying Hyppolite; but the legends of her later reappearances—as Libussa at Prague, &c.,—follow the less mythological story of the Amazons given by Herodotus (IV. 112), who represents the Scythians as gradually disarming them by sending out their youths to meet them with dalliance instead of with weapons. The youths went off with their captured captors, and from their union sprang the Sauromatæ, among whom the men and women dressed alike, and fought and hunted together. But of the real outcome of that truce and union Tennyson can tell us more than Herodotus: in his *Princess* we see the woman whom maternity and war have combined to produce, her independence betrayed by the tenderness of her nature. The surrender, once secured, was made permanent for ages by the sentiments and sympathies born of the child's appeal for compassion.

In primitive ages the child must in many cases have been a burthen even to man in the struggle for existence; the population question could hardly have failed to press its importance upon men, as it does even upon certain animals; and it would be an especial interest to a man not to have his hut overrun with offspring not his own,—turning his fair labour into drudgery for their support, and so cursing the earth for him. Thus, while Polyandry was giving rise to the obvious complications under which it must ultimately disappear, it would be natural that devils of lust should be invented to restrain the maternal instinct. But as time went on the daughters of Eve would have taken the story of her fall and hardships too much to heart. The pangs and perils of childbirth were ever-present monitors whose warnings might be followed too closely. The early Jewish laws bear distinct traces of the necessity which had arrived for insisting on the command to increase and multiply. Under these changed circumstances it would be natural that the story of a recusant and passionless Eve should arise and suffer the penalties undergone by Lilith,—the necessity of bearing, as captive, a vast progeny against her will only to lose them again, and to long for human children she did not bring forth and could not cherish. The too passionate and the passionless woman are successively warned in the origin and outcome of the myth.[7]

It is a suggestive fact that the descendants of Adam should trace their fall not to the independent Lilith, who asserted her equality at cost of becoming the Devil's bride, but to the apparently submissive Eve who stayed inside the garden. The serpent found out the guarded and restrained woman as well as the free and defiant, and with much more formidable results. For craft is the only weapon of the weak against the strong. The submissiveness of the captive woman must have been for a long time outward only. When Adam found himself among thorns and briars he might have questioned whether much had been gained by calling Eve his rib, when after all she really was a woman, and prepared to take her intellectual rights from the Serpent if denied her in legitimate ways. The question is, indeed, hardly out of date yet when the genius of woman is compelled to act with subtlety and reduced to exert its influence too often by intrigue.

It is remarkable that we find something like a similar development to the two wives of Adam in Hindu mythology also. Káli and Dúrga have the same origin: the former is represented dancing on the prostrate form of her 'lord and master,' and she becomes the demoness of violence, the mother of the diabolical 'Calas' of Singhalese demonolatry. Dúrga sacrificed herself for her husband's honour, and is now adored. The counterpart of Dúrga-worship is the Zenana system. In countries where the Zenana system has not survived, but some freedom has been gained for woman, it is probable that Káli will presently not be thought of as necessarily trampling on man, and Lilith not be regarded as the Devil's wife because she will not submit to be the slave of man. When man can make him a home and garden which shall not be a prison, and in which knowledge is unforbidden fruit, Lilith will not have to seek her liberty by revolution against his society, nor Eve hers by intrigue; unfitness for co-operation with the ferocities of nature will leave her a help meet for the rearing of children, and for the recovery and culture of every garden, whether within or without the man who now asserts over woman a lordship unnatural and unjust.

---

**NOTES**

1 Hist. Arabûm.
2 Entdeckes Judenthum.
3 This legend may have been in the mind of the writer of the Book of Revelations when (xii. 14) he describes the Woman who received wings that she might escape the Serpent. Lilith's wings bore her to the Serpent.
4 Inferno, ix. 56–64.
5 She was a Lybian Queen beloved by Zeus, whose children were victims of Hera's jealousy. She was daughter of Belus, and it is a notable coincidence, if no more, that in Gen. xxxvi. 'Bela' is mentioned as a king of Edom, the domain of Samaël, who married Lilith.
6 The martial and hunting customs of the German women, as well as their equality with men, may be traced in the vestiges of their decline. Hexe (witch) is from hag (forest): the priestesses who carried the Broom of Thor were called Hagdissen. Before the seventeenth century the Hexe was called Drud or Trud (red folk, related to the Lightning-god). But the famous female hunters and warriors of Wodan, the Valkyries, were so called also; and the preservation of the epithet (Trud) in the noble name Gertrude is a connecting link between the German Amazons and the political power so long maintained by women in the same country. Their office as priestesses probably marks a step downward from their outdoor equality. By this route, as priestesses of diabolised deities, they became witches; but many folk-legends made these witches still great riders, and the Devil was said to transform and ride them as dapplegrey mares. The chief charge against the witches, that of carnal commerce with devils, is also significant. Like Lilith, women became devils' brides whenever they were not content with sitting at home with the distaff and the child.
7 Mr. W. B. Scott has painted a beautiful picture of Eve gazing up with longing at a sweet babe in the tree, whose serpent coils beneath she does not see.

# Chapter X
## War in Heaven

The 'Other' — Tiamat, Bohu, 'the Deep' — Ra and Apophis — Hathors —
Bel's combat — Revolt in Heaven — Lilith — Myth of the Devil
at the creation of Light

IN NONE OF the ancient scriptures do we get back to any theory or explanation of the origin of evil or of the enemies of the gods. In a Persian text at Persepolis, of Darius I., Ahriman is called with simplicity 'the Other' (*Aniya*), and 'the Hater' (*Duvaisañt*, Zend *thaīsat*), and that is about as much as we are really told about the devils of any race. Their existence is taken for granted. The legends of rebellion in heaven and of angels cast down and transformed to devils may supply an easy explanation to our modern theologians, but when we trace them to their origin we discover that to the ancients they had no such significance. The angels were cast down to Pits prepared for them from the foundation of the world, and before it, and when they fell it was into the hands of already existing enemies eager to torment them. Nevertheless these accounts of rebellious spirits in heaven are of great importance and merit our careful consideration.

It is remarkable that the Bible opens with an intimation of the existence of this 'Other.' Its second verse speaks of a certain 'darkness upon the face of the deep.' The word used here is *Bohu*, which is identified as the Assyrian *Bahu*, the Queen of Hades. In the inscription of Shalmaneser the word is used for 'abyss of chaos.'[1] Bahu is otherwise Gula, a form of Ishtar or Allat, 'Lady of the House of Death,' and an epithet of the same female demon is Nin-cigal, 'Lady of the Mighty Earth.' The story of the Descent of Ishtar into Hades, the realm of Nin-cigal, has already been told (p. 77); in that version Ishtar is the same as Astarte, the Assyrian Venus. But like the moon with which she was associated she waned and declined, and the beautiful legend of her descent (like Persephone) into Hades seems to have found a variant in the myth of Bel and the Dragon. There she is a sea-monster and is called Tiamat (Thalatth of Berosus),—that is, 'the Deep,' over which rests the darkness described in Genesis i. 2. The process by which the moon would share the evil repute of Tiamat is obvious. In the Babylonian belief the dry land rested upon the abyss of watery chaos from which it was drawn. This underworld ocean was shut in by gates. They were opened when the moon was created to rule the night—therefore Prince of Darkness. The formation by Anu of this Moon-god (Uru) from Tiamat, might even have been suggested by the rising of the tides under his sway. The Babylonians represent the Moon as having been created before the Sun, and he emerged from 'a boiling' in the abyss. 'At the beginning of the month, at the rising of the night, his horns are breaking through to shine on heaven.'[2] In the one Babylonian design, a seal in the British Museum,[3] which seems referable to the legend of the Fall of Man, the male figure has horns. It may have been that this male Moon (Uru) was supposed to have been corrupted by some female emanation of Tiamat, and to have fallen from a 'ruler of the night' to an ally of the night. This female corrupter, who would correspond to Eve, might in this way have become mistress of the Moon, and ultimately identified with it.

Although the cause of the original conflict between the Abyss beneath and the Heaven above is left by ancient inscriptions and scriptures to imagination, it is not a very strained hypothesis that ancient Chaos regarded the upper gods as aggressors on her domain in the work of creation. 'When above,' runs the Babylonian legend, 'were not raised the heavens, and below on the earth a plant had not grown ... the chaos (or water) Tiamat was the producing mother of the whole of them.' 'The gods had not sprung up, any one of them.'[4] Indeed in the legend of the conflict between Bel and the Dragon, on the Babylonian cylinders, it appears that the god Sar addressed her as wife, and said, 'The tribute to thy maternity shall be forced upon them by thy weapons.'[5] The Sun and Moon would naturally be drawn into any contest between Overworld (with Light) and Underworld (with Darkness).

Though Tiamat is called a Dragon, she was pictured by the Babylonians only as a monstrous Griffin. In the Assyrian account of the fight it will be seen that she is called a 'Serpent.' The link between the two—Griffin and Serpent—will be found, I suspect, in Typhonic influence on the fable. In a hymn to Amen-Ra (the Sun), copied about fourteenth century B.C. from an earlier composition, as its translator, Mr. Goodwin, supposes, we have the following:—

> The gods rejoice in his goodness who exalts those who are lowly:
> Lord of the boat and barge,
> They conduct thee through the firmament in peace.
> Thy servants rejoice:
> Beholding the overthrow of the wicked:

His limbs pierced with the sword:
Fire consumes him:
His soul and body are annihilated.
NAKA (the serpent) saves his feet:
The gods rejoice:
The servants of the Sun are in peace.

The allusion in the second line indicates that this hymn relates to the navigation of Ra through Hades, and the destruction of Apophis.

We may read next the Accadian tablet (p. 256) which speaks of the seven Hathors as neither male nor female, and as born in 'the Deep.'

Another Accadian tablet, translated by Mr. Sayce, speaks of these as the 'baleful seven destroyers;' as 'born in the mountain of the sunset;' as being Incubi. It is significantly said:—'Among the stars of heaven their watch they kept not, in watching was their office.' Here is a primæval note of treachery.[6]

We next come to a further phase, represented in a Cuneiform tablet, which must be quoted at length:—

Days of storm, Powers of Evil,
Rebellious spirits, who were born in the lower part of heaven,
They were workers of calamity.

(The lines giving the names and descriptions of the spirits are here broken.)

The third was like a leopard,
The fourth was like a snake ...
The fifth was like a dog ...
The sixth was an enemy to heaven and its king.
The seventh was a destructive tempest.

These seven are the messengers of Anu [7] their king.
From place to place by turns they pass.
They are the dark storms in heaven, which into fire unite themselves.
They are the destructive tempests, which on a fine day sudden darkness cause.
With storms and meteors they rush.
Their rage ignites the thunderbolts of Im.[8]
From the right hand of the Thunderer they dart forth.
On the horizon of heaven like lightning they ...
Against high heaven, the dwelling-place of Anu the king, they plotted evil, and had none to withstand them.
When Bel heard this news, he communed secretly with his own heart.
Then he took counsel with Hea the great Inventor (or Sage) of the gods.
And they stationed the Moon, the Sun, and Ishtar to keep guard over the approach to heaven.
Unto Anu, ruler of heaven, they told it.
And those three gods, his children,
To watch night and day unceasingly he commanded them.
When those seven evil spirits rushed upon the base of heaven,
And close in front of the Moon with fiery weapons advanced,
Then the noble Sun and Im the warrior side by side stood firm.
But Ishtar, with Anu the king, entered the exalted dwelling, and hid themselves in the summit of heaven.


## Column II.

Those evil spirits, the messengers of Anu their king ...
They have plotted evil ...
From mid-heaven like meteors they have rushed upon the earth.
Bel, who the noble Moon in eclipse
Saw from heaven,
Called aloud to Paku his messenger:
O my messenger Paku, carry my words to the Deep.[9]
Tell my son that the Moon in heaven is terribly eclipsed!
To Hea in the Deep repeat this!

Paku understood the words of his Lord.
Unto Hea in the Deep swiftly he went.
To the Lord, the great Inventor, the god Nukimmut,
Paku repeated the words of his Lord.
When Hea in the Deep heard these words,
He bit his lips, and tears bedewed his face.
Then he sent for his son Marduk to help him.
Go to my son Marduk,
Tell my son that the Moon in heaven is terribly eclipsed!
That eclipse has been seen in heaven!
They are seven, those evil spirits, and death they fear not!
They are seven, those evil spirits, who rush like a hurricane,
And fall like firebrands on the earth!
In front of the bright Moon with fiery weapons (*they draw nigh*);
But the noble Sun and Im the warrior (*are withstanding them*).

**[The rest of the legend is lost.]**

Nukimmut is a name of Hea which occurs frequently: he was the good genius of the earth, and his son Marduk was his incarnation—a Herakles or Saviour. It will be noted that as yet Ishtar is in heaven. The next Tablet, which shows the development of the myth, introduces us to the great female dragon Tiamat herself, and her destroyer Bel.

... And with it his right hand he armed.
His naming sword he raised in his hand.
He brandished his lightnings before him.
A curved scymitar he carried on his body.
And he made a sword to destroy the Dragon,
Which turned four ways; so that none could avoid its rapid blows.
It turned to the south, to the north, to the east, and to the west.
Near to his sabre he placed the bow of his father Anu.
He made a whirling thunderbolt, and a bolt with double flames,
impossible to extinguish.

And a quadruple bolt, and a septuple bolt, and a ... bolt of crooked
fire.
He took the thunderbolts which he had made, and there were
seven of them,
To be shot at the Dragon, and he put them into his quiver behind
him.
Then he raised his great sword, whose name was 'Lord of the
Storm.'
He mounted his chariot, whose name was 'Destroyer of the
Impious.'
He took his place, and lifted the four reins
In his hand.

[Bel now offers to the Dragon to decide their quarrel by single
combat, which the Dragon accepts. This agrees with the representations of the combat on Babylonian cylinders in Mr. Smith's 'Chaldean
Genesis,' p. 62, etc.]

(Why seekest thou thus) to irritate me with blasphemies?
Let thy army withdraw: let thy chiefs stand aside:
Then I and thou (alone) we will do battle.
When the Dragon heard this.
Stand back! she said, and repeated her command.
Then the tempter rose watchfully on high.
Turning and twisting, she shifted her standing point,
She watched his lightnings, she provided for retreat.
The warrior angels sheathed their swords.
Then the Dragon attacked the just Prince of the gods.
Strongly they joined in the trial of battle,
The King drew his sword, and dealt rapid blows,
Then he took his whirling thunderbolt, and looked well behind and
before him:
And when the Dragon opened her mouth to swallow him,
He flung the bolt into her, before she could shut her lips.
The blazing lightning poured into her inside.
He pulled out her heart; her mouth he rent open;
He drew his (falchion), and cut open her belly.

He cut into her inside and extracted her heart;
He took vengeance on her, and destroyed her life.
When he knew she was dead he boasted over her.
After that the Dragon their leader was slain,
Her troops took to flight: her army was scattered abroad,
And the angels her allies, who had come to help her,
Retreated, grew quiet, and went away.
They fled from thence, fearing for their own lives,
And saved themselves, flying to places beyond pursuit.
He followed them, their weapons he broke up.
Broken they lay, and in great heaps they were captured.
A crowd of followers, full of astonishment,
Its remains lifted up, and on their shoulders hoisted.
And the eleven tribes pouring in after the battle
In great multitudes, coming to see,
Gazed at the monstrous serpent....


In the fragment just quoted we have the 'flaming sword which turned every way' (Gen. iii. 24). The seven distinct forms of evil are but faintly remembered in the seven thunderbolts taken by Bel: they are now all virtually gathered into the one form he combats, and are thus on their way to form the seven-headed dragon of the Apocalypse, where Michael replaces Bel.[10] 'The angels, her allies who had come to help her,' are surely that 'third part of the stars of heaven' which the apocalyptic dragon's tail drew to the earth in its fall (Rev. xii. 4). Bel's dragon is also called a 'Tempter.'

At length we reach the brief but clear account of the 'Revolt in Heaven' found in a cuneiform tablet in the British Museum, and translated by Mr. Fox Talbot:[11]—

The Divine Being spoke three times, the commencement of a
psalm.
The god of holy songs, Lord of religion and worship
seated a thousand singers and musicians: and established a choral
band
who to his hymn were to respond in multitudes....
With a loud cry of contempt they broke up his holy song spoiling,
confusing, confounding his hymn of praise.
The god of the bright crown with a wish to summon his adherents
sounded a trumpet blast which would wake the dead,
which to those rebel angels prohibited return
he stopped their service, and sent them to the gods who were his
enemies.
In their room he created mankind.
The first who received life, dwelt along with him.
May he give them strength never to neglect his word,
following the serpent's voice, whom his hands had made.
And may the god of divine speech expel from his five thousand
that wicked thousand
who in the midst of his heavenly song had shouted evil
blasphemies!

It will be observed that there were already hostile gods to
whom these riotous angels were sent. It is clear that in both the
Egyptian and Assyrian cosmogonies the upper gods had in their
employ many ferocious monsters. Thus in the Book of Hades, Horus
addresses a terrible serpent: 'My Kheti, great fire, of which this flame
in my eye is the emission, and of which my children guard the folds,
open thy mouth, draw wide thy jaws, launch thy flame against the
enemies of my father, burn their bodies, consume their souls!'[12] Many
such instances could be quoted. In this same book we find a great
serpent, Saa-Set, 'Guardian of the Earth.' Each of the twelve pylons
of Hades is surmounted by its serpent-guards—except one. What has

become of that one? In the last inscription but one, quoted in full, it will be observed (third line from the last) that *eleven* (angel) tribes came in after Bel's battle to inspect the slain dragon. The twelfth had revolted. These, we may suppose, had listened to 'the serpent's voice' mentioned in the last fragment quoted.

We have thus distributed through these fragments all the elements which, from Egyptian and Assyrian sources gathered around the legend of the Serpent in Eden. The Tree of Knowledge and that of Life are not included, and I have given elsewhere my reasons for believing these to be importations from the ancient Aryan legend of the war between the Devas and Asuras for the immortalising Amrita.

In the last fragment quoted we have also a notable statement, that mankind were created to fill the places that had been occupied by the fallen angels. It is probable that this notion supplied the basis of a class of legends of which Lilith is type. She whose place Eve was created to fill was a serpent-woman, and the earliest mention of her is in the exorcism already quoted, found at Nineveh. In all probability she is but another form of Gula, the fallen Istar and Queen of Hades; in which case her conspiracy with the serpent Samaël would be the Darkness which was upon the face of Bahu, 'the Deep,' in the second verse of the Bible.

The Bible opens with the scene of the gods conquering the Dragon of Darkness with Light. There is a rabbinical legend, that when Light issued from under the throne of God, the Prince of Darkness asked the Creator wherefore he had brought Light into existence? God answered that it was in order that he might be driven back to his abode of darkness. The evil one asked that he might see that; and entering the stream of Light, he saw across time and the world, and beheld the face of the Messiah. Then he fell upon his face and cried, 'This is he who shall lay low in ruin me and all the inhabitants of hell!'

What the Prince of Darkness saw was the vision of a race: beginning with the words (Gen. i. 3, 4), 'God said, Let there be Light; and there was Light; and God saw the Light that it was good; and God divided between the Light and the Darkness;' ending with Rev. xx. 1, 2, 'And I saw an angel come down from heaven having the key of the bottomless pit, and a great chain in his hand. And he laid hold on the dragon, that old serpent, which is the Devil and Satan, and bound him a thousand years.'

---

NOTES
1  'Records of the Past,' iii. p. 83. See also i. p. 135.
2  'Chaldean Genesis,' by George Smith, p. 70.
3  Copied in 'Chald. Gen.,' p. 91. As to the connection of this design with the legend of Eden, see chap. vii. of this volume.
4  'Chaldean Genesis,' pp. 62, 63.
5  Ib., 97.
6  'Records of the Past,' ix. 141.
7  Anu was the ruler of the highest heaven. Meteors and lightnings are similarly considered in Hebrew poetry as the messengers of the Almighty. (Psalm civ. 4, 'Who maketh his ministers a flaming fire,' quoted in Heb. i. 7.)
8  Im, the god of the sky, sometimes called Rimmon (the Thunderer). He answers to the Jupiter Tonans of the Latins.
9  The abyss or ocean where the god Hea dwelt.
10 The late Mr. G. Smith says that the Chaldean dragon was seven-headed. 'Chaldean Genesis,' p. 100.
11 'Records of the Past,' vii. 123.
12 'Records of the Past,' x. 127.

# Chapter XI
## War on Earth

'REJOICE, YE HEAVENS, and ye that dwell in them! Woe to the earth and the sea! for the devil is come down to you, having great wrath, because he knoweth that he hath but a short time.' This passage from the Book of Revelations is the refrain of many and much earlier scriptures. The Assyrian accounts of the war in heaven, given in the preceding chapter, by no means generally support the story that the archdragon was slain by Bel. Even the one that does describe the chief dragon's death leaves her comrades alive, and the balance of testimony is largely in favour of the theory which prevailed, that the rebellious angels were merely cast out of heaven, and went to swell the ranks of the dark and fearful abode which from the beginning had been peopled by the enemies of the gods. The nature of this abode is described in various passages of the Bible, and in many traditions.

'Out of the north an evil shall break forth upon all the inhabitants of the land.' So said Jeremiah (i. 14), in pursuance of nearly universal traditions as to the region of space in which demons and devils had their abode. 'Hell is naked before him,' says Job (xxvi. 6), 'and destruction hath no covering. He stretcheth out the north over the empty place.' According to the Hebrew mythology this habitation of demons was a realm of perpetual cold and midnight, which Jehovah, in creating the world, purposely left chaotic; so it was prepared for the Devil and his angels at the foundation of the world.

Although this northern hell was a region of disorder, so far as the people of Jehovah and the divine domain were concerned, they had among themselves a strong military and aristocratic government. It was disorder perfectly systematised. The anarchical atmosphere of the region is reflected in the abnormal structures ascribed to the many devils with whose traits Jewish and Arabic folklore is familiar, and which are too numerous to be described here. Such a devil, for instance, is Bedargon, 'hand-high,' with fifty heads and fifty-six hearts, who cannot strike any one or be struck, instant death ensuing to either party in such an attack. A more dangerous devil is Ketef, identified as the 'terror from the chambers' alluded to by Jeremiah (xxxii. 25), 'Bitter Pestilence.' His name is said to be from *kataf*, 'cut and split,' because he divides the course of the day; and those who are interested to compare Hebrew and Hindu myths may find it interesting to note the coincidences between Ketef and Ketu, the cut-off tail of Ráhu, and source of pestilence.[1] Ketef reigns neither in the dark or day, but between the two; his power over the year is limited to the time between June 17 and July 9, during which it was considered dangerous to flog children or let them go out after four P.M. Ketef is calf-headed, and consists of hide, hair, and eyes; he rolls like a cask; he has a terrible horn, but his chief terror lies in an evil eye fixed in his heart which none can see without instant death. The arch-fiend who reigns over the infernal host has many Court

Fools—probably meteors and comets—who lead men astray.

All these devils have their regulations in their own domain, but, as we have said, their laws mean disorder in that part of the universe which belongs to the family of Jehovah. In flying about the world they are limited to places which are still chaotic or waste. They haunt such congenial spots as rocks and ruins, and frequent desert, wilderness, dark mountains, and the ruins of human habitations. They can take possession of a wandering star.

There is a pretty Talmudic legend of a devil having once gone to sleep, when some one, not seeing him of course, set down a cask of wine on his ears. In leaping up the devil broke the cask, and being tried for it, was condemned to repay the damage at a certain period. The period having elapsed before the money was brought, the devil was asked the cause of the delay. He replied that it was very difficult for devils to obtain money, because men were careful to keep it locked or tied up; and 'we have no power,' he said, 'to take from anything bound or sealed up, nor can we take anything that is measured or counted; we are permitted to take only what is free or common.'

According to one legend the devils were specially angered, because Jehovah, when he created man, gave him dominion over things in the sea (Gen. i. 28), that being a realm of unrest and tempest which they claimed as belonging to themselves. They were denied control of the life that is in the sea, though permitted a large degree of power over its waters. Over the winds their rule was supreme, and it was only by reducing certain demons to slavery that Solomon was able to ride in a wind-chariot.

Out of these several realms of order and disorder in nature were evolved the angels and the devils which were supposed to beset man. The first man is said to have been like an angel. From the instant of his creation there attended him two spirits, whom the rabbins found shadowed out in the sentence, 'Jehovah-Elohim formed man of the dust of the ground, and breathed into his nostrils the breath of life; and man became a living soul' (Gen. ii. 7). This 'breath of life' was a holy spirit, and stood on Adam's right; the 'living soul' was a restless spirit on his left, which continually moved up and down. When Adam had sinned, this restless spirit became a diabolical spirit, and it has ever acted as mediator between man and the realm of anarchy.

It has been mentioned that in the Assyrian legends of the Revolt in Heaven we find no adequate intimation of the motive by which the rebels were actuated. It is said they interrupted the heavenly song, that they brought on an eclipse, that they afflicted human beings with disease; but why they did all this is not stated. The motive of the serpent in tempting Eve is not stated in Genesis. The theory which Cædmon and Milton have made so familiar, that the dragons aspired to rival Jehovah, and usurp the throne of Heaven, must, however, have been already popular in the time of Isaiah. In his rhapsody concerning the fall of Babylon, he takes his rhetoric from the story of Bel and the Dragon, and turns a legend, as familiar to every Babylonian as that of St. George and the Dragon now is to Englishmen, into an illustration of their own doom. The invective is directed against the King of Babylon, consequently the sex of the devil is changed; but the most remarkable change is in the ascription to Lucifer of a clear purpose to rival the Most High, and seize the throne of heaven.

'Hell from beneath is moved for thee to meet thee at thy coming, it stirreth up the (spirits of) the dead, even all the chief ones (great goats) of the earth: it hath raised up from their thrones all the kings of the nations (demon-begotten aliens). All these shall say unto thee, Art thou also become weak as we? Art thou become like unto us? Thy splendour is brought down to the underworld, and the noise of thy viols: the worm is spread under thee, and the worms cover thee. How art thou fallen, O Lucifer (Daystar), son of the morning! how art thou cut down to the ground which didst weaken the nations! For thou hast said in thy heart, I will ascend into (the upper) heaven, I will exalt my throne above the stars (archangels) of God: I will sit (reign) also upon the mount of the congregation (the assembly of the enemies of God) in the sides of the north. I will ascend above the heights of the clouds (the thunder-throne of Jehovah); I will be like the Most High. Yet shalt thou be brought down to hell, to the sides of the pit.'[2]

In this passage we mark the arena of the combat shifted from heaven to earth. It is not the throne of heaven but that of the world at which the fiends now aim. Nay, there is confession in every line of the prophecy that the enemy of Jehovah *has* usurped his throne. Hell has prevailed, and Lucifer is the Prince of this World. The celestial success has not been maintained on earth. This would be the obvious fact to a humiliated, oppressed, heavily-taxed people, who believed themselves the one family on earth sprung from Jehovah, and their masters the offspring of demons. This situation gave to the vague traditions of a single combat between Bel and the Dragon, about an eclipse or a riot, the significance which it retained ever afterward of a mighty conflict on earth between the realms of Light and Darkness, between which the Elohim had set a boundary-line (Gen. i. 4) in the beginning.

A similar situation returned when the Jews were under the sway of Rome, and then all that had ever been said of Babylon was repeated against Rome under the name of Edom. It recurred in the case of those Jews who acknowledged Jesus as their Messiah: in the pomp and glory of the Cæsars they beheld the triumph of the Powers of Darkness, and the burthen of Isaiah against Lucifer was raised again in that of the Apocalypse against the seven-headed Dragon. It is notable how these writers left out of sight the myth of Eden so far as it did not belong to their race. Isaiah does not say anything even of the serpent. The Apocalypse says nothing of the two wonderful trees, and the serpent appears only as a Dragon from whom the woman is escaping, by whom she is not at all tempted. The shape of the Devil, and the Combat with him, have always been determined by dangers and evils that are actual, not such as are archæological.

A gipsy near Edinburgh gave me his version of the combat between God and Satan as follows. 'When God created the universe and all things in it, Satan tried to create a rival universe. He managed to match everything pretty well except man. There he failed; and God to punish his pride cast him down to the earth and bound him with a chain. But this chain was so long that Satan was able to move over the whole face of the earth!' There had got into this wanderer's head some bit of the Babylonian story, and it was mingled with Gnostic traditions about Ildabaoth; but there was also a quaint suggestion in Satan's long chain of the migration of this mythical combat not only round the world, but through the ages.

The early followers of Christ came before the glories of Paganism with the legend that the lowly should inherit the earth. And though they speedily surrendered to the rulers of the world in Rome, and made themselves into a christian aristocracy, when they came into Northern Europe the christians were again brought to confront with an humble system the religion of thrones and warriors. St. Gatien celebrating mass in a cavern beside the Loire, meant as much weakness in presence of Paganism as the Huguenots felt twelve centuries later hiding in the like caverns from St. Gatien's priestly successors.

The burthen of Isaiah is heard again, and with realistic intensity, in the seventh century, and in the north, with our patriarchial poet Cædmon.

> The All-powerful had
> Angel-tribes,
> Through might of hand,
> The holy Lord,
> Ten established,
> In whom he trusted well
> That they his service
> Would follow,
> Work his will;
> Therefore gave he them wit,
> And shaped them with his hands,
> The holy Lord.
> He had placed them so happily,
> One he had made so powerful,
> So mighty in his mind's thought,
> He let him sway over so much,

Highest after himself in heaven's kingdom.
He had made him so fair,
So beauteous was his form in heaven,
That came to him from the Lord of hosts,
He was like to the light stars.
It was his to work the praise of the Lord,
It was his to hold dear his joys in heaven,
And to thank his Lord
For the reward that he had bestowed on him in that light;
Then had he let him long possess it;
But he turned it for himself to a worse thing,
Began to raise war upon him,
Against the highest Ruler of heaven,
Who sitteth in the holy seat.
Dear was he to our Lord,
But it might not be hidden from him
That his angel began
To be presumptuous,
Raised himself against his Master,
Sought speech of hate,
Words of pride towards him,
Would not serve God,
Said that his body was
Light and beauteous,
Fair and bright of hue:
He might not find in his mind
That he would God
In subjection,
His Lord, serve:
Seemed to himself
That he a power and force
Had greater
Than the holy God
Could have
Of adherents.
Many words spake
The angel of presumption:
Thought, through his own power,
How he for himself a stronger

Seat might make,
Higher in heaven:
Said that him his mind impelled,
That he west and north
Would begin to work,
Would prepare structures:
Said it to him seemed doubtful
That he to God would
Be a vassal.
'Why shall I toil?' said he;
'To me it is no whit needful.
To have a superior;
I can with my hands as many
Wonders work;
I have great power
To form
A diviner throne,
A higher in heaven.
Why shall I for his favour serve,
Bend to him in such vassalage?
I may be a god as he
Stand by me strong associates,
Who will not fail me in the strife,
Heroes stern of mood,
They have chosen me for chief,
Renowned warriors!
With such may one devise counsel,
With such capture his adherents;
They are my zealous friends,
Faithful in their thoughts;
I may be their chieftain,
Sway in this realm:
Thus to me it seemeth not right
That I in aught
Need cringe
To God for any good;
I will no longer be his vassal.'
When the All-powerful it
All had heard,

That his angel devised
Great presumption
To raise up against his Master,
And spake proud words
Foolishly against his Lord,
Then must he expiate the deed,
Share the work of war,
And for his punishment must have
Of all deadly ills the greatest.
So doth every man
Who against his Lord
Deviseth to war,
With crime against the great Ruler.
Then was the Mighty angry;
The highest Ruler of heaven
Hurled him from the lofty seat;
Hate had he gained at his Lord,
His favour he had lost,
Incensed with him was the Good in his mind,
Therefore must he seek the gulf
Of hard hell-torment,
For that he had warred with heaven's Ruler,
He rejected him then from his favour,
And cast him into hell,
Into the deep parts,
Where he became a devil:
The fiend with all his comrades
Fell then from heaven above,
Through as long as three nights and days,
The angels from heaven into hell;
And them all the Lord transformed to devils,
Because they his deed and word
Would not revere;
Therefore them in a worse light,
Under the earth beneath,
Almighty God
Had placed triumphless
In the swart hell;
There they have at even,

Immeasurably long,
Each of all the fiends,
A renewal of fire;
Then cometh ere dawn
The eastern wind,
Frost bitter-cold,
Ever fire or dart;
Some hard torment
They must have,
It was wrought for them in punishment,
Their world was changed:
For their sinful course
He filled hell
With the apostates.

*Fig. 3.—Satan Punished*

Whether this spirited description was written by Cædmon, and whether it is of his century, are questions unimportant to the present inquiry. The poem represents a mediæval notion which long prevailed, and which characterised the Mysteries, that Satan and his comrades were humiliated from the highest angelic rank to a hell already prepared and peopled with devils, and were there, and by those devils, severely punished. One of the illuminations of the Cædmon manuscript, preserved in the Bodleian Library, shows Satan undergoing his torment (Fig. 3). He is bound over something like a gridiron, and four devils are torturing him, the largest using a scourge with six prongs. His face manifests great suffering. His form is mainly human, but his bushy tail and animal feet indicate that he has been transformed to a devil similar to those who chastise him.

On Cædmon's foundation Milton built his gorgeous edifice. His Satan is an ambitious and very English lord, in whom are reflected the whole aristocracy of England in their hatred and contempt of the holy Puritan Commonwealth, the Church of Christ as he deemed it. The ages had brought round a similar situation to that which confronted the Jews at Babylon, the early Christians of Rome, and their missionaries among the proud pagan princes of the north. The Church had long allied itself with the earlier Lucifers of the north, and now represented the proud empire of a satanic aristocracy, and the persecuted Nonconformists represented the authority of the King of kings. In the English palace, and in the throne of Canterbury, Milton saw his Beelzebub and his Satan.

> Th' infernal serpent; he it was, whose guile,
> Stirred up with envy and revenge, deceived
> The mother of mankind, what time his pride
> Had cast him out from heav'n, with all his host
> Of rebel angels, by whose aid aspiring
> To set himself in glory above his peers

He trusted to have equall'd the Most High,
If he opposed; and with ambitious aim
Against the throne and monarchy of God
Raised impious war in heav'n, and battle proud,
With vain attempt. Him the almighty Power
Hurl'd headlong flaming from th' ethereal sky,
With hideous ruin and combustion, down
To bottomless perdition, there to dwell
In adamantine chains and penal fire,
Who durst defy th' Omnipotent to arms.[3]

This adaptation of the imagery of Isaiah concerning Lucifer has in it all the thunder hurled by Cromwell against Charles. Even a Puritan poet might not altogether repress admiration for the dash and daring of a Prince Rupert, to which indeed even his prosaic co-religionists paid the compliment of ascribing to it a diabolical source.[4] Not amid conflicts that raged in ancient Syria broke forth such lines as—

Better to reign in hell, than serve in heav'n.
With rallied arms to try what may be yet
Regain'd in heav'n, or what more lost in hell.

The Bel whom Milton saw was Cromwell, and the Dragon that serpent of English oppression which the Dictator is trampling on in a well-known engraving of his time. In the history of the Reformation the old legend did manifold duty again, as in the picture (Fig. 13) by Luther's friend Lucas Cranach.

It would seem that in the course of time Bel and the Dragon became sufficiently close allies for their worshippers to feed and defend them both with equal devotion, and for Daniel to explode them both in carrying on the fight of his deity against the gods of Babylon. This story of Bel is apocryphal as to the canon, but highly significant as to the history we are now considering. Although the Jews maintained their struggle against 'principalities and powers' long after it had been a forlorn hope, and never surrendered, nor made alliance with the Dragon, the same cannot be said of those who appropriated their title of 'the chosen of God,' counterfeited their covenant, and travestied their traditions. The alliance of Christianity and the Dragon has not been nominal, but fearfully real. In fulfilling their mission of 'inheriting the earth,' the 'meek' called around them and pressed into their service agents and weapons more diabolical than any with which the Oriental imagination had peopled the abode of devils in the north.

At a Fair in Tours (August 1878) I saw two exhibitions which were impressive enough in the light they cast through history. One was a shrunken and sufficiently grotesque production by puppets of the Mediæval 'Mystery' of Hell. Nearly every old scheme and vision of the underworld was represented in the scene. The three Judges sat to hear each case. A devil rang a bell whenever any culprit appeared at the gate. The accused was ushered in by a winged devil—Satan, the Accuser—who, by the show-woman's lips, stated the charges against each with an eager desire to make him or her out as wicked as possible. A devil with pitchfork received the sentenced, and shoved them down into a furnace. There was an array of brilliant dragons around, but they appeared to have nothing to do beyond enjoying the spectacle. But this exhibition which was styled 'Twenty minutes in Hell,' was poor and faint beside the neighbouring exhibition of the real Hell, in which Europe had been tortured for fifteen centuries. Some industrious Germans had got together in one large room several hundreds of the instruments of torture by which the nations of the West were persuaded to embrace Christianity. Every limb, sinew, feature, bone, and nerve of the human frame had suggested to christian inventiveness some ingenious device by which it might be tortured. Wheels on which to break bones, chairs of anguish, thumbscrews, the iron Virgin whose embrace pierced through every vital part; the hunger-mask which renewed for Christ's sake the exact torment of Tantalus; even the machine which bore the very name of the enemy that was cast down—the Dragon's Head! By such instrumentalities came those quasi-miraculous 'Triumphs of the Cross,' of which so much has been said and sung! The most salient phenomenon of christian history is the steady triumph of the Dragon. Misleader and Deceiver to the last, he is quite willing to sprinkle his fork and rack with holy water, to cross himself, to label his caldrons 'divine justice,' to write CHRIST upon his forehead; by so doing he was able to spring his infernal engine on the best nations, and cow the strongest hearts, till from their pallid lips were wrung the 'confessions of faith,' or the last cry of martyred truth. So was he able to assault the pure heavens once more, to quench the stars of human faith and hope, and generate a race of polite, learned, and civilised hypocrites. But the ancient sunbeams are after him: the mandate has again gone forth, 'Let there be light,' and the Light that now breaks forth is not of that kind which respects the limit of Darkness.

## NOTES

1 See i. pp. 46 and 255. Concerning Ketef see Eisenmenger, ii. p. 435.

2 Isaiah xiv. It may appear as if in this personification of a fallen star we have entered a different mythological region from that represented by the Assyrian tablets; but it is not so. The demoniac forms of Ishtar, Astarte, are fallen stars also. She appears in Greece as Artemis Astrateia, whose worship Pausanias mentions as coming from the East. Her development is through Asteria (Greek form of Ishtar), in whose myth is hidden much valuable Babylonian lore. Asteria was said to have thrown herself into the sea, and been changed into the island called Asteria, from its having fallen like a star from heaven. Her suicide was to escape from the embraces of Zeus, and her escape from him in form of a quail, as well as her fate, may be instructively compared with the story of Lilith, who flew out of Eden on wings to escape from Adam, and made an effort to drown herself in the Red Sea. The diabolisation of Asteria (the fallen star) was through her daughter Hecate. Hecate was the female Titan who was the most potent ally of the gods. Her rule was supreme under Zeus, and all the gifts valued by mortals were believed to proceed from her; but she was severely judicial, and rigidly withheld all blessings from such as did not deserve them. Thus she was, as the searching eye of Zeus, a star-spy upon earth. Such spies, as we have repeatedly had occasion to mention in this work, are normally developed into devils. From professional detectives they become accusers and instigators. Ishtar of the Babylonians, Asteria of the Greeks, and the Day-star of the Hebrews are male and female forms of the same personification: Hecate with her torch (ἕκατος, 'far-shooting') and Lucifer ('light-bringer' on the deeds of darkness) are the same in their degradation.

3 'Paradise Lost,' i. 40–50.

4 And foremost rides Prince Rupert, darling of fortune and of war, with his beautiful and thoughtful face of twenty-three, stern and bronzed already, yet beardless and dimpled, his dark and passionate eyes, his long love-locks drooping over costly embroidery, his graceful scarlet cloak, his white-plumed hat, and his tall and stately form. His high-born beauty is preserved to us for ever on the canvas of Vandyck, and as the Italians have named the artist 'Il Pittore Cavalieresco,' so will this subject of his skill remain for ever the ideal of Il Cavaliere Pittoresco. And as he now rides at the head of this brilliant array, his beautiful white dog bounds onward joyously beside him, that quadruped renowned in the pamphlets of the time, whose snowy skin has been stained by many a blood-drop in the desperate forays of his master, but who has thus far escaped so safely that the Puritans believe him a familiar spirit, and try to destroy him 'by poyson and extempore prayer, which yet hurt him no more than the plague plaster did Mr. Pym.' Failing in this, they pronounce the pretty creature to be 'a divell, not a very downright divell, but some Lapland ladye, once by nature a handsome white ladye, now by art a handsome white dogge.'—A Charge with Prince Rupert. Col. Higginson's 'Atlantic Essays.'

# Chapter XII
# **Strife**

Hebrew god of War — Samaël — The father's blessing and curse — Esau — Edom
— Jacob and the Phantom — The planet Mars — Tradesman and Huntsman —
'The Devil's Dream'

Who is this that cometh from Edom,
In dyed garments from Bozrah?
This that is glorious in his apparel,
Travelling in the greatness of his strength?
I who promise deliverance, mighty to save.
Wherefore art thou red in thine apparel,
And thy garments like him that treadeth the wine-vat?
I have trodden the wine-press alone;
And of the peoples there was none with me:
And I will tread them in mine anger,
And trample them in my fury;
And their blood shall be sprinkled upon my garments,
And I will stain all my raiment.
For the day of vengeance is in my heart,
And the year of mine avenged is come.
And I looked, and there was none to help;
And I wondered that there was none to uphold;
Therefore mine own arm gained me the victory,
And mine own fury, it upheld me.
And I will tread down the peoples in mine anger,
And make them drunk in my wrath,
And will bring down their strength to the earth.[1]

This is the picture of the god of War. Upon it the comment in *Emek Hammelech* is: 'The colour of the godless Samaël and of all his princes and lords has the aspect of red fire; and all their emanations are red. Samaël is red, also his horse, his sword, his raiment, and the ground beneath him, are red. In the future the Holy God shall wear his raiment.'[2] Samaël is leader of the Opposition. He is the Soul of the fiery planet Mars. He is the Creator and inspirer of all Serpents. Azazel, demon of the Desert, is his First Lord. He was the terrestrial Chief around whom the fallen angels gathered, and his great power was acknowledged. All these characters the ancient Rabbins found blended in his name. Simmé (dazzling), Sóme (blinding), Semól (the left side), and Samhammaveth (deadly poison), were combined in the terrible name of Samaël. He ruled over the *sinister* Left. When Moses, in war with the Amalekites, raised his ten fingers, it was a special invocation to the Ten Sephiroth, Divine Emanations, because he knew the power which the Amalekites got from Samaël might turn his own left hand against Israel.[3] The scapegoat was a sacrifice to him through Azazel.

Samaël is the mythologic expression and embodiment of the history of Esau, afterward Edom. Jacob and Esau represented the sheep and the goat, divided in the past and to be sundered for ever. As Jacob by covering his flesh with goat-skins obtained his father's blessing due to Esau, the Israelites wandering through the wilderness (near Edom's forbidden domain) seemed to have faith that the offering of a goat would convince his Viceroy Azazel that they were orthodox Edomites. The redness of Samaël begins with the red pottage from which Esau was called Edom. The English version does not give the emphasis with which Esau is said to have called for the pottage—"the red! the red!" The characteristics ascribed to Esau in the legend are merely a saga built on the local names with which he was associated. 'Edom' means red, and 'Seir' means hairy. It probably meant the 'Shaggy Mountains.'[4]

It is interesting to observe the parting of the human and the theological myths in this story. Jacob is the third person of a patriarchal trinity,—Abraham the Heavenly Father, Isaac the Laugher (the Sun), and Jacob the Impostor or Supplanter. As the moon supplants the sun, takes hold of his heel, shines with his light, so does Jacob supplant his elder brother; and all the deadliness ascribed to the Moon, and other Third Persons of Trinities, was inherited by Jacob until his name was changed by euphemism. As the impartial sun shines for good and evil, the smile of Isaac, the Laugher, promised great blessings to both of his sons. The human myth therefore represents both of them gaining great power and wealth, and after a long feud they are reconciled. This feature of the legend we shall consider hereafter. Jehovah has another interest to be secured. He had declared that one should serve the other; that they should be cursed who cursed Jacob; and he said, 'Jacob have I loved, Esau have I hated.' Jahvistic theology had here something more important than two brothers to harmonise; namely a patriarch's blessing and a god's curse. It was contrary to all orthodoxy that a man whom Jehovah hated should possess the blessings of life; it was equally unorthodox that a father's blessing should not carry with it every advantage promised. It had to be recorded that Esau became powerful, lived by his sword, and had great possessions.

It had also to be recorded that 'Edom revolted from under the hand of Judah and made a king unto themselves,' and that such independence continued 'unto this day' (2 Kings viii. 20, 22). There was thus no room for the exhibition of Jacob's superiority,—that is of Israel's priority over Edom,—in this world; nor yet any room to carry out Isaac's curse on all who cursed Jacob, and the saying: 'Jacob have I loved, Esau have I hated, and laid his mountains and his heritage waste for the dragons of the wilderness' (Mal. i.).

Answers to such problems as these evolve themselves slowly but inevitably. The agonised cry of the poor girl in Browning's poem—'There may be heaven, there must be hell'—marks the direction in which necessity led human speculation many ages before her. A future had to be invented for the working out of the curse on Esau, who on earth had to fulfil his father's blessing by enjoying power, wealth, and independence of his brother. In that future his greatness while living was repaid by his relegation to the desert and the rock with the he-goat for his support. Esau was believed to have been changed into a terrible hairy devil.[5] But still there followed him in his phantasmal transformation a ghostly environment of his former power and greatness; the boldest and holiest could not afford to despise or set aside that 'share' which had been allotted him in the legend, and could not be wholly set aside in the invisible world.

Jacob's share began with a shrewd bargain with his imprudent brother. Jacob by his cunning in the breeding of the streaked animals (Gen. xxx.), by which he outwitted Laban, and other manœuvres, was really the cause of bringing on the race called after him that repute for extortion, affixed to them in such figures as Shylock, which they have found it so hard to live down. In becoming the great barterers of the East, their obstacle was the plunderer sallying forth from the mountain fastnesses or careering over the desert. These were the traditional descendants of Esau, who gradually included the Ishmaelites as well as the Edomites, afterwards merged in the Idumeans. But as the tribal distinctions became lost, the ancient hostility survived in the abstract form of this satan of Strife—Samaël. He came to mean the spirit that stirs up antagonism between those who should be brethren. He finally became, and among the more superstitious Jews still is, instigator of the cruel persecutions which have so long pursued their race, and the prejudices against them which survive even in countries to whose wealth, learning, and arts they have largely contributed. In Jewish countries Edom has long been a name for the power of Rome and Romanism, somewhat in the same way as the same are called 'Babylon' by some christians. Jacob, when passing into the wilderness of Edom, wrestled with the invisible power of Esau, or Samaël, and had not been able to prevail except with a lame thigh,—a part which, in every animal, Israel thereafter held sacred to the Opposing Power and abstained from eating. A rabbinical legend represents Jacob as having been bitten by a serpent while he was lingering about the boundary of Edom, and before his gift of goats and other cattle had been offered to his brother. The fiery serpents which afflicted Israel were universally attributed to Samaël, and the raising of the Brazen Serpent for the homage of the people was an instance of the uniform deference to Esau's power in his own domain which was long inculcated.

As I write, fiery Mars, near enough for the astronomer to

detect its moons, is a wondrous phenomenon in the sky. Beneath it fearful famine is desolating three vast countries, war is raging between two powerful nations, and civil strife is smiting another ere it has fairly recovered from the wounds of a foreign struggle. The dismal conditions seem to have so little root in political necessity that one might almost be pardoned even now for dreaming that some subtle influence has come among men from the red planet that has approached the earth. How easy then must it have been in a similar conjunction of earthly and celestial phenomena to have imagined Samaël, the planetary Spectre, to be at work with his fatal fires! Whatever may have been the occasion, the red light of Mars at an early period fixed upon that planet the odium of all the burning, blighting, desert-producing powers of which it was thought necessary to relieve the adorable Sun. It was believed that all 'born under' that planet were quarrelsome. And it was part of the popular Jewish belief in the ultimate triumph of good over evil that under Mars the Messias was to be born.

We may regard Esau-Samaël then as the Devil of Strife. His traditional son Cain was like himself a 'murderer from the beginning;'[6] but in that early period the conflict was between the nomad and the huntsman on one side, on the other the agriculturist and the cattle-breeder, who was never regarded as a noble figure among the Semitic tribes. In the course of time some Semitic tribes became agriculturists, and among them, in defiance of his archæological character, Samaël was saddled with the evils that beset them. As an ox he brought rinderpest. But his visible appearance was still more generally that of the raven, the wild ass, the hog which brought scurvy; while in shape of a dog he was so generally believed to bring deadly disease, that it would seem as if 'hydrophobia' was specially attributed to him.

In process of time benignant Peace dwelt more and more with the agriculturists, but still among the Israelites the tradesman was the 'coming man,' and to him peace was essential. The huntsman, of the Esau clan, figures in many legends, of which the following is translated from the Arabic by Lane:—There was a huntsman who from a mountain cave brought some honey in his water-skin, which he offered to an oilman; when the oilman opened the skin a drop of honey fell which a bird ate; the oilman's cat sprang on the bird and killed it; the huntsman's hound killed the cat; the oilman killed the dog; the huntsman killed the oilman; and as the two men belonged to different villages, their inhabitants rose against each other in battle, 'and there died of them a great multitude, the number of whom none knoweth but God, whose name be exalted!'[7]

Esau's character as a wild huntsman is referred to in another chapter. It is as the genius of strife and nomadic war that he more directly stands in contrast with his 'supplanter.'

From the wild elemental demons of storm and tempest of the most primitive age to this Devil of Strife, the human mind has associated evil with unrest. 'The wicked are like the troubled sea when it cannot rest.' Such is the burthen of the Japanese Oni throned in the heart of the hurricane, of the wild huntsman issuing forth at the first note of war, of Edom hating the victories of peace, living by the sword. The prophecy that the Prince of Peace should be born under the planet Mars is a strange and mystical suggestion. In a powerful poem by Thomas Aird, 'The Devil's Dream,' the last fearful doom of Satan's vision is imprisonment beneath a lake for ever still,—the Spirit of Unrest condemned for ever to the realm of absolute stillness!

There all is solemn idleness: no music here, no jars,
Where Silence guards the coast, e'er thrill her everlasting bars.
No sun here shines on wanton isles; but o'er the burning sheet
A rim of restless halo shakes, which marks the internal heat;
As, in the days of beauteous earth, we see with dazzled sight
The red and setting sun o'erflow with rings of welling light.

Oh! here in dread abeyance lurks of uncreated things
The last Lake of God's Wrath, where He His first great Enemy brings.
Deep in the bosom of the gulf the Fiend was made to stay,
Till, as it seemed, ten thousand years had o'er him rolled away;
In dreams he had extended life to bear the fiery space;
But all was passive, dull, and stern within his dwelling-place.

Oh! for a blast of tenfold ire to rouse the giant surge,
Him from that flat fixed lethargy impetuously to urge!
Let him but rise, but ride upon the tempest-crested wave
Of fire enridged tumultuously, each angry thing he'd brave!
The strokes of Wrath, thick let them fall! a speed so glorious dread
Would bear him through, the clinging pains would strip from off his head.

The vision of this Last Stern Lake, oh! how it plagued his soul,
Type of that dull eternity that on him soon must roll,
When plans and issues all must cease that earlier care beguiled,
And never era more shall stand a landmark on the wild:
Nor failure nor success is there, nor busy hope nor fame,
But passive fixed endurance, all eternal and the same.

## NOTES

1 Isa. lxiii. 1–6.
2 Fol. 84, col. 1.
3 Maarecheth haëlahuth, fol. 257, col. 1.
4 Gesenius, Heb. Lexic.
5 Hairiness was a pretty general characteristic of devils; hence, possibly, the epithet 'Old Harry,' i.e., hairy, applied to the Devil. In 'Old Deccan Days,' p. 50, a Rakshasa is described as hairy:—'Her hair hangs around her in a thick black tangle.' But the beard has rarely been accorded to devils.
6 Buslaef has a beautiful mediæval picture of a devil inciting Cain to hurl stones on his prostrate brother's form.
7 Forty-one Eastern Tales.

# Chapter XIII
# Barbaric Aristocracy

IN THE PRECEDING chapter it was noted that there were two myths wrapped up in the story of Jacob and Esau,—the one theological, the other human. The former was there treated, the latter may be considered here. Rabbinical theology has made the Jewish race adopt as their founder that tricky patriarch whom Shylock adopted as his model; but any censure on them for that comes with little grace from christians who believe that they are still enjoying a covenant which Jacob's extortions and treacheries were the divinely-adopted means of confirming. It is high time that the Jewish people should repudiate Jacob's proceedings, and if they do not give him his first name ('Impostor') back again, at least withdraw from him the name Israel. But it is still more important for mankind to study the phases of their civilisation, and not attribute to any particular race the spirit of a legend which represents an epoch of social development throughout the world.

When Rebekah asked Jehovah why her unborn babes struggled in her womb, he answered, 'Two nations are in thy womb. One people shall be stronger than the other people; the elder shall be subject to the younger.' What peoples these were is described in the blessings of Jacob on the two representatives when they had grown up to be, the one red and hairy, a huntsman; the other a quiet man, dwelling in tents and builder of cattle-booths.

Jacob—cunning, extortionate, fraudulent in spirit even when technically fair—is not a pleasing figure in the eyes of the nineteenth century. But he does not belong to the nineteenth century. His contest was with Esau. The very names of them belong to mythology; they are not individual men; they are conflicting tendencies and interests of a primitive period. They must be thought of as Israel and Edom historically; morally, as the Barter principle and the Bandit principle.

High things begin low. Astronomy began as Astrology; and when Trade began there must have been even more trickery about it than there is now. Conceive of a world made up of nomadic tribes engaged in perpetual warfare. It is a commerce of killing. If a tribe desires the richer soil or larger possessions of another, the method is to exterminate that other. But at last there rises a tribe either too weak or too peaceful to exterminate, and it proposes to barter. It challenges its neighbours to a contest of wits. They try to get the advantage of each other in bargains; they haggle and cheat; and it is not heroic at all, but it is the beginning of commerce and peace.

But the Dukes of Edom as they are called will not enter into this compact. They have not been used to it; they are always outwitted at a bargain; just like those other red men in the West of America, whose lands are bought with beads, and their territorial birthright taken for a mess of pottage. They prefer to live by the hunt and by the sword. Then between these two peoples is an eternal feud, with an occasional truce, or, in biblical phrase, 'reconciliation.'

Surrounded by a commercial civilisation, with its prosaic virtues and its petty vices, we cannot help admiring much about the Duke of Edom, non-producer though he be. Brave, impulsive, quick to forgive as to resent; generous, as people can afford to be when they may give what they never earned; his gallant qualities cast a certain meanness over his grasping brother, the Israelite. It is a healthy sign in youth to admire such qualities. The boy who delights in Robin Hood; the youth who feels a stir of enthusiasm when he reads Schiller's *Robbers*; the *ennuyés* of the clubs and the roughs, with unfulfilled capacities for adventure in them, who admire 'the gallant Turk,' are all lingering in the nomadic age. They do not think of things but of persons. They are impressed by the barbaric dash. The splendour of warriors hides trampled and decimated peasantries; their courage can gild atrocities. Beside such captivating qualities and thrilling scenes how poor and commonplace appear thrifty rusticity, and the cautious, selfish, money-making tradesmen!

But fine and heroic as the Duke of Edom may appear in the distance, it is best to keep him at a distance. When Robin Hood reappeared on Blackheath lately, his warmest admirers were satisfied to hear he was securely lodged in gaol. The Jews had just the same sensations about the Dukes of Edom. They saw that tribe near to, and lived in daily dread of them. They were hirsute barbarians, dwelling amid mountain fastnesses, and lording it over a vast territory. The weak tribe of the plains had no sooner got together some herds and a little money, than those dashing Edomites fell upon them and carried away their savings and substance in a day. This made the bartering tribe all the more dependent on their cunning. They had to match their wits against, the world; and they have had to do the same to this day, when it is a chief element of their survival that their thrift is of importance to the business and finance of Europe. But in the myth it is shown that Trade, timorous as it is in presence of the sword, may have a magnanimity of its own. The Supplanter of Edom is haunted by the wrong he has done his elder brother, and driven him to greater animosity. He resolves to seek him, offer him gifts, and crave reconciliation. It is easy to put an unfavourable construction upon his action, but it is not necessary. The Supplanter, with droves of cattle, a large portion of his possessions, passes out towards perilous Edom, unarmed, undefended, except by his amicable intentions towards the powerful chieftain he had wronged. At the border of the hostile kingdom he learns that the chieftain is coming to meet him with four hundred men. He is now seized, with a mighty spirit of Fear. He sends on the herdsmen with the herds, and remains alone. During the watches of the night there closes upon him this phantom of Fear, with its presage of Death. The tricky tradesman has met his Conscience, and it is girt about with Terror. But he feels that his nobler self is with it, and that he will win. Finely has Charles Wesley told the story in his hymn:—

> Come, O thou traveller unknown,
> Whom still I hold but cannot see!
> My company before is gone
> And I am left alone with thee:
> With thee all night I mean to stay
> And wrestle till the break of day.

'Confident in self-despair,' the Supplanter conquers his Fear; with the dawn he travels onward alone to meet the man he had outraged and his armed men, and to him says, 'I have appeared before thee as though I had appeared before God, that thou mightest be favourable to me.' The proud Duke is disarmed. The brothers embrace and weep together. The chieftain declines the presents, and is only induced to accept them as proof of his forgiveness. The Tradesman learns for all time that his mere cleverness may bring a demon to his side in the night, and that he never made so good a bargain as when he has restored ill-gotten gains. The aristocrat and warrior returns to his mountain, aware now that magnanimity and courage are not impossible to quiet men living by merchandise. The hunting-ground must make way now for the cattle-breeder. The sword must yield before the balances.

Whatever may have been the tribes which in primitive times had these encounters, and taught each other this lesson, they were long since reconciled. But the ghosts of Israel and Edom, of Barter and Plunder, fought on through long tribal histories. Israel represented by the archangel Michael, and Edom by dragon Samaël, waged their war. One characteristic of the opposing power has been already considered. Samaël embodied Edom as the genius of Strife. He was the especial Accuser of Israel, their Antichrist, so to say, as Michael was their Advocate. But the name 'Edom' itself was retained as a kind of personification of the barbaric military and lordly Devil. The highwayman in epaulettes, the heroic spoiler, with his hairy hand which Israel itself had imitated many a time in its gloves, were summed up as 'Edom.'

This personification is the more important since it has characterised the more serious idea of Satan which prevails in the world. He is mainly a moral conception, and means the pride and pomp of the world, its natural wildness and ferocities, and the glory of them. The Mussulman fable relates that when Allah created man, and placed him in a garden, he called all the angels to worship this crowning work of his hands. Iblis alone refused to worship Adam. The very idea of a garden is hateful to the spirit of Nomadism.[1] Man the gardener receives no reverence from the proud leader of the Seraphim. God said unto him (Iblis), What hindered thee from worshipping Adam, since I commanded thee? He answered, I am more excellent than he: thou hast created me of (ethereal) fire, and hast created him of clay (black mud). God said, Get thee down therefore from paradise, for it is not fit that thou behave thyself proudly therein.[2]

The earnestness and self-devotion of the northern pagans in their resistance to Christianity impressed the finest minds in the Church profoundly. Some of the Fathers even quoted the enthusiasm of those whom they regarded as devotees of the Devil, to shame the apathy of christians. The Church could show no martyr braver than Rand, down whose throat St. Olaf made a viper creep, which gnawed through his side; and Rand was an example of thousands. This gave many of the early christians of the north a very serious view of the realm of Satan, and of Satan himself as a great potentate

It was increased by their discovery that the pagan kings—Satan's subjects—had moral codes and law-courts, and energetically maintained justice. In this way there grew up a more dignified idea of Hell.

*Fig. 4.—Hierarchy of Hell (Russian, Sixteenth Century)*

The grotesque imps receded before the array of majestic devils, like Satan and Beelzebub; and these were invested with a certain grandeur and barbaric pride. They were regarded as rival monarchs who had refused to submit themselves to Jehovah, but they were deemed worthy of heroic treatment. The traces of this sentiment found in the ancient frescoes of Russia are of especial importance.

Nothing can exceed the grandeur of the Hierarchy of Hell as they appear in some of these superb pictures. Satan is generally depicted with similar dignity to the king of heaven, from whom he is divided by a wall's depth, sometimes even resembling him in all but complexion and hair (which is fire on Satan). There are frequent instances, as in the accompanying figure (4), where, in careful correspondence with the attitude of Christ on the Father's knees, Satan supports the betrayer of Christ. Beside the king of Hell, seated in its Mouth, are personages of distinction, some probably representing those poets and sages of Greece and Rome, the prospect of whose damnation filled some of the first christian Fathers with such delight.

In Spain, when a Bishop is about to baptize one of the European Dukes of the Devil, he asks at the font what has become of his ancestors, naming them—all heathen. 'They are all in hell!' replies the Bishop. 'Then there will I follow them,' returns the Chief, and thereafter by no persuasion can he be induced to fare otherwise than to Hell. Gradually the Church made up its mind to ally itself with this obstinate barbaric pride and ambition. It was willing to give up anything whatever for a kingdom of this world, and to worship any number of Princes of Darkness, if they would give unto the Bishops such kingdoms, and the glory of them. They induced Esau to be baptized by promise of their aid in his oppressions, and free indulgences to all his passions; and then, by his help, they were able to lay before weaker Esaus the christian alternatives—Be baptized or burnt!

Not to have known how to conquer in bloodless victories the barbaric Esaus of the world by a virtue more pure, a heroism more patient, than theirs, and with that 'sweet reasonableness of Christ,' which is the latest epitaph on his tomb among the rich; not to have recognised the true nobility of the Dukes, and purified their pride to self-reverence, their passion to moral courage, their daring and freedom to a self-reliance at once gentle and manly; this was no doubt the necessary failure of a dogmatic and irrational system. But it is this which has made the christian Israel more of an impostor than its prototype, in every country to which it came steadily developing to a hypocritical imitator of the Esau whose birthright it stole by baptism. It speedily lost his magnanimity, but never his sword, which however it contrived to make at once meaner and more cruel by twisting it into thumbscrews and the like. For many centuries its voice has been, in a thin phonographic way, the voice of Jesus, but the hands are the hands of Esau with Samaël's claw added.

---

NOTES
1  The contest between the agriculturist and the (nomadic) shepherd is expressed in the legend that Cain and Abel divided the world between them, the one taking possession of the movable and the other of the immovable property. Cain said to his brother, 'The earth on which thou standest is mine, then betake thyself to the air;' but Abel replied, 'The garments which thou wearest are mine, take them off.'—Midrash.
2  Sale's Koran, vii. Al Araf. Iblis, the Mussulman name for the Devil, is probably a corruption of the word diabolus.

# Chapter XIV
## Job and the Divider

> Israel is a flourishing vine,
> Which bringeth forth fruit to itself;
> According to the increase of his fruit
> He hath multiplied his altars;
> According to the goodness of his land
> He hath made goodly images.
> Their heart is divided: now shall they be found guilty;
> He will break down their altars, he will spoil their images.

These words of the prophet Hosea (x. 1, 2) foreshadow the devil which the devout Jahvist saw growing steadily to enormous strength through all the history of Israel. The germ of this enemy may be found in our chapter on Fate; one of its earliest developments is indicated in the account already given of the partition between Jacob and Esau, and the superstition to which that led of a ghostly Antagonist, to whom a share had been irreversibly pledged. From the principle thus adopted, there grew a host of demons whom it was believed necessary to propitiate by offering them their share. A divided universe had for its counterpart a divided loyalty in the heart of the people. The growth of a belief in the supremacy of one

God was far from being a real monotheism; as a matter of fact no primitive race has been monotheistic. In 2 Kings xvii. it is stated as a belief of the Jews that some Assyrians who had been imported into their territory (Samaria) were slain by lions because they knew not 'the manner of the God of the land.' Spinoza noticed the indications given in this and other narratives that the Jews believed that gods whose worship was intolerable within their own boundaries were yet adapted to other regions (Tractatus, ii.). With this state of mind it is not wonderful that when the Jews found themselves in those alien regions they apprehended that the gods of those countries might also employ lions on such as knew not their manner, but adhered to the worship of Jehovah too exclusively.

Among the Jews grew up a more spiritual class of minds, whose feeling towards the mongrel worship around them was that of abhorrence; but these had a very difficult cause to maintain. The popular superstitions were firmly rooted in the fact that terrible evils afflicted mankind, and in the further fact that these did not spare the most pious. Nay, it had for a long time been a growing belief that the bounties and afflictions of nature, instead of following the direction promised by the patriarchs,—rewarding the pious, punishing the wicked,—were distributed in a reverse way. Dives and Lazarus seemed to have their respective lots before any future paradise was devised for their equalisation—as indeed is natural, since Dives attends to his business, while Lazarus is investing his powers in Abraham's bosom. Out of this experience there came at last the demand for a life beyond the grave, without whose redress the pious began to deem themselves of all men the most miserable. But before this heavenly future became a matter of common belief, there were theories which prepared, the way for it. It was held by the devout that the evils which afflicted the righteous were Jehovah's tests of their loyalty to him, and that in the end such trials would be repaid. And when observation, following the theory, showed that they were not so repaid, it was said the righteousness had been unreal, the devotee was punished for hidden wickedness. When continued observation had proved that this theory too was false, and that piety was not paid in external bounties, either to the good man or his family, the solution of a future settlement was arrived at.

This simple process may be traced in various races, and in its several phases.

The most impressive presentation of the experiences under which the primitive secular theory of rewards and punishments perished, and that of an adjustment beyond the grave arose, is found in the Book of Job. The solution here reached—a future reward in this life—is an impossible one for anything more than an exceptional case. But the Book of Job displays how beautiful such an instance would be, showing afflictions to be temporary and destined to be followed by compensations largely outweighing them. It was a tremendous statement of the question—If a man die, shall he live again? Jehovah answered, 'Yes' out of the whirlwind, and raised Job out of the dust. But for the millions who never rose from the dust that voice was heard announcing their resurrection from a trial that pressed them even into the grave. It is remarkable that Job's expression of faith that his Vindicator would appear on earth, should have become the one text of the Old Testament which has been adapted by christians to express faith in immortality. Job strongly disowns that faith.

> There is hope for a tree,
> If it be cut down, that it will sprout again,
> And that its tender branches will not fail;
> Though its root may have grown old in the earth,
> And though its trunk be dead upon the ground,
> At the scent of water it will bud,
> And put forth boughs, like a young plant.
> But man dieth and is gone for ever!
> Yet I know that my Vindicator liveth,
> And will stand up at length on the earth;
> And though with my skin this body be wasted away,
> Yet in my flesh shall I see God.
> Yea, I shall see him my friend;
> My eyes shall behold him no longer an adversary;
> For this my soul panteth within me.[1]

The scenery and details of this drama are such as must have made an impression upon the mind of the ancient Jews beyond what is now possible for any existing people. In the first place, the locality was the land of Uz, which Jeremiah (Lam. iv. 21) points out as part of Edom, the territory traditionally ruled over by the great invisible Accuser of Israel, who had succeeded to the portion of Esau, adversary of their founder, Jacob. Job was within the perilous bounds. And yet here, where scape-goats were offered to deprecate Samaël, and where in ordinary sacrifices some item entered for the devil's share, Job refused to pay any honour to the Power of the Place. He offered burnt-offerings alone for himself and his sons, these being exclusively given to Jehovah.[2] Even after his children and his possessions were destroyed by this great adversary, Job offered his sacrifice without even omitting the salt, which was the Oriental seal of an inviolable compact between two, and which so especially recalled and con-secrated the covenant with Jehovah.[3] Among his twenty thousand animals, Azazel's animal, the goat, is not even named. Job's distinction was an absolute and unprecedented singleness of loyalty to Jehovah.

This loyalty of a disciple even in the enemy's country is made the subject of a sort of boast by Jehovah when the Accuser enters. Postponing for the moment consideration of the character and office of this Satan, we may observe here that the trial which he challenges is merely a test of the sincerity of Job's allegiance to Jehovah. The Accuser claims that it is all given for value received. These posses-sions are taken away.

This is but the framework around the philosophical poem in which all theories of the world are personified in grand council.


First of all Job (the Troubled) asks—Why? Orthodoxy answers. (Eliphaz was the son of Esau (Samaël), and his name here means that he was the Accuser in disguise. He, 'God's strength,' stands for the Law. It affirms that God's ways are just, and consequently afflictions imply previous sin.) Eliphaz repeats the question put by the Accuser in heaven—'Was not thy fear of God thy hope?' And he brings Job to the test of prayer, in which he has so long trusted. Eliphaz rests on revelation; he has had a vision; and if his revelation be not true, he challenges Job to disprove it by calling on God to answer him, or else securing the advocacy of some one of the heavenly host. Eliphaz says trouble does not spring out of the dust.

Job's reply is to man and God—Point out the error! Grant my troubles are divine arrows, what have I done to thee, O watcher of men! Am I a sea-monster—and we imagine Job looking at his wasted limbs—that the Almighty must take precautions and send spies against me?

Then follows Bildad the Shuhite,—that is the 'contentious,' one of the descendants of Keturah (Abraham's concubine), traditionally supposed to be inimical to the legitimate Abrahamic line, and at a later period identified as the Turks. Bildad, with invective rather than argument, charges that Job's children had been slain for their sins, and otherwise makes a personal application of Eliphaz's theology.

Job declares that since God is so perfect, no man by such standard could be proved just; that if he could prove himself just, the argument would be settled by the stronger party in his own favour; and therefore, liberated from all temptation to justify himself, he affirms that the innocent and the guilty are dealt with much in the same way. If it is a trial of strength between God and himself, he yields. If it is a matter of reasoning, let the terrors be withdrawn, and he will then be able to answer calmly. For the present, even if he were righteous, he dare not lift up his head to so assert, while the rod is upon him.

Zophar 'the impudent' speaks. Here too, probably, is a disguise: he is (says the LXX.) King of the Minæans, that is the Nomades, and his designation 'the Naamathite,' of unknown significance, bears a suspicious resemblance to Naamah, a mythologic wife of Samaël and mother of several devils. Zophar is cynical. He laughs at Job for even suggesting the notion of an argument between himself and God, whose wisdom and ways are unsearchable. He (God) sees man's iniquity even when it looks as if he did not. He is deeper than hell.

What can a man do but pray and acknowledge his sinfulness?

But Job, even in his extremity, is healthy-hearted enough to laugh too. He tells his three 'comforters' that no doubt Wisdom will die with them. Nevertheless, he has heard similar remarks before, and he is not prepared to renounce his conscience and common-sense on such grounds. And now, indeed, Job rises to a higher strain. He has made up his mind that after what has come upon him, he cares not if more be added, and challenges the universe to name his offence. So long as his transgression is 'sealed up in a bag,' he has a right to consider it an invention.[4]

Temanite Orthodoxy is shocked at all this. Eliphaz declares that Job's assertion that innocent and guilty suffer alike makes the fear of God a vain thing, and discourages prayer. 'With us are the aged and hoary-headed.' (Job is a neologist.) Eliphaz paints human nature in Calvinistic colours.

> Behold, (God) putteth no trust in his ministering spirits,
> And the heavens are not pure in his sight;
> Much less abominable and polluted man,
> Who drinketh iniquity as water!

The wise have related, and they got it from the fathers to whom the land was given, and among whom no stranger was allowed to bring his strange doctrines, that affliction is the sign and punishment of wickedness.

Job merely says he has heard enough of this, and finds no wise man among them. He acknowledges that such reproaches add to his sorrows. He would rather contend with God than with them, if he could. But he sees a slight indication of divine favour in the remarkable unwisdom of his revilers, and their failure to prove their point.

Bildad draws a picture of what he considers would be the proper environment of a wicked man, and it closely resembles the situation of Job.

But Job reminds him that he, Bildad, is not God. It is God that has brought him so low, but God has been satisfied with his flesh. He has not yet uttered any complaint as to his conduct; and so he, Job, believes that his vindicator will yet appear to confront his accusers—the men who are so glib when his afflictor is silent.[5]

Zophar harps on the old string. Pretty much as some preachers go on endlessly with their pictures of the terrors which haunted the deathbeds of Voltaire and Paine, all the more because none are present to relate the facts. Zophar recounts how men who seemed good, but were not, were overtaken by asps and vipers and fires from heaven.

But Job, on the other hand, has a curious catalogue of examples in which the notoriously wicked have lived in wealth and gaiety. And if it be said God pays such off in their children, Job denies the justice of that. It is the offender, and not his child, who ought to feel it. The prosperous and the bitter in soul alike lie down in the dust at last, the good and the evil; and Job is quite content to admit that he does not understand it. One thing he does understand: 'Your explanations are false.'

But Eliphaz insists on Job having a dogma. If the orthodox dogma is not true, put something in its place! Why *are* you afflicted? What is, *your* theory? Is it because God was afraid of your greatness? It must be as we say, and you have been defrauding and injuring people in secret.

Job, having repeated his ardent desire to meet God face to face as to his innocence, says he can only conclude that what befalls him and others is what is 'appointed' for them. His terror indeed arises from that: the good and the evil seem to be distributed without reference to human conduct. How darkness conspires with the assassin! If God were only a man, things might be different; but as it is, 'what he desireth that he doeth,' and 'who can turn him?'

Bildad falls back on his dogma of depravity. Man is a 'worm,' a 'reptile.' Job finds that for a worm Bildad is very familiar with the divine secrets. If man is morally so weak he should be lowly in mind also. God by his spirit hath garnished the heavens; his hand formed the 'crooked serpent'—

> Lo! these are but the borders of his works;
> How faint the whisper we have heard of him!
> But the thunder of his power who can understand?

Job takes up the position of the agnostic, and the three 'Comforters' are silenced. The argument has ended where it had to end. Job then proceeds with sublime eloquence. A man may lose all outward things, but no man or god can make him utter a lie, or take from him his integrity, or his consciousness of it. Friends may reproach him, but he can see that his own heart does not. That one superiority to the wicked he can preserve. In reviewing his arguments Job is careful to say that he does *not* maintain that good and evil men are on an equality. For one thing, when the wicked man is in trouble he cannot find resource in his innocence. 'Can he delight himself in the Almighty?' When such die, their widows do not bewail them. Men do not befriend oppressors when they come to want. Men hiss them. And with guilt in their heart they feel their sorrows to be the arrows of God, sent in anger. In all the realms of nature, therefore, amid its powers, splendours, and precious things, man cannot find the wisdom which raises him above misfortune, but only in his inward loyalty to the highest, and freedom from moral evil.

Then enters a fifth character, Elihu, whose plan is to mediate between the old dogma and the new agnostic philosophy. He is Orthodoxy rationalised. Elihu's name is suggestive of his ambiguity; it seems to mean one whose '*God* is *He*' and he comes from the tribe of Buz, whose Hebrew meaning might almost be represented in that English word which, with an added *z*, would best convey the windiness of his remarks. Buz was the son of Milkah, the Moon, and his descendant so came fairly by his theologic 'moonshine' of the kind which Carlyle has so well described in his account of Coleridgean casuistry. Elihu means to be fair to both sides! Elihu sees some truth in both sides! Eclectic Elihu! Job is perfectly right in thinking he had not done anything to merit his sufferings, but he did not know what snares were around him, and how he might have done something wicked but for his affliction. Moreover, God ruins people now and then just to show how he can lift them up again. Job ought to have taken this for granted, and then to have expressed it in the old abject phraseology, saying, 'I have received chastisement; I will offend no more! What I see not, teach thou me!' (A truly Elihuic or 'contemptible' answer to Job's sensible words, 'Why is light given to a man whose way is hid?' Why administer the rod which enlightens as to the anger but not its cause, or as to the way of amend?) In fact the casuistic Elihu casts no light whatever on the situation. He simply overwhelms him with metaphors and generalities about the divine justice and mercy, meant to hide this new and dangerous solution which Job had discovered—namely, that the old dogmatic theories of evil were proved false by experience, and that a good man amid sorrow should admit his ignorance, but never allow terror to wring from him the voice of guilt, nor the attempt to propitiate divine wrath.

When Jehovah appears on the scene, answering Job out of the whirlwind, the tone is one of wrath, but the whole utterance is merely an amplification of what Job had said—what we see and suffer are but fringes of a Whole we cannot understand. The magnificence and wonder of the universe celebrated in that voice of the whirlwind had to be given the lame and impotent conclusion of Job 'abhorring himself,' and 'repenting in dust and ashes.' The conventional Cerberus must have his sop. But none the less does the great heart of this poem reveal the soul that was not shaken or divided in prosperity or adversity. The burnt-offering of his prosperous days, symbol of a worship which refused to include the supposed powers of mischief, was enjoined on Job's Comforters. They must bend to him as nearer God than they. And in his high philosophy Job found what is symbolised in the three daughters born to him: Jemima (the Dove, the voice of the returning Spring); Kezia (Cassia, the sweet incense); Kerenhappuch (the horn of beautiful colour, or decoration).

From the Jewish point of view this triumph of Job represented a tremendous heresy. The idea that afflictions could befall a man without any reference to his conduct, and consequently not to be influenced by the normal rites and sacrifices, is one fatal to a priesthood. If evil may be referred in one case to what is going on far away among gods in obscurities of the universe, and to some purpose beyond the ken of all sages, it may so be referred in all cases, and though burnt-offerings may be resorted to formally, they must cease when their powerlessness is proved. Hence the Rabbins have taken the side of Job's Comforters. They invented a legend that Job had been a great magician in Egypt, and was one of those whose sorceries so long prevented the escape of Israel. He was converted afterwards, but it is hinted that his early wickedness required the retribution he suffered. His name was to them the troubler troubled.

Heretical also was the theory that man could get along without any Angelolatry or Demon-worship. Job in his singleness of service, fearing God alone, defying the Seraphim and Cherubim from Samaël down to do their worst, was a perilous figure. The priests got no part of any burnt-offering. The sin-offering was of almost sumptuary importance. Hence the rabbinical theory, already noticed, that it was through neglect of these expiations to the God of Sin that the morally spotless Job came under the power of his plagues.

But for precisely the same reasons the story of Job became representative to the more spiritual class of minds of a genuine as contrasted with a nominal monotheism, and the piety of the pure, the undivided heart. Its meaning is so human that it is not necessary to discuss the question of its connection with the story of Hariśchandra, or whether its accent was caught from or by the legends of Zoroaster and of Buddha, who passed unscathed through the ordeals of Ahriman and Mara. It was repeated in the encounters of the infant Christ with Herod, and of the adult Christ with Satan. It was repeated in the unswerving loyalty of the patient Griselda to her husband. It is indeed the heroic theme of many races and ages, and it everywhere points to a period when the virtues of endurance and patience rose up to match the agonies which fear and weakness had tried to propitiate,—when man first learned to suffer and be strong.

**NOTES**

1  Noyes' Translation.
2  Eisenmenger, Entd. Jud. i. 836.
3  Job. i. 22, the literal rendering of which is, 'In all this Job sinned not, nor gave God unsalted.' This translation I first heard from Dr. A. P. Peabody, sometime President of Harvard University, from whom I have a note in which he says:—'The word which I have rendered gave is appropriate to a sacrifice. The word I have rendered unsalted means so literally; and is in Job vi. 6 rendered unsavory. It may, and sometimes does, denote folly, by a not unnatural metaphor; but in that sense the word gave—an offertory word—is out of place.' Waltonus (Bib. Polyg.) translates 'nec dedit insulsum Deo;' had he rendered תפלה by insalsum it would have been exact. The horror with which demons and devils are supposed to regard salt is noticed, i. 288.
4  Gesenius so understands verse 17 of chap. xiv.
5  The much misunderstood and mistranslated passage, xix. 25–27 (already quoted), is certainly referable to the wide-spread belief that as against each man there was an Accusing Spirit, so for each there was a Vindicating Spirit. These two stood respectively on the right and left of the balances in which the good and evil actions of each soul were weighed against each other, each trying to make his side as heavy as possible. But as the accusations against him are made by living men, and on earth, Job is not prepared to consider a celestial acquittal beyond the grave as adequate.

# Chapter XV
# Satan

THERE IS NOTHING about the Satan of the Book of Job to indicate him as a diabolical character. He appears as a respectable and powerful personage among the sons of God who present themselves before Jehovah, and his office is that of a public prosecutor. He goes to and fro in the earth attending to his duties. He has received certificates of character from A. Schultens, Herder, Eichorn, Dathe, Ilgen, who proposed a new word for Satan in the prologue of Job, which would make him a faithful but too suspicious servant of God.

Such indeed he was deemed originally; but it is easy to see how the degradation of such a figure must have begun. There is often a clamour in England for the creation of Public Prosecutors; yet no doubt there is good ground for the hesitation which its judicial heads feel in advising such a step. The experience of countries in which Prosecuting Attorneys exist is not such as to prove the institution one of unmixed advantage. It is not in human nature for an official person not to make the most of the duty intrusted to him, and the tendency is to raise the interest he specially represents above that of justice itself. A defeated prosecutor feels a certain stigma upon his reputation as much as a defeated advocate, and it is doubtful whether it be safe that the fame of any man should be in the least identified with personal success where justice is trying to strike a true balance. The recent performances of certain attorneys in England and America retained by Societies for the Suppression of Vice strikingly illustrate the dangers here alluded to. The necessity that such salaried social detectives should perpetually parade before the community as purifiers of society induces them to get up unreal cases where real ones cannot be easily discovered. Thus they become Accusers, and from this it is an easy step to become Slanderers; nor is it a very difficult one which may make them instigators of the vices they profess to suppress.

The first representations of Satan show him holding in his hand the scales; but the latter show him trying slyly with hand or foot to press down that side of the balance in which the evil deeds of a soul are being weighed against the good. We need not try to track archæologically this declension of a Prosecutor, by increasing ardour in his office, through the stages of Accuser, Adversary, Executioner, and at last Rival of the legitimate Rule, and tempter of its subjects. The process is simple and familiar. I have before me a little twopenny book,[1] which is said to have a vast circulation, where one may trace the whole mental evolution of Satan. The ancient Devil-worshipper who has reappeared with such power in England tells us that he was the reputed son of a farmer, who had to support a wife and eleven children on from 7s. to 9s. per week, and who sent him for a short time to school. 'My schoolmistress reproved me for something wrong, telling me that God Almighty took notice of children's sins. This stuck to my conscience a great while; and who this God Almighty could be I could not conjecture; and how he could know my sins without asking my mother I could not conceive. At that time there was a person named Godfrey, an exciseman, in the town, a man of a stern and hard-favoured countenance, whom I took notice of for having a stick covered with figures, and an ink-bottle hanging at the button-hole of his coat. I imagined that man to be employed by God Almighty to take notice and keep an account of children's sins; and once I got into the market-house and watched him very narrowly, and found that he was always in a hurry, by his walking so fast; and I thought he had need to hurry, as he must have a deal to do to find out all the sins of children!' This terror caused the little Huntington to say his prayers. 'Punishment for sin I found was to be inflicted after death, therefore I hated the churchyard, and would travel any distance round rather than drag my guilty conscience over that enchanted spot.'

The child is father to the man. When Huntington, S.S., grew up, it was to record for the thousands who listened to him as a prophet his many encounters with the devil. The Satan he believes in is an exact counterpart of the stern, hard-favoured exciseman whom he had regarded as God's employé. On one occasion he writes, 'Satan began to tempt me violently that there was no God, but I reasoned against the belief of that from my own experience of his dreadful wrath, saying, How can I credit this suggestion, when (God's) wrath is already revealed in my heart, and every curse in his book levelled at my head.' (That seems his only evidence of God's existence—his wrath!) 'The Devil answered that the Bible was false, and only wrote by cunning men to puzzle and deceive people. 'There is no God,' said the adversary, 'nor is the Bible true.' ... I asked, 'Who, then, made the world?' He replied, 'I did, and I made men too.' Satan, perceiving my rationality almost gone, followed me up with another temptation; that as there was no God I must come back to his work again, else when he had brought me to hell he would punish me more than all the rest. I cried out, 'Oh, what will become of me! what will become of me!' He answered that there was no escape but by praying to him; and that he would show me some lenity when he took me to hell. I went and sat in my tool-house halting between two opinions; whether I should petition Satan, or whether I should keep praying to God, until I could ascertain the consequences. While I was thinking of bending my knees to such a cursed being as Satan, an uncommon fear of God sprung up in my heart to keep me from it.'

In other words, Mr. Huntington wavered between the petitions 'Good Lord! Good Devil!' The question whether it were more moral, more holy, to worship the one than the other did not occur to him. He only considers which is the strongest—which could do him the most mischief—which, therefore, to fear the most; and when Satan has almost convinced him in his own favour, he changes round to God. Why? Not because of any superior goodness on God's part. He says, 'An uncommon fear of God sprung up in my heart.' The greater terror won the day; that is to say, of two demons he yielded to the stronger. Such an experience, though that of one living in our own time, represents a phase in the development of the relation between God and Satan which would have appeared primitive to an Assyrian two thousand years ago. The ethical antagonism of the two was then much more clearly felt. But this bit of contemporary superstition may bring before us the period when Satan, from having been a Nemesis or Retributive Agent of the divine law, had become a mere personal rival of his superior.

Satan, among the Jews, was at first a generic term for an adversary lying in wait. It is probably the furtive suggestion at the root of this Hebrew word which aided in its selection as the name for the invisible adverse powers when they were especially distinguished. But originally no special personage, much less any antagonist of Jehovah, was signified by the word. Thus we read: 'And God's anger was kindled because he (Balaam) went; and the angel of the Lord stood in the way for a Satan against him.... And the ass saw the angel of the Lord standing in the way and his sword drawn in his hand.'[2] The eyes of Balaam are presently opened, and the angel says, 'I went out to be a Satan to thee because the way is perverse before me.' The Philistines fear to take David with them to battle lest he should prove a Satan to them, that is, an underhand enemy or traitor.[3] David called those who wished to put Shimei to death Satans;[4] but in this case the epithet would have been more applicable to himself for affecting to protect the honest man for whose murder he treacherously provided.[5]

That it was popularly used for adversary as distinct from evil appears in Solomon's words, 'There is neither Satan nor evil occurrent.'[6] Yet it is in connection with Solomon that we may note the entrance of some of the materials for the mythology which afterwards invested the name of Satan. It is said that, in anger at his idolatries, 'the Lord stirred up a Satan unto Solomon, Hadad the Edomite: he was of the king's seed in Edom.'[7] Hadad, 'the Sharp,' bore a name next to that of Esau himself for the redness of his wrath, and, as we have seen in a former chapter, Edom was to the Jews the land of 'bogeys.' 'Another Satan,' whom the Lord 'stirred up,' was the Devastator, Prince Rezon, founder of the kingdom of Damascus, of whom it is said, 'he was a Satan to Israel all the days of Solomon.'[8] The human characteristics of supposed 'Scourges of God' easily pass away. The name that becomes traditionally associated with calamities whose agents were 'stirred up' by the Almighty is not allowed the glory of its desolations. The word 'Satan,' twice used in this chapter concerning Solomon's fall, probably gained here a long step towards distinct personification as an eminent national enemy, though there is no intimation of a power daring to oppose the will of Jehovah. Nor, indeed, is there any such intimation anywhere in the 'canonical' books of the Old Testament. The writer of Psalm cix., imprecating for his adversaries, says: 'Set thou a wicked man over him; and let Satan stand at his right hand. When he shall be judged, let him be condemned; and let his prayer become sin.' In this there is an indication of a special Satan, but he is supposed to be an agent of Jehovah. In the catalogue of the curses invoked of the Lord, we find the evils which were afterwards supposed to proceed only from Satan. The only instance in the Old Testament in which there is even a faint suggestion of hostility towards Satan on the part of Jehovah is in Zechariah. Here we find the following remarkable words: 'And he showed me Joshua the high priest standing before the angel of Jehovah, and the Satan standing at his right hand to oppose him. And Jehovah said unto Satan, Jehovah rebuke thee, O Satan; even Jehovah, that hath chosen Jerusalem, rebuke thee: is not this a brand plucked out of the fire? Now Joshua was clothed with filthy garments, and stood before the angel. And he answered and spake to those that stood before him, saying, Take away the filthy garments from him. And to him he said, Lo, I have caused thine iniquity to pass from thee, and I will clothe thee with goodly raiment."[9]

Here we have a very fair study and sketch of that judicial trial of the soul for which mainly the dogma of a resurrection after death was invented. The doctrine of future rewards and punishments is not one which a priesthood would invent or care for, so long as they possessed unrestricted power to administer such in this life. It is when an alien power steps in to supersede the priesthood—the Gallio too indifferent whether ceremonial laws are carried out to permit the full application of terrestrial cruelties—that the priest requires a tribunal beyond the grave to execute his sentence. In this picture of Zechariah we have this invisible Celestial Court. The Angel of Judgment is in his seat. The Angel of Accusation is present to prosecute. A poor filthy wretch appears for trial. What advocate can he command? Where is Michael, the special advocate of Israel? He does not recognise one of his clients in this poor Joshua in his rags. But lo! suddenly Jehovah himself appears; reproves his own commissioned Accuser; declares Joshua a brand plucked from the burning (Tophet); orders a change of raiment, and, condoning his offences, takes him into his own service. But in all this there is nothing to show general antagonism between Jehovah and Satan, but the reverse.

When we look into the Book of Job we find a Satan sufficiently different from any and all of those mentioned under that name in other parts of the Old Testament to justify the belief that he has been mainly adapted from the traditions of other regions. The plagues and afflictions which in Psalm cix. are invoked from Jehovah, even while Satan is mentioned as near, are in the Book of Job ascribed to Satan himself. Jehovah only permits Satan to inflict them with a proviso against total destruction. Satan is here named as a personality in a way not known elsewhere in the Old Testament, unless it be in 1 Chron. xxi. 1, where Satan (the article being in this single case absent) is said to have 'stood up against Israel, and provoked David to number Israel.' But in this case the uniformity of the passage with the others (excepting those in Job) is preserved by the same incident being recorded in 2 Sam. xxiv. 1, 'The anger of Jehovah was kindled against Israel, and he (Jehovah) moved David against them to say, Go number Israel and Judah.'

It is clear that, in the Old Testament, it is in the Book of Job alone that we find Satan as the powerful prince of an empire which is distinct from that of Jehovah,—an empire of tempest, plague, and fire,—though he presents himself before Jehovah, and awaits permission to exert his power on a loyal subject of Jehovah. The formality of a trial, so dear to the Semitic heart, is omitted in this case. And these circumstances confirm the many other facts which prove this drama to be largely of non-Semitic origin. It is tolerably clear that the drama of Hariśchandra in India and that of Job were both developed from the Sanskrit legends mentioned in our chapter on Viswámitra; and it is certain that Aryan and Semitic elements are both represented in the figure of Satan as he has passed into the theology of Christendom.

Nor indeed has Satan since his importation into Jewish literature in this new aspect, much as the Rabbins have made of him, ever been assigned the same character among that people that has been assigned him in Christendom. He has never replaced Samaël as their Archfiend. Rabbins have, indeed, in later times associated him with the Serpent which seduced Eve in Eden; but the absence of any important reference to that story in the New Testament is significant of the slight place it had in the Jewish mind long after the belief in Satan had become popular. In fact, that essentially Aryan myth little accorded with the ideas of strife and immorality which the Jews had gradually associated with Samaël. In the narrative, as it stands in Genesis, it is by no means the Serpent that makes the worst appearance. It is Jehovah, whose word—that death shall follow on the day the apple is eaten—is falsified by the result; and while the Serpent is seen telling the truth, and guiding man to knowledge, Jehovah is represented as animated by jealousy or even fear of man's attainments. All of which is natural enough in an extremely primitive myth of a combat between rival gods, but by no means possesses the moral accent of the time and conditions amid which Jahvism certainly originated. It is in the same unmoral plane as the contest of the Devas and Asuras for the Amrita, in Hindu mythology, a contest of physical force and wits.

The real development of Satan among the Jews was from an accusing to an opposing spirit, then to an agent of punishment—a hated executioner.

*Fig. 5.—Gnostic Figure (Ste. Genevieve Collection)*

The fact that the figure here given (Fig. 5) was identified by one so familiar with Semitic demonology as Calmet as a representation of him, is extremely interesting. It was found among representations of Cherubim, and on the back of one somewhat like it is a formula of invocation against demons. The countenance is of that severe beauty which the Greeks ascribed to Nemesis. Nemesis has at her feet the wheel and rudder, symbols of her power to overtake the evil-doer by land or sea; the feet of this figure are winged for pursuit. He has four hands. In one he bears the lamp which, like Lucifer, brings light on the deed of darkness. As to others, he answers Baruch's description (Ep. 13, 14) of the Babylonian god, 'He hath a sceptre in his hand like a man, like a judge of the kingdom—he hath in his hand a sword and an axe.' He bears nicely-graduated implements of punishment, from the lash that scourges to the axe that slays; and his retributive powers are supplemented by the scorpion tail. At his knees are signets; whomsoever he seals are sealed. He has the terrible eyes which were believed able to read on every forehead a catalogue of sins invisible to mortals, a power that made women careful of their veils, and gave meaning to the formula 'Get thee behind me!'[10]

Now this figure, which Calmet believed to be Satan, bears on its reverse, 'The Everlasting Sun.' He is a god made up of Egyptian and Magian forms, the head-plumes belonging to the one, the multiplied wings to the other. Matter (*Hist. Crit. de Gnost.*) reproduces it, and says that 'it differs so much from all else of the kind as to prove it the work of an impostor.' But Professor C. W. King has a (probably fifth century) gem in his collection evidently a rude copy of this (reproduced in his 'Gnostics,' Pl. xi. 3), on the back of which is 'Light of Lights;' and, in a note which I have from him, he says that it sufficiently proves Matter wrong, and that this form was primitive. In one gem of Professor King's (Pl. v. 1) the lamp is also carried, and means the 'Light of Lights.' The inscription beneath, within a coiled serpent, is in corrupt cuneiform characters, long preserved by the Magi, though without understanding them. There is little doubt, therefore, that the instinct of Calmet was right, and that we have here an early form of the detective and retributive Magian deity ultimately degraded to an accusing spirit, or Satan.

Although the Jews did not identify Satan with their Scapegoat, yet he has been veritably the Scapegoat among devils for two thousand years. All the nightmares and phantasms that ever haunted the human imagination have been packed upon him unto this day, when it is almost as common to hear his name in India and China as in Europe and America. In thus passing round the world, he has caught the varying features of many fossilised demons: he has been horned, hoofed, reptilian, quadrupedal, anthropoid, anthropomorphic, beautiful, ugly, male, female; the whites painted him black, and the blacks, with more reason, painted him white. Thus has Satan been made a miracle of incongruities. Yet through all these protean shapes there has persisted the original characteristic mentioned. He is prosecutor and executioner under the divine government, though his office has been debased by that mental confusion which, in the East, abhors the burner of corpses, and, in the West, regards the public hangman with contempt; the abhorrence, in the case of Satan, being intensified by the supposition of an overfondness for his work, carried to the extent of instigating the offences which will bring him victims.

In a well-known English Roman Catholic book [11] of recent times, there is this account of St. Francis' visit to hell in company with the Angel Gabriel:—'St. Francis saw that, on the other side of (a certain) soul, there was another devil to mock at and reproach it. He said, Remember where you are, and where you will be for ever; how short the sin was, how long the punishment. It is your own fault; when you committed that mortal sin you knew how you would be punished. What a good bargain you made to take the pains of eternity in exchange for the sin of a day, an hour, a moment. You cry now for your sin, but your crying comes too late. You liked bad company; you will find bad company enough here. Your father was a drunkard, look at him there drinking red-hot fire. You were too idle to go to mass on Sundays; be as idle as you like now, for there is no mass to go to. You disobeyed your father, but you dare not disobey him who is your father in hell.'

This devil speaks as one carrying out the divine decrees. He preaches. He utters from his chasuble of flame the sermons of Father Furniss. And, no doubt, wherever belief in Satan is theological, this is pretty much the form which he assumes before the mind (or what such believers would call their mind, albeit really the mind of some Syrian dead these two thousand years). But the Satan popularly personalised was man's effort to imagine an enthusiasm of inhumanity. He is the necessary appendage to a personalised Omnipotence, whose thoughts are not as man's thoughts, but claim to coerce these. His degradation reflects the heartlessness and the ingenuity of torture which must always represent personal government with its catalogue of fictitious crimes. Offences against mere Majesty, against iniquities framed in law, must be doubly punished, the thing to be secured being doubly weak. Under any theocratic government law and punishment would become the types of diabolism. Satan thus has a twofold significance. He reports what powerful priesthoods found to be the obstacles to their authority; and he reports the character of the priestly despotisms which aimed to obstruct human development.

## NOTES

1 'The Kingdom of Heaven Taken by Prayer.' By William Huntington, S.S. This title is explained to be 'Sinner Saved,' otherwise one might understand the letters to signify a Surviving Syrian.
2 Num. xxii. 22.
3 1 Sam. xxix. 4.
4 2 Sam. xix. 22.
5 1 Kings ii. 9.
6 1 Kings v. 4.
7 1 Kings xi. 14.
8 1 Kings xi. 25.
9 Zech. iii.
10 Cf. Rev. vii. 3.
11 'The Sight of Hell,' prepared, as one of a 'Series of Books for Children and Young Persons,' by the Rev. Father Furniss, C.S.S.R., by authority of his Superiors.

# Chapter XVI
## Religious Despotism

Pharaoh and Herod — Zoroaster's mother — Ahriman's emissaries —
Kansa and Krishna — Emissaries of Kansa — Astyages and Cyrus —
Zohák — Bel and the Christian

THE JEWS HAD already, when Christ appeared, formed the theory that the hardening of Pharaoh's heart, and his resistance to the departure of Israel from Egypt, were due to diabolical sorcery. The belief afterwards matured; that Edom (Esau or Samaël) was the instigator of Roman aggression was steadily forming. The mental conditions were therefore favourable to the growth of a belief in the Jewish followers of Christ that the hostility to the religious movement of their time was another effort on the part of Samaël to crush the kingdom of God. Herod was not, indeed, called Satan or Samaël, nor was Pharaoh; but the splendour and grandeur of this Idumean (the realm of Esau), notwithstanding his oppressions and crimes, had made him a fair representative to the people of the supernatural power they dreaded. Under these circumstances it was a powerful appeal to the sympathies of the Jewish people to invent in connection with Herod a myth exactly similar to that associated with Pharaoh,—namely, a conspiracy with sorcerers, and consequent massacre of all new-born children.

The myths which tell of divine babes supernaturally saved

from royal hostility are veritable myths, even where they occur so late in time that historic names and places are given; for, of course, it is impossible that by any natural means either Pharaoh or Herod should be aware of the peculiar nature of any particular infant born in their dominions. Such traditions, when thus presented in historical guise, can only be explained by reference to corresponding fables written out in simpler mythic form; while it is especially necessary to remember that such corresponding narratives may be of independent ethnical origin, and that the later in time may be more primitive spiritually.

In the Legend of Zoroaster [1] his mother Dogdo, previous to his birth, has a dream in which she sees a black cloud, which, like the wing of some vast bird, hides the sun, and brings on frightful darkness. This cloud rains down on her house terrible beasts with sharp teeth,—tigers, lions, wolves, rhinoceroses, serpents. One monster especially attacks her with great fury, and her unborn babe speaks in reassuring terms. A great light rises and the beasts fall. A beautiful youth appears, hurls a book at the Devas (Devils), and they fly, with exception of three,—a wolf, a lion, and a tiger. These, however, the youth drives away with a luminous horn. He then replaces the holy infant in the womb, and says to the mother: 'Fear nothing! The King of Heaven protects this infant. The earth waits for him. He is the prophet whom Ormuzd sends to his people: his law will fill the world with joy: he will make the lion and the lamb drink in the same place. Fear not these ferocious beasts; why should he whom Ormuzd preserves fear the enmity of the whole world?' With these words the youth vanished, and Dogdo awoke. Repairing to an interpreter, she was told that the Horn meant the grandeur of Ormuzd; the Book was the Avesta; the three Beasts betokened three powerful enemies.

Zoroaster was born laughing. This prodigy being noised abroad, the Magicians became alarmed, and sought to slay the child. One of them raised a sword to strike him, but his arm fell to the ground. The Magicians bore the child to the desert, kindled a fire and threw him into it, but his mother afterwards found him sleeping tranquilly and unharmed in the flames. Next he was thrown in front of a drove of cows and bulls, but the fiercest of the bulls stood carefully over the child and protected him. The Magicians killed all the young of a pack of wolves, and then cast the infant Zoroaster to them that they might vent their rage upon him, but the mouths of the wolves were shut. They abandoned the child on a lonely mountain, but two ewes came and suckled him.

Zoroaster's father respected the ministers of the Devas (Magi), but his child rebuked him. Zoroaster walked on the water (crossing a great river where was no bridge) on his way to Mount Iran where he was to receive the Law. It was then he had the vision of the battle between the two serpent armies,—the white and black adders, the former, from the South, conquering the latter, which had come from the North to destroy him.

The Legend of the Infant Krishna is as follows:—The tyrant Kansa, having given his sister Devaki in marriage to Vasudéva, as he was returning from the wedding heard a voice declare, 'The eighth son of Devaki is destined to be thy destroyer.' Alarmed at this, Kansa cast his sister and her husband into a prison with seven iron doors, and whenever a son was born he caused it to be instantly destroyed.

When Devaki became pregnant the eighth time, Brahma and Siva, with attending Devas, appeared and sang: 'O favoured among women! in thy delivery all nature shall have cause to exult! How ardently we long to behold that face for the sake of which we have coursed round three worlds!' When Krishna was born a chorus of celestial spirits saluted him; the room was illumined with supernatural light. While Devaki was weeping at the fatal decree of Kansa that her son should be destroyed, a voice was heard by Vasudéva saying: 'Son of Yadu, carry this child to Gokul, on the other side of the river Jumna, to Nauda, whose wife has just given birth to a daughter. Leave him and bring the girl hither.' At this the seven doors swung open, deep sleep fell on the guards, and Vasudéva went forth with the holy infant in his arms. The river Jumna was swollen, but the waters, having kissed the feet of Krishna, retired on either side, opening a pathway. The great serpent of Vishnu held its hood over this new incarnation of its Lord. Beside sleeping Nauda and his wife the daughter was replaced by the son, who was named Krishna, the Dark.

When all this had happened a voice came to Kansa saying: 'The boy destined to destroy thee is born, and is now living.' Whereupon Kansa ordered all the male children in his kingdom to be destroyed. This being ineffectual, the whereabouts of Krishna were discovered; but the messenger who was sent to destroy the child beheld its image in the water and adored it. The Rakshasas worked in the interest of Kansa. One approached the divine child in shape of a monstrous bull whose head he wrung off; and he so burned in the stomach of a crocodile which had swallowed him that the monster cast him from his mouth unharmed.

Finally, as a youth, Krishna, after living some time as a herdsman, attacked the tyrant Kansa, tore the crown from his head, and dragged him by his hair a long way; with the curious result that Kansa became liberated from the three worlds, such virtue had long thinking about the incarnate one, even in enmity!

The divine beings represented in these legends find their complement in the fabulous history of Cyrus; and the hostile powers which sought their destruction are represented in demonology by the Persian tyrant-devil Zohák. The name of Astyages, the grandfather of Cyrus, has been satisfactorily traced to Ashdahák, and Ajis Daháka, the 'biting snake.' The word thus connects him with Vedic Ahi and with Iranian Zohák, the tyrant out of whose shoulders a magician evoked two serpents which adhered to him and became at once his familiars and the arms of his cruelty. As Astyages, the last king of Media, he had a dream that the offspring of his daughter Mandane would reign over Asia. He gave her in marriage to Cambyses, and when she bore a child (Cyrus), committed it to his minister Harpagus to be slain. Harpagus, however, moved with pity, gave it to a herdsman of Astyages, who substituted for it a still-born child, and having so satisfied the tyrant of its death, reared Cyrus as his own son.

The luminous Horn of the Zoroastrian legend and the diabolism of Zohák are both recalled in the Book of Daniel (viii.) in the terrific struggle of the ram and the he-goat. The he-goat, ancient symbol of hairy Esau, long idealised into the Invisible Foe of Israel, had become associated also with Babylon and with Nimrod its founder, the Semitic Zohák. But Bel, conqueror of the Dragon, was the founder of Babylon, and to Jewish eyes the Dragon was his familiar;

to the Jews he represented the tyranny and idolatry of Nimrod, the two serpents of Zohák. When Cyrus supplanted Astyages, this was the idol he found the Babylonians worshipping until Daniel destroyed it. And so, it would appear, came about the fact that to the Jews the power of Christendom came to be represented as the Reign of Bel. One can hardly wonder at that. If ever there were cruelty and oppression passing beyond the limit of mere human capacities, it has been recorded in the tragical history of Jewish sufferings. The disbeliever in præternatural powers of evil can no less than others recognise in this 'Bel and the Christian,' which the Jews substituted for 'Bel and the Dragon,' the real archfiend—Superstition, turning human hearts to stone when to stony gods they sacrifice their own humanity and the welfare of mankind.

**NOTES**

1   M. Anquetil Du Perron's 'Zendavesta et Vie de Zoroastre.'

# Chapter XVII

# The Prince of this World

Temptations — Birth of Buddha — Mara — Temptation of power — Asceticism and Luxury — Mara's menaces — Appearance of the Buddha's Vindicator — Ahriman tempts Zoroaster — Satan and Christ — Criticism of Strauss — Jewish traditions — Hunger — Variants

THE DEVIL, HAVING shown Jesus all the kingdoms of this world, said, 'All this power will I give thee, and the glory of them: for that is delivered unto me, and to whomsoever I will I give it.' The theory thus announced is as a vast formation underlying many religions. As every religion begins as an ideal, it must find itself in antagonism to the world at large; and since the social and political world are themselves, so long as they last, the outcome of nature, it is inevitable that in primitive times the earth should be regarded as a Satanic realm, and the divine world pictured elsewhere. A legitimate result of this conclusion is asceticism, and belief in the wickedness of earthly enjoyments. To men of great intellectual powers, generally accompanied as they are with keen susceptibilities of enjoyment and strong sympathies, the renunciation of this world must be as a living burial. To men who, amid the corruptions of the world, feel within them the power to strike in with effect, or who, seeing 'with how little wisdom the world is governed,' are stirred by the sense of power, the struggle against the temptation to lead in the kingdoms of this world is necessarily severe. Thus simple is the sense of those temptations which make the almost invariable ordeal of the traditional founders of religions. As in earlier times the god won his spurs, so to say, by conquering some monstrous beast, the saint or saviour must have overcome some potent many-headed world, with gems for scales and double-tongue, coiling round the earth, and thence, like Lilith's golden hair, round the heart of all surrendered to its seductions.

It is remarkable to note the contrast between the visible and invisible worlds which surrounded the spiritual pilgrimage of Sakya Muni to Buddhahood or enlightenment. At his birth there is no trace of political hostility: the cruel Kansa, Herod, Magicians seeking to destroy, are replaced by the affectionate force of a king trying to retain his son. The universal traditions reach their happy height in the ecstatic gospels of the Siamese.[1] The universe was illumined; all jewels shown with unwonted lustre; the air was full of music; all pain ceased; the blind saw, the deaf heard; the birds paused in their flight; all trees and plants burst into bloom, and lotus flowers appeared in every place. Not under the dominion of Mara [2] was this beautiful world. But by turning from all its youth, health, and life, to think only of its decrepitude, illness, and death, the Prince Sakya Muni surrounded himself with another world in which Mara had his share of power. I condense here the accounts of his encounters with the Prince, who was on his way to be a hermit.

When the Prince passed out at the palace gates, the king Mara, knowing that the youth was passing beyond his evil power, determined to prevent him. Descending from his abode and floating in the air, Mara cried, 'Lord, thou art capable of such vast endurance, go not forth to adopt a religious life, but return to thy kingdom, and in seven days thou shalt become an emperor of the world, ruling over the four great continents.' 'Take heed, O Mara!' replied the Prince; 'I also know that in seven days I might gain universal empire, but I have no desire for such possessions. I know that the pursuit of religion is better than the empire of the world. See how the world is moved, and quakes with praise of this my entry on a religious life! I shall attain the glorious omniscience, and shall teach the wheel of the law, that all teachable beings may free themselves from transmigratory existence. You, thinking only of the lusts of the flesh, would force me to leave all beings to wander without guide into your power. Avaunt! get thee away far from me!'

Mara withdrew, but only to watch for another opportunity. It came when the Prince had reduced himself to emaciation and agony by the severest austerities. Then Mara presented himself, and pretending compassion, said, 'Beware, O grand Being! Your state is pitiable to look on; you are attenuated beyond measure, and your skin, that was of the colour of gold, is dark and discoloured. You are practising this mortification in vain. I can see that you will not live through it. You, who are a Grand Being, had better give up this course, for be assured you will derive much more advantage from sacrifices of fire and flowers.' Him the Grand Being indignantly answered, 'Hearken, thou vile and wicked Mara! Thy words suit not the time. Think not to deceive me, for I heed thee not. Thou mayest mislead those who have no understanding, but I, who have virtue, endurance, and intelligence, who know what is good and what is evil, cannot be so misled. Thou, O Mara! hast eight generals. Thy first is delight in the five lusts of the flesh, which are the pleasures of appearance, sound, scent, flavour, and touch. Thy second general is wrath, who takes the form of vexation, indignation, and desire to injure. Thy third is concupiscence. Thy fourth is desire. Thy fifth is impudence. Thy sixth is arrogance. Thy seventh is doubt. And thine eighth is ingratitude. These are thy generals, who cannot be escaped by those whose hearts are set on honour and wealth. But I know that he who can contend with these thy generals shall escape beyond all sorrow, and enjoy the most glorious happiness. Therefore I have not ceased to practise mortification, knowing that even were I to die whilst thus engaged, it would be a most excellent thing.'

It is added that Mara 'fled in confusion,' but the next incident seems to show that his suggestion was not unheeded; for 'after he had departed,' the Grand Being had his vision of the three-stringed guitar—one string drawn too tightly, the second too loosely, the third moderately—which last, somewhat in defiance of orchestral ideas, alone gave sweet music, and taught him that moderation was better than excess or laxity. By eating enough he gained that pristine strength and beauty which offended the five Brahmans so that they left him. The third and final effort of Mara immediately preceded the Prince's attainment of the order of Buddha under the Bo-tree. He now sent his three daughters, Raka (Love), Aradi (Anger), Tanha (Desire). Beautifully bedecked they approached him, and Raka said, 'Lord, fearest thou not death?' But he drove her away. The two others also he drove away as they had no charm of sufficient power to entice him. Then Mara assembled his generals, and said, 'Listen, ye Maras, that know not sorrow! Now shall I make war on the Prince, that man without equal. I dare not attack him in face, but I will circumvent him by approaching on the north side. Assume then all manner of shapes, and use your mightiest powers, that he may flee in terror.'

Having taken on fearful shapes, raising awful sounds, headed by Mara himself, who had assumed immense size, and mounted his elephant Girimaga, a thousand miles in height, they advanced; but they dare not enter beneath the shade of the holy Bo-tree. They frightened away, however, the Lord's guardian angels, and he was left alone. Then seeing the army approaching from the north, he reflected, 'Long have I devoted myself to a life of mortification, and now I am alone, without a friend to aid me in this contest. Yet may I escape the Maras, for the virtue of my transcendent merits will be my army.' 'Help me,' he cried, 'ye thirty Barami! ye powers of accumulated merit, ye powers of Almsgiving, Morality, Relinquishment, Wisdom, Fortitude, Patience, Truth, Determination, Charity, and Equanimity, help me in my fight with Mara!' The Lord was seated on his jewelled throne (the same that had been formed of the grass on which he sat), and Mara with his army exhausted every resource of terror—monstrous beasts, rain of missiles and burning ashes, gales that blew down mountain peaks—to inspire him with fear; but all in vain! Nay, the burning ashes were changed to flowers as they fell.

'Come down from thy throne,' shouted the evil-formed one; 'come down, or I will cut thine heart into atoms!' The Lord replied, 'This jewelled throne was created by the power of my merits, for I am he who will teach all men the remedy for death, who will redeem all beings, and set them free from the sorrows of circling existence.'

Mara then claimed that the throne belonged to himself, and

had been created by his own merits; and on this armed himself with the Chakkra, the irresistible weapon of Indra, and Wheel of the Law. Yet Buddha answered, 'By the thirty virtues of transcendent merits, and the five alms, I have obtained the throne. Thou, in saying that this throne was created by thy merits, tellest an untruth, for indeed there is no throne for a sinful, horrible being such as thou art.'

Then furious Mara hurled the Chakkra, which clove mountains in its course, but could not pass a canopy of flowers which rose over the Lord's head.

And now the great Being asked Mara for the witnesses of his acts of merit by virtue of which he claimed the throne. In response, Mara's generals all bore him witness. Then Mara challenged him, 'Tell me now, where is the man that can bear witness for thee?' The Lord reflected, 'Truly here is no man to bear me witness, but I will call on the earth itself, though it has neither spirit nor understanding, and it shall be my witness.' Stretching forth his hand, he thus invoked the earth: 'O holy Earth! I who have attained the thirty powers of virtue, and performed the five great alms, each time that I have performed a great act have not failed to pour water on thee. Now that I have no other witness, I call upon thee to give thy testimony!'

The angel of the earth appeared in shape of a lovely woman, and answered, 'O Being more excellent than angels or men! it is true that, when you performed your great works, you ever poured water on my hair.' And with these words she wrung her long hair, and from it issued a stream, a torrent, a flood, in which Mara and his hosts were overturned, their insignia destroyed, and King Mara put to flight, amid the loud rejoicings of angels.

Then the evil one and his generals were conquered not only in power but in heart; and Mara, raising his thousand arms, paid reverence, saying, 'Homage to the Lord, who has subdued his body even as a charioteer breaks his horses to his use! The Lord will become the omniscient Buddha, the Teacher of angels, and Brahmas, and Yakkhas (demons), and men. He will confound all Maras, and rescue men from the whirl of transmigration!'

The menacing powers depicted as assailing Sakya Muni appear only around the infancy of Zoroaster. The interview of the latter with Ahriman hardly amounts to a severe trial, but still the accent of the chief temptation both of Buddha and Christ is in it, namely, the promise of worldly empire. It was on one of those midnight journeys through Heaven and Hell that Zoroaster saw Ahriman, and delivered from his power 'one who had done both good and evil.'[3] When Ahriman met Zoroaster's gaze, he cried, 'Quit thou the pure law; cast it to the ground; thou wilt then be in the world all that thou canst desire. Be not anxious about thy end. At least, do not destroy my subjects, O pure Zoroaster, son of Poroscharp, who art born of her thou hast borne!' Zoroaster answered, 'Wicked Majesty! it is for thee and thy worshippers that Hell is prepared, but by the mercy of God I shall bury your work with shame and ignominy.'

Fig. 6.—Temptation of Christ (Lucas van Leyden)

In the account of Matthew, Satan begins his temptation of Jesus in the same way and amid similar circumstances to those we find in the Siamese legends of Buddha. It occurs in a wilderness, and the appeal is to hunger. The temptation of Buddha, in which Mara promises the empire of the world, is also repeated in the case of Satan and Jesus (Fig. 6). The menaces, however, in this case, are relegated to the infancy, and the lustful temptation is absent alto-gether. Mark has an allusion to his being in the wilderness forty days 'with the beasts,' which may mean that Satan 'drove' him into a region of danger to inspire fear. In Luke we have the remarkable claim of Satan that the authority over the world has been delivered to himself, and he gives it to whom he will; which Jesus does not deny, as Buddha did the similar claim of Mara. As in the case of Buddha, the temptation of Jesus ends his fasting; angels bring him food (διηκόνουν ἀυτῷ probably means that), and thenceforth he eats and drinks, to the scandal of the ascetics.

The essential addition in the case of Jesus is the notable temp-tation to try and perform a crucial act. Satan quotes an accredited messianic prophecy, and invites Jesus to test his claim to be the pre-dicted deliverer by casting himself from the pinnacle of the Temple, and testing the promise that angels should protect the true Son of God. Strauss,[4] as it appears to me, has not considered the importance of this in connection with the general situation. 'Assent,' he says, 'cannot be withheld from the canon that, to be credible, the narrative must ascribe nothing to the devil inconsistent with his established cunning. Now, the first temptation, appealing to hunger, we grant, is not ill-conceived; if this were ineffectual, the devil, as an artful tactician, should have had a yet more alluring temptation at hand; but instead of this, we find him, in Matthew, proposing to Jesus the neck-breaking feat of casting himself down from the pinnacle of the Temple—a far less inviting miracle than the metamorphosis of the stones. This proposition finding no acceptance, there follows, as a crowning effort, a suggestion which, whatever might be the bribe, every true Israelite would instantly reject with abhorrence—to fall down and worship the devil.'

Not so! The scapegoat was a perpetual act of worship to the Devil. In this story of the temptation of Christ there enter some characteristic elements of the temptation of Job.[5] Uz in the one case and the wilderness in the other mean morally the same, the region ruled over by Azazel. In both cases the trial is under divine direction. And the trial is in both cases to secure a division of worship between the good and evil powers, which was so universal in the East that it was the test of exceptional piety if one did not swerve from an un-mixed sacrifice. Jesus is apparently abandoned by the God in whom he trusted; he is 'driven' into a wilderness, and there kept with the beasts and without food. The Devil alone comes to him; exhibits his own miraculous power by bearing him through the air to his own Mount Seir, and showing him the whole world in a moment of time; and now says to him, as it were, 'Try your God! See if *he* will even turn stones into bread to save his own son, to whom I offer the king-doms of the world!' Then bearing him into the 'holy hill' of his own God—the pinnacle of the Temple—says, 'Try now a leap, and see if *he* saves from being dashed to pieces, even in his own precincts, his so trustful devotee, whom I have borne aloft so safely! Which, then, has the greater power to protect, enrich, advance you,—he who has left you out here to starve, so that you dare not trust yourself to him, or I? Fall down then and worship me as your God, and all the world is yours! It is the world you are to reign over: rule it in my name!

When St. Anthony is tempted by the Devil in the form of a lean monk, it was easy to see that the hermit was troubled with a vision of his own emaciation. When the Devil appears to Luther under guise of a holy monk, it is an obvious explanation that he was impressed by a memory of the holy brothers who still remained in the Church, and who, while they implored his return, pointed out the strength and influence he had lost by secession. Equally simple are the moral elements in the story of Christ's temptation. While a member of John's ascetic community, for which 'though he was rich he became poor,' hunger, and such anxiety about a living as victimises many a young thinker now, must have assailed him. Later on his Devil meets him on the Temple, quotes scripture, and warns him that his visionary God will not raise him so high in the Church as the Prince of this World can.[6] And finally, when dreams of a larger union, including Jews and Gentiles, visited him, the power that might be gained by connivance with universal idolatry would be reflected in the offer of the kingdoms of the world in payment for the purity of his aims and singleness of his worship.

That these trials of self-truthfulness and fidelity, occurring at various phases of life, would be recognised, is certain. A youth of high position, as Christ probably was,[7] or even one with that great power over the people which all concede, was, in a worldly sense, 'throwing away his prospects;' and this voice, real in its time, would naturally be conventionalised. It would put on the stock costume of devils and angels; and among Jewish christians it would naturally be associated with the forty-days' fast of Moses (Exod. xxxiv. 28; Deut. ix. 9), and that of Elias (1 Kings xix. 8), and the forty-years' trial of Israel in the wilderness. Among Greek christians some traces of the legend of Herakles in his seclusion as herdsman, or at the cross-roads between Vice and Virtue, might enter; and it is not impossible that some touches might be added from the Oriental myth which invested Buddha.

However this may be, we may with certainty repair to the common source of all such myths in the higher nature of man, and recognise the power of a pure genius to overcome those temptations to a success unworthy of itself. We may interpret all such legends with a clearness proportioned to the sacrifices we have made for truth and ideal right; and the endless perplexities of commentators and theologians about the impossible outward details of the New Testament story are simple confessions that the great spirit so tried is now made to label with his name his own Tempter—namely, a Church grown powerful and wealthy, which, as the Prince of this World, bribes the conscience and tempts away the talent necessary to the progress of mankind.

## NOTES

1 As given in Mr. Alabaster's 'The Wheel of the Law' (Trübner & Co., 1871). In the Apocryphal Gospels, some of the signs of nature's joy attending the birth of Buddha are reported at the birth of Mary and that of Christ, as the pausing of birds in their flight, &c. Anna is said to have conceived Mary under a tree, as Maia under a tree brought forth Buddha.

2 'Mara, or Man (Sanscrit Màra, death, god of love; by some authors translated 'illusion,' as if it came from the Sanscrit Màya), the angels of evil, desire, of love, death, &c. Though King Mara plays the part of our Satan the tempter, he and his host were formerly great givers of alms, which led to their being born in the highest of the Deva heavens, called Paranimit Wasawatti, there to live more than nine thousand million years, surrounded by all the luxuries of sensuality. From this heaven the filthy one, as the Siamese describe him, descends to the earth to tempt and excite to evil.'—Alabaster.

3 Some say Djemschid, others Guenschesp, a warrior sent to hell for beating the fire.

4 Leben Jesu, ii. 54. The close resemblance between the trial of Israel in the wilderness and this of Jesus is drawn in his own masterly way.

5 A passage of the Pesikta (iii. 35) represents a conversation between Jehovah and Satan with reference to Messias which bears a resemblance to the prologue of Job. Satan said: Lord, permit me to tempt Messias and his generation. 'To him the Lord said: You could have no power over him. Satan again said: Permit me because I have the power. God answered: If you persist longer in this, rather would I destroy thee from the world, than that one soul of the generation of Messias should be lost.' Though the rabbin might report the trial declined, the Christian would claim it to have been endured.

6 In his fresco of the Temptation at the Vatican, Michael Angelo has painted the Devil in the dress of a priest, standing with Jesus on the Temple.

7 'Idols and Ideals.' London: Trübner & Co. New York: Henry Holt & Co. In the Essay on Christianity I have given my reasons for this belief.

# Chapter XVIII
## Trial of the Great

A REPRESENTATION OF the Temptation of St. Anthony (marionettes), which I witnessed at Tours (1878), had several points of
significance. It was the mediæval 'Morality' as diminished by centuries, and conventionalised among those whom the centuries mould
in ways and for ends they know not. Amid a scenery of grotesque
devils, rudely copied from Callot, St. Anthony appeared, and was
tempted in a way that recalled the old pictures. There was the same
fair Temptress, in this case the wife of Satan, who warns her lord
that his ugly devils will be of no avail against Anthony, and that the
whole affair should be confided to her. She being repelled, the rest of
the performance consisted in the devils continually ringing the bell
of the hermitage, and finally setting fire to it. This conflagration was
the supreme torment of Anthony—and, sooth to say, it was a fairly
comfortable abode—who utters piteous prayers and is presently
comforted by an angel bringing him wreaths of evergreen.

The prayers of the saint and the response of the angel were
meant to be seriously taken; but their pathos was generally met
with pardonable laughter by the crowd in the booth. Yet there was

a pathos about it all, if only this, that the only temptations thought of for a saint were a sound and quiet house and a mistress. The bell-noise alone remained from the great picture of Spagnoletto at Siena, where the unsheltered old man raises his deprecating hand against the disturber, but not his eyes from the book he reads. In Spagnoletto's picture there are five large books, pen, ink, and hour-glass; but there is neither hermitage to be burnt nor female charms to be resisted.

But Spagnoletto, even in his time, was beholding the vision of exceptional men in the past, whose hunger and thirst was for knowl-edge, truth, and culture, and who sought these in solitude. Such men have so long left the Church familiar to the French peasantry that any representation of their temptations and trials would be out of place among the marionettes. The bells which now disturb them are those that sound from steeples.

Another picture loomed up before my eyes over the puppet performance at Tours, that which for Bunyan frescoed the walls of Bedford Gaol. There, too, the old demons, giants, and devils took on grave and vast forms, and reflected the trials of the Great Hearts who withstood the Popes and Pagans, the armed political Apollyons and the Giant Despairs, who could make prisons the hermitages of men born to be saviours of the people.

Such were the temptations that Milton knew; from his own heart came the pigments with which he painted the trial of Christ in the wilderness. 'Set women in his eye,' said Belial:—

Women, when nothing else, beguiled the heart
Of wisest Solomon, and made him build,
And made him bow to the gods of his wives.
To whom quick answer Satan thus returned.
Belial, in much uneven scale thou weigh'st
All others by thyself....
But he whom we attempt is wiser far
Than Solomon, of more exalted mind,
Made and set wholly on the accomplishment
Of greatest things....
Therefore with manlier objects we must try
His constancy, with such as have more show
Of worth, of honour, glory, and popular praise;
Rocks whereon greatest men have oftest wrecked.[1]

The progressive ideas which Milton attributed to Satan have not failed. That Celestial City which Bunyan found it so hard to reach has now become a metropolis of wealth and fashion, and the trials which once beset pilgrims toiling towards it are now transferred to those who would pass beyond it to another city, seen from afar, with temples of Reason and palaces of Justice.

The old phantasms have shrunk to puppets. The trials by personal devils are relegated to the regions of insanity and disease. It is everywhere a dance of puppets though on a cerebral stage. A lady well known in Edinburgh related to me a terrible experience she had with the devil. She had invited some of her relations to visit her for some days; but these relatives were Unitarians, and, after they had gone, having entered the room which they had occupied, she was seized by the devil, thrown on the floor, and her back so strained that she had to keep her bed for some time. This was to her 'the Unitarian fiend' of which the Wesleyan Hymn-Book sang so long;

but even the Wesleyans have now discarded the famous couplet, and there must be few who would not recognise that the old lady at Edinburgh merely had a tottering body representing a failing mind.

I have just read a book in which a lady in America relates her trial by the devil. This lady, in her girlhood, was of a christian family, but she married a rabbi and was baptized into Judaism. After some years of happy life a terrible compunction seized her; she imagined herself lost for ever; she became ill. A christian (Baptist) minister and his wife were the evil stars in her case, and with what terrors they surrounded the poor Jewess may be gathered from the following extract.

'She then left me—that dear friend left me alone to my God, and to him I carried a lacerated and bleeding heart, and laid it at the foot of the cross, as an atonement for the multiplied sins I had committed, whether of ignorance or wilfulness; and how shall I proceed to portray the heart-felt agonies of that night preceding my deliverance from the shafts of Satan? Oh! this weight, this load of sin, this burden so intolerable that it crushed me to the earth; for this was a dark hour with me—the darkest; and I lay calm, to all appearance, but with cold perspiration drenching me, nor could I close my eyes; and these words again smote my ear, No redemption, no redemption; and the tempter came, inviting me, with all his blandishment and power, to follow him to his court of pleasure. My eyes were open; I certainly saw him, dressed in the most phantastic shape. This was no illusion; for he soon assumed the appearance of one of the gay throng I had mingled with in former days, and beckoned me to follow. I was awake, and seemed to lie on the brink of a chasm, and spirits were dancing around me, and I made some slight outcry, and those dear girls watching with me came to me, and looked at me. They said I looked at them but could not speak, and they moistened my lips, and said I was nearly gone; then I whispered, and they came and looked at me again, but would not disturb me. It was well they did not; for the power of God was over me, and angels were around me, and whispering spirits near, and I whispered in sweet communion with them, as they surrounded me, and, pointing to the throne of grace, said, 'Behold!' and I felt that the glory of God was about to manifest itself; for a shout, as if a choir of angels had tuned their golden harps, burst forth in, 'Glory to God on high,' and died away in softest strains of melody. I lifted up my eyes to heaven, and there, so near as to be almost within my reach, the brightest vision of our Lord and Saviour stood before me, enveloped with a light, ethereal mist, so bright and yet transparent that his divine figure could be seen distinctly, and my eyes were riveted upon him; for this bright vision seemed to touch my bed, standing at the foot, so near, and he stretched forth his left hand toward me, whilst with the right one he pointed to the throne of grace, and a voice came, saying, 'Blessed are they who can see God; arise, take up thy cross and follow me; for though thy sins be as scarlet they shall be white as wool.' And with my eyes fixed on that bright vision, I saw from the hand stretched toward me great drops of blood, as if from each finger; for his blessed hand was spread open, as if in prayer, and those drops fell distinctly, as if upon the earth; and a misty light encircled me, and a voice again said, 'Take up *thy* cross and follow me; for though thy sins be as scarlet they shall be white as wool.' And angels were all around me, and I saw the throne of heaven. And, oh! the sweet calm that stole over my senses. It must have been a foretaste of heavenly bliss. How long I lay after this beautiful vision I know not; but when I opened my eyes it was early dawn, and I felt so happy and well. My young friends pressed around my bedside, to know how I felt, and I said, 'I am well and so happy.' They then said I was whispering with some one in my dreams all night. I told them angels were with me; that I was not asleep, and I had sweet communion with them, and would soon be well.'[2]

That is what the temptation of Jesus in the wilderness comes to when dislocated from its time and place, and, with its gathered ages of fable, is imported at last to be an engine of torture sprung on the nerves of a devout woman. This Jewess was divorced from her husband by her Christianity; her child died a victim to precocious piety; but what were home and affection in ruins compared with salvation from that frightful devil seen in her holy delirium?

History shows that it has always required unusual courage for a human being to confront an enemy believed to be præternatural. This Jewess would probably have been able to face a tiger for the sake of her husband, but not that fantastic devil. Not long ago an English actor was criticised because, in playing Hamlet, he cowered with fear on seeing the ghost, all his sinews and joints seeming to give way; but to me he appeared then the perfect type of what mankind have always been when believing themselves in the presence of præternatural powers. The limit of courage in human nature was passed when the foe was one which no earthly power or weapon could reach.

In old times, nearly all the sorcerers and witches were women; and it may have been, in some part, because woman had more real courage than man unarmed. Sorcery and witchcraft were but the so-called pagan rites in their last degradation, and women were the last to abandon the declining religion, just as they are the last to leave the superstition which has followed it. Their sentiment and affection were intertwined with it, and the threats of eternal torture by devils which frightened men from the old faith to the new were less powerful to shake the faith of women. When pagan priests became christians, priestesses remained, to become sorceresses. The new faith had gradually to win the love of the sex too used to martyrdom on earth to fear it much in hell. And now, again, when knowledge clears away the old terrors, and many men are growing indifferent to all religion, because no longer frightened by it, we may expect the churches to be increasingly kept up by women alone, simply because they went into them more by attraction of saintly ideals than fear of diabolical menaces.

Thomas Carlyle has selected Luther's boldness in the presence of what he believed the Devil to illustrate his valour. 'His defiance of the 'Devils' in Worms,' says Carlyle, 'was not a mere boast, as the like might be if spoken now. It was a faith of Luther's that there were Devils, spiritual denizens of the Pit, continually besetting men. Many times, in his writings, this turns up; and a most small sneer has been grounded on it by some. In the room of the Wartburg, where he sat translating the Bible, they still show you a black spot on the wall; the strange memorial of one of these conflicts. Luther sat translating one of the Psalms; he was worn down with long labour, with sickness, abstinence from food; there rose before him some hideous indefinable Image, which he took for the Evil One, to forbid his work; Luther started up with fiend-defiance; flung his inkstand at the spectre, and it disappeared! The spot still remains there; a curious monument of several things. Any apothecary's apprentice can now tell us what we are to think of this apparition, in a scientific sense; but the man's heart that dare rise defiant, face to face, against Hell itself, can give no higher proof of fearlessness. The thing he will quail before exists not on this earth nor under it—fearless enough! 'The Devil is aware,' writes he on one occasion, 'that this does not proceed out of fear in me. I have seen and defied innumerable Devils. Duke George,'—of Leipzig, a great enemy of his,—'Duke George is not equal to one Devil,' far short of a Devil! 'If I had business at Leipzig, I would ride into Leipzig, though it rained Duke Georges for nine days running.' What a reservoir of Dukes to ride into!'[3]

Although Luther's courage certainly appears in this, it is plain that his Devil was much humanised as compared with the fearful phantoms of an earlier time. Nobody would ever have tried an inkstand on the Gorgons, Furies, Lucifers of ancient belief. In Luther's Bible the Devil is pictured as a monk—a lean monk, such as he himself was only too likely to become if he continued his rebellion against the Church (Fig. 17). It was against a Devil liable to resistance by physical force that he hurled his inkstand, and against whom he also hurled the contents of his inkstand in those words which Richter said were half-battles.

Luther's Devil, in fact, represents one of the last phases in the reduction of the Evil Power from a personified phantom with which no man could cope, to that impersonal but all the more real moral obstruction with which every man can cope—if only with an inkstand. The horned monster with cowl, beads, and cross, is a mere transparency, through which every brave heart may recognise the practical power of wrong around him, the established error, disguised as religion, which is able to tempt and threaten him.

The temptations with menace described—those which, coming upon the weak nerves of women, vanquished their reason and heart; that which, in a healthy man, raised valour and power—may be taken as side-lights for a corresponding experience in the life of a great man now living—Carlyle himself. It was at a period of youth when, amid the lonely hills of Scotland, he wandered out of harmony with the world in which he lived. Consecrated by pious parents to the ministry, he had inwardly renounced every dogma of the Church. With genius and culture for high work, the world demanded of him low work. Friendless, alone, poor, he sat eating his heart, probably with little else to eat. Every Scotch parson he met unconsciously propounded to that youth the question whether he could convert his heretical stone into bread, or precipitate himself from the pinnacle of the Scotch Kirk without bruises? Then it was he roamed in his mystical wilderness, until he found himself in the gayest capital of the world, which, however, on him had little to bestow but a further sense of loneliness.

'Now, when I look back, it was a strange isolation I then lived in. The men and women around me, even speaking with me, were but Figures; I had practically forgotten that they were alive, that they were not merely automatic. In the midst of their crowded streets and assemblages, I walked solitary; and (except as it was my own heart, not another's, that I kept devouring) savage also, as is the tiger in his jungle. Some comfort it would have been, could I, like a Faust, have fancied myself tempted and tormented of a Devil; for a Hell, as I imagine, without Life, though only diabolic Life, were more frightful: but in our age of Downpulling and Disbelief, the very Devil has been pulled down—you cannot so much as believe in a Devil. To me the Universe was all void of Life, of Purpose, of Volition, even of Hostility: it was one huge, dead, immeasurable, Steam-engine, rolling on, in its dead indifference, to grind me limb from limb. Oh, the vast gloomy, solitary Golgotha, and Mill of Death! Why was the Living banished thither, companionless, conscious? Why, if there is no Devil; nay, unless the Devil is your God?' ...

'From suicide a certain aftershine of Christianity withheld me.'...

'So had it lasted, as in bitter, protracted Death-agony, through long years. The heart within me, unvisited by any heavenly dewdrop, was smouldering in sulphurous, slow-consuming fire. Almost since earliest memory I had shed no tear; or once only when I, murmuring half-audibly, recited Faust's Deathsong, that wild *Selig der den er im Siegesglanze findet* (Happy whom *he* finds in Battle's splendour), and thought that of this last Friend even I was not forsaken, that Destiny itself could not doom me not to die. Having no hope, neither had I any definite fear, were it of Man or of Devil; nay, I often felt as if it might be solacing could the Arch-Devil himself, though in Tartarean terrors, rise to me that I might tell him a little of my mind. And yet, strangely enough, I lived in a continual, indefinite, pining fear; tremulous, pusillanimous, apprehensive of I knew not what; it seemed as if all things in the Heavens above and the Earth beneath would hurt me; as if the Heavens and the Earth were but boundless jaws of a devouring monster, wherein I, palpitating, waited to be devoured.

'Full of such humour, and perhaps the miserablest man in the whole French Capital or Suburbs, was I, one sultry Dogday, after much perambulation, toiling along the dirty little *Rue Sainte Thomas de l'Enfer*, among civic rubbish enough, in a close atmosphere, and over pavements hot as Nebuchadnezzar's Furnace; whereby doubtless my spirits were little cheered; when all at once there rose a Thought in me, and I asked myself, 'What *art* thou afraid of? Wherefore, like a coward, dost thou for ever pip and whimper, and go cowering and trembling? Despicable biped! what is the sum-total of the worst that lies before thee? Death? Well, Death; and say the pangs of Tophet too, and all that the Devil or Man may, will, or can do against thee! Hast thou not a heart; canst thou not suffer whatsoever it be; and, as a Child of Freedom, though outcast, trample Tophet itself under thy feet, while it consumes thee! Let it come, then; I will meet it and defy it!' And as I so thought, there rushed like a stream of fire over my whole soul; and I shook base Fear away from me for ever. I was strong, of unknown strength; a spirit, almost a god. Ever from that time the temper of my misery was changed: not Fear or whining Sorrow was it, but Indignation and grim fire-eyed Defiance.

'Thus had the Everlasting No pealed authoritatively through all the recesses of my Being, of my Me; and then was it that my whole Me stood up, in native God-created majesty and with emphasis recorded its Protest. Such a Protest, the most important transaction in Life, may that same Indignation and Defiance, in a psychological point of view, be fitly called. The Everlasting No had said, 'Behold thou art fatherless, outcast, and the Universe is mine (the Devil's);' to which my whole Me now made answer, '*I* am not thine, but Free, and for ever hate thee!'

'It is from this hour that I incline to date my spiritual New Birth, or Baphometic fire-baptism; perhaps I directly thereupon began to be a Man.'[4]

Perhaps he who so uttered his *Apage Satana* did not recognise amid what haunted Edom he wrestled with his Phantom. Saint Louis, having invited the Carthusian monks to Paris, assigned them a habitation in the Faubourg Saint-Jacques, near the ancient chateau of Vauvert, a manor built by Robert (le Diable), but for a long time then uninhabited, because infested by demons, which had, perhaps, been false coiners. Fearful howls had been heard there, and spectres seen, dragging chains; and, in particular, it was frequented by a fearful green monster, serpent and man in one, with a long white beard, wielding a huge club, with which he threatened all who passed that way. This demon, in common belief, passed along the road to and from the chateau in a fiery chariot, and twisted the neck of every human being met on his way. He was called the Devil of Vauvert. The Carthusians were not frightened by these stories, but asked Louis to give them the Manor, which he did, with all its dependencies. After that nothing more was heard of the Diable Vauvert or his imps. It was but fair to the Demons who had assisted the friars in obtaining a valuable property so cheaply that the street should thenceforth bear the name of Rue d'Enfer, as it does. But the formidable genii of the place haunted it still, and, in the course of time, the Carthusians proved that they could use with effect all the terrors which the Devils had left behind them. They represented a great money-coining Christendom with which free-thinking Michaels had to contend, even to the day when, as we have just read, one of the bravest of these there encountered his Vauvert devil and laid him low for ever.

I well remember that wretched street of St. Thomas leading into Hell Street, as if the Parisian authorities, remembering that Thomas was a doubter, meant to remind the wayfarer that whoso doubteth is damned. Near by is the convent of St. Michael, who makes no war on the neighbouring Rue Dragon. All names—mere idle names! Among the thousands that crowd along them, how many pause to note the quaintness of the names on the street-lamps, remaining there from fossil fears and phantom battles long turned to fairy lore. Yet amid them, on that sultry day, in one heart, was fought and won a battle which summed up all their sense and value. Every Hell was conquered then and there when Fear was conquered. There, when the lower Self was cast down beneath the poised spear of a Free Mind, St. Michael at last chained his dragon. There Luther's inkstand was not only hurled, but hit its mark; there, 'Get thee behind me,' was said, and obeyed; there Buddha brought the archfiend Mara to kneel at his feet.

And it was by sole might of a Man. Therefore may this be emphasised as the temptation and triumph which have for us to-day the meaning of all others.

A young man of intellectual power, seeing beyond all the conventional errors around him, without means, feeling that ordinary work, however honourable, would for him mean failure of his life—because failure to contribute his larger truth to mankind—he finds the terrible cost of his aim to be hunger, want, a life passed amid suspicion and alienation, without sympathy, lonely, unloved—and, alas! with a probability that all these losses may involve loss of just what they are incurred for, the power to make good his truth. After giving up love and joy, he may, after all, be unable to give living service to his truth, but only a broken body and shed blood. Similar trials in outer form have been encountered again and again; not only in the great temptations and triumphs of sacred tradition, but perhaps even more genuinely in the unknown lives of many pious people all over the world, have hunger, want, suffering, been conquered by faith. But rarely amid doubts. Rarely in the way of Saint Thomas, in no fear of hell or devil, nor in any hope of reward in heaven, or on earth; rarely indeed without any feeling of a God taking notice, or belief in angels waiting near, have men or women triumphed utterly over self. All history proves what man can sacrifice on earth for an eternal weight of glory above. We know how cheerfully men and women can sing at the stake, when they feel the fire consuming them to be a chariot bearing them to heaven. We understand the valour of Luther marching against his devils with his hymn, 'Ein feste Burg ist unser Gott.' But it is important to know what man's high heart is capable of without any of these encouragements or aids, what man's moral force when he feels himself alone. For this must become an increasingly momentous consideration.

Already the educated youth of our time have followed the wanderer of threescore years ago into that St. Thomas d'Enfer Street, which may be morally translated as the point where man doubts every hell he does not feel, and every creed he cannot prove. The old fears and hopes are fading faster from the minds around us than from their professions. There must be very few sane people now who are restrained by fear of hell, or promises of future reward. What then controls human passion and selfishness? For many, custom; for others, hereditary good nature and good sense; for some, a sense of honour; for multitudes, the fear of law and penalties. It is very difficult indeed, amid these complex motives, to know how far simple human nature, acting at its best, is capable of heroic endurance for truth, and of pure passion for the right. This cannot be seen in those who intellectually reject the creed of the majority, but conform to its standards and pursue its worldly advantages. It must be seen, if at all, in those who are radically severed from the conventional aims of the world,—who seek not its wealth, nor its honours, decline its proudest titles, defy its authority, share not its prospects for time or eternity. It must be proved by those, the grandeur of whose aims can change the splendours of Paris to a wilderness. These may show what man, as man, is capable of, what may be his new birth, and the religion of his simple manhood. What they think, say, and do is not prescribed either by human or supernatural command; in them you do not see what society thinks, or sects believe, or what the populace applaud. You see the individual man building his moral edifice, as genuinely as birds their nests, by law of his own moral constitution. It is a great thing to know what those edifices are, for so at last every man will have to build if he build at all. And if noble lives cannot be so lived, we may be sure the career of the human race will be downhill henceforth. For any unbiassed mind may judge whether the tendency of thought and power lies toward or away from the old hopes and fears on which the regime of the past was founded.

A great and wise Teacher of our time, who shared with Carlyle his lonely pilgrimage, has admonished his generation of the temptations brought by talent,—selfish use of it for ambitious ends on the one hand, or withdrawal into fruitless solitude on the other; and I cannot forbear closing this chapter with his admonition to his young countrymen forty years ago.[5]

'Public and private avarice makes the air we breathe thick and fat. The scholar is decent, indolent, complacent. See already the tragic consequence. The mind of this country, taught to aim at low objects, eats upon itself. There is no work for any but the decorous and the complacent. Young men of the fairest promise, who begin life upon our shores, inflated by the mountain winds, shined upon by all the stars of God, find the earth below not in unison with these,— but are hindered from action by the disgust which the principles on which business is managed inspire and turn drudges, or die of disgust,—some of them suicides. What is the remedy? They did not yet see, and thousands of young men as hopeful, now crowding to the barriers for the career, do not yet see, that if the single man plant himself indomitably on his instincts, and there abide, the huge world will come round to him. Patience—patience;—with the shades of all the good and great for company; and for solace, the perspective of your own infinite life; and for work, the study and the communication of principles, the making those instincts prevalent, the conversion of the world. Is it not the chief disgrace in the world—not to be an unit; not to be reckoned one character; not to yield that peculiar fruit which each man was created to bear,—but to be reckoned in the gross, in the hundred, in the thousand of the party, the section, to which we belong; and our opinion predicted geographically, as the north or the south? Not so, brothers and friends,—please God, ours shall not be so. We will walk on our own feet; we will work with our own hands; we will speak our own minds.'

**NOTES**
1  'Paradise Regained,' ii.
2  'Henry Luria; or, the Little Jewish Convert: being contained in the Memoir of Mrs. S. T. Cohen, relict of the Rev. Dr. A. H. Cohen, late Rabbi of the Synagogue in Richmond, Va.' 1860.
3  'Heroes and Hero-worship,' iv.
4  'Sartor Resartus.' London: Chapman & Hall, 1869, p. 160.
5  'The American Scholar.' An Oration delivered before the Phi Beta Kappa Society at Cambridge (Massachusetts), August 31, 1837. By Ralph Waldo Emerson.

# Chapter XIX
## The Man of Sin

Hindu myth — Gnostic theories — Ophite scheme of redemption — Rabbinical traditions of primitive man — Pauline Pessimism — Law of death — Satan's ownership of man — Redemption of the elect — Contemporary statements — Baptism — Exorcism — The 'new man's' food — Eucharist — Herbert Spencer's explanation — Primitive ideas — Legends of Adam and Seth — Adamites — A Mormon 'Mystery' of initiation

IN A HINDU myth, Dhrubo, an infant devotee, passed much time in a jungle, surrounded by ferocious beasts, in devotional exercises of such extraordinary merit that Vishnu erected a new heaven for him as the reward of his piety. Vishnu even left his own happy abode to superintend the construction of this special heaven. In Hebrew mythology the favourite son, the chosen people, is called out of Egypt to dwell in a new home, a promised land, not in heaven but on earth. The idea common to the two is that of a contrast between a natural and a celestial environment,—a jungle and beasts, bondage and distress; a new heaven, a land flowing with milk and honey,—and the correspondence with these of the elect child, Dhrubo or Israel.

The tendency of Christ's mind appears to have been rather in the Aryan direction; he pointed his friends to a kingdom not of this world, and to his Father's many mansions in heaven. But the Hebrew faith in a messianic reign in this world was too strong for his dream; a new earth was appended to the new heaven, and became gradually paramount, but this new earth was represented only by the small society of believers who made the body of Christ, the members in which his blood flowed.

That great cauldron of confused superstitions and mysticisms which the Roman Empire became after the overthrow of Jerusalem, formed a thick scum which has passed under the vague name of Gnosticism. The primitive notions of all races were contained in it, however, and they gathered in the second and third centuries a certain consistency in the system of the Ophites. In the beginning existed *Bythos* (the Depth); his first emanation and consort is *Ennoia* (Thought); their first daughter is *Pneuma* (Spirit), their second *Sophia* (Wisdom). Sophia's emanations are two—one perfect, Christos; the other imperfect, Sophia-Achamoth,—who respectively guide all that proceed from God and all that proceed from Matter. Sophia, unable to act directly upon anything so gross as Matter or unordered as Chaos, employs her imperfect daughter Sophia-Achamoth for that purpose. But she, finding delight in imparting life to inert Matter, became ambitious of creating in the abyss a world for herself. To this end she produced the Demiurgus Ildabaoth (otherwise Jehovah) to be creator of the material world. After this Sophia-Achamoth shook off Matter, in which she had become entangled; but Ildabaoth ('son of Darkness') proceeded to produce emanations corresponding to those of Bythos in the upper universe. Among his creations was Man, but his man was a soulless monster crawling on the ground. Sophia-Achamoth managed to transfer to Man the small ray of divine light which Ildabaoth had inherited from her. The 'primitive Man' became thus a divine being. Ildabaoth, now entirely evil, was enraged at having produced a being who had become superior to himself, and his envy took shape in a serpent-formed Satan, *Ophiomorphos*.

He is the concentration of all that is most base in Matter, conjoined with a spiritual intelligence. Their anti-Judaism led the Ophites to identify Ildabaoth as Jehovah, and this serpent-son of his as Michael; they also called him Samaël. Ildabaoth then also created the animal, vegetable, and mineral kingdoms, with all their evils. Resolving to confine man within his own lower domain, he forbade him to eat of the Tree of Knowledge. To defeat his scheme, which had all been evolved out of her own temporary fall, Sophia-Achamoth sent her own genius, also in form of a serpent, Ophis, to induce Man to transgress the tyrant's command. Eve supposing Ophis the same as Ophiomorphos, regarded the prohibition against the fruit as withdrawn and readily ate of it. Man thus became capable of understanding heavenly mysteries, and Ildabaoth made haste to imprison him in the dungeon of Matter. He also punished Ophis by making him eat dust, and this heavenly serpent, contaminated by Matter, changed from Man's friend to his foe. Sophia-Achamoth has always striven against these two Serpents, who bind man to the body by corrupt desires; she supplied mankind with divine light, through which they became sensible of their nakedness—the misery of their condition. Ildabaoth's seductive agents gained control over all the offspring of Adam except Seth, type of the Spiritual Man. Sophia-Achamoth moved Bythos to send down her perfect brother Christos to aid the Spiritual Race of Seth. Christos descended through the seven planetary regions, assuming successively forms related to each, and entered into the man Jesus at the moment of his baptism. Ildabaoth, discovering him, stirred up the Jews to put him to death; but Christos and Sophia, abandoning the material body of Jesus on the cross, gave him one made of ether. Hence his mother and disciples could not recognise him. He ascended to the Middle Space, where he sits by the right hand of Ildabaoth, though unperceived by the latter, and, putting forth efforts for purification of mankind corresponding to those put forth by Ildabaoth for evil, he is collecting all the Spiritual elements of the world into the kingdom which is to overthrow that of the Enemy.[1]

Notwithstanding the animosity shown by the Ophites towards the Jews, most of the elements in their system are plagiarised from the Jews. According to ancient rabbinical traditions, Adam and Eve, by eating the fruit of the lowest region, fell through the six regions to the seventh and lowest; they were there brought under control of the previously fallen Samaël, who defiled them with his spittle. Their nakedness consisted in their having lost a natural protection of which only our finger-nails are left; others say they lost a covering of hair.[2] The Jews also from of old contended that Seth was the son of Adam, in whom returned the divine nature with which man was originally endowed. We have, indeed, only to identify Ildabaoth with Elohim instead of Jehovah to perceive that the Ophites were following Jewish precedents in attributing the natural world to a fiend. The link between, the two conceptions may be discovered in the writings of Paul.

Paul's pessimistic conception of this world and of human nature was radical, and it mainly formed the mould in which dogmatic Christianity subsequently took shape. His general theology is a travesty of the creation of the world and of man. All that work of Elohim was, by implication, natural, that is to say, diabolical. The earth as then created belonged to the Prince of this world, who was the author of sin, and its consequence, death. In Adam all die. The natural man is enmity against God; he is of the earth earthy; his father is the devil; he cannot know spiritual things. All mankind are born spiritually dead. Christ is a new and diviner Demiurgos, engaged in the work of producing a new creation and a new man. For his purpose the old law, circumcision or uncircumcision, are of no avail or importance, but a new creature. His death is the symbol of man's death to the natural world, his resurrection of man's rising into a new world which mere flesh and blood cannot inherit. As God breathed into Adam's nostrils the breath of life, the Spirit breathes upon the elect of Christ a new mind and new heart.

The 'new creature' must inhale an entirely new physical atmosphere. When Paul speaks of 'the Prince of the Power of the Air,' it must not be supposed that he is only metaphorical. On this, however, we must dwell for a little.

'The air,' writes Burton in his 'Anatomy of Melancholy,' 'The air is not so full of flies in summer as it is at all times of invisible devils. They counterfeit suns and moons, and sit on ships' masts. They cause whirlwinds of a sudden, and tempestuous storms, which though our meteorologists generally refer to natural causes, yet I am of Bodine's mind, they are more often caused by those aerial devils in their several quarters. Cardan gives much information concerning them. His father had one of them, an aerial devil, bound to him for eight and twenty years; as Agrippa's dog had a devil tied to his collar. Some think that Paracelsus had one confined in his sword pommel. Others wear them in rings;' and so the old man runs on, speculating about the mysterious cobwebs collected in the ceiling of his brain.

The atmosphere mentally breathed by Burton and his authorities was indeed charged with invisible phantasms; and every one of them was in its origin a genuine intellectual effort to interpret the phenomena of nature. It is not wonderful that the ancients should have ascribed to a diabolical source the subtle deaths that struck at them from the air. A single breath of the invisible poison of the air might lay low the strongest. Even after man had come to understand his visible foes, the deadly animal or plant, he could only cower and pray before the lurking power of miasma and infection, the power of the air. The Tyndalls of a primitive time studied dust and disease, and called the winged seeds of decay and death 'aerial devils,' and prepared the way for Mephistopheles (devil of *smells*), as he in turn for the *bacterial* demon of modern science.

There were not wanting theologic explanations why these malignant beings should find their dwelling-place in the air. They had been driven out of heaven. The etherial realm above the air was reserved for the good. Of the demons the Hindus say, 'Their feet touch not the ground.' 'What man of virtue is there,' said Titus to his soldiers, 'who does not know that those souls which are severed from their fleshy bodies in battles by the sword are received by the æther—that purest of elements—and joined to that company which are placed among the stars; that they become gods, dæmons, and propitious heroes, and show themselves as such to their posterity afterwards?'[3] Malignant spirits were believed to hold a more undisputed sway over the atmosphere than over the earth, although our planet was mainly in their power, and the subjects of the higher empire always a small colony.[4] Moreover, there was a natural tendency of demons, which originally represented earthly evils, when these were conquered by human intelligence, to pass into the realm least accessible to science or to control by man. The uncharted winds became their refuge.

This belief was general among the Christian Fathers,[5] lasted a very long time even among the educated, and is still the teaching of the Roman Catholic Church, as any one may see by reading the authorised work of Mgr. Gaume on 'Holy Water' (p. 305). So long as it was admitted among thinking people that the mind was as competent to build facts upon theory as theories on fact, a great deal might be plausibly said for this atmospheric diabolarchy. In the days when witchcraft was first called in question, Glanvil argued 'that since this little Spot is so thickly peopled in every Atome of it, 'tis weakness to think that all the vast spaces Above and hollows under Ground are desert and uninhabited,' and he anticipated that, as microscopic science might reveal further populations in places seemingly vacant, it would necessitate the belief that the regions of the upper air are inhabited.[6] Other learned men concluded that the spirits that lodge there are such as are clogged with earthly elements; the baser sort; dwelling in cold air, they would like to inhabit the more sheltered earth. In repayment for broth, and various dietetic horrors proffered them by witches, they enable them to pass freely through their realm—the air.

Out of such intellectual atmosphere came Paul's sentence (Eph. ii. 2) about 'the Prince of the Power of the Air.' It was a spiritualisation of the existing aerial demonology. When Paul and his companions carried their religious agitation into the centres of learning and wealth, and brought the teachings of a Jew to confront the temples of Greece and Rome, they found themselves unrelated to that great world. It had another habit of mind and feeling, and the idea grew in him that it was the spirits of the Satanic world counteracting the spirit sent on earth from the divine world. This animated its fashions, philosophy, science, and literature. He warns the Church at Ephesus that they will need the whole armour of God, because they are wrestling not with mere flesh and blood, but against the rulers of the world's darkness, the evil spirits in high places—that is, in the Air.

*Fig. 7.—Adam Signing Contract for his Posterity To Satan*

As heirs of this new nature and new world, with its new atmosphere, purchased and endowed by Christ, the Pauline theory further presupposes, that the natural man, having died, is buried with Christ in baptism, rises with him, and is then sealed to him by the Holy Ghost. For a little time such must still bear about them their fleshy bodies, but soon Christ shall come, and these vile bodies shall be changed into his likeness; meanwhile they must keep their bodies in subjection, even as Paul did, by beating it black and blue (ὑπωπιάζω), and await their deliverance from the body of the dead world they have left, but which so far is permitted to adhere to them. This conception had to work itself out in myths and dogmas of which Paul knew nothing. 'If any man come after me and hate not his father and mother, and his own (natural) life also, he cannot be my disciple.' The new race with which the new creation was in travail was logically discovered to need a new Mother as well as a new Father. Every natural mother was subjected to a stain that it might be affirmed that only one mother was immaculate—she whose conception was supernatural, not of the flesh. Marriage became an indulgence to sin (whose purchase-money survives still in the marriage-fee). The monastery and the nunnery represented this new ascetic kingdom; that perilous word 'worldliness' was transmitted to be the source of insanity and hypocrisy.

Happily, the common sense and sentiment of mankind have so steadily and successfully won back the outlawed interests of life and the world, that it requires some research into ecclesiastical archæology to comprehend the original significance of the symbols in which it survives. The ancient rabbins limited the number of souls which hang on Adam to 600,000, but the Christian theologians extended the figures to include the human race. Probably even some orthodox people may be scandalised at the idea of the fathers (Irenæus, for example), that, at the Fall, the human race became Satan's rightful property, did they see it in the picture copied by Buslaef, from an ancient Russian Bible, in possession of Count Uvarof. Adam gives Satan a written contract for himself and his descendants (Fig. 7). And yet, according to a recent statement, the Rev. Mr. Simeon recently preached a sermon in the Church of St. Augustine, Kilburn, London, 'to prove that the ruler of the world is the devil. He stated that the Creator of the world had given the control of the world to one of his chief angels, Lucifer, who, however, had gone to grief, and done his utmost to ruin the world. Since then the Creator and Lucifer had been continually striving to checkmate each other. As Lucifer is still the Prince of this world, it would seem that it is not he who has been beaten yet.'[7] A popular preacher in America, Rev. Dr. Talmage, states the case as follows:—

'I turn to the same old book, and I find out that the Son of Mary, who was the Son of God, the darling of heaven, the champion of the ages, by some called Lord, by some called Jesus, by others called Christ, but this morning by us called by the three blessed titles, Lord Jesus Christ, by one magnificent stroke made it possible for us all to be saved. He not only told us that there was a hell, but he went into it. He walked down the fiery steeps. He stepped off the bottom rung of the long ladder of despair. He descended into hell. He put his bare foot on the hottest coal of the fiercest furnace.

'He explored the darkest den of eternal midnight, and then He came forth lacerated and scarified, and bleeding and mauled by the hands of infernal excruciation, to cry out to all the ages, 'I have paid the price for all those who would make me their substitute. By my piled-up groans, by my omnipotent agony, I demand the rescue of all those who will give up sin and trust in me,' Mercy! mercy! mercy! But how am I to get it? Cheap. It will not cost you as much as a loaf of bread. Only a penny? No, no. Escape from hell, and all the harps, and mansions, and thrones, and sunlit fields of heaven besides in the bargain, 'without money, and without price.'"

These preachers are only stating with creditable candour the original significance of the sacraments and ceremonies which were the physiognomy of that theory of 'a new creature.' Following various ancient traditions, that life was produced out of water, that water escaped the primal curse on nature, that devils hate and fear it because of this and the saltness of so much of it, many religions have used water for purification and exorcism.[8] Baptism is based on the notion that every child is offspring of the Devil, and possessed of his demon; the Fathers agreed that all unbaptized babes, even the still-born, are lost; and up to the year 1550 every infant was subjected at baptism to the exorcism, 'I command thee, unclean spirit, in the name of the Father, of the Son, and of the Holy Ghost, that thou come out, and depart from, these infants whom our Lord Jesus Christ has vouchsafed to call to his holy baptism, to be made members of his body and of his holy congregation,' &c.

A clergyman informed me that he knew of a case in which a man, receiving back his child after christening, kissed it, and said, 'I never kissed it before, because I knew it was not a child of God; but now that it is, I love it dearly.' But why not? Some even now teach that a white angel follows the baptized, a black demon the unbaptized.

The belief was wide-spread that unbaptized children were turned into elves at death. In Iceland it is still told as a bit of folk-lore, that when God visited Eve, she kept a large number of her children out of sight, 'because they had not been washed,' and these children were turned into elves, and became the progenitors of that uncanny race. The Greek Church made so much of baptism, that there has been developed an Eastern sect which claims John the Baptist as its founder, making little of Christ, who baptized none; and to this day in Russia the peasant regards it as almost essential to a right reception of the benedictions of Sunday to have been under water on the previous day—soap being sagaciously added. The Roman Catholic Church, following the provision of the Council of Carthage, still sets a high value on baptismal exorcism; and Calvin refers to a theological debate at the Sorbonne in Paris, whether it would not be justifiable for a priest to throw a child into a well rather than have it die unbaptized. Luther preserved the Catholic form of exorcism; and, in some districts of Germany, Protestants have still such faith in it, that, when either a child or a domestic animal is suspected of being possessed, they will send for the Romish priest to perform the rite of exorcism.

Mr. Herbert Spencer has described the class of superstitions out of which the sacrament of the Eucharist has grown. 'In some cases,' he says, 'parts of the dead are swallowed by the living, who seek thus to inspire themselves with the good qualities of the dead; and we saw (§ 133) that the dead are supposed to be honoured by this act. The implied notion was supposed to be associated with the further notion that the nature of another being, inhering in all the fragments of his body, inheres too in the unconsumed part of anything consumed with his body; so that an operation wrought on the remnants of his food becomes an operation wrought on the food swallowed, and therefore on the swallower. Yet another implication is, that between those who swallow different parts of the same food some community of nature is established. Hence such beliefs as that ascribed by Bastian to some negroes, who think that, 'on eating and drinking consecrated food, they eat and drink the god himself'—such god being an ancestor, who has taken his share. Various ceremonies among savages are prompted by this conception; as, for instance, the choosing a totem. Among the Mosquito Indians, 'the manner of obtaining this guardian was to proceed to some secluded spot and offer up a sacrifice: with the beast or bird which thereupon appeared, in dream or in reality, a compact for life was made, by drawing blood from various parts of the body.' This blood, supposed to be taken by the chosen animal, connected the two, and the animal's life became so bound up with their own that the death of one involved that of the other.'[9] And now mark that, in these same regions, this idea re-appears as a religious observance. Sahagun and Herrera describe a ceremony of the Aztecs called 'eating the god.' Mendieta, describing this ceremony, says, 'They had also a sort of eucharist.... They made a sort of small idols of seeds, ... and ate them as the body or memory of their gods.' As the seeds were cemented partly by the blood of sacrificed boys; as their gods were cannibal gods; as Huitzilopochtli, whose worship included this rite, was the god to whom human sacrifices were most extensive; it is clear that the aim was to establish community with gods by taking blood in common.'[10]

When, a little time ago, a New Zealand chief showed his high appreciation of a learned German by eating his eyes to improve his own intellectual vision, the case seemed to some to call for more and better protected missionaries; but the chief might find in the sacramental communion of the missionaries the real principle of his faith. The celebration of the 'Lord's Supper' when a Bishop is ordained has only to be 'scratched,' as the proverb says, to reveal beneath it the Indians choosing their episcopal totem. As Israel observed the Passover—eating together of the lamb whose blood sprinkled on their door-posts had marked those to be preserved from the Destroying Angel in Egypt—they who believed that Jesus was Messias tasted the body and blood of their Head, as indicating the elect out of a world otherwise given over to the Destroyer spiritually, and finally to be delivered up to him bodily. 'He that eateth my flesh and drinketh my blood dwelleth in me and I in him.' These were to tread on serpents, or handle them unharmed, as it is said Paul did. They were not really to die, but to fall asleep, that they might be changed as a seed to its flower, through literal resurrection from the earth.

We should probably look in vain after any satisfactory vestiges of the migration of the superstition concerning the mystical potency of food. It is found fully developed in the ancient Hindu myth of the struggle between the gods and demons for the Amrita, the immortalising nectar, one stolen sip of which gave the monster Ráhu the imperishable nature which no other of his order possesses. It is found in corresponding myths concerning the gods of Asgard and of

Olympus. The fall of man in the Iranian legend was through a certain milk given by Ahriman to the first pair, Meschia and Meschiane. In Buddhist mythology, it was eating rice that corrupted the nature of man. It was the process of incarnation in the Gilghit legend (i. 398). The whole story of Persephone turns upon her having eaten the seed of a pomegranate in Hades, by which she was bound to that sphere. There is a myth very similar to that of Persephone in Japan. There is a legend in the Scottish Highlands that a woman was conveyed into the secret recesses of the 'men of peace'—the Daoine Shi', euphemistic name of uncanny beings, who carry away mortals to their subterranean apartments, where beautiful damsels tempt them to eat of magnificent banquets. This woman on her arrival was recognised by a former acquaintance, who, still retaining some portion of human benevolence, warned her that, if she tasted anything whatsoever for a certain space of time, she would be doomed to remain in that underworld for ever. The woman having taken this counsel, was ultimately restored to the society of mortals. It was added that, when the period named by her unfortunate friend had elapsed, a disenchantment of this woman's eyes took place, and the viands which had before seemed so tempting she now discovered to consist only of the refuse of the earth.[11]

The difficulty of tracing the ethnical origin of such legends as these is much greater than that of tracing their common natural origin. The effect of certain kinds of food upon the human system is very marked, even apart from the notorious effects of the drinks made from the vegetative world.

*Fig. 8.—Seth Offering a Branch to Adam*

The effects of mandrake, opium, tobacco, various semi-poisonous fungi, the simplicity with which differences of race might be explained by their vegetarian or carnivorous customs, would be enough to suggest theories of the potency of food over the body and soul of man such as even now have their value in scientific speculation.

The Jewish opinion that Seth was the offspring of the divine part of Adam was the germ of a remarkable christian myth. Adam, when dying, desired Seth to procure the oil of mercy (for his extreme unction) from the angels guarding Paradise. Michael informs Seth that it can only be obtained after the lapse of the ages intervening the Fall and the Atonement. Seth received, however, a small branch of the Tree of Knowledge, and was told that when it should bear fruit, Adam would recover. Returning, Seth found Adam dead, and planted the branch in his grave. It grew to a tree which Solomon had hewn down for building the temple; but the workmen could not adapt it, threw it aside, and it was used as a bridge over a lake. The Queen of Sheba, about to cross this lake, beheld a vision of Christ on the cross, and informed Solomon that when a certain person had been suspended on that tree the fall of the Jewish nation would be near. Solomon in alarm buried the wood deep in the earth, and the spot was covered by the pool of Bethesda. Shortly before the crucifixion the tree floated on that water, and ultimately, as the cross, bore its fruit.[12]

In our old Russian picture (Fig. 8) Seth is shown offering a branch of the Tree of Knowledge to his father Adam. That it should spring up to be the Tree of Life is simply in obedience to Magian and Gnostic theories, which generally turn on some scheme by which the Good turns against the Evil Mind the point of his own weapon. These were the influences which gave to christian doctrines on the subject their perilous precision. The universal tradition was that Adam was the first person liberated by Christ from hell; and this corresponded with an equally wide belief that all who were saved by the death of Christ and his descent into hell were at once raised into the moral condition of Adam and Eve before the Fall,—to eat the food and breathe the holy air of Paradise.

An honest mirror was held up before this theology by the christian Adamites. Their movement (second and third centuries) was a most legitimate outcome of the Pauline and Johannine gospel. The author of this so-called 'heresy,' Prodicus, really anticipated the Methodist doctrine of 'sanctification,' and he was only consistent in admonishing his followers that clothing was, in the Bible, the original badge of carnal guilt and shame, and was no longer necessary for those whom Christ had redeemed from the Fall and raised to the original innocence of Adam and Eve. These believers, in the appropriate climate of Northern Africa, had no difficulty in carrying out their doctrine practically, and having named their churches 'Paradises,' assembled in them quite naked. There is still a superstition in the East that a snake will never attack one who is naked. The same Adamite doctrine—a prelapsarian perfection symbolised by nudity—was taught by John Picard in Bohemia, and a flourishing sect of 'Adamites' arose there in the fifteenth century. The Slavonian Adamites of the last century—and they are known to carry on their services still in secret—not only dispense with clothing, but also with sacraments and ceremonies, which are for the imperfect, not for the perfected. Again and again has this logical result of the popular theology appeared, and with increasingly gross circumstances, as the refined and intelligent abandon except in name the corresponding dogmas. It is an impressive fact that Paul's central doctrine of 'a new creature' is now adopted with most realistic orthodoxy by the Mormons of

Utah, whose initiation consists of a dramatic performance on each candidate of moulding the body out of clay, breathing in the nostrils, the 'deep sleep' presentation of an Eve to each Adam, the temptation, fall, and redemption. The 'saints' thus made, unfortunately, seem to have equally realistic ideas that the Gentiles are adherents of the Prince of this world, and their sacramental bands have shown some striking imitations of those events of history which, when not labelled 'Christian,' are pronounced barbarous. Now that the old dogmatic system is being left more and more to the ignorant and vulgar to make over into their own image and likeness, it may be hoped that elsewhere also the error that libels and outrages nature will run to seed; for error, like the aloe, has its period when it shoots up a high stem and—dies.

---

NOTES
1  The relations of this system to those of various countries are stated by Professor King in his work 'The Gnostics and their Remains.'
2  In the Architectural Museum, Westminster, there is an old picture which possibly represents the hairy Adam.
3  Josephus; 'Wars of the Jews,' vi. 1.
4  Those who wish to pursue the subject may consult Plutarch, Philo, Josephus, Diog. Laertius; also Eisenmenger, Wetstein, Elsner, Doughtæi, Lightfoot, Sup. Relig., &c.
5  See 'Supernatural Religion,' vol. i. ch. 4 and 5, for ample references concerning these superstitions among both Jews and Christians.
6  'Saducismus,' p. 53.
7  'Eastern Morning News,' quoted in the 'National Reformer,' December 17, 1877.

8   Much curious information is contained in the work already referred to, 'L'Eau Benite au Dix-neuvième Siècle.' Par Monsignor Gaume, Protonotaire Apostolique. Paris, 1866. It is there stated that water escaped the curse; that salt produces fecundity; that devils driven off temporarily by the cross are effectually dismissed by holy water; that St. Vincent, interrupted by a storm while preaching, dispersed it by throwing holy water at it; and he advises the use of holy water against the latest devices of the devil—spirit-rapping. It must not, however, be supposed that these notions are confined to Catholics. Every element in the disquisition of Monsignor Gaume is represented in the region where his church is most hated. Mr. James Napier, in his recent book on Folklore, shows us the Scotch hastening new-born babes to baptism lest they become 'changelings,' and the true meaning of the rite is illustrated in a reminiscence of his own childhood. He was supposed to be pining under an Evil Eye, and the old woman, or 'skilly,' called in, carefully locked the door, now unlocked by her patient, and proceeded as follows:— 'A sixpence was borrowed from a neighbour, a good fire was kept burning in the grate, the door was locked, and I was placed upon a chair in front of the fire. The operator, an old woman, took a tablespoon and filled it with water. With the sixpence she then lifted as much salt as it would carry, and both were put into the water in the spoon. The water was then stirred with the forefinger till the salt was dissolved. Then the soles of my feet and the palms of my hands were bathed with this solution thrice, and after these bathings I was made to taste the solution three times. The operator then drew her wet forefinger across my brow—called scoring aboon the breath. The remaining contents of the spoon she then cast right over the fire, into the hinder part of the fire, saying as she did so, 'Guid preserve frae a' skaith.' These were the first words permitted to be spoken during the operation. I was then put in bed, and, in attestation of the charm, recovered. To my knowledge this operation has been performed within these forty years, and probably in many outlying country places it is still practised. The origin of this superstition is probably to be found in ancient fire-worship. The great blazing fire was evidently an important element in the transaction; nor was this a solitary instance in which regard was paid to the fire. I remember being taught that it was unlucky to spit into the fire, some evil being likely shortly after to befall those who did so. Crumbs left upon the table after a meal were carefully gathered and put into the fire. The cuttings from the nails and hair were also put into the fire. These freaks certainly look like survivals of fire-worship.' It may be well here to refer the reader to what has been said in vol. i. on Demons of Fire. The Devil's fear of salt and consequently of water confirmed the perhaps earlier apprehension of all fiery phantoms of that which naturally quenches flame.

9   We here get a clue to the origin of various strange ceremonies by which men bind themselves to one another. Michelet, in his 'Origines du Droit Français,' writes: 'Boire le sang l'un de l'autre, c'etait pour ainsi dire se faire même chair. Ce symbole si expressif se trouve chez un grand nombre de peuples;' and he gives instances from various ancient races. But, as we here see, this practice is not originally adopted as a symbol (no practices begin as symbols), but is prompted by the belief that a community of nature is thus established, and a community of power over one another.

10  'Principles of Sociology,' i. ch. xix. Origen says, that a man eats and drinks with demons when he eats flesh and drinks wine offered to idols. (Contra Cels. viii. 31.)

11  Dr. James Browne's 'History of the Highlands,' ed. 1855, i. 108.

12  'Aurea Legenda.' The story, as intertwined with that of the discovery of the true cross by the Empress Helena, was a fruitful theme for artists. It has been painted in various versions by Angiolo Gaddi in S. Croce at Florence, by Pietro della Francesca at Arezzo, and in S. Croce in Ger. at Rome are frescoes celebrating Helena in a chapel named from her, but into which persons of her sex are admitted only once a year.

## Chapter XX
# The Holy Ghost

A Hanover relic — Mr. Atkinson on the Dove — The Dove in the Old Testament — Ecclesiastical symbol — Judicial symbol — A vision of St. Dunstan's — The witness of chastity — Dove and Serpent — The unpardonable sin — Inexpiable sin among the Jews — Destructive power of Jehovah — Potency of the breath — Third persons of Trinities — Pentecost — Christian superstitions — Mr. Moody on the sin against the Holy Ghost — Mysterious fear — Idols of the cave

THERE IS IN the old town of Hanover, in Germany, a schoolhouse in which, above the teacher's chair, there was anciently the representation of a dove perched upon an iron branch or rod; and beneath the inscription—'THIS SHALL LEAD YOU INTO ALL TRUTH.' In the course of time the dove fell down and was removed to the museum; but there is still left before the children the rod, with the admonition that it will lead them into all truth. This is about as much as for a long time was left in the average christian mind of the symbolical Dove, the Holy Ghost. Half of its primitive sense departed, and there remained only an emblem of mysterious terror. More spiritual minds have introduced into the modern world a conception of the Holy Ghost as a life-giving influence or a spirit of love, but the ancient view which regarded it as the Iron Rod of judgment and execution still survives in the notion of the 'sin against the Holy Ghost.'

Mr. Henry G. Atkinson writes as follows:[1]—'My old friend Barry Cornwall, the fine poet, once said to me, 'My dear Atkinson, can you tell me the meaning of the Holy Ghost; what can it possibly mean?' 'Well,' I said, 'I suppose it means a pigeon. We have never heard of it in any other form but that of the dove descending from heaven to the Virgin Mary. Then we have the pretty fable of the dove returning to the ark with the olive-branch, so that the Christian religion may be called the Religion of the Pigeon. In the Greek Church the pigeon is held sacred. St. Petersburgh is swarming with pigeons, but they are never killed or disturbed. I knew a lady whose life was made wretched in the belief that she had sinned the unpardonable sin against the Holy Ghost, and neither priest nor physician could persuade her out of the delusion, though in all other respects she was quite sensible. She regarded herself as such a wretch that she could not bear to see herself in the glass, and the looking-glasses had all to be removed, and when she went to an hotel, her husband had to go first and have the looking-glasses of the apartments covered over. But what is the Holy Ghost—what is its office? Sitting with Miss Martineau at her house at Ambleside one day, a German lady, who spoke broken English, came in. She was a neighbour, and had a large house and grounds, and kept fowls. 'Oh!' she said, quite excited, 'the beast has taken off another chicken (meaning the hawk). I saw it myself. The wretch! it came down just like the Holy Ghost, and snatched off the chicken.' How Miss Martineau did laugh; but I don't know that this story throws much light upon the subject, since it does but bring us back to the pigeon.'

It would require a volume to explain fully all the problems suggested in this brief note, but the more important facts may be condensed.

It is difficult to show how far the natural characteristics and habits of the dove are reflected in its wide-spread symbolism. Its

plaintive note and fondness for solitudes are indicated in the Psalm-
ist's aspiration, 'Oh that I had the wings of a dove, then would I fly
away and be at rest; lo, then would I wander far off, and remain in
the wilderness.'[2] It is not a difficult transition from this association
with the wilderness to investment with a relationship with the demon of the wilderness—Azazel. So we find it in certain passages
in Jeremiah, where the word has been suppressed in the ordinary
English version. 'The land is desolate because of the fierceness of
the dove.' 'Let us go again to our own people to avoid the sword of
the dove.' 'They shall flee away every one for fear of the sword of
the dove.'[3] In India its lustres—blue and fiery—may have connected
it with azure-necked Siva.

The far-seeing and wonderful character of the pigeon as a carrier was well known to the ancients. On Egyptian bas-reliefs priests
are shown sending them with messages. They appear in the branches
of the oaks of Dodona, and in old Russian frescoes they sometimes
perch on the Tree of Knowledge in paradise. It is said that, in order to
avail himself of this universal symbolism, Mohammed trained a dove
to perch on his shoulder. As the raven was said to whisper secrets
to Odin, so the dove was often pictured at the ear of God. In Nôtre
Dame de Chartres, its beak is at the ear of Pope Gregory the Great.

It passed—and did not have far to go—to be the familiar of
kings. It brought the chrism from heaven at the baptism of Clovis.
White doves came to bear the soul of Louis of Thuringia to heaven.
The dove surmounted the sceptre of Charlemagne. At the consecration of the kings of France, after the ceremony of unction, white
doves were let loose in the church. At the consecration of a monarch

in England, a duke bears before the sovereign the sceptre with the dove.

By association with both ecclesiastical and political sovereignty, it came to represent very nearly the old fatal serpent power which had lurked in all its transformations. When the Holy Ghost was represented as a crowned man, the dove was pictured on his wrist like that falcon with which the German lady, mentioned by Mr. Atkinson, identified it. But in this connection its symbolism is more especially referable to a passage in Isaiah:[4] 'There shall come forth a rod out of the stem of Jesse, and a branch shall grow out of his roots; and the Spirit of the Lord shall rest upon him, the spirit of wisdom and understanding, the spirit of counsel and might, the spirit of the knowledge and of the fear of the Lord.' The sanctity of the number seven led to the partition of the last clause into three spirits, making up the seven, which were: Wisdom, Understanding, Counsel, Strength, Knowledge, Piety, Fear. In some of the representations of these where each of the seven Doves is labelled with its name, 'Fear' is at the top of their arch, a Psalm having said, 'The fear of the Lord is the beginning of wisdom.' When the knightly Order of the Holy Ghost was created in 1352, it was aristocratic, and, when reorganised by Henry III. of France in 1579, it was restricted to magisterial and political personages. With them was the spirit of Fear certainly; and the Order shows plainly what had long been the ideas connected with the Holy Ghost.

M. Didron finds this confirmed in the legends of every country, and especially refers to a story of St. Dunstan, Archbishop of Canterbury, in the tenth century. Three men, convicted of coining false money, had been condemned to death. Immediately before the celebration of mass on the day of Pentecost, the festival of the Holy Ghost, St. Dunstan inquired whether justice had been done upon the three criminals: he was informed in reply that the execution had been delayed on account of the solemn feast of Pentecost then in celebration. 'It shall not be thus,' cried the indignant archbishop, and gave orders for the immediate execution of the guilty men. Several of those who were present remonstrated against the cruelty of that order; it was nevertheless obeyed.

After the execution of the criminals, Dunstan washed his face, and turned with a joyful countenance towards his oratory. 'I now hope,' said he, 'that God will be pleased to accept the sacrifice I am about to offer;' and in fact, during the celebration of mass, at the moment when the Saint raised his hands to implore that God the Father would be pleased to give peace to his Church, to guide, guard, and keep it in unity throughout the world, 'a dove, as white as snow, was seen to descend from heaven, and during the entire service remained with wings extended, floating silently in air above the head of the archbishop.'[5]

The passionate sexual nature of the dove made it emblem of Aphrodite, and it became spiritualised in its consecration to the Madonna. From its relation to the falsely-accused Mary, there grew around the Dove a special class of legends which show it attesting female innocence or avenging it. The white dove said to have issued from the mouth of Joan of Arc is one of many instances. There is still, I believe, preserved in the Lyttleton family the picture painted by Dowager Lady Lyttleton in 1780, in commemoration of the warning of death given to Lord Lyttleton by the mother of two girls he had seduced, the vision being attended by a fluttering dove. The original account of his vision or dream, attributed to Lord Lyttleton, mentions only 'a bird.' When next told, it is that he 'heard a noise resembling the fluttering of a dove,' and on looking to the window saw 'an unhappy female whom he had seduced.' But the exigencies of orthodoxy are too strong for original narratives. As the 'bird' attested an announcement that on the third day (that too was gradually added) he would die, it must have been a dove; and as the dove attends only the innocent, it must have been the poor girl's mother that appeared. It was easy to have the woman die at the precise hour of appearance.[6] When in Chicago in 1875, I read in one of the morning papers a very particular account of how a white dove flew into the chamber window of a young unmarried woman in a neighbouring village, she having brought forth a child, and solemnly declaring that she had never lost her virginity.

In this history of the symbolism of the Dove the theological development of the Holy Ghost has been outlined. We have seen in the previous chapter that the Holy Spirit is in opposition to the Natural Air,—repository of evils. The Dove symbolised this aspect of it in hovering over the world emerging from its diluvial baptism, and also over the typical new Adam (Jesus) coming from his baptism. But in this it corresponds with the serpent-symbol of life in Egyptian mythology brooding over the primal mundane egg (as in Fig. 23, vol. i.). Nathaniel Hawthorne found a mystical meaning in the beautiful group at Rome representing a girl pressing a dove to her bosom while she is attacked by a serpent. But in their theological aspects the

Dove and the Serpent blend; they are at once related and separated in Christ's words, 'Be ye wise as serpents and harmless as doves;' but in the office of the Holy Ghost as representing a divine Intelligence, and its consequent evolution as executor of divine judgments, it fulfils in Christendom much the same part as the Serpent in the more primitive mythologies.

'Every sin and blasphemy will be forgiven unto men,' said a legendary Christ;[7] 'but the blasphemy against the Spirit will not be forgiven. And whosoever shall speak a word against the Son of man, it will be forgiven him, but whosoever shall speak against the Holy Ghost, it will not be forgiven him, neither in this world nor in that to come.' In Mark [8] it is said, 'All things shall be forgiven unto the sons of men, the sins and the blasphemies wherewith they shall blaspheme: but whosoever shall blaspheme against the Holy Ghost has never forgiveness, but will be guilty of everlasting sin; (because they said, He has an unclean spirit).' When Christ uttered these tremendous words, no disciple seems to have been startled, or to have inquired into the nature of that sin, so much worse than any offence against himself or the Father, which has since employed so much theological speculation.

In fact, they needed no explanation: it was an old story; the unpardonable sin was a familiar feature of ancient Jewish law. Therein the sin excluded from expiation was any presumptuous language or action against Jehovah. It is easy to see why this was so. Real offences, crimes against man or society, were certain of punishment, through the common interest and need. But the honour and interests of Jehovah, not being obvious or founded in nature, required special and severe statutes. The less a thing is protected by its intrinsic and practical importance, the more it must, if at all, be artificially protected. This is illustrated in the story of Eli and his two sons. These youths were guilty of the grossest immoralities, but not a word was said against them, they being sons of the High Priest, except a mild remonstrance from Eli himself. But when on an occasion these youths tasted the part of the sacrificial meat offered to Jehovah, the divine wrath was kindled. Eli, much more terrified at this ceremonial than the moral offence, said to his sons, 'If one man sin against another, the judge shall judge him, but if a man sin against Jehovah, who shall entreat for him?' In protecting his interests, Jehovah's destroying angel does not allude to any other offence of Eli's sons except that against himself. But when the priestly guardians of the divine interests came with their people under the control of successive Gallios,—aliens who cared not for their ceremonial law, and declined to permit the infliction of its penalties, as England now forbids *suttee* in India,—the priests could only pass sentences; execution of them had to be adjourned to a future world.

The doctrine of a future state of rewards and punishments is not one which a priesthood would naturally prefer or invent. So long as a priesthood possesses the power of life and death over the human body, they would not, by suggesting future awards, risk the possibility of a heresy arising to maintain *Deorum injuria diis cura*. But where an alien jurisdiction has relegated to local deities the defence of their own majesty, there must grow up the theory that such offences as cannot be expiated on earth are unpardonable, and must, because of the legal impunity with which they can be committed, be all the more terribly avenged somewhere else.

Under alien influences, also, the supreme and absolute government of Jehovah had been divided, as is elsewhere described. He who originally claimed the empire of both light and darkness, good and evil, when his rivalry against other gods was on a question of power, had to be relieved of responsibility for earthly evils when the moral sense demanded dualism. Thus there grew up a separate personification of the destructive power of Jehovah, which had been supposed to lodge in his breath. The last breath of man obviously ends life; there is nothing more simple in its natural germ than the association of the first breath and the last with the Creative Spirit.[9] This potency of the breath or spirit is found in many ancient regions. It is the natural teaching of the destructive simoom,[10] or even of the annual autumnal breath which strikes the foliage with death. Persia especially abounded with superstitions of this character. By a sorcerer's breath the two serpents were evoked from the breast of Zohák. Nizami has woven the popular notion into his story of the two physicians who tried to destroy each other; one of whom survived his rival's poisonous draught, and killed that rival by making him smell a flower on which he had breathed.[11] Such notions as these influenced powerfully the later development of the idea of Jehovah, concerning whom it was said of old, 'With the breath of his mouth shall he slay the wicked;' 'the breath of the Lord like a stream of brimstone doth kindle (Tophet).'

Meanwhile in all the Trinitarian races which were to give form to christian Mythology, destructiveness had generally (not invariably) become the traditional rôle of the Third Person.[12] In Egypt there were Osiris the Creator, Horus the Preserver, Typhon the Destroyer; in Babylonia, Anu the Upper Air, Sin (Uri) the Moon, Samis the Sun.

In Assyria the Sun regains his place, and deadly influences were as-cribed to the Moon. In India, Brahma the Father, Vishnu the Saviour, Siva the Destroyer; in Persia, Zeruâne-Akrane Infinite Time, Ormuzd the Good, Ahriman the Evil; in Greece Zeus, Poseidôn, and Hadês, or Heaven, Ocean, and Hell, were the first-born of Time. The Trinitarian form had gradually crept in among the Jews, though their Jahvistic theology only admitted its application to inferior deities—Cain, Abel, Seth; Moses, Aaron, Hur; Abraham, Isaac, Jacob. As time went on, these succeeded the ideas of Jehovah, Messias, and Wisdom. But already the serpent was the wisest of all the beasts of the field in Jewish mythology; and the personified Wisdom was fully prepared to be identified with Athene, the Greek Wisdom, who sprang armed from the head of Zeus (the Air), and whose familiar was a serpent.

On the other hand, however, the divine Breath had also its benign significance. Siva ('the auspicious') inherited the character of Rudra ('roaring storm'), but it was rather supported later on by his wife Káli. Athena though armed was the goddess of agriculture. The breath of Elohim had given man life. 'I now draw in and now let forth,' says Krishna;[13] 'I am generation and dissolution; I am death and immortality.' 'Thou wilt fancy it the dawning zephyr of an early spring,' says Sàdi; 'but it is the breath of Isa, or Jesus; for in that fresh breath and verdure the dead earth is reviving.'[14] 'The voice of the turtle is heard in the land,' sings Solomon.

When the Third Person of the Christian Trinity was consti-tuted, it inherited the fatality of all the previous Third Persons—the Destroyers—while it veiled them in mystery. When the Holy Ghost inspired the disciples the account is significant.[15] 'Suddenly there came a sound from heaven as of a rushing mighty wind, ... and there appeared unto them cloven tongues like as of fire, and it sat upon each of them. And they were all filled with the Holy Ghost.' This was on the Day of Pentecost, the harvest festival, when the first-fruits were offered to the quickening Spirit or Breath of nature; but the destructive feature is there also—the tongues are cloven like those of serpents. The beneficent power was manifest at the gate called Beautiful when the lame man was made to walk by Peter's power; but its fatal power was with the same apostle, and when he said, 'Why hath Satan filled thy heart to lie to the Holy Ghost?' instantly Ananias fell down and gave up the ghost.[16] The spirit was carried, it is said, in the breath of the apostles. Its awfulness had various illustrations. Mary offered up two doves in token of her conception by the Holy Ghost. Jesus is described as scourging from the temple those that sold doves, and the allegory is repeated in Peter's denunciation of Simon Magus, who offered money for the gift of the Holy Ghost.[17]

In one of his sermons Mr. Moody said, 'Nearly every day we have somebody coming into the inquiry-room very much discouraged and disheartened and cast down, because they think they have committed a sin against the Holy Ghost, and that there is no hope for them.' Mr. Moody said he believed the sin was nearly impossible, but he adds this remarkable statement, 'I don't remember of ever hearing a man swear by the Holy Ghost except once, and then I looked upon him expecting him to fall dead, and my blood ran cold when I heard him.' But it is almost as rare to hear prayers addressed to the Holy Ghost; and both phenomena—for praying and swearing are radically related—are no doubt survivals of the ancient notions which I have described. The forces of nature out of which the symbol grew, the life that springs from death and grows by decay, is essentially repeated again by those who adhere to the letter that kills, and also by those who ascend with the spirit that makes alive. It is probable that no more terrible form of the belief in a Devil survives than this Holy Ghost Dogma, which, lurking in vagueness and mystery, like the serpent of which it was born, passes by the self-righteous to cast its shadows over the most sensitive and lowly minds, chiefly those of pure women prone to exaggerate their least blemishes.

In right reason the fatal Holy Ghost stands as the type of that Fear by which priesthoods have been able to preserve their institutions after the deities around whom they grew had become unpresentable, and which could best be fostered beneath the veil of mystery. They who love darkness rather than light because their deeds cannot bear the light, veil their gods not to abolish them but to preserve them. Calvinism is veiled, and Athanasianism, and Romanism; they are all veiled idols, whose power lives by being hid in a mass of philology and casuistry. So long as Christianity can persuade the Pope and Dr. Martineau, Dean Stanley and Mr. Moody, Quakers, Shakers, Jumpers, all to describe themselves alike as 'Christians,' its real nature will be veiled, its institutions will cumber the ground, and draw away the strength and intellect due to humanity; the indefinable 'infidel' will be a devil. This process has been going on for a long time. The serpent-god, accursed by the human mind which grew superior to it, has crept into its Ark; but its fang and venom linger with that Bishop breathing on a priest, the priest breathing on a sick child, and bears down side by side with science that atmosphere of mystery in which creep all the old reptiles that throttle common sense and send their virus through all the social frame.

In demonology the Holy Ghost is not a Devil, but in it are reflected the diabolisation of Culture and Progress and Art. It was these 'Devils' which compelled the gods to veil themselves through successive ages, and to spiritualise their idols and dogmas to save their institutions. The deities concealed have proved far more potent over the popular imagination than when visible. The indefinable terrible menace of the Holy Ghost was a consummate reply to that equally indefinable spirit of loathing and contempt which rises among the cultured and refined towards things that have become unreal, their formalities and their cant. It is this ever-recurring necessity that enables clergymen to denounce belief in Hell and a Devil in churches which assuredly would never have been built but for the superstition so denounced. The ancient beliefs and the present denunciation of them are on the same thread,—the determination of a Church to survive and hold its power at any and every cost. The jesuitical power to veil the dogma is the most successful method of confronting the Spirit of an Age, which in the eye of reason is the only holy spirit, but which to ecclesiastical power struggling with enlightenment is the only formidable Satan.

---

NOTES
1  To the 'Secular Chronicle,' February 11, 1877.
2  Psalm lv.
3  Jer. xxv. 38; xlvi. 16; l. 16.
4  Isaiah xi. 2, 3.
5  The more fatal aspect of the dove has tended to invest the pigeon, especially wild pigeons, which in Oldenburg, and many other regions, are supposed to bode calamity and death if they fly round a house.

6   Sir Nathaniel Wraxall's Memoirs.

7   Matt. xii. 31.

8   Mark iii. 28.

9   I have before me an account by a christian mother of the death of her child, whom she had dedicated to the Lord before his birth, in which she says, 'A full breath issued from his mouth like an etherial flame, a slight quiver of the lip, and all was over.'

10  'Serpent poison.' It is substantially the same word as the demonic Samaël. The following is from Colonel Campbell's 'Travels,' ii. p. 130:—'It was still the hot season of the year, and we were to travel through that country over which the horrid wind I have before mentioned sweeps its consuming blasts; it is called by the Turks Samiel, is mentioned by the holy Job under the name of the East wind, and extends its ravages all the way from the extreme end of the Gulf of Cambaya up to Mosul; it carries along with it flakes of fire, like threads of silk; instantly strikes dead those that breathe it, and consumes them inwardly to ashes; the flesh soon becoming black as a coal, and dropping off the bones. Philosophers consider it as a kind of electric fire, proceeding from the sulphurous or nitrous exhalations which are kindled by the agitations of the winds. The only possible means of escape from its fatal effects is to fall flat on the ground, and thereby prevent the drawing it in; to do this, however, it is necessary first to see it, which is not always practicable.'

11  The 'Sacred Anthology,' p. 425. Nizami uses his fable to illustrate the effect of even an innocent flower on one whom conscience has made a coward.

12  Nothing is more natural than the Triad: the regions which may be most simply distinguished are the Upper, Middle, and Lower.

13  Bhàgavàt-Gita.

14  Gulistan.

15  Acts ii.

16  Compare Gen. vi. 3. Jehovah said, 'My breath shall not always abide in man.'

17  Among the many survivals in civilised countries of these notions may be noticed the belief that, in order to be free from a spell it is necessary to draw blood from the witch above the breath, i.e., mouth and nostrils; to 'score aboon the breath' is a Scottish phrase. This probably came by the 'pagan' route; but it meets its christian kith and kin in the following story which I find in a (MS.) Memorial sent to the House of Lords in 1869 by the Rev. Thomas Berney, Rector of Bracon Ash, Diocese of Norwich:—'I was sent for in haste to privately baptize a child thought to be dying, and belonging to parents who lived 'on the Common' at Hockering. It indeed appeared to be very ill, and its eyes were fixed, and remarkably clouded and dull. Having baptized, I felt moved with a longing desire to be enabled to heal the child; and I prayed very earnestly to the Lord God Almighty to give me faith and strength to enable me to do so. And I put my hands on its head and drew them down on to its arms; and then breathed on its head three times, in the name of the Lord Jesus Christ. And as I held its arms and looked on it anxiously, its face became exceedingly red and dark, and as the child gradually assumed a natural colour, the eyes became clear again; and then it gently closed its eyes in sleep. And I told the mother not to touch it any more till it awoke; but to carry it up in the cradle as it was. The next morning I found the child perfectly well. She had not touched it, except at four in the morning to feed it, when it seemed dead asleep, and it did not awake till ten o'clock.' This was written by an English Rector, and dated from the Carlton Club! The italics are in the original MS. now before me. The importance that no earthly hand should profanely touch the body while the spirit was at work in it shows how completely systematised is that insanity which consists of making a human mind an arena for the survival of the unfittest.

# Chapter XXl
# Antichrist

IN THE 'PADMA PURANA' it is recorded that when King Vena embraced heretical doctrine and abjured the temples and sacrifices, the
people following him, seven powerful Rishis, high priests, visited him
and entreated him to return to their faith. They said, 'These acts, O
king, which thou art performing, are not of our holy traditions, nor
fit for our religion, but are such as shall be performed by mankind
at the entrance of Kali, the last and sinful age, when thy new faith
shall be received by all, and the service of the gods be utterly relin-
quished.' King Vena, being thus in advance of his time, was burned
on the sacred grass, while a mantra was performed for him.

This theory of Kali is curious as indicating a final triumph of
the enemies of the gods. In the Scandinavian theory of 'Ragnarok,'
the Twilight of the gods, there also seems to have been included no
hope of the future victory of the existing gods. In the Parsi faith we
first meet with the belief in a general catastrophe followed by the
supremacy and universal sway of good. This faith characterised the
later Hebrew prophecies, and is the spirit of Paul's brave saying,
'When all things shall be subjected unto him, then also shall the Son

himself be subject unto him that put all things under him, that God may be all in all.'

When, however, theology and metaphysics advanced and modelled this fiery lava of prophetic and apostolic ages into dogmatic shapes, evil was accorded an equal duration with good. The conflict between Christ and his foes was not to end with the conversion or destruction of his foes, but his final coming as monarch of the world was to witness the chaining up of the Archfiend in the Pit.

Christ's own idea of Satan, assuming certain reported expressions to have been really uttered by him, must have been that which regarded him as a Tempter to evil, whose object was to test the reality of faith. 'Simon, Simon, behold, Satan asked you for himself, that he might sift you as the wheat; but I made supplication for thee, that thy faith fail not; and when once thou hast returned, confirm thy brethren. And he said unto him, Lord, I am ready to go with thee, both into prison and into death. And he said, I tell thee, Peter, a cock will not crow this day till thou wilt thrice deny that thou knowest me.'[1] Such a sentiment could not convey to Jewish ears a degraded notion of Satan, except as being a nocturnal spirit who must cease his work at cock-crow. It is an adaptation of what Jehovah himself was said to do, in the prophecy of Amos. 'I will not utterly destroy the house of Jacob, saith the Lord.... I will sift the house of Israel among all nations, like as corn is sifted in a sieve, yet shall not the least grain fall upon the earth.'[2]

Paul, too, appears to have had some such conception of Satan, since he speaks of an evil-doer as delivered up to Satan 'for the destruction of the flesh that the spirit may be saved.'[3] There is, however, in another passage an indication of the distinctness with which Paul and his friends had conceived a fresh adaptation of Satan as obstacle of their work. 'For such,' he says, 'are false apostles, deceitful workers, transforming themselves into apostles of Christ. And no marvel: for Satan transforms himself into an angel of light. It is no great thing therefore if his ministers also transform themselves as ministers of righteousness; whose end will be according to their works.'[4] It may be noted here that Paul does not think of Satan himself as transforming himself to a minister of righteousness, but of Satan's ministers as doing so. It is one of a number of phrases in the New Testament which reveal the working of a new movement towards an expression of its own. Real and far-reaching religious revolutions in history are distinguished from mere sectarian modifications, which they sum up in nothing more than in their new phraseology. When Jehovah, Messias, and Satan are gradually supplanted by Father, Christ, and Antichrist (or Man of Sin, False Christ, Withholder (κατέχον), False Prophet, Son of Perdition, Mystery of Iniquity, Lawless One), it is plain that new elements are present, and new emergencies. These varied phrases just quoted could not, indeed, crystallise for a long time into any single name for the new Obstacle to the new life, for during the same time the new life itself was too living, too various, to harden in any definite shape or be marked with any special name. The only New Testament writer who uses the word Antichrist is the so-called Apostle John; and it is interesting to remark that it is by him connected with a dogmatic statement of the nature of Christ and definition of heresy. 'Every spirit that confesses Jesus Christ is come in the flesh is of God; and every spirit that confesses not

Jesus is not of God: and this is the spirit of Antichrist, whereof ye have heard that it comes; and now it is in the world already.'[5] This language, characteristic of the middle and close of the second century,[6] is in strong contrast with Paul's utterance in the first century, describing the Man of Sin (or of lawlessness, the son of perdition), as one 'who opposeth and exalteth himself above all that is called God, or that is worshipped; so that he sat in the temple of God, showing himself that he is God.'[7] Christ has not yet begun to supplant God; to Paul he is the Son of God confronting the Son of Destruction, the divine man opposed by the man of sin. When the *nature* of Christ becomes the basis of a dogma, the man of sin is at once defined as the opponent of that dogma.

As this dogma struggled on to its consummation and victory, it necessarily took the form of a triumph over the Cæsars, who were proclaiming themselves gods, and demanding worship as such. The writer of the second Epistle bearing Peter's name saw those christians who yielded to such authority typified in Balaam, the erring prophet who was opposed by the angel;[8] the writer of the Gospel of John saw the traitor Judas as the 'son of perdition,'[9] representing Jesus as praying that the rest of his disciples might be kept 'out of the evil one;' and many similar expressions disclose the fact that, towards the close of the second century, and throughout the third, the chief obstacle of those who were just beginning to be called 'Christians' was the temptation offered by Rome to the christians themselves to betray their sect. It was still a danger to name the very imperial gods who successively set themselves up to be worshipped at Rome, but the pointing of the phrases is unmistakable long before the last of the pagan emperors held the stirrup for the first christian Pontiff to mount his horse.

Nero had answered to the portrait of 'the son of perdition sitting in the temple of God' perfectly. He aspired to the title 'King of the Jews.' He solemnly assumed the name of Jupiter. He had his temples and his priests, and shared divine honours with his mistress Poppæa. Yet, when Nero and his glory had perished under those phials of wrath described in the Apocalypse, a more exact image of the insidious 'False Christ' appeared in Vespasian. His alleged miracles ('lying wonders'), and the reported prediction of his greatness by a prophet on Mount Carmel, his oppression of the Jews, who had to contribute the annual double drachma to support the temples and gods which Vespasian had restored, altogether made this decorous and popular emperor a more formidable enemy than the 'Beast' Nero whom he succeeded. The virtues and philosophy of Marcus Aurelius still increased the danger. Political conditions favoured all those who were inclined to compromise, and to mingle the popular pagan and the Jewish festivals, symbols, and ceremonies. In apocalyptic metaphor, Vespasian and Aurelius are the two horns of the Lamb who spake like the Dragon, *i.e.*, Nero (Rev. xiii. 11).

The beginnings of that mongrel of superstitions which at last gained the name of Christianity were in the liberation, by decay of parts and particles, of all those systems which Julius Cæsar had caged together for mutual destruction. 'With new thrones rise new altars,' says Byron's Sardanapalus; but it is still more true that, with new thrones all altars crumble a little. At an early period the differences between the believers in Christ and those they called idolaters were mainly in name; and, with the increase of Gentile converts, the adoption of the symbolism and practices of the old religions was so universal that the quarrel was about originality. 'The Devil,' says Tertullian, 'whose business it is to pervert the truth, mimics the exact circumstances of the Divine Sacraments in the mysteries of idols. He himself baptizes some, that is to say, his believers and followers: he promises forgiveness of sins from the *sacred fount*, and thus initiates them into the religion of Mithras; he thus marks on the forehead his own soldiers: he then celebrates the *oblation of bread*; he brings in the symbol of resurrection, and wins the crown with the sword.'[10]

What masses of fantastic nonsense it was possible to cram into one brain was shown in the time of Nero, the brain being that of Simon the Magician. Simon was, after all, a representative man; he reappears in christian Gnosticism, and Peter, who denounced him, reappears also in the phrenzy of Montanism. Take the followers of this Sorcerer worshipping his image in the likeness of Jupiter, the Moon, and Minerva; and Montanus with his wild women Priscilla and Maximilla going about claiming to be inspired by the Holy Ghost to re-establish Syrian orthodoxy and asceticism; and we have fair specimens of the parties that glared at each other, and apostrophised each other as children of Belial. They competed with each other by pretended miracles. They both claimed the name of Christ, and all the approved symbols and sacraments. The triumph of one party turned the other into Antichrist.

Thus in process of time, as one hydra-head fell only to be followed by another, there was defined a Spirit common to and working through them all—a new devil, whose special office was hostility to Christ, and whose operations were through those who claimed to be christians as well as through open enemies.

As usual, when the phrases, born of real struggles, had lost their meaning, they were handed up to the theologians to be made into perpetual dogmas. Out of an immeasurable mass of theories and speculations, we may regard the following passage from Jerome as showing what had become the prevailing belief at the beginning of the fifth century. 'Let us say that which all ecclesiastical writers have handed down, viz., that at the end of the world, when the Roman Empire is to be destroyed, there will be ten kings, who will divide the Roman world among them; and there will arise an eleventh little king who will subdue three of the ten kings, that is, the king of Egypt, of Africa, and of Ethiopia; and on these having been slain, the seven other kings will submit.' 'And behold,' he says, 'in the ram were the eyes of a man'—this is that we may not suppose him to be a devil or a dæmon, as some have thought, but a man in whom Satan will dwell utterly and bodily—'and a mouth speaking great things;' for he is the 'man of sin, the son of perdition, who sitteth in the temple of God making himself as God.'[11]

The 'Little Horn' of Daniel has proved a cornucopia of Antichrists. Not only the christians but the Jews and the mussulmans have definite beliefs on the subject. The rabbinical name for Antichrist is Armillus, a word found in the Targum (Isa. xi. 4): 'By the word of his mouth the wicked Armillus shall die.' There will be twelve signs of the Messiah's coming—appearance of three apostate kings, terrible heat of the sun, dew of blood, healing dew, the sun darkened for thirty days, universal power of Rome with affliction for Jews, and the appearance of the first Messias (Joseph's tribe), Nehemiah. The next and seventh sign will be the appearance of Armillus, born of a marble statue in a church at Rome. The Romans will accept him as their god, and the whole world be subject to him. Nehemiah alone will refuse to worship him, and for this will be slain, and the Jews suffer terrible things. The eighth sign will be the appearance of the angel Michael with three blasts of his trumpet—which shall call forth Elias, the forerunner, and the true Messias (Ben David), and bring on the war with Armillus who shall perish, and all christians with him. The ten tribes shall be gathered into Paradise. Messias shall wed the fairest daughter of their race, and when he dies his sons shall succeed him, and reign in unbroken line over a beatified Israel.

The mussulman modification of the notion of Antichrist is very remarkable. They call him *Al Dajjail*, that is, the impostor. They say that Mohammed told his follower Tamisri Al-Dari, that at the end of the world Antichrist would enter Jerusalem seated on an ass; but that Jesus will then make his second coming to encounter him. The Beast of the Apocalypse will aid Antichrist, but Jesus will be joined by Imam Mahadi, who has never died; together they will subdue Antichrist, and thereafter the mussulmans and christians will for ever be united in one religion. The Jews, however, will regard Antichrist as their expected Messias. Antichrist will be blind of one eye, and deaf of one ear. 'Unbeliever' will be written on his forehead. In that day the sun will rise in the west.[12]

The christians poorly requited this amicable theory of the mussulmans by very extensively identifying Mohammed as Antichrist, at one period. From that period came the English word *mawmet* (idol), and *mummery* (idolatry), both of which, probably, are derived from the name of the Arabian Prophet. Daniel's 'Little Horn' betokens, according to Martin Luther, Mohammed. 'But what are the Little Horn's Eyes? The Little Horn's Eyes,' says he, 'mean Mohammed's Alkoran, or Law, wherewith he ruleth. In the which Law there is nought but sheer human reason (eitel menschliche Vernunft).' ... 'For his Law,' he reiterates, 'teaches nothing but that which human understanding and reason may well like.' ... Wherefore 'Christ will come upon him with fire and brimstone.' When he wrote this—in his 'army sermon' against the Turks—in 1529, he had never seen a Koran. 'Brother Richard's' (Predigerordens) *Confutatio Alcoran*, dated 1300, formed the exclusive basis of his argument. But in Lent of 1540, he relates, a Latin translation, though a very unsatisfactory one, fell into his hands, and once more he returned to Brother Richard, and did his Refutation into German, supplementing his version with brief but racy notes. This Brother Richard had, according to his own account, gone in quest of knowledge to 'Babylon, that beautiful city of the Saracens,' and at Babylon he had learnt Arabic and been inured in the evil ways of the Saracens. When he had safely returned to his native land he set about combating the same. And this is his exordium:—'At the time of the Emperor Heraclius there arose a man, yea, a Devil, and a first-born child of Satan, ... who wallowed in ... and he was dealing in the Black Art, and his name it was Machumet.' ... This work Luther made known to his countrymen by translating and commenting, prefacing, and rounding it off by an epilogue. True, his notes amount to little more but an occasional 'Oh fie, for shame, you horrid Devil, you damned Mahomet,' or 'O Satan, Satan, you shall pay for that,' or, 'That's it, Devils, Saracens, Turks, it's all the same,' or, 'Here the Devil smells a rat,' or briefly, 'O Pfui Dich, Teufel!' except when he modestly, with a query, suggests whether those Assassins, who, according to his text, are regularly educated to go out into the world in order to kill and slay all Worldly Powers, may not, perchance, be the Gypsies or the 'Tattern' (Tartars); or when he breaks down with a 'Hic nescio quid dicat translator.' His epilogue, however, is devoted to a special disquisition as to whether Mohammed or the Pope be worse. And in the twenty-second chapter of this disquisition he has arrived at the final conclusion that, after all, the Pope is worse, and that he, and not Mohammed, is the real 'Endechrist.' '*Wohlen,*' he winds up, 'God grant us his grace, and punish both the Pope and Mohammed, together with their devils. I have done my part as a true prophet and teacher. Those who won't listen may leave it alone.' In similar strains speaks the learned and gentle Melancthon. In an introductory epistle to a reprint of that same Latin Koran which displeased Luther so much, he finds fault with Mohammed, or rather, to use his own words, he thinks that 'Mohammed is inspired by Satan,' because he 'does not explain what sin is,' and further, since he 'showeth not the reason of human misery.' He agrees with Luther about the Little Horn: though in another treatise he is rather inclined to see in Mohammed both Gog and Magog. And 'Mohammed's sect,' he says, 'is altogether made up (*conflata*) of blasphemy, robbery, and shameful lusts.' Nor does it matter in the least what the Koran is all about. 'Even if there were anything less scurrilous in the book, it need not concern us any more than the portents of the Egyptians, who invoked snakes and cats.... Were it not that partly this Mohammedan pest, and partly the Pope's idolatry, have long been leading us straight to wreck and ruin—may God have mercy upon *some* of us!"[13]

'Mawmet' was used by Wicliffe for idol in his translation of the New Testament, Acts vii. 41, 'And they made a calf in those days and offered a sacrifice to the Mawmet' (idol). The word, though otherwise derived by some, is probably a corruption of Mohammed. In the 'Mappa Mundi' of the thirteenth century we find the representation of the golden calf in the promontory of Sinai, with the superscription 'Mahum' for Mohammed, whose name under various corruptions, such as Mahound, Mawmet, &c., became a general byword in the mediæval languages for an idol. In a missionary hymn of Wesley's Mohammed is apostrophised as—

That Arab thief, as Satan bold,
Who quite destroyed Thy Asian fold;
and the Almighty is adjured to—
The Unitarian fiend expel,
And chase his doctrine back to Hell.

In these days, when the very mention of the Devil raises a smile, we can hardly realise the solemnity with which his work was once viewed. When Goethe represents Mephistopheles as undertaking to teach Faust's class in theology and dwells on his orthodoxy, it is the refrain of the faith of many generations. The Devil was not 'God's Ape,' as Tertullian called him, in any comical way; not only was his ceremonial believed to be modelled on that of God, but his inspiration of his followers was believed to be quite as potent and earnest. Tertullian was constrained to write in this strain—'Blush, my Roman fellow-soldiers, even if ye are not to be judged by Christ, but by any soldier of Mithras, who when he is undergoing initiation in the cave, the very camp of the Powers of Darkness, when the wreath is offered him (a sword being placed between as if in semblance of martyrdom), and then about to be set on his head, he is warned to put forth his hand and push the wreath away, transferring it to, perchance, his shoulder, saying at the same time, My only crown is Mithras. And thenceforth he never wears a wreath; and this is a mark he has for a test, whenever tried as to his initiation, for he is immediately proved to be a soldier of Mithras if he throws down the wreath offered him, saying his crown is in his god. Let us therefore acknowledge the craft of the Devil, who mimics certain things of those that be divine, in order that he may confound and judge us by the faith of his own followers.'

This was written before the exaltation of Christianity under Constantine. When the age of the martyrdom of the so-called pagans came on, these formulæ became real, and the christians were still more confounded by finding that the worshippers of the Devil, as they thought them, could yield up their lives in many parts of Europe as bravely for their faith as any christian had ever done. The 'Prince of this world' became thus an unmeaning phrase except for the heretics. Christ had become the Prince of this world; and he was opposed by religious devotees as earnest as any who had suffered under Nero. The relation of the Opposition to the Devil was yet more closely defined when it claimed the christian name for its schism or heresy, and when it carried its loyalty to the Adversary of the Church to the extent of suffering martyrdom. 'Tell me, holy father,' said Evervinus to St. Bernard, concerning the Albigenses, 'how is this? They entered to the stake and bore the torment of the fire not only with patience, but with joy and gladness. I wish your explanation, how these members of the Devil could persist in their heresy with a courage and constancy scarcely to be found in the most religious of the faith of Christ?'

Under these circumstances the personification of Antichrist had a natural but still wonderful development. He was to be born of a virgin, in Babylon, to be educated at Bethsaida and Chorazin, and to make a triumphal entry into Jerusalem, proclaiming himself the Son of God. In the interview at Messina (1202) between Richard I. and the Abbot Joachim of Floris, the king said, 'I thought that Antichrist would be born at Antioch or in Babylon, and of the tribe of Dan, and would reign in the temple of the Lord in Jerusalem, and would walk in that land in which Christ walked, and would reign in it for three years and a half, and would dispute against Elijah and Enoch, and would kill them, and would afterwards die; and that after his death God would give sixty days of repentance, in which those might repent which should have erred from the way of truth, and have been seduced by the preaching of Antichrist and his false prophets.'

This belief was reflected in Western Europe in the belief that the congregation of Witches assembled on their Sabbath (an institution then included among paganisms) to celebrate grand mass to the Devil, and that all the primitive temples were raised in honour of Satan.

*Fig 9.—Procession of the Serpent of Sins*

In the Russian Church the correspondence between the good and evil powers, following their primitive faith in the conflict between Byelbog and Tchernibog (white god and black god), went to the curious extent of picturing in hell a sort of infernal Trinity. The Father throned in Heaven with the Son between his knees and the Dove beside or beneath him, was replied to by a majestic Satan in hell, holding his Son (Judas) on his knees, and the Serpent acting as counteragent of the Dove. This singular arrangement may still be seen in many of the pictures which cover the walls of the oldest Russian churches (Fig. 9). The infernal god is not without a solemn majesty answering to that of his great antagonist above. The Serpent of Sins proceeds from the diabolical Father and Son, passing from beneath their throne through one of the two mouths of Hell, and then winds upward, hungrily opening its jaws near the terrible Balances where souls are weighed (Fig. 10). Along its hideous length are seated at regular intervals nine winged devils, representing probably antagonists of the nine Sephiroth or Æons of the Gnostic theology. Each is armed with a hook whereby the souls weighed and found wanting may be dragged. The sins which these devils represent are labelled, generally on rings around the serpent, and increase in heinousness towards the head. It is a curious fact that the Sin nearest the head is marked 'Unmercifulness.' Strange and unconscious sarcasm on an Omnipotent Deity under whose sway exists this elaboration of a scheme of sins and tortures precisely corresponding to the scheme of virtues and joys!

Truly said the Epistle of John, there be many Antichrists. If this was true before the word Christianity had been formed, or the system it names, what was the case afterwards? For centuries we find vast systems denouncing each other as Antichrist. And ultimately, as a subtle hardly-conscious heresy spread abroad, the great excommunicator of antichrists itself, Rome, acquired that title, which it has never shaken off since. The See of Rome did not first receive that appellation from Protestants, but from its own chiefs.

*Fig. 10.—Ancient Russian Wall-Painting*

Fig. 11.—Alexander VI. as Antichrist.

Gregory himself (A.C. 590) started the idea by declaring that any man who held even the shadow of such power as the Popes arrogated to themselves after his time would be the forerunner of Antichrist. Arnulphus, Bishop of Orleans, in an invective against John XV. at Rheims (A.C. 991), intimated that a Pope destitute of charity was Antichrist. But the stigma was at length fixed (twelfth century) by Amalrich of Bena ('Quia Papa esset Antichristus et Roma Babylon et ipse sedit in Monte Oliveti, *i.e.*, in pinguedine potestatis'); and also by the Abbot Joachim (A.C. 1202). The theory of Richard I., as stated to Joachim concerning Antichrist, has already been quoted. It was in the presence of the Archbishops of Rouen and Auxerre, and the Bishop of Bayonne, and represented their opinion and the common belief of the time. But Joachim said the Second Apocalyptic Beast represented some great prelate who will be like Simon Magus, and, as it were, universal Pontiff, and that very Antichrist of whom St. Paul speaks. Hildebrand was the first Pope to whom this ugly label was affixed, but the career of Alexander VI. (Roderic Borgia) made it for ever irremovable for the Protestant mind. There is in the British Museum a volume of caricatures, dated 1545, in which occurs an ingenious representation of Alexander VI. The Pope is first seen in his ceremonial robes; but a leaf being raised, another figure is joined to the lower part of the former, and there appears the papal devil, the cross in his hand being changed to a pitchfork (Fig. 11). Attached to it is an explanation in German giving the legend of the Pope's death. He was poisoned (1503) by the cup he had prepared for another man. It was afterwards said that he had secured the papacy by aid of the Devil. Having asked how long he would reign, the Devil returned an equivocal answer; and though Alexander understood that it was to be fifteen years, it proved to be only eleven. When in 1520 Pope Leo X. issued his formal bull against Luther, the reformer termed it 'the execrable bull of Antichrist.' An Italian poem of the time having represented Luther as the offspring of Megæra, the Germans returned the invective in a form more likely to impress the popular mind; namely, in a caricature (Fig. 12), representing the said Fury as nursing the Pope. This caricature is also of date 1545, and with it were others showing Alecto and Tisiphone acting in other capacities for the papal babe.

*Fig. 12.—The Pope Nursed by Megæra.*

The Lutherans had made the discovery that the number of the Apocalyptic Beast, 666, put into Hebrew numeral letters, contained the words *Aberin Kadescha Papa* (our holy father the Pope). The downfall of this Antichrist was a favourite theme of pulpit eloquence, and also with artists. A very spirited pamphlet was printed (1521), and illustrated with designs by Luther's friend Lucas Cranach. It was entitled *Passional Christi und Antichristi*. The fall of the papal Antichrist (Fig. 13), has for its companion one of Christ washing the feet of his disciples.

But the Catholics could also make discoveries; and among many other things they found that the word 'Luther' in Hebrew numerals also made the number of the Beast. It was remembered that one of the earliest predictions concerning Antichrist was that he would travesty the birth of Christ from a virgin by being born of a nun by a Bishop. Luther's marriage with the nun Catharine von Bora came sufficiently near the prediction to be welcomed by his enemies. The source of his inspiration as understood by Catholics is cleverly indicated in a caricature of the period (Fig. 14).

The theory that the Papacy represents Antichrist has so long been the solemn belief of rebels against its authority, that it has become a vulgarised article of Protestant faith. On the other hand, Catholics appear to take a political and prospective view of Antichrist. Cardinal Manning, in his pastoral following the election of Leo XIII., said: 'A tide of revolution has swept over all countries. Every people in Europe is inwardly divided against itself, and the old society of Christendom, with its laws, its sanctities, and its stability, is giving way before the popular will, which has no law, or rather which claims to be a law to itself. This is at least the forerunning sign of the Lawless One, who in his own time shall be revealed.'

*Fig. 13.—Antichrist's Descent (L. Cranach)*

*Fig. 14.—Luther's Devil as seen by Catholics*

Throughout the endless exchange of epithets, it has been made clear that Antichrist is the *reductio ad absurdum* of the notion of a personal Devil. From the day when the word was first coined, it has assumed every variety of shape, has fitted with equal precision the most contrarious things and persons; and the need of such a novel form at one point or another in the progress of controversy is a satire on the inadequacy of Satan and his ancient ministers. Bygone Devils cannot represent new animosities. The ascent of every ecclesiastical or theological system is traceable in massacres and martyrdoms; each of these, whether on one side or the other, helps to develop a new devil. The story of Antichrist shows devils in the making. Meantime, to eyes that see how every system so built up must sacrifice a virtue at every stage of its ascent, it will be sufficiently clear that every powerful Church is Adversary of the religion it claims to represent. Buddhism is Antibuddha; Islam is Antimohammed; Christianity is Antichrist.

**NOTES**

1  Luke xxii. 31.
2  Amos ix. 8, 9.
3  1 Cor. v. 5.
4  2 Cor. xi. 13.
5  1 John iv. 2, 3.
6  Polycarp, Ep. to Philippians, vii.
7  2 Thess. ii.
8  2 Peter ii. 15.
9  John xvii. 12.
10 'But,' says Professor King (Gnostics, p. 52), 'a dispassionate examiner will discover that these two zealous Fathers somewhat beg the question in assuming that the Mithraic rites were invented as counterfeits of the Christian Sacraments; the former having really been in existence long before the promulgation of Christianity.' Whatever may have been the incidents in the life of Christ connected with such things, it is certainly true, as Professor King says, that these 'were afterwards invested with the mystic and supernatural virtues, in a later age insisted upon as articles of faith, by succeeding and unscrupulous missionaries, eager to outbid the attractions of more ancient ceremonies of a cognate character.' In the porch of the Church Bocca della Verita at Rome, there is, or was, a fresco of Ceres shelling corn and Bacchus pressing grapes, from them falling the elements of the Eucharist to a table below. This was described to me by a friend, but when I went to see it in 1872, it had just been whitewashed over! I called the attention of Signor Rosa to this shameful proceeding, and he had then some hope that this very interesting relic might be recovered.
11 Op. iv. 511. Col. Agrip. 1616.
12 For full details of all these superstitions see Eisenmenger (Entd. Jud. li. Armillus); D'Herbelot (Bib. Orient. Daggiel); Buxtorf (Lexicon, Armillus); Calmet, Antichrist; and on the same word, Smith; also a valuable article in M'Clintock and Strong's Cyc. Bib. Lit. (American).
13 Deutsch, 'Lit. Remains.' Islam.

# Chapter XXII
## The Pride of Life

The curse of Iblis — Samaël as Democrat — His vindication by Christ and Paul — Asmodäus — History of the name — Aschmedai of the Jews — Book of Tobit — Doré's 'Triumph of Christianity' — Aucassin and Nicolette — Asmodeus in the convent — The Asmodeus of Le Sage — Mephistopheles — Blake's 'Marriage of Heaven and Hell' — The Devil and the artists — Sádi's Vision of Satan — Arts of the Devil — Suspicion of beauty — Earthly and heavenly mansions — Deacon *versus* Devil

ON THE PARAPET of the external gallery of Nôtre Dame in Paris is the carved form, of human size, represented in our figure (15). There is in the face a remarkable expression of pride and satisfaction as he looks forth on the gay city and contemplates all the wickedness in it, but this satisfaction is curiously blended with a look of envy and lust. His elegant head-dress gives him the pomp becoming the Asmodeus presiding over the most brilliant capital in the world.

His seat on the fine parapet is in contrast with the place assigned him in Eastern traditions—ruins and desert places,—but otherwise he fairly fulfilled, no doubt, early ideas in selecting his headquarters at Paris. A mussulman legend says that when, after the Fall of Man, Allah was mitigating the sentences he had pronounced, Iblis (who, as the Koran relates, pleaded and obtained the deferment of his consignment to Hell until the resurrection, and unlimited power over sinners who do not accept the word of Allah) asked—

'Where shall I dwell in the meantime?
'In ruins, tombs, and all other unclean places shunned by man.

'What shall be my food?
'All things slain in the name of idols.
'How shall I quench my thirst?
'With wine and intoxicating liquors.
'What shall occupy my leisure hours?
'Music, song, love-poetry, and dancing.
'What is my watchword?
'The curse of Allah until the day of judgment.
'But how shall I contend with man, to whom thou hast granted
two guardian angels, and who has received thy revelation?
'Thy progeny shall be more numerous than his,—for for every
man that is born, there shall come into the world seven evil
spirits—but they shall be powerless against the faithful.'
Iblis with wine, song, and dance—the 'pride of life'—is also said
to have been aided in entering Paradise by the peacock, which he
flattered.[1]

This fable, though later than the era of Mohammed in form, is as ancient as the myth of Eden in substance. The germ of it is already in the belief that Jehovah separated from the rest of the earth a garden, and from the human world a family of his own, and from the week a day of his own. The reply of the elect to the proud Gentile aristocracy was an ascetic caste established by covenant with the King of kings. This attitude of the pious caste turned the barbaric aristocrats, in a sense, to democrats. Indeed Samaël, in whom the execrated Dukes of Edom were ideally represented, might be almost described as the Democratic Devil. According to an early Jewish legend, Jehovah, having resolved to separate 'men' (*i.e.*, Jews) from 'swine' (*i.e.*, idolaters, Gentiles), made circumcision the seal on them as children of Abraham. There having been, however, Jews who were necessarily never circumcised, their souls, it was arranged, should pass at death into the forms of certain sacred birds where they would be purified, and finally united to the elect in Paradise.

Now, Samaël, or Adam Belial as he was sometimes called, is said to have appealed to the Creator that this arrangement should include all races of beings. 'Lord of the world!' he said, 'we also are of your creation. Thou art our father. As thou savest the souls of Israel by transforming them that they may be brought back again and made immortal, so also do unto us! Why shouldst thou regard the seed of Abraham before us?' Jehovah answered, 'Have you done the same that Abraham did, who recognised me from his childhood and went into Chaldean fire for love of me? You have seen that I rescued him from your hands, and from the fiery oven which had no power over him, and yet you have not loved and worshipped me. Henceforth speak no more of good or evil.'[2]

The old rabbinical books which record this conversation do not report Samaël's answer; nor is it necessary: that answer was given by Jesus and Paul breaking down the partitions between Jew and Gentile. It was quite another thing, however, to include the world morally. Jesus, it would seem, aimed at this also; he came 'eating and drinking,' and the orthodox said Samaël was in him. Personally, he declined to substitute even the cosmopolitan rite of baptism for the discredited national rite of circumcision. But Paul was of another mind. His pharisaism was spiritualised and intensified in his new faith, to which the great world was all an Adversary.

It was a tremendous concession, this giving up of the gay and beautiful world, with its mirth and amusements, its fine arts and romance—to the Devil.

Fig. 15.—The Pride of Life

Unswerving Nemesis has followed that wild theorem in many forms, of which the most significant is Asmodeus.

Asmodäus, or Aêshma-daêva of the Zend texts, the modern Persian Khasm, is etymologically what Carlyle might call 'the god Wish;' *aêsha* meaning 'wish,' from the Sanskrit root *ish*, 'to desire.' An almost standing epithet of Aêshma is Khrvîdra, meaning apparently 'having a hurtful weapon or lance.' He is occasionally mentioned immediately after Anrô-mainyus (Ahriman); sometimes is expressly named as one of his most prominent supporters. In the remarkable combat between Ahuro-mazda (Ormuzd) and Anrô-mainyus, described in Zam. Y. 46, the good deity summons to his aid Vohumano, Ashavahista, and Fire; while the Evil One is aided by Akômano, Aêshma, and Aji-Daháka.[3] Here, therefore, Aêshma appears as opposed to Ashavahista, 'supreme purity' of the Lord of Fire. Aêshma is the spirit of the lower or impure Fire, Lust and Wrath. A Sanskrit text styles him Kossa-deva, 'the god of Wrath.' In Yaçna 27, 35, Śraosha, Aêshma's opponent, is invoked to shield the faithful 'in both worlds from Death the Violent, from Aêshma the Violent, from the hosts of Violence that raise aloft the terrible banner—from the assaults of Aêshma that he makes along with Vídátu ('Divider, Destroyer'), the demon-created.' He is thus the leading representative of dissolution, the fatal power of Ahriman. Ormuzd is said to have created Śraosha to be the destroyer of 'Aêshma of the fatal lance.' Śraosha ('the Hearer') is the moral vanquisher of Aêshma, in distinction from Haoma, who is his chief opponent in the physical domain.

Such, following Windischmann,[4] is the origin of the devil whom the apocryphal book of Tobit has made familiar in Europe as Asmodeus. Aschmedai, as the Jews called him, appears in this story as precisely that spirit described in the Avesta—the devil of Violence and Lust, whose passion for Sara leads him to slay her seven husbands on their wedding-night. The devils of Lust are considered elsewhere, and Asmodeus among them; there is another aspect of him which here concerns us. He is a fastidious devil. He will not have the object of his passion liable to the embrace of any other. He cannot endure bad smells, and that raised by the smoke of the fish-entrails burnt by Tobit drives him 'into the utmost parts of Egypt, where the angel bound him.' It is, however, of more importance to read the story by the light of the general reputation of Aschmedai among the Jews and Arabians. It was notably that of the devil represented in the Moslem tradition at the beginning of this chapter. He is the Eastern Don Giovanni and Lothario; he plies Noah and Solomon with wine, and seduces their wives, and always aims high with his dashing intrigues. He would have cried Amen to Luther's lines—

> Who loves not wine, woman, and song,
> He lives a fool his whole life long.

Besides being an aristocrat, he is a scholar, the most learned Master of Arts, educated in the great College of Hell, founded by Asa and Asael, as elsewhere related. He was fond of gaming; and so fashionable that Calmet believed his very name signifies fine dress.

Now, the moral reflections in the Book of Tobit, and its casual intimations concerning the position of the persons concerned, show that they were Jewish captives of the humblest working class, whose religion is of a type now found chiefly among the more ignorant sectarians. Tobit's moral instructions to his son, 'In pride is destruction and much trouble, and in lewdness is decay and much want,' 'Drink not wine to make thee drunken,' and his careful instructions about finding wealth in the fear of God, are precisely such as would shape a devil in the image of Asmodeus. Tobit's moral truisms are made falsities by his puritanism: 'Prayer is good with fasting and alms and righteousness;' 'but give nothing to the wicked;' 'If thou serve God he will repay thee.'

'Cakes and ale' do not cease to exist because Tobits are virtuous; but unfortunately they may be raised from their subordinate to an insubordinate place by the transfer of religious restraints to the hands of Ignorance and Cant. Asmodeus, defined against Persian and Jewish asceticism and hypocrisy, had his attractions for men of the world. Through him the devil became perilously associated with wit, gallantry, and the one creed of youth which is not at all consumptive—

> Grey is all Theory,
> Green Life's golden-fruited tree!

Especially did Asmodeus represent the subordination of so-called 'religious' and tribal distinctions to secular considerations. As Samaël had petitioned for an extension of the Abrahamic Covenant to all the world and failed to secure it from Jehovah, Asmodeus proposed to disregard the distinction. There is much in the Book of Tobit which looks as if it were written especially with the intention of persuading Jewish youth, tempted by Babylonians to marriage, that their lovers might prove to be succubi or incubi. Tobit implores his son to marry in his own tribe, and not take a 'strange woman.' Asmodeus was as cosmopolitan as the god of Love himself, and many of his uglier early characteristics were hidden out of sight by such later developments.

Gustave Doré has painted in his vivid way the 'Triumph of Christianity.' In it we see the angelic hosts with drawn swords overthrowing the forms adored of paganism—hurling them headlong into an abyss. So far as the battle and victory go, this is just the conception which an early christian would have had of what took place through the advent of Christ. It filled their souls with joy to behold by Faith's vision those draped angels casting down undraped goddesses; they would delight to imagine how the fall might break the bones of those beautiful limbs. For they never thought of these gods and goddesses as statues, but as real seductive devils; and when these christians had brought over the arts, they often pictured the black souls coming out of these fair idols as they fell.

Doré may have tried to make the angels as beautiful as the goddesses, but he has not succeeded. In this he has interpreted the heart behind every deformity which was ever added to a pagan deity. The horror of the monks was transparent homage. Why did they starve and scourge their bodies, and roll them in thorns? Because not even by defacing the beautiful images were they able to expel from their inward worship the lovely ideals they represented.

It is not difficult now to perceive that the old monks were consigning the pagan ideals to imaginary and themselves to actual hells, in full hope of thereby gaining permanent possession of the same beauty abjured on earth. The loveliness of the world was transient. They grew morbid about death; beneath the rosiest form they saw the skeleton. The heavenly angels they longed for were Venuses and Apollos, with no skeletons visible beneath their immortalised flesh. They never made sacrifices for a disembodied heaven. The force of self-crucifixion lay in the creed—'I believe in the resurrection of the body, and the life everlasting.'

The world could not generally be turned into a black procession at its own funeral. In proportion to the conquests of Christianity must be its progressive surrender to the unconquerable—to human nature. Aphrodite and Eros, over whose deep graves nunneries and monasteries had been built, were the first to revive, and the story, as Mr. Pater has told it, is like some romantic version of Ishtar's Descent into Hades and her resurrection.[5] While as yet the earth seemed frostbound, long before the Renaissance, the song of the turtle was heard in the ballad of Aucassin and Nicolette. The christian knight will marry the beautiful Saracen, and to all priestly warnings that he will surely go to hell, replies, 'What could I do in Paradise? I care only to go where I can be with Nicolette. Who go to Paradise? Old priests, holy cripples, dried-up monks, who pass their lives before altars. I much prefer Hell, where go the brave, the gay, and beautiful. There will be the players on harps, the classic poets and singers; and there I shall not be parted from Nicolette!'

Along with pretty Saracen maidens, or memories of them, were brought back into Europe legends of Asmodeus. Aphrodite and Eros might disguise themselves in his less known and less anathematised name, so that he could manage to sing of his love for Sara, of Parsi for Jewess, under the names of christian Aucassin and saracen Nicolette. In the Eastern Church he reappeared also. There are beautiful old pictures which show the smart cavalier, feather-in-cap, on the youth's left, while on his right stands 'grey Theory' in the form of a long-bearded friar. Such pictures, no doubt, taught for many a different lesson from that intended—namely, that the beat of the heart is on the left.

Where St. Benedict rolled himself in thorns for dreaming of *his* (deserted) 'Nicolette,' St. Francis planted roses; and the Latin Church had to recognise this evolution of seven centuries. They hid the thorns in the courts of convents, and sold the roses to the outside world as indulgences. But as Asmodeus had not respected the line between Jew and Gentile in Nineveh, so he passed over that between priest, nun, and worldling in the West. In the days of Witchcraft the Church was scandalised by the rumour that the nuns of the Franciscan Convent of Louviers had largely taken to sorcery, and were attending the terrible 'Witches' Sabbaths.' The nun most prominent in this affair was one Madeleine Bavent. The priests announced that she had confessed that she was borne away to the orgies by the demon Asmodeus, and that he had induced her to profane the sacred host. It turned out that the nuns had engaged in intrigues with the priests who had charge of them—especially with Fathers David, Picard, and Boulé—but Asmodeus was credited with the crime, and the nuns were punished for it. Madeleine was condemned to life-long penance, and Picard anticipated the fire by a suicide, in which he was said to have been assisted by the devil.

Following the rabbinical tradition which represented him as continually passing from the high infernal College of Asa and Asael to the earth to apply his arts of sorcery, Asmodeus gained a respectable position in European literature through the romance of Le Sage ('Le Diable Boiteux'), and his fame so gained did much to bring about in France that friendly feeling for the Devil which has long been a characteristic of French literature. A very large number of books, periodicals, and journals in France have gained popularity through the Devil's name. Asmodeus was, in fact, the Arch-bohemian. As such, he largely influenced the conception of Mephistopheles as rendered by Goethe—himself the Prince of Bohemians. The old horror of Asmodeus for bad smells is insulted in the name Mephistopheles, and this devil is many rolled into one; yet in many respects his kinship to Asmodeus is revealed. All the dried starveling Anthonys and Benedicts are, in a cultured way, present in the theologian and scholar Faust; all the sweet ladies that haunted their seclusion became realistic in Gretchen. She is the Nemesis of suppressed passions.

One province of nature after another has been recovered from Asceticism. In this case Ishtar has had to regain her apparel and ornaments at successive portals that are centuries, and they are not all recovered yet. But we have gone far enough, even in puritanised England, to produce a 'madman' far-seeing enough to behold *The Marriage of Heaven and Hell*. The case of Asmodeus is stated well, albeit radically, by William Blake, in that proverb which was told him by the devils, whom he alone of midnight travellers was shrewd enough to consult: 'The pride of the peacock is the glory of God; the lust of the goat is the bounty of God; the wrath of the lion is the wisdom of God.' When that statement is improved, as it well may be, it will be when those who represent religion shall have learned that human like other nature is commanded by obedience.

In this connection may be mentioned a class of legends indicating the Devil's sensitiveness with regard to his personal appearance. The anxiety of the priests and hermits to have him represented as hideous was said to have been warmly resented by Satan, one of the most striking being the legend of many versions concerning a

Sacristan, who was also an artist, who ornamented an abbey with a devil so ugly that none could behold it without terror. It was believed he had by inspiration secured an exact portrait of the archfiend. The Devil appeared to the Sacristan, reproached him with having made him so ugly, and threatened to punish him grievously if he did not make him better looking. Although this menace was thrice repeated, the Sacristan refused to comply. The Devil then tempted him into an intrigue with a lady of the neighbourhood, and they eloped after robbing the abbey of its treasure. But they were caught, and the Sacristan imprisoned. The Devil then appears and offers to get him out of his trouble if he will only destroy the ugly likeness, and make another and handsomer. The Sacristan consented, and suddenly found himself in bed as if nothing had happened, while the Devil in his image lay in chains. The Devil when discovered vanished; the Sacristan got off on the theory that crimes and all had been satanic juggles. But the Sacristan took care to substitute a handsome devil for the ugly one. In another version the Sacristan remained faithful to his original portraiture of the Devil despite all menaces of the latter, who resolved to take a dire revenge. While the artist was completing his ornamentation of the abbey with an image of the Virgin, made as beautiful as the fiend near it was ugly, the Devil broke the ladder on which he was working, and a fatal fall was only prevented by the hand of the Madonna he had just made, which was outstretched to sustain him. The accompanying picture of this scene (Fig. 16) is from 'Queen Mary's Psalter' in the British Museum.

Vasari relates that when Spinello of Arezzo, in his famous fresco of the fall of the rebellious angels, had painted the hideous devil with seven faces about his body, the fiend appeared to him in the same form, and asked the artist where he had seen him in so frightful an aspect, and why he had treated him so ignominiously. When Spinello awoke in horror, he fell into a state of gloom, and soon after died.

*Fig. 16.—The Artist's Rescue*

The Persian poet Sádi has a remarkable passage conceived in the spirit of these legends, but more kindly.

I saw the demon in a dream,
But how unlike he seemed to be
To all of horrible we dream,
And all of fearful that we see.
His shape was like a cypress bough,

His eyes like those that Houris wear,
His face as beautiful as though
The rays of Paradise were there.
I near him came, and spoke—'Art thou,'
I said, 'indeed the Evil One?
No angel has so bright a brow,
Such yet no eye has looked upon.
Why should mankind make thee a jest,
When thou canst show a face like this?
Fair as the moon in splendour drest,
An eye of joy, a smile of bliss!
The painter draws thee vile to sight,
Our baths thy frightful form display;
They told me thou wert black as night,
Behold, thou art as fair as day!'
The lovely vision's ire awoke,
His voice was loud and proud his mien:
'Believe not, friend!' 'twas thus he spoke,
'That thou my likeness yet hast seen:
The pencil that my portrait made
Was guided by an envious foe;
In Paradise I man betrayed,
And he, from hatred, paints me so.'

Boehme relates that when Satan was asked the cause of God's enmity to him and his consequent downfall, he replied, 'I wished to be an artist.' There is in this quaint sentence a very true intimation of the allurements which, in ancient times, the arts of the Gentile possessed for the Jews and christian judaisers. Indeed, a similar feeling towards the sensuous attractions of the Catholic and Ritualistic Churches is not uncommon among the prosaic and puritanical sects whose younger members are often thus charmed away from them. Dr. Donne preached a sermon before Oliver Cromwell at Whitehall, in which he affirmed that the Muses were damned spirits of devils;

and the discussion on the Drama which occurred at Sheffield Church Congress (1878), following Dr. Bickerstith's opening discourse on 'the Devil and his wiles,' shows that the Low Church wing cherishes much the same opinion as that of Dr. Donne. The dread of the theatre among some sects amounts to terror. The writer remembers the horror that spread through a large Wesleyan circle, with which he was connected, when a distinguished minister of that body, just returned from Europe, casually remarked that 'the theatre at Rome seemed to be poorly supported.' The fearful confession spread through the denomination, and it was understood that the observant traveller had 'made shipwreck of faith.' The Methodist instinct told true: the preacher became an accomplished Gentile.

Music made its way but slowly in the Church, and the suspicion of it still lingers among many sects. The Quakers took up the burthen of Epiphanius who wrote against the flute-players, 'After the pattern of the serpent's form has the flute been invented for the deceiving of mankind. Observe the figure that the player makes in blowing his flute. Does he not bend himself up and down to the right hand and to the left, like unto the serpent? These forms hath the Devil used to manifest his blasphemy against things heavenly, to destroy things upon earth, to encompass the world, capturing right and left such as lend an ear to his seductions.' The unregenerate birds that carol all day, be it Sabbath or Fast, have taught the composer that his best inspiration is from the Prince of the Air. Tartini wrote over a hundred sonatas and as manyconcertos, but he rightly valued above them all his 'Sonata del Diavolo.' Concerning this he wrote to the astronomer Lalande:—'One night, in the year 1713, I dreamed that

I had made a compact with his Satanic Majesty, by which he was received into my service. Everything succeeded to the utmost of my desires, and my every wish was anticipated by my new domestic. I thought that, in taking up my violin to practise, I jocosely asked him if he could play on this instrument. He answered that he believed he was able to pick out a tune; when, to my astonishment, he began a sonata, so strange, and yet so beautiful, and executed in so masterly a manner, that in the whole course of my life I had never heard anything so exquisite. So great was my amazement that I could scarcely breathe. Awakened by the violence of my feelings, I instantly seized my violin, in the hope of being able to catch some part of the ravishing melody which I had just heard, but all in vain. The piece which I composed according to my scattered recollections is, it is true, the best I ever produced. I have entitled it, 'Sonata del Diavolo;' but it is so far inferior to that which had made so forcible an impression on me, that I should have dashed my violin into a thousand pieces, and given up music for ever in despair, had it been possible to deprive myself of the enjoyments which I receive from it.'

The fire and originality of Tartini's great work is a fine example of that power which Timoleon called *Automatia*, and Goethe the *Dämonische*,—'that which cannot be explained by reason or understanding; it is not in my nature, but I am subject to it.' 'It seems to play at will with all the elements of our being.'

The Puritans brought upon England and America that relapse into the ancient asceticism which was shown in the burning of great pictures by Cromwell's Parliament. It is shown still in the jealousy with which the puritanised mind in both countries views all that aims at the simple decoration of life, and whose ministry is to the sense of beauty. On that day of the week when England and New England hebraise, as Matthew Arnold says, it is observable that the sabbatarian fury is especially directed against everything which proposes to give simple pleasure or satisfy the popular craving for beauty. Sabbatarianism sees a great deal of hard work going on, but is not much troubled so long as it is ugly and dismal work. It utters no cry at the thousands of hands employed on Sunday railways, but is beside itself if one of the trains takes excursionists to the seaside, and is frantic at the thought of a comparatively few persons being employed on that day in Museums and Art Galleries. It is a survival of the old feeling that the Devil lurks about all beauty and pleasure.

A money-making age has measurably dispersed the superstitions which once connected the Devil with all great fortunes. For a long time, and in many regions of the world, the Jews suffered grievously by being supposed to get their wealth by the Devil's help. Their wealth (largely the result of their not exchanging it for worldly enjoyments) so often proved their misfortune, that it was easy to illustrate by their case the monkish theory that devil's gifts turn to ashes. Princes were indefatigable in relieving the Jews of such ashes, however. The Lords of Triar, who possessed the mines of Glucksbrunn, were believed to have been guided to them by a gold stag which often appeared to them—of course the Devil. It is related that when St. Wolfram went to convert the Frislanders, their king, Radbot, was prevented from submitting to baptism by a diabolical deception. The Devil appeared to him as an angel clothed in a garment woven of gold, on his head a jewelled diadem, and said, 'Bravest of men!

what has led thee to depart from the Prince of thy gods? Do it not; be steadfast to thy religion and thou shalt dwell in a house of gold which I will give into thy possession to all eternity. Go to Wolfram to-morrow, ask him about those bright dwellings he promises thee. If he cannot show them, let both parties choose an ambassador; I will be their leader and will show them the gold house I promise thee.' St. Wolfram being unable to show Radbot the bright dwellings of Paradise, one of his deacons was sent along with a representative of the king, and the Devil (disguised as a traveller) took them to the house of gold, which was of incredible size and splendour. The Deacon exclaimed, 'If this house be made by God it will stand for ever; if by the Devil, it must vanish speedily.' Whereupon he crossed himself; the house vanished, and the Deacon found himself with the Frislander in a swamp. It took them three days to extricate themselves and return to King Radbot, whom they found dead.

The ascetic principle which branded the arts, interests, pursuits, and pleasures of the world as belonging to the domain of Satan, involved the fatal extreme of including among the outlawed realms all secular learning. The scholar and man of science were also declared to be inspired by the 'pride of life.' But this part of our subject requires a separate chapter.

---

NOTES

1 Weil's 'Biblical Legends.'
2 Eisenmenger, ii. 60.
3 See vol. i. pp. 58 and 358.
4 'Zoroastrische Studien,' pp. 138–147. With which comp. Spiegel, Transl. of Avesta, III. xlvii.
5 'Studies in the Hist. of the Renaissance.' Macmillan.

# Chapter XXIII
## The Curse on Knowledge

A Bishop on intellect — The Bible on learning — The Serpent and Seth —
A Hebrew Renaissance — Spells — Shelley at Oxford — Book-burning —
Japanese ink-devil — Book of Cyprianus — Devil's Bible — Red letters —
Dread of Science — Roger Bacon — Luther's Devil — Lutherans and Science

IN LUCAS VAN LEYDEN'S picture of Satan tempting Christ (Fig. 6), the fiend is represented in the garb of a University man of the time. From his head falls a streamer which coils on the ground to a serpent. From that serpent to the sceptical scholar demanding a miracle the evolution is fully traceable. The Serpent, of old the 'seer,' was in its Semitic adaptation a tempter to forbidden knowledge. This was the earliest priestly outcry against 'godless education.'

During the Shakespere tercentenary festival at Stratford-on-Avon, the Bishop of St. Andrews declared that there is not a word in the Bible warranting homage to Intellect, and such a boast beside the grave of the most intellectual of Englishmen is in itself a survival illustrating the tremendous curse hurled by jealous Jehovah on man's first effort to obtain knowledge. That same Serpent of knowledge has passed very far, and his curse has many times been repeated. In the Accadian poem of the fatal Seven, as we have seen, it is said, 'In watching was their office;' and the Assyrian version says, 'Unto heaven that which was not seen they raised.' On the Babylonian cylinders is inscribed the curse of the god of Intelligence

(Hea) upon man—'Wisdom and knowledge hostilely may they injure him.'[1] The same Serpent twined round the staff of Æsculapius and whispered those secrets which made the gods jealous, so that Jove killed the learned Physician with a flash of lightning. Its teeth were sown when Cadmus imported the alphabet into Greece; and when these alphabetical dragon's-teeth had turned to type, the ancient curse was renewed in legends which connected Fust with the Devil.

The Hebrews are least among races responsible for the legend which has drifted into Genesis. Nor was the Bishop's boast about their Bible correct. The homage paid to Solomon was hardly on account of his moral character. 'He spake of trees, from the cedar-tree that is in Lebanon, even unto the hyssop that springeth out of the wall; he spake also of beasts, and of fowl, and of creeping things, and of fishes.'[2] While the curse on man for eating the fruit of knowledge is never quoted in the Hebrew scriptures, there are many indications of their devotion to knowledge; and their prophets even heard Jehovah saying, 'My people are destroyed through lack of knowledge.' It is not wonderful, therefore, that we find among the Jews the gradual growth of a legend concerning Seth, which may be regarded as a reply to the curse on the Serpent.

The apotheosis of Seth in rabbinical and mussulman mythology represents a sort of Semitic Renaissance. As we have seen in a former chapter, the Egyptians and Greeks identified Set with Typhon, but at the same time that demon was associated with science. He is astronomically located in Capricorn, the sphere of the hierophants in the Egyptian Mysteries, and the mansion of the guardians of science. Thus he would correspond with the Serpent, who, as adapted by the

Hebrews in the myth of Eden, whispers to Eve of divine knowledge. But, as detached from Typho, Seth, while leaving behind the malignancy, carried away the reputation for learning usually ascribed to devils. Thus, while we have had to record so many instances of degraded deities, we may note in Seth a converted devil. In the mussulman and rabbinical traditions Seth is a voluminous author; he receives a library from heaven; he is the originator of astronomy and of many arts; and, as an instructor in cultivation, he restores many an acre which as Set he had blighted. In the apocryphal Genesis he is represented as having been caught up to heaven and shown the future destiny of mankind. Anastasius of Sinai says that when God created Adam after his own image, he breathed into him grace and illumination, and a ray of the Holy Spirit. But when he had sinned this glory left him. Then he became the father of Cain and Abel. But afterwards it is said Adam 'begat a son in his own likeness, after his image, and called his name 'Seth,' which is not said of Cain and Abel; and this means that Seth was begotten in the likeness of unfallen man in paradise—Seth meaning 'Resurrection.' And all those then living, when they saw how the face of Seth shone with divine light, and heard him speak with divine wisdom, said, He is God; therefore his sons were commonly called the sons of God.[3]

That this 'Resurrection' of departed glory and wisdom was really, as I have said, a Renaissance—a restoration of learning from the curse put upon it in the story of the Serpent—is indicated by its evolution in the Gnostic myth wherein Seth was made to avenge Satan. He took under his special care the Tree of the Knowledge of Good and Evil, and planted it in his father's grave (Fig. 8). Rabbins carried their homage to Seth even to the extent of vindicating Saturn, the most notorious of planets, and say that Abraham and the Prophets were inspired by it.[4] The Dog (Jackal) was, in Egyptian symbols, emblem of the Scribe; Sirius was the Dog-star domiciled with Saturn; Seth was by them identified with Sirius, as the god of occult and infernal knowledge. He was near relative of the serpent Sesha, familiar of Æsculapius, and so easily connected with the subtlest of the beasts in Eden which had crept in from the Iranian mythology.

This reaction was instituted by scholars, who, in their necessarily timid way of fable, may be said to have recovered the Tree of Knowledge under guise of homage to Seth. It flourished, as we have seen (chap. xi.), to the extent of finally raising the Serpent to be a god, and lowering Jehovah who cursed him to a jealous devil!

But the terror with which Jehovah is said to have been inspired when he said, 'The man has become as one of us, to know good and evil,' never failed to reappear among priesthoods when anything threatened to remove the means of learning from under their control. The causes of this are too many to be fully considered here; but the main cause unquestionably was the tendency of learning to release men from the sway of the priest. The primitive man of science would speedily discover how many things existed of which his priest was ignorant, and thus the germ of Scepticism would be planted. The man who possessed the Sacred Books, in whole or in part, might become master of the 'spells' supposed to be contained in its words and sentences, and might use them against the priests; or, at any rate, he might feel independent of the ordinary apparatus of salvation.

The anxiety of priests to keep fast hold of the keys of learning, so that no secular son of Adam should become 'as one of them,' coupled with the wonderful powers they professed ability to exercise, powerfully stimulated the curiosity of intellectual men, and led them to seek after this forbidden fruit in subtle ways, which easily illustrated the story of the Serpent. The poet Shelley, who was suspected at Oxford because of his fondness for chemistry, recognised his mythological ancestry, and used to speak of 'my cousin, the Serpent.' The joke was born of circumstances sufficiently scandalous in the last generation to make the Oxonian of to-day blush; but the like histories of earlier ages are so tragical that, when fully known by the common people, they will change certain familiar badges into brands of shame. While the cant goes on about the Church being the protector of learning through the dark ages, the fact is that, from the burning of valuable books at Ephesus by christian fanatics (Acts xix. 19) to the present day, the Church has destroyed tenfold more important works than it ever produced, and almost suffocated the intellectual life of a thousand years. Amid the unbroken persecution of the Jews by christian cruelty, which lasted from the early eleventh century for five hundred years, untold numbers of manuscripts were destroyed, which might have now been giving the world full and clear knowledge concerning ages, for whose records archæological scholars are painfully exploring the crumbled ruins of the East. Synagogues were believed to be temples of Satan; they were plundered and razed to the ground, and their precious archives strewed the streets of many cities. On the 17th of June 1244 twenty-four cartloads of these ancient MSS. were burned in Paris alone. "And all this by our holy 'protector of learning' through the Middle Ages!

The Japanese have pictures of a famous magician who conjured up a demon—vast, vague, and terrible—out of his inkstand. They call it latterly 'emblem of a licentious press,' but, no doubt, it was originally used to terrify the country generally concerning the press. That Devil has also haunted the ecclesiastical imagination in Europe. Nearly every book written without priestly command was associated with the Devil, and there are several old books in Europe, laboriously and honestly written, which to this day are invested with popular superstitions reporting the denunciations with which they were visited. For some centuries it has been believed in Denmark and neighbouring countries that a strange and formidable book exists, by means of which you can raise or lay the Devil. It is vulgarly known as the *Book of Cyprianus*. The owner of it can neither sell, bury, or burn it, and if he cannot get rid of it before his death, he becomes the prey of the fiend. The only way of getting rid of it is to find somebody who will accept it as a present, well knowing what it is. Cyprianus is said to have been a clever and virtuous young student, but he studied the black art in Norway, and came under the power of the Devil, who compelled him to use his unholy learning to evil ends. This grieved him sorely, and he wrote a book, in which he shows first, how evil shall be done, and then how to counteract it. The book is probably one which really exists or existed, and professed to teach the art of sorcery, and likewise the charms against it. It consists of three parts, severally called *Cyprianus*, *Dr. Faust*, and *Jacob Ramel*. The two latter are written in cypher. It teaches everything appertaining to 'signing,' conjuring, second sight, and all the charms alluded to in

Deuteronomy xviii. 10–12. The person possessing Cyprianus' book is said never to be in need of money, and none can harm him. The only way of getting rid of it is to put it away in a secret place in a church along with a clerk's fee of four shillings.

In Stockholm I saw the so-called *Devil's Bible*, the biggest book in the world, in the Royal Library. It is literally as they describe it, *'gigas librorum'*: no single man can lift it from the floor. It was part of the booty carried off by the Swedes after the surrender of Prague, A.D. 1648. It contains three hundred parchment leaves, each one made of an ass's hide, the cover being of oak planks, 1½ inches thick. It contains the Old and New Testaments; *Josephi Flavii Antiquitates Judaicæ; Isidori Episcopi L. XX. de diversis materiis; Confessio peccatorum*; and some other works. The last-named production is written on black and dark brown ground with red and yellow letters. Here and there sentences are marked *'hæc sunt suspecta,' 'superstitiosa,' 'prohibita.'* One MS., which is headed, *'Experimentum de furto et febribus'*, is a treatise in Monkish Latin on the exorcism of ghosts and evil spirits, charms against thieves and sickness, and various prescriptions in 'White Magic.' The age of the book is considerably over three hundred years. The autograph of a German emperor is in it: 'Ferdinandus Imperator Romanorum, A.D. 1577.' The volume is known in Sweden as *Fan's Bibel* (Devil's Bible). The legend says, that a monk, suspected of black arts, who had been condemned to death, begged for life, and his judge mockingly told him that he would be pardoned only if he should produce next morning all the books here found and in this vast size. The monk invoked the Devil's assistance, and the ponderous volume was written in a single night. This Devil

must have been one who prided himself more on his literary powers than his personal appearance; for the face and form said to be
his portrait, frontispiece of the volume, represent a most hideous
ape, green and hairy, with horrible curled tusks. It is, no doubt, the
ape*Anerhahn* of the Wagner legends; Burns's 'towzie tyke, black,
grim, and large.'[5]

I noticed particularly in this old work the recurrence of deep
red letters and sentences similar to the ink which Fust used at the
close of his earliest printed volumes to give his name, with the place
and date of printing. Now Red is sacred in one direction as symbolis-
ing the blood of Christ, but it is also the colour of Judas, who betrayed
that blood. Hence, while red letters might denote sacred days and
sentences in priestly calendars, they might be supposed mimicry
of such sanctities by 'God's Ape' if occurring in secular works or
books of magic. It is said that these red letters were especially noted
in Paris as indications of the diabolical origin of the works so easily
produced by Fust; and, though it is uncertain whether he suffered
imprisonment, the red lines with his name appear to have been regarded as his signature in blood.

For a long time every successive discovery of science, every
invention of material benefit to man, was believed by priest-ridden
peoples to have been secured by compact with the devil. The fate of
the artist Prometheus, fettered by jealous Jove, was repeated in each
who aspired to bring light to man, and some men of genius—such as
Cornelius Agrippa, and Paracelsus—appear to have been frightened
away from legitimate scientific research by the first connection of
their names with sorcery. They had before them the example of the

greatest scientific man of the Middle Ages, Roger Bacon, and knew how easily, in the priestly whisper, the chemist's crucible grew to a wizard's cauldron. The time may come when Oxford University will have learned enough to build a true memorial of the grandest man who ever wrote and taught within its walls. It would show Roger Bacon—rectifier of the Julian Calendar, analyst of lenses, inventor of spectacles and achromatic lenses, probable constructor of the first telescope, demonstrator of the chemical action of air in combustion, inventor of the mode of purifying saltpetre and crystallising it into gunpowder, anticipator of the philosophical method with which his namesake is credited—looking on a pile of his books for whose researches he had paid two thousand French livres, to say nothing of a life's labour, only to see them condemned by his University, their circulation prohibited; and his sad gaze might be from the prison to which the Council of Franciscans at Paris sentenced him whom Oxford gladly delivered into their hands. He was condemned, says their historian Wadding, *'propter novitates quasdam suspectas.'* The suspected novelties were crucibles, retorts, and lenses that made the stars look larger. So was it with the Oxford six hundred years ago. Undeniably some progress had been made even in the last generation, for Shelley was only forbidden to study chemistry, and expelled for his metaphysics. But now that it is claimed that Oxford is no longer partaker with them that stoned investigators and thinkers from Bacon to Shelley, it would be in order to build for its own great martyr of science a memorial, that superstition may look on one whom it has pierced.

Fig. 17.—Luther's Devil

Referring to Luther's inkstand thrown at the Devil, Dr. Zerffii, in his lecture on the Devil, says, 'He (the devil) hates nothing so much as writing or printer's ink.' But the truth of this remark depends upon which of two devils be considered. It would hardly apply to the Serpent who recommended the fruit of knowledge, or to the University man in Lucas van Leyden's picture (Fig. 6). But if we suppose the Devil of Luther's Bible (Fig. 17) to be the one at which the inkstand was thrown, the criticism is correct. The two pictures mentioned may be instructively compared. Luther's Devil is the reply of the University to the Church. These are the two devils—the priest and the scholar—who glared at each other in the early sixteenth century. 'The Devil smelled the roast,' says Luther, 'that if the languages revived, his kingdom would get a hole which he could not easily stop again.' And it must be admitted that some of the monkish execrations of the time, indeed of many times since, have an undertone of Jahvistic jealousy. 'These Knowers will become as one of us.' It must also be admitted that the clerical instinct told true: the University man held in him that sceptical devil who is always the destroyer of the priest's paradise. These two devils which struggled with each other through the sixteenth century still wage their war in the arena of Protestantism. Many a Lutheran now living may remember to have smiled when Hofmann's experiments in discovering carbonic acid gas gained him repute for raising again Mephosto; but perhaps they did not recognise Luther's devil when, at the annual assembly of Lutheran Pastors in Berlin (Sept. 1877), he reappeared as the Rev. Professor Grau, and said, 'Not a few listen to those striving to combine Christ with Belial, to reconcile redeeming truth with modern science and culture.' But though they who take the name of Luther in vain may thus join hands with the Devil, at whom the Reformer threw his inkstand, the combat will still go on, and the University Belial do the brave work of Bel till beneath his feet lies the dragon of Darkness whether disguised as Pope or Protestant.

If the Church wishes to know precisely how far the roughness pardonable in the past survives unpardonably in itself, let its clergy peruse carefully the following translation by Mr. Leland of a poem by Heine; and realise that the Devil portrayed in it is, by grace of its own prelates, at present the most admired personage in every Court and fashionable drawing-room in Christendom.

I called the Devil, and he came:
In blank amaze his form I scan.
He is not ugly, is not lame,
But a refined, accomplished man,—
One in the very prime of life,
At home in every cabinet strife,
Who, as diplomatist, can tell
Church and State news extremely well.
He is somewhat pale—and no wonder either,
Since he studies Sanskrit and Hegel together.
His favourite poet is still Fonqué.
Of criticism he makes no mention,
Since all such matters unworthy attention
He leaves to his grandmother, Hecaté.
He praised my legal efforts, and said
That he also when younger some law had read,
Remarking that friendship like mine would be
An acquisition, and bowed to me,—
Then asked if we had not met before,
At the Spanish Minister's soirée?
And, as I scanned his face once more,
I found I had known him for many a day.

**NOTES**

1 'Chald. Genesis,' by George Smith, p. 84.
2 This text was engraved by Mrs. Rose Mary Crawshay on a tomb she had erected in hon-our of her humble neighbour, Mr. Norbury, who sought knowledge for its own sake. Few ancient scriptures could have supplied an inscription so appropriate.
3 Mr. Baring-Gould, quoting this (from Anastasius Sinaita, Ὀδηγός, ed. Gretser, Ingolst. 1606, p. 269), attributes this shining face of Seth to his previous character as a Sun-god. ('Old Test. Legends,' i. 84.)
4 King's 'Gnostics,' p. 53, n.
5 Tertullian's phrase, 'The Devil is God's Ape,' became popular at one time, and the Ape-devil had frequent representation in art—as, for instance, in Holbein's 'Crucifixion' (1477), now at Augsburg, where a Devil with head of an ape, bat-wings, and flaming red legs is carrying off the soul of the impenitent thief. The same subject is found in the same gallery in an Altdorfer, where the Devil's face is that of a gorilla.

# Chapter XXIV
# Witchcraft

**ST. CYPRIAN SAW** the devil in a flower.[1] That little vision may report more than many more famous ones the consistency with which the first christians had developed the doctrine that nature is the incarnation of the Evil Spirit. It reports to us the sense of many sounds and sights which were heard and seen by ears and eyes trained for such and no other, all showing that the genii of nature and beauty were vanishing from the earth. Over the Ægean sea were heard lamentations and the voice, 'Great Pan is dead!' Augustus consults the oracle of Apollo and receives reply—

> Me puer Hebræus, Divos Deus ipse gubernans,
> Cedere sede jubet, tristremque redire sub orcum;
> Aris ergo dehinc tacitis abscedito nostris.

But while the rage of these Fathers towards all the great gods and goddesses, who in their grand temples represented 'the pride of life,' was remorseless, they were comparatively indifferent to the belief or disbelief of the lower classes in their small tutelary divinities. They appear almost to have encouraged belief in these, perhaps appreciating the advantages of the popular custom of giving generous offerings to such personal and domestic patrons. At a very early period there seems to have arisen an idea of converting these more plebeian spirits into guardian angels with christian names. Thus Jerome relates in his Life of the first Hermit Paul, that when St. Anthony was on his way to visit that holy man, he encountered a Centaur who pointed out the way; and next a human-like dwarf with horns, hooked fingers, and feet like those of a goat. St. Anthony believing this to be an apparition of the Devil, made the sign of the Cross; but the little man, nowise troubled by this, respectfully approached the monk, and having been asked who he was, answered: 'I am a mortal, and one of those inhabitants of the Desert whom the Gentiles in their error worship under the names of Fauns, Satyrs, and Incubi: I am delegated by my people to ask of thee to pray for us to our common God, who we know has descended for the salvation of the world, and whose praises resound in all the earth.' At this glorification of Christ St. Anthony was transported with joy, and turning towards Alexandria he cried, 'Woe to thee, adulterous city, which adorest animals as gods!'

Perhaps the evolution of these desert demons into good christians would have gone on more rapidly and completely if the primitive theologians had known as much of their history as comparative mythology has disclosed to the modern world. St. Anthony was, however, fairly on the track of them when he turned towards Alexandria. Egypt appears to have been the especial centre from which were distributed through the world the fetish guardians of provinces, towns, households and individuals. Their Serapes reappear in the Teraphim of Laban, and many of the forms they used reappear in the Penates, Lares, and genii of Latin countries. All these in their several countries were originally related to its ancient religion or mythology, but before the christian era they were very much the same in Egypt, Greece, and Italy. They were shaped in many different, but usually natural forms, such as serpents, dogs, boys, and old men, though often some intimation was given of their demonic character. They were so multiplied that even plants and animals had their guardians. The anthropomorphic genii called the Patrii, who were supposed to preside over provinces, were generally represented bearing weapons with which they defended the regions of which they were patrons. These were the Averrunci or Apotropæi.

There are many interesting branches of this subject which cannot be entered into here, and others have already been considered in the foregoing parts of this work. It is sufficient for my present purpose to remark, that, in the course of time, all the households of the world had traditional guardians; these were generally represented in some shape on amulets and talismans, on which were commonly inscribed the verbal charms by which the patron could be summoned. In the process of further time the amulets—especially such as were reproduced by tribes migrating from the vicinity of good engravers—might be marked only with the verbal charms; these again were, in the end, frequently represented only by some word or name. This was the 'spell.' Imagination fails in the effort to conceive how many strata of extinct deities had bequeathed to the ancient Egyptians those mystical names whose exact utterance they believed would constrain each god so named to appear and bind him to serve the invoker's purpose whether good or evil.[2] This idea continued among the Jews and shaped the commandment, 'Thou shalt not take the name of the Lord thy God in vain.'

It was in these diminutive forms that great systems survived among the common people. Amid natural convulsions ancient formations of faith were broken into fragments; in the ebb and flow of time these fragments were smoothed, as it were, into these talismanic pebbles. Yet each of these conveyed all the virtue which had been derived from the great and costly ceremonial system from which it originally crumbled; the virtue of soothing the mind and calming the nerves of sufferers with the feeling that, though they might have been assailed by hostile powers, they had friendly powers too who were active in their behalf—Vindicators, to recall Job's phrase—who at last would stand by them to the end. In the further ebb and flow of generations the mass of such charms are further pulverised into sand or into mud; but not all of them: amid the mud will be found many surviving specimens, and such mud of accumulated superstitions is always susceptible of being remoulded after such lingering models, should occasion demand.

Erasmus, in his 'Adages,' suggests that it was from these genii of 'the Gentiles' that the christians derived their notion of each person being attended by two angels, a good and a bad. Probably he was but half right. The peoples to whom he refers did not generally believe that each man was attended by a bad spirit, a personal enemy.

That was an honour reserved for individuals particularly formidable to the evil powers,—Adam, Jacob, Hercules, or Zoroaster. The one preternatural power attending each ordinary individual defended him from the general forces of evil. But it was Christianity which, in the gradual effort to substitute patron-saints and guardian-angels of its own for the pagan genii, turned the latter from friends to enemies, and their protecting into assailing weapons.

All the hereditary household gods of what is now called Christendom were diabolised. But in order that the masses might turn from them and invoke christian guardians, the Penates, Lares, and genii had to be belittled on the one hand, and the superior power of the saints and angels demonstrated. When Christianity had gained the throne of political power, it was easy to show that the 'imps,' as the old guardians were now called, could no longer protect their invokers from christian punishment, or confer equal favours.

Christianity conquered Europe by the sword, but at first that sword was not wielded against the humble masses. It was wielded against their proud oppressors. To the common people it brought glad tidings of a new order, in which, under the banner of a crucified working-man and his (alleged) peasant mother, all caste should disappear but that of piety and charity. Christ eating with publicans and sinners and healing the wayside cripples reappeared in St. Martin dividing his embroidered cloak with a beggar—type of a new aristocracy. They who worshipped the Crucified Peasant in the rock-cave of Tours which St. Martin had consecrated, or in little St. Martin's Church at Canterbury where Bertha was baptized, could not see the splendid cathedrals now visible from them, built of their bones and cemented with their blood. King Ethelbert surrendered the temple of his idol to the consecration of Augustine, and his baptized subjects had no difficulty in seeing the point of the ejected devil's talons on the wall which he assailed when the first mass was therein celebrated.

Glad tidings to the poor were these that the persecuted first missionaries brought to Gaul, Britain, and Germany. But they did not last. The christians and the pagan princes, like Herod and Pilate, joined hands to crucify the European peasant, and he was reduced to a worse serfdom than he had suffered before. Every humble home in Europe was trampled in the mire in the name of Christ. The poor man's wife and child, and all he possessed were victims of the workman of Jerusalem turned destroyer of his brethren. Michelet has well traced Witchcraft to the Despair of the Middle Ages.[3] The decay of the old religions, which Christianity had made too rapid for it to be complete, had left, as we have seen, all the trains laid for that terrible explosion; and now its own hand of cruelty brought the torch to ignite them. Let us, at risk of some iteration, consider some of these combustible elements.

Fig. 18.—Devils (Old Missal)

In the first place the Church had recognised the existence of the pagan gods and goddesses, not wishing to imbreed in the popular mind a sceptical habit, and also having use for them to excite terror. Having for this latter purpose carved and painted them as ugly and bestial, it became further of importance that they should be represented as stupid and comparatively impotent. Baptism could exorcise them, and a crucifix put thousands of them to flight. This tuition was not difficult. The peasantries of Europe had readily been induced to associate the newly announced (christian) Devil with their most mischievous demons. But we have already considered the forces under which these demons had entered on their decline before they were associated with Satan. Many conquered obstructions had rendered the Demons which represented them ridiculous. Hence the 'Dummeteufel' of so many German fables and of the mediæval miracle-plays. 'No greater proof,' says Dr. Dasent, 'can be given of the small hold which the christian Devil has taken of the Norse mind, than the heathen aspect under which he constantly appears, and the ludicrous way in which he is always outwitted.'[4] 'The Germans,' says Max Müller, 'indoctrinated with the idea of a real devil, the Semitic Satan or Diabolus, treated him in the most good-humoured manner.'[5] A fair idea of the insignificance he and his angels reached may be gained from the accompanying picture (Fig. 18), with which a mediæval Missal now in possession of Sir Joseph Hooker is illuminated. It could not be expected that the masses would fear beings whom their priests thus held up to ridicule. It is not difficult to imagine the process of evolution by which the horns of such insignificant devils turned to the asinine ears of such devils as this stall carving at Corbeil, near Paris (Fig. 19), which represented the popular view of the mastery obtained by witches over devils. It must be remembered also that this power over devils was in accordance with the traditions concerning Solomon, and the subserviency of Oriental demons generally to the lamps or charms to which they were bound.

*Fig. 19.—Carving at Corbeil*

What the popular christian devil had become in all the Northern nations is sufficiently shown in the figure he presented in most of the old miracle-plays and 'Moralities.' 'The Devill in his fethers all ragged and rent,'[6] had horns, wide mouth, long (sometimes up-turned) nose, red beard, cloven foot, and tail. He was attended by a buffoon called Vice. 'And,' says Harsenet, 'it was a pretty part in the old Church playes when the nimble Vice would skip up nimbly like a Jackanapes into the Devil's necke, and ride the Devil a course, and be-labour him with a wooden dagger, till he made him roar, whereat the people would laugh to see the Devil so Vice-haunted.[7] The two must have nearly resembled the clown and his unhappy victim Pantaloon in our pantomimes, as to their antics. It would seem that sometimes holy personages were caricatured in the make-up of the stage-devil. Thus in 'Gammer Gurton's Needle' we have this conversation:—

*Gammer.* But, Hodge, had he no horns to push?

*Hodge.* As long as your two armes. Saw ye never fryer Rushe
Painted on cloth, with a side long cowe's tayle
And crooked cloven feet, and many a hooked nayle?
For all the world (if I should judge) should reckon him his brother;
Loke, even what face fryer Rushe had, the devil had such another.

In the scene of Christ's delivering souls from purgatory, the Devil is represented as blowing lustily a horn to alarm his comrades, and crying, 'Out, out, aronzt!' to the invader. He fights with a three-pronged fork. He and his victims are painted black,[8] in contrast with the souls of the saved, which are white. The hair was considered very important.[9] When he went to battle, even his fiery nature was sometimes represented in a way that must have been more ludicrous than impressive.[10]

The insignificance to which the priests had reduced the devil in the plays, where they were usually the actors, reflected their own petty routine of life. They could conceive of nothing more terrible than their own mean mishaps and local obstructions. One great of-fice of the Devil was to tempt some friar to sleep when he should be at prayer,[11] make another drink too much, or a third cast warm glances at a village beauty. The*Revelations* of the Abbot Richalmus, written seven hundred years ago, shows the Devil already far gone in his process of diminution. The Devil here concentrates the energies which once made the earth tremble on causing nausea to the Abbot, and making the choir cough while he is preaching. 'When I sit down to holy studies,' he says, 'the devils make me heavy with sleep. Then I stretch my hands beyond my cuffs to give them a chill. Forthwith the spirits prick me under my clothes like so many fleas, which causes me to put my hands on them; and so they get warm again, and my reading grows careless.' 'Come, just look at my lip; for twenty years has an imp clung to it just to make it hang down.' It is ludicrous to find that ancient characteristic of the gods of Death already adverted to—their hatred of salt, the agent of preservation—descended from being the sign of Job's constancy to Jehovah into a mere item of the Abbot's appetite. 'When I am at dinner, and the devil has taken away my appetite, as soon as I have tasted a little salt it comes back to me; and if, shortly afterwards, I lose it again, I take some more salt, and am once more an hungered.'[12]

One dangerous element was the contempt into which, by many causes, the infernal powers had been brought. But a more dangerous one lay in another direction. Though the current phrases of the New Testament and of the Fathers of the Church, declaring this world, its wealth, loves, and pleasures, to be all the kingdom of Satan, had become cant in the mouths of priests ruling over Europe, it had never been cant to the humble peasantries. Although they had degraded many devils imported by the priests, it had been in connection with the declining terrors of their native demonologies. But above these degraded and hated gnomes and elves, whose paternity had been transferred from Sœtere to Satan, there was an array of beautiful deities—gentle gods and goddesses traditionally revered and loved as protectors of the home and the family—which had never really lost their hold on the common people. They might have shrunk before the aggressive victories of the Saints into little Fairies, but their continued love for the poor and the oppressed was the romance of every household. What did these good fairies do? They sometimes loaded the lowly with wealth, if summoned in just the right way; they sang secrets to them from trees as little birds, they smoothed the course of love, clothed ash-maidens in fine clothes, transported people through the air, enabled them to render themselves invulnerable, or invisible, to get out of prisons, to vanquish 'the powers that be,' whether 'ordained of God' or not. Now all these were benefits which, by christian theory, could only be conferred by that Prince of this World who ministered to 'the pride of life.'

Into homes which the priest and his noble had stripped of happiness and hope,—whose loving brides were for baptized Bluebeards, whose hard earnings were taken as the price of salvation from devils whose awfulness was departing,—there came from afar rumours of great wealth and splendour conferred upon their worshippers by Eastern gods and goddesses. The priests said all those were devils who would torture their devotees eternally after death; yet it could not be denied that the Moors had the secret of lustres and ornamentation, that the heathen East was gorgeous, that all Christendom was dreaming of the wealth of Ormus and of Ind. Granted that Satan had come westward and northward, joined the scurvy crew of Loki, and become of little importance; but what of Baal or Beelzebub, of Asmodeus, of the genii who built Solomon's temple, of rich Pluto, of august Ahriman? Along with stories of Oriental magnificence there spread through Christendom names of many deities and demons; many of them beautiful names, too, euphemism having generally managed to bestow melodious epithets alike on deities feared and loved. In Faust's 'Miraculous Art and Book of Marvels, or the Black Raven' (1469), the infernal heirarchy are thus named:—*King*, Lucifer; *Viceroy*, Belial; *Gubernatores*, Satan, Beelzebub, Astaroth, Pluto; *Chief Princes*, Aziel, Mephistopheles, Marbuel, Ariel, Aniguel, Anisel, Barfael. Seductive meanings, too, corresponding to these names, had filtered in some way from the high places they once occupied into the minds of the people. Lucifer was a fallen star that might rise again; Belial and Beelzebub were princes of the fire that rendered possible the arts of man, and the Belfires never went out in the cold North; Astarte meant beauty, and Pluto wealth; Aziel (Asael) was President of the great College of occult arts, from whom Solomon learned the secrets by which he made the jinni his slaves; Marbuel was the artist and mechanic, sometimes believed to aid artisans who produced work beyond ordinary human skill; Ariel was the fine spirit of the air whose intelligence corresponded to that of the Holy Ghost on the other side; Aniguel is the serpent of Paradise, generally written Anisel; Anizazel is probably a fanciful relative of Azazel, 'the strong god;' and Barfael, who in a later Faust book is Barbuel, is an orientalised form of the 'demon of the long beard' who holds the secret of the philosopher's stone.

In a later chapter the growth of favourable views of the devil is considered. Some of the legends therein related may be instructively read in connection with the development of Witchcraft. Many rumours were spread abroad of kindly assistance brought by demons to persons in distress. But even more than by hopes so awakened was the witch aided by the burning desire of the people for vengeance. They wanted Zamiel (Samaël) to help them to mould the bullet that would not miss its mark. The Devil and all his angels had long been recognised by their catechists as being utilised by the Deity to execute his vengeance on the guilty; and to serfs in their agony that devil who would not spare prince or priest was more desired than even the bestower of favours to their starving minds and bodies.

Under the long ages of war in Europe, absorbing the energies of men, women had become the preservers of letters. The era of witchcraft in Europe found that sex alone able to read and write, arts disesteemed in men, among the peasantry at least. To them men turned when it had become a priestly lesson that a few words were more potent than the weapons of princes. Besides this, women were the chief sorcerers, because they were the chief sufferers. In Alsace (1615), out of seventy-five who perished as witches, sixty-two were women. The famous *Malleus Maleficorum*, which did more evil than any work ever published, derives *femina* from *fide minus*. Although in the Faust legend Mephistopheles objects to marriage, many stories represent diabolical weddings. Particular details were told of the marriage of Satan with the daughter of a Sorceress at Egnischen (1585), on which occasion the three towers of the castle there were said to have been illuminated, and a splendid banquet spread, the favourite dish being a ragout of bats. There was exquisite music, and a 'beautiful man' blessed the nuptials. How many poor peasant girls must have had such dreams as they looked up from their drudgery to the brilliant chateaux?

*Fig. 20.—Lilith as Cat*

In the illuminated manuscript known as 'Queen Mary's Psalter' (1553) there is a picture of the Fall of Man (Fig. 20) which possesses far-reaching significance. It is a modification of that idea, which gained such wide currency in the Middle Ages, that it was the serpent-woman Lilith who had tempted Adam to eat the forbidden fruit. In this picture, while the beautiful face and ample hair of Lilith are given, instead of the usual female bust she has the body of a cat. This nocturnal animal, already sacred to Freyja, the Teutonic Venus, whose chariot it drew, gained a new mythological career in the North by the large number of Southern and Oriental stones which related it to the lunar and amorous demonesses. When the gods fled before the Titans, Diana, as Ovid relates, changed herself to a cat, and as infernal Hecate that animal was still beside her. If my reader will turn to vol. i. p. 130, some of the vast number of myths which prepared the cat to take its place as familiar of the witch may be found. Whether the artist had Lilith in his mind or not, the illumination in 'Queen Mary's Psalter' represents a remarkable association of myths. For Lilith was forerunner of the mediæval mothers weeping for their children; her voice of perpetual lamentation at the cruel fate allotted her by the combined tyranny of God and man was heard on every sighing wind; and she was the richly dressed bride of the Prince of Devils, ever seeking to tempt youth. Such stories floated through the mind of the Middle Ages, and this infernal Madonna is here seen in association with the cat, beneath whose soft sparkling fur the goddess of Love and Beauty was supposed to be still lurking near the fireside of many a miserable home. Some fragrance of the mystical East was with this feline beauty, and nothing can be more striking than the contrast which the ordinary devils beside her present. Their unseductive ugliness and meanness is placed out of sight of the pair tempted to seek the fruit of forbidden knowledge. They inspire the man and woman in their evidently eager grasping after the fruit, which here means the consultation of fair fortune-tellers and witches to obtain that occult knowledge for which speculative men are seeking in secret studies and laboratories.

Those who have paid attention to the subject of Witchcraft need not be reminded that its complexity and vastness would require a larger volume than the present to deal with it satisfactorily. The present study must be limited to a presentation of some of the facts which induce the writer to believe that, beneath the phenomena, lay a profound alienation from Christianity, and an effort to recall the banished gods which it had superseded.

The first christian church was mainly Jewish, and this is also to say that it inherited the vast Angelolatry and the system of spells which that tribe had brought from Babylon. To all this was now superadded the accumulation of Assyrian and Egyptian lore which was re-edited in the form of Neoplatonicism. This mongrel mass, constituted of notions crumbled from many systems, acquired a certain consistency in Gnosticism. The ancient Egyptians had colleges set apart for astrological study, and for cultivation of the art of healing by charms. Every month, decade, day of the year had its special guardian in the heavens. The popular festivals were astronomic. To the priests in the colleges were reserved study of the sacred books in which the astrological secrets were contained, and whose authorship was attributed to the god Thoth, inventor of writing, the Greek Hermes, and, later, Egyptian Hermes Trismegistus. The zodiac is a memorial of the influence which the stars were supposed to exert upon the human body. Alchemy (the word is Egyptian, *Kémi* meaning 'black earth') was also studied in connection with solar, lunar, and stellar influences. The Alchemists dreamed of discovering the philosopher's stone, which would change base metals to gold; and Diocletian, in burning the Alchemists' books, believed that, in so doing, he would deprive the Egyptians of their source of wealth.[13]

Imported into Greece, these notions and their cult had a twofold development. Among the Platonists they turned to a naturalistic and allegorical Demonology; among the uncultivated they formed a Diabolarchy, which gathered around the terrible lunar phantasm—Hecate.

The astrological College of Egypt gave to the Jews their strange idea of the high school maintained among the devils, already referred to in connection with Asmodeus, who was one of its leading professors. The rabbinical legend was, that two eminent angels, Asa and Asael, remonstrated with the Creator on having formed man only to give trouble. The Creator said they would have done the same as man under similar circumstances; whereupon Asa and Asael proposed that the experiment should be tried. They went to earth, and the Creator's prediction was fulfilled: they were the first 'sons of God' who fell in love with the daughters of men (Gen. vi. 2). They were then embodied. In heaven they had been angels of especial knowledge in divine arts, and they now used their spells to reascend. But their sin rendered the spells powerless for that, so they repaired to the Dark Mountains, and there established a great College of Sorcery. Among the many distinguished graduates of this College were Job, Jethro, and Bileam. It was believed that these three instructed the soothsayers who attempted to rival the miracles of Moses before Pharaoh. Job and Jethro were subsequently converted, but Bileam continued his hostility to Israel, and remains a teacher in the College. Through knowledge of the supreme spell—the *Shem-hammphorásch*, or real name of God—Solomon was able to chain Professor Asmodeus, and wrest from him the secret of the worm Schámir, by whose aid the Temple was built.

Traditions of the learning of the Egyptians, and of the marvels learned by Solomon from Asa and Asael by which he compelled demons to serve him, and the impressive story of the Witch of Endor, powerfully influenced the inquisitive minds of Europe. The fierce denunciations of all studies of these arts of sorcery by the early Church would alone reveal how prevalent they were. The wonderful story of Apollonius of Tyana,[14] as told by Philostratus, was really a kind of gospel to the more worldly-minded scholars. Some rabbins, following the outcry against Jesus, 'He casteth out devils by Beelzebub,' circulated at an early date the story that Jesus had derived his power to work miracles from the spell *Shem-hammphorásch*, which he found on one of the stones of the Temple where Solomon had left it. Though Eusebius cast doubt upon them, the christians generally do not appear to have denied the miracles of Apollonius, which precisely copy those of Jesus from the miraculous birth to the ascension, but even to have quoted them as an evidence of the possibility of miracles. Celsus having attributed the miracles of Jesus to sorcery, and said that magic influenced only the ignorant and immoral, Origen replies that, in order to convince himself of the contrary, he has only to read the memoirs of Apollonius by Mæragenes, who speaks of him as a philosopher and magician, who repeatedly exercised his powers on philosophers. Arnobius and the fathers of the fourth century generally believed in the Apollonian thaumaturgy and attributed it to magic. Aldus Manutius published the book of Philostratus in the fifteenth century, and the degree to which the fascinating and marvellous stories concerning Apollonius fired the European imagination just awaking under the breath of the Renaissance, may be estimated by the fury with which the 'magician' was anathematised by Pico della Mirandola, Jean Bodin, and Baronius. The book and the controversy attracted much attention, and while the priests still continued to charge Apollonius with being a 'magician,' they appear to have perceived that it would have been more to the point, so far as their real peril was concerned, to have proved him an impostor. Failing that, Dr. Faustus and his fellow-professors in the 'black art' were left masters of the situation. The people had to digest the facts admitted, that a Pagan had learned, by initiations into the astrological schools of Egypt and India, the means of healing the sick, raising the dead, flying through the air, throwing off chains, opening locks, rendering himself invisible, and discerning the future.

There was a call for some kind of Apollonius, and Faustus arose. Side by side flourished Luther and Faustus. To Roman Catholic eyes they were twin sons of the Devil;[15] that they were characteristic products of one moral age and force appears to me certain, even as to-day the negations of Science and the revival of 'Spiritualism' have a common root in radical disbelief of the hereditary dogmas and forms of so-called religion. It is, however, not surprising that Protestantism felt as much horror of its bastard brother as Science has of the ghostly seances. Through the early sixteenth century we can trace this strange Dr. Faustus ('auspicious,' he had chosen that name) going about Germany, not omitting Erfurth, and talking in taverns about his magic arts and powers. More is said of him in the following chapter; it is sufficient to observe here, and it is the conclusion of Professor Morley, who has sifted the history with his usual care, that about him, as a centre of crystallisation, tales ascribed in the first place to other conjurers arranged themselves, until he became the popular ideal of one who sought to sound the depths of this world's knowledge and enjoyments without help from the Church or its God. The priests did not doubt that this could be done, nor did the Protestants; they generally agreed that it could be accomplished at cost of the soul. As angels of the good God must answer to the formulas of invocation to those who had made a sacramental compact with their Chief, so was it possible to share a sacrament of Satan, and by certain invocations summon his infernal angels to obtain the pleasures of this world of which he is Prince. A thousand years' experience of the Church had left the poor ready to sign the compact if they could secure some little earthly joy. As for Heaven, if it were anything like what its ministers had provided for the poor on earth, Hell might be preferable after all.

Dr. Wuttke, while writing his recent work on German super-stitions, was surprised to learn that there still exist in France and in Wurtemberg schools for teaching the Black Art. A priest in the last-named country wrote him that a boy had confessed to having passed the lower grade of such a school, but, scared by the horrid ceremonies, had pronounced some holy words which destroyed the effect of the wicked practices, and struck the assembled Devil-wor-shippers with consternation. The boy said he had barely escaped with his life. I have myself passed an evening at a school in London 'for the development of Spirit-mediums,' and possibly Dr. Wuttke's correspondent would describe these also as Devil-worshippers. No doubt all such circles might be traced archæologically to that Sor-cerers' College said by the rabbins to have been kept by Asa and

Asael. But what moral force preserved them? They do but represent a turning of methods made familiar by the Church to coax benefits from other supernatural powers in the hope that they would be less dilatory than the Trinity in bestowing their gifts. What is the difference between St. Wolfram's God and King Radbot's Devil? The one offers a golden mansion on earth warranted to last through eternity, the other a like mansion in the skies receivable after death. The Saint agrees that if Radbot's Devil can build him such a house the king would be quite right to worship the architect. The question of the comparative moral merits of the two invisible Powers is not mentioned. This legend, related in a preceding chapter, is characteristic of the motives to which the priesthood appealed through the Middle Ages. It is no wonder that the people began to appeal to the gods of their traditional Radbots, nor that they should have used the ceremonial and sacramental formulas around them.

But to these were added other formulas borrowed from different sources. The 'Compact with the Devil' had in it various elements. It appears to have been a custom of the Odinistic religion for men to sign acts of self-dedication to trusted deities, somewhat corresponding to the votive tablets of Southern religion. It was a legend of Odin that when dying he marked his arm with the point of a spear, and this may have been imitated. In the 'Mysteries' of pagan and christian systems blood played an important part—the human blood of earlier times being symbolised by that of animals, and ultimately, among christians, in wine of the Eucharist. The primitive history of this blood-covenant is given in another chapter. Some astrological formulas, and many of the deities invoked, spread through Europe with the Jews. The actual, and quite as often fabulous, wealth of that antichristian race was ascribed to Antichrist, and while christian princes thought of such gold as legitimate spoil, the honest peasants sought from their astrologers the transmitted 'key of Solomon,' in virtue of which the demons served him. The famous 'Compact' therefore was largely of christian-judaic origin, and only meant conveyance of the soul in consideration of precisely the same treasures as those promised by the Church to all whose names were written in the Lamb's Book,—the only difference being in the period when redemption of the respective issues of priest and astrologer should fall due. One was payable during this life, the other after death.

The ceremonial performances of Witchcraft have also always existed in some form. What we are familiar with of late as Spirit-seances are by no means new. More than a hundred years ago, Mr. Wesley and various clergymen were sitting at a table in Cock Lane, asking the spirit 'Fanny' to rap twice if she were 'in a state of progressive happiness.' Nay, a hundred years before that (1661), Sir Thomas Chamberlain and others, sitting in a haunted house at Tedworth, Wilts, asked 'Satan, if the Drummer set thee to work, give three knocks, and no more, which it did very distinctly, and stopped.'[16] We also learn that, in another town and case (1654), 'a naked arm and hand appeared and beat the floor.' It would not be difficult to go further back and find that the dark circle of our Spiritualists with much of its apparatus has existed continuously through the Middle Ages. The dark seance which Goethe has represented in Faust, Part II., at which the spirits of Helen and Paris are evoked, is a very accurate picture of the 'materialisations' now exhibited by mediums, more than forty years after its publication. These outer resemblances are physiognomical. The seance of to-day has lost the darker features of its mediæval prototype, because the Present has not a real and temporal, but only a speculative and sentimental despair, and this is the kind that possesses chiefly the well-to-do and idle classes. It is not difficult to meet the eye of our everyday human nature amid those frenzied periods when whole districts seemed afflicted with epidemic madness, and look deep in that eye to the fathomless heart of humanity.

In an old parish register of Fewston, Yorkshire, are the following entries:—'1621. Anne, daughter of Edward Fairfax, baptized the 12th June.' '1621. Edward Fairfax, Esq., a child named Anne, buried the 9th October.' Then in the History of Knaresborough we read of this child, 'She was held to have died through witchcraft.' In what dreams did that child, supposed to have been snatched away by diabolic malice, return as a pure spirit uplifted in light, yet shadowed by the anxiety and pain of the bereaved family! A medium is at hand, one through whose mind and heart all the stormy electricities of the time are playing. The most distinguished representative of the Fairfax family is off fighting for Parliament against the King. Edward Fairfax is a zealous Churchman. His eldest daughter, Helen, aged twenty-one, is a parishioner of the Rev. Mr. Smithson, yet she has come under the strong influence of a Nonconformist preacher, Mr. Cook. The scholarly clergyman and his worldly Church on one side, and the ignorant minister with his humble followers on the other, are unconscious personifications of Vice and Virtue, while between them poor Helen is no Heraklea.

Nineteen days after the burial of her little sister Anne, as mentioned above, Helen is found 'in a deadly trance.' After a little she begins to speak, her words showing that she is, by imagination, 'in the church at Leeds, hearing a sermon by Mr. Cook.' On November 3, as she lies on her bed, Helen exclaims, 'A white cat hath been long upon me and drawn my breath, and hath left in my mouth and throat so filthy a smell that it doth poison me!' Next we have the following in the father's diary: '*Item.* Upon Wednesday, the 14th of November, she saw a black dog by her bedside, and, after a little sleep, she had an apparition of one like a young gentleman, very brave, his apparel all laid with gold lace, a hat with a golden band, and a ruff in fashion. He did salute her with the same compliment as she said Sir Fernandino Fairfax useth when he cometh to the house and saluteth her mother.... He said he was a Prince, and would make her Queen of England and of all the world if she would go with him. She refused, and said, 'In the name of God, what art thou?' He presently did forbid her to name God; to which she replied, 'Thou art no man if thou canst not abide the name of God; but if thou be a man, come near, let me feel of thee;' which he would not do, but said, 'It is no matter for feeling.' She proceeded, 'If thou wert a man, thou wouldst not deny to be felt; but thou art the devil, and art but a shadow.'

It is possible that Helen Fairfax had read in Shakspere's 'Lear,' printed twelve years before, that

> The Prince of Darkness is a gentleman;
> Modo he's called, and Mahu.[17]

But the reader will remark how her vision anticipates that of Faust, the transformation of the poodle to finely-dressed Mephistopheles. On the next apparition a bit from Patmos is interpolated, the Devil appearing as a beast with many horns; but the folklore of Yorkshire prevails, and 'presently he was like a very little dog, and desired her to open her mouth and let him come into her body, and then he would rule all the world.' Lastly, he 'filled the room with fire.'

In the account thus far we have the following items of ancient mythology:—1, the Cat; 2, the Dog; 3, the Pride of Life (Asmodeus), represented in the fine dress and manners of the fiend; 4, the Prince of this World, offering its throne; 5, the Egyptian belief in potency of the Name; 6, the Hunger-Demon, who dares not be felt, because his back is hollow, and, though himself a shadow, casts none; 7, the disembodied devil of the rabbins, who seeks to enter a human form, in order to enjoy the higher powers of which man is capable; 8, the fiend of fire.

The period in which Helen Fairfax lived supplied forms for the 'materialisation' of these notions flitting from the ancient cemeteries of theology. The gay and gallant Asmodeus had been transformed into a goat under the ascetic eye of Europe; his mistress is a naked witch; her familiar and slave is a cat. This is the conventionalised theologic theory, as we find it in many examples, one of which is here shown (Fig. 21), as copied from a stone panel at the entrance of Lyons Cathedral. This is what Helen's visions end in. She and her younger sister of seven years, and a young neighbour, a girl of twelve, who have become infected with Helen's hysterics, identify six poor women as witches, and Edward Fairfax would have secured their execution had it not been for the clergyman Smithson.

*Fig. 21.—A Witch (Lyons Cathedral)*

Cats played a large part in this as in other witch-trials. They had long been regarded as an insurance of humble households. In many regions still may be found beliefs that a three-coloured cat protects against fire; a black cat cures epilepsy, protects gardens; and in Bohemia a cat is the favourite bridal gift to procure a happy wedded life. One who kills a cat has no luck for seven years. The Yorkshire women called witches remembered these proverbs to their cost. Among the cats regarded by the Fairfaxes as familiars of the accused, some names are notable. One is called 'Gibbe.' This is the Icelandic *gabba*, to 'delude,' and our gibber; it is the 'Gib' cat of Reinicke Fuchs, and of the 'Romaunt of the Rose.' In 'Gammer Gurton' we read, 'Hath no man gelded Gyb, her cat;' and in Henry IV. i. 2, 'I am as melancholy as a gib cat.' Another of the cats is called *Inges*. That is, *ignis*, fire—Agni maintaining his reign of terror.

Helen's devil hates the dissenter, and says, 'Cook is a lying villain,' because Cook exorcises him with a psalm. On the other hand, the devil praises the clergyman, but Helen breaks out with 'He is not worthy to be a vicar who will bear with witches.' Amid the religious controversies then exciting all households, mourning for his dead child, humiliated by the suspicions of his best neighbours that his daughter was guilty of deception, Edward Fairfax, Gentleman, a scholar and author, lent an ear to the vulgar superstitions of his neighbourhood. Could he have stood on the shoulders of Grimm, he would have left us a very different narrative than that preserved by the Philobiblion Society.[18]

It is hardly possible to determine now the value of the alleged confessions of witches. They were extorted by torture or by promises of clemency (the latter rarely fulfilled); they were shaped by cross-examiners rather than by their victims; and their worth is still more impaired where, as is usual, they are not given in detail, but recorded in 'substance,' the phraseology in such case reflecting the priest's preconceived theory of witches and their orgies. It is to be feared, for instance, that 'devil' is often written instead of some name that might now be interesting. Nevertheless, there seems to be ground for believing that in many cases there were seances held to invoke supernatural powers.

Among the vast number of trials and confessions, I have found none more significant than the following. In February 1691 a daughter and niece of Mr. Parris, minister in Salem (Massachusetts), girls of ten or eleven years, and several other girls, complained of various bodily torments, and as the physicians could find no cause for them, they were pronounced bewitched. The Rev. Mr. Parris had once been in business at the Barbadoes, and probably brought thence his two slaves, Spanish Indians, man and wife. When the children were declared bewitched, the Indian woman, Tituba, tried an experiment, probably with fetishes familiar in the Barbadoes, to find out the witch. Whereupon the children cried out against the Indian woman as appearing to them and tormenting them. Tituba said her mistress, in her own country, had taught her how to find out a witch, but denied being one herself; but afterwards (urged, as she subsequently declared, by her master) she confessed; and the marks of Spanish cruelty on her body were assumed to be the Devil's wounds. The Rev. Mr. Parris in a calmer time might have vindicated poor Tituba by taking for text of his sermon on the subject Christ's saying about a house divided against itself, and reminding the colony, which held public fast against Satan, that the devil was too clever to cover his Salem agent with wounds; but instead of that he preached on the words, 'Have I not chosen you twelve, and one of you is a devil.' During this sermon a woman left the church; she was sister of a woman who had also been accused by the children, and, being offended by something Mr. Parris said, went out of meeting; of course, also to prison. There were three other women involved with Tituba, in whose fetish experiments a well-informed writer thinks the Salem delusion began.[19] The examination before the Deputy-Governor (Danforth) began at Salem, April 11, 1692, and there are several notable points in it. Tituba's husband, the Indian John, cunningly escaped by pretending to be one of the afflicted. He charged Goody Proctor, and said, 'She brought the book to me.' No one asked what book! Abigail Williams, also one of the accusers of Goody, was asked, 'Does she bring the book to you? A. Yes. Q. What would she have you do with it? A. To write in it, and I shall be well.' Not a descriptive word is demanded or given concerning this book. The examiners are evidently well acquainted with it. In the alleged confessions preserved in official reports, but not in the words of the accused, the nature of the book is made clear. Thus Mary Osgood 'confesses that about eleven years ago, when she was in a melancholy state and condition, she used to walk abroad in her orchard, and, upon a certain time she saw the appearance of a cat at the end of the house, which yet she thought was a real cat. However, at that time it diverted her from praying to God, and instead thereof she prayed to the Devil; about which time she made a covenant with the Devil, who, as a black man, came to her, and presented her a book, upon which she laid her finger, and that left a red spot. And that upon her signing that book, the devil told her that he was her god.' This is not unlikely to be a paraphrase of some sermon on the infernal Book of Satan corresponding to the Book of Life, the theory being too conventional for the court to inquire about the mysterious volume. Equally well known was the Antichrist theory which had long represented that avatar of Satan as having organised a church. Thus we read:—'Abigail Williams, did you see a company at Mr. Parris's house eat and drink? A. Yes, sir; that was their sacrament. Q. What was it? A. They said it was our blood.' 'Mary Walcot, have you seen a white man? A. Yes, sir, a great many times. *Q.*What sort of man was he? *A.* A fine grave man, and when he came he made all the witches to tremble.' When it is remembered that Mary Osgood had described the Devil as 'a black man' (all were thinking of the Indians), this Antiblackman suggests Christ resisting Antichrist. Again, although nothing seems to have been said in the court previously about baptism, one of the examiners asks 'Goody Laccy how many years ago since they were baptized? *A.* Three or four years ago I suppose. *Q.* Who baptized them? *A.* The old serpent. *Q.* How did he do it? *A.*He dipped their heads in the water, saying they were his, and that he had power over them; ... there were six (who) baptized. *Q.* Name them. *A.*I think they were of the higher powers.'

There are interspersed through the proceedings suggestions of mercy on condition of confession, which, joined to these theoretical questions, render it plain that the retractations which the so-called witches made were true, and that in New England, at least, there was little if any basis for the delusion beyond the experiment of the two Spanish Indians. The terrible massacre of witches which occurred there was the result of the decision of English judges and divines that witchcraft is recognised in the Bible, and there assigned the death-penalty.

It will be observed here that ancient mythology to Salem is chiefly that of the Bible, modified by local conditions. White man and black man represent Christ and Antichrist, and we have the same symbols on both sides,—eucharists, baptisms, and names written in books. The survivals from European folklore met with in the New England trials are—the cat, the horse (rarely), and the dog. In one case a dog suffered from the repute of being a witch, insomuch that some who met him fell into fits; he was put to death. Riding through the air continues, but the American witches ride upon a stick or pole. The old-fashioned broom, the cloud-symbol of the Wild Huntsman, is rarely mentioned. One thing, however, survives from England, at least; the same sharp controversy that is reflected in the Fairfax case. Cotton Mather tried one of the possessed with the Bible, the 'Assembly's Catechism,' his grandfather's 'Milk for Babes,' his father's 'Remarkable Providence,' and a book to prove there were witches. 'And when any of those were offered for her to read in, she would be struck dead and fall into convulsions.' But when he tried her with Popish and Quaker books, the English Prayer-Book, and a book to prove there were no witches, the devil permitted her to read these as long as she pleased. One is at a loss which most to admire, the astuteness of the accused witch in bearing testimony to the Puritan religion, or the phenomenon of its eminent representative seeking a witness to it in the Father of lies.

If now we travel towards the East we find the survivals growing clearer, as in the West they become faint.

In 1669 the people of the villages of Mohra and Elfdale in Sweden, believing that they were troubled by witches, were visited by a royal commission, the result of whose investigations was the execution of twenty-three adults and fifteen children; running of the gauntlet by thirty-six between the ages of nine and sixteen years; the lashing on the hand of twenty children for three Sundays at the church-door, and similarlashing of the aforesaid thirty-six once a week for a year. Portions of the confessions of the witches are given below from the Public Register as translated by Anthony Horneck, D.D., and printed in London, anno 1700. I add a few words in brackets to point out survivals.

'We of the province of Elfdale do confess that we used to go to a gravel-pit which lay hard by a cross-way (Hecate), and there we put on a vest (Wolf-girdle) over our heads, and then danced round, and after this ran to the cross-way, and called the Devil thrice, first with a still voice, the second time somewhat louder, and the third time very loud, with these words—*Antecessor, come and carry us to Blockula.* Whereupon immediately he used to appear, but in different habits; but for the most part we saw him in a grey coat and red and blue stockings: he had a red beard (Barbarossa), a high-crowned hat (Turn-cap), with linen of divers colours wrapt about it, and long garters upon his stockings.

'Then he asked us whether we would serve him with soul and body. If we were content to do so, he set us upon a beast which he had there ready, and carried us over churches and high walls; and after all we came to a green meadow where Blockula lies. We must procure some scrapings of altars, and filings of church clocks; and then he gives us a horn with a salve in it, wherewith we do anoint ourselves (chrism); and a saddle with a hammer (Thor's), and a wooden nail, thereby to fix the saddle (Walkyr's); whereupon we call upon the Devil and away we go.'

'For their journey, they said they made use of all sorts of instruments, of beasts, of men, of spits, and posts, according as they had opportunity: if they do ride upon goats (Azazel) and have many children with them, that all may have room, they stick a spit into the backside of the Goat, and then are anointed with the aforesaid ointment. What the manner of their journey is, God only knows. Thus much was made out, that if the children did at any time name the names (Egyptian spells) of those that had carried them away, they were again carried by force either to Blockula, or to the cross-way, and there miserably beaten, insomuch that some of them died of it.'

'A little girl of Elfdale confessed that, naming the name of JESUS as she was carried away, she fell suddenly upon the ground, and got a great hole in her side, which the Devil presently healed up again, and away he carried her; and to this day the girl confessed she had exceeding great pain in her side.'

'They unanimously confessed that Blockula is situated in a delicate large meadow, whereof you can see no end. The place or house they met at had before it a gate painted with divers colours; through this gate they went into a little meadow distinct from the other, where the beasts went that they used to ride on; but the men whom they made use of in their journey stood in the house by the gate in a slumbering posture, sleeping against the wall (castle of Waldemar). In a huge large room of this house, they said, there stood a very long table, at which the witches did sit down; and that hard by this room was another chamber where there were very lovely and delicate beds. The first thing they must do at Blockula was, that they must deny all, and devote themselves body and soul to the Devil, and promise to serve him faithfully, and confirm all this with an oath (initiation). Hereupon they cut their fingers (Odinism), and with their blood write their name in his book (Revelations). They added that he caused them to be baptized, too, by such priests as he had there (Antichrist's Sacraments).'

'And he, the Devil, bids them believe that the day of judgment will come speedily, and therefore sets them on work to build a great house of stone (Babel), promising that in that house he will preserve them from God's fury, and cause them to enjoy the greatest delights and pleasures (Moslem). But while they work exceeding hard at it, there falls a great part of the wall down again.'

'They said, they had seen sometimes a very great Devil like a Dragon, with fire round about him, and bound with an iron chain (Apocalyptic), and the Devil that converses with them tells them that if they confess anything he will let that great Devil loose upon them, whereby all Sweedeland shall come into great danger.

'They added that the Devil had a church there, such another as in the town of Mohra. When the Commissioners were coming he told the Witches they should not fear them; for he would certainly kill them all. And they confessed that some of them had attempted to murther the Commissioners, but had not been able to effect it.

'Some of the children talked much of a white Angel (Frigga as christian tutelary), which used to forbid them what the Devil had bid them do, and told them that those doings should not last long. What had been done had been permitted because of the wickedness of the people.

'Those of Elfdale confessed that the Devil used to play upon an harp before them (Tannhauser), and afterwards to go with them that he liked best into a chamber, when he committed venerous acts with them (Asmodeus); and this indeed all confessed, that he had carnal knowledge of them, and that the Devil had sons and daughters by them, which he did marry together, and they ... brought forth toads and serpents (Echidna).

'After this they sat down to table, and those that the Devil esteemed most were placed nearest to him; but the children must stand at the door, where he himself gives them meat and drink (Sacrament). After meals they went to dancing, and in the meanwhile swore and cursed most dreadfully, and afterwards went to fighting one with another (Valhalla).

'They also confessed that the Devil gives them a beast about the bigness and shape of a young cat (Hecate), which they call a carrier; and that he gives them a bird as big as a raven (Odin's messenger), but white;[20] and these two creatures they can send anywhere, and wherever they come they take away all sorts of victuals they can get, butter, cheese, milk, bacon, and all sorts of seeds, whatever they find, and carry it to the witch. What the bird brings they may keep for themselves, but what the carrier brings they must reserve for the Devil, and that is brought to Blockula, where he doth give them of it so much as he thinks fit. They added likewise that these carriers fill themselves so full sometimes, that they are forced to spue ('Odin's booty') by the way, which spuing is found in several gardens, where colworts grow, and not far from the houses of these witches. It is of a yellow colour like gold, and is called butter of witches.

'The Lords Commissioners were indeed very earnest, and took great pains to persuade them to show some of their tricks, but to no purpose; for they did all unanimously confess that since they had confessed all, they found that all their witchcraft was gone, and that the Devil at this time appeared to them very terrible, with claws on his hands and feet, and with horns on his head, a long tail behind, and showed to them a pit burning, with a hand put out; but the Devil did thrust the person down again with an iron fork; and suggested to the witches that if they continued in their confession, he would deal with them in the same manner.'

The ministers of both Elfdale and Mohra were the chief inciters of this investigation, and both testified that they had suffered many tortures in the night from the witches. One was taken by the throat and so violently used that 'for some weeks he was not able to speak or perform divine service.'

We have in this narrative the official and clerical statement, and can never know to what the victims really confessed. Blockula seems to be a Swedish edition of Blocksberg, of old considered a great resort of witches. But we may especially note the epithet by which the witches are said to have first appealed to the Devil—*Antecessor*. Dr. Horneck has not given us the Swedish term of which this is a translation, but we may feel assured that it was not a phrase coined by the class among whom reputed witches were found. In all probability it was a learned phrase of the time for some supposed power which preceded and was conquered by Christianity; and if we knew its significance it might supply a clue to the reality with which the Commissioners were dealing. There would seem to be strong probabilities that in Sweden also, as elsewhere, there had been a revival of faith in the old religion whose barbaric rites had still survived in a few holes and corners where they were practised by night. The Antecessor was still present to hold out promises where the Successor had broken all that his sponsors had made when the populace accepted his baptism. This probability is further suggested by the fact that some of these uncanny events happened at Elfdale, a name which hints at a region of especial sanctity under the old religion, and also by the statement that the Devil had a church there, a sort of travesty of the village church. About the same time we find John Fiene confessing in Scotland that the Devil appeared to him in 'white raiment,' and it is also testified that John heard 'the Devil preach in a kirk in the pulpit in the night by candlelight, the candle burning blue.'[21]

The names used by the Scotch witches are often suggestive of pagan survivals. Thus in the trial at the Paisley Assizes, 1678, concerning the alleged bewitching of Sir George Maxwell, Margaret Jackson testified to giving up her soul by renouncing her baptism to a devil named Locas (Loki?); another raised a tempest to impede the king's voyage to Denmark by casting into the sea a cat, and crying Hola (Hela?); and Agnes Sampson called the Devil to her in the shape of a dog by saying, 'Elva (Elf?), come and speak to me!'

It is necessary to pass by many of the indications contained in the witch-trials that there had been an effort to recur to the pleasures and powers traditionally associated with the pagan era of Europe, and confirmed by the very denunciations of contemporary paganism with its pomp and luxury by the priesthood. The promises held out by the 'Devil' to Elfdale peasants and puritanised Helen Fairfax are unmistakable. But it is necessary to remark also that the ceremonies by which, as was clearly proved in various cases, the fortune-tellers or 'witches' endeavoured to imitate the spells of Dr. Faustus were archæological.

Around the cauldron, which was used in imitation of the Alchemists, a rude Zodiac was marked, some alchemic signs being added; and in the cauldron were placed ingredients concerning many of which the accounts are confused. It is, however, certain that the chief ingredients were plants which, precisely as in ancient Egypt, had been gathered at certain phases of the moon, or seasons of the year, or from some spot where the sun was supposed not to have shone on it. It was clearly proved also that the plants chiefly used by the sorceresses were rue and vervain. Vervain was sacred to the god of war in Greece and Rome, and made the badge of ambassadors sent to make treaties of peace. In Germany it was sacred to Thor, and he would not strike with his lightning a house protected by it. The Druids called it 'holy herb;' they gathered it when the dog-star rose, from unsunned spots, and compensated the earth for the deprivation with a sacrifice of honey. Its reputation was sufficient in Ben Jonson's day for him to write—

Bring your garlands, and with reverence place
The vervain on the altar.

The charm which vervain had for the mediæval peasant was that it was believed, if it had first touched a Bel-fire, to snap iron; and, if boiled with rue, made a liquid which, being poured on a gunflint, made the shot as sure to take effect as any Freischütz could desire.

Rue was supposed to have a potent effect on the eye, and to bestow second sight. So sacred was it once in England that missionaries sprinkled holy water from brushes made up of it, whence it was called 'herb of grace.' Milton represents Michael as purging Adam's eyes with it. In the Tyrol it is believed to confer fine vision and used with agrimony (flowers of Argos, the many-eyed); in Posen it is said also to heal serpent-bites. By this route it came into the cauldron of the wizard and witch. In Drayton's incantation it is said—

> Then sprinkles she the juice of rue,
> With nine drops of the midnight dew
> From lunary distilling.

This association of lunary, or moon-wort, once supposed to cure lunacy, with rue is in harmony with the mythology of both. An old oracle, said to have been revealed by Hecate herself, ran thus:—'From a root of wild rue fashion and polish a statue; adorn it with household lizards; grind myrrh, gum, and frankincense with the same reptiles, and let the mixture stand in the air during the waning of a moon; then address your vows in the following terms' (the formula is not preserved). 'As many forms as I have, so many lizards let there be; do these things exactly; you will build me an abode with branches of laurel, and having addressed fervent prayers to the image, you will see me in your sleep.'[22]

Rue was thus consecrated as the very substance of Hecate, the mother of all European witches. M. Maury supposes that it was because it was a narcotic and caused hallucinations. Hallucinations were, no doubt, the basis of belief in second sight. But whatever may be the cause, rue was the plant of witchcraft; and Bishop Taylor speaks of its being used by exorcists to try the devil, and thence deriving its appellation 'herb of grace.' More probably it was used to sprinkle holy water because of a traditional sanctity. All narcotics were supposed to be children of the night; and if, in addition, they were able to cause hallucinations, they were supposed to be under more especial care of the moon.

After reading a large number of reports concerning the ordeals and trials of witches, and also many of their alleged confessions, I have arrived at the conclusion that there were certainly gatherings held in secret places; that some of the ordinary ceremonies and prayers of the Church were used, with names of traditional deities and Oriental demons substituted for those of the Trinity and saints; that with these were mingled some observances which had been preserved from the ancient world by Gnostics, Astrologists, and Alchemists. That at these gatherings there was sometimes direct devil-worship is probable, but oftener the invocations were in other names, and it is for the most part due to the legal reporters that the 'Devil' is so often named. As to the 'confessions,' many, no doubt, admitted they had gone to witches' Sabbaths who had been there only in feverish dreams, as must have been the case of many young children and morbid pietists who were executed; others confessed in hope of escape from charges they could not answer; and others were weary of their lives.

The writer of this well remembers, in a small Virginian village (Falmouth), more than thirty years ago, the terrible persecutions to which an old white woman named Nancy Calamese was subjected because of her reputation as a witch. Rumours of lizards vomited by her poor neighbours caused her to be dreaded by the ignorant; the negroes were in terror of her; she hardly dared pass through the streets for fear of being hooted by boys. One morning she waded into the Rappahannock river and drowned herself, and many of her neighbours regarded the suicide as her confession. Probably it was a similar sort of confession to many that we read in the reports of witch trials.

The retribution that followed was more ferocious than could have visited mere attempts by the poor and ignorant to call up spirits to their aid. Every now and then the prosecutions disclose the well-known animus of heresy, persecution, and also the fury of magistrates suspicious of conspiracies. In England, New England, and France, particularly, an incipient rationalism was revealed in the party called 'Saducees,' who tried to cast discredit on the belief in witchcraft. This was recognised by Sir Mathew Hale in England and Cotton Mather in New England, consequently by the chief authorities of church and state in both countries, as an attack on biblical infallibility, since it was said in the Bible, 'Thou shalt not suffer a witch to live.' The leading wizards and witches were probably also persons who had been known in connection with the popular discontent and revolutionary feeling displayed in so many of the vindictive conjurations which were brought to light.

The horrors which attended the crushing out of this last revival of paganism are such as recall the Bartholomew massacre and the recent slaughter of Communists in Paris, so vividly that one can hardly repress the suspicion that the same sort of mingled panic and fanaticism were represented in them all. Dr. Réville has summed up the fearful history of three hundred years as follows:—'In the single year 1485, and in the district of Worms alone, eighty-five witches were delivered to the flames. At Geneva, at Basle, at Hamburg, at Ratisbon, at Vienna, and in a multitude of other towns, there were executions of the same kind. At Hamburg, among other victims, a physician was burnt alive, because he saved the life of a woman who had been given up by the midwife. In Italy, during the year 1523, there were burnt in the diocese of Como alone more than two hundred witches. This was after the new bull hurled at witchcraft by Pope Adrian VI. In Spain it was still worse; there, in 1527, two little girls, of from nine to eleven years of age, denounced a host of witches, whom they pretended to detect by a mark in their left eye. In England and Scotland political influence was brought to bear upon sorcery; Mary Stuart was animated by a lively zeal against witches. In France the Parliament of Paris happily removed business of this kind from the ecclesiastical tribunals; and under Louis XI., Charles VIII., and Louis XII. there were but few condemnations for the practice of magic; but from the time of Francis I., and especially from Henry II., the scourge reappeared. Jean Bodin, a man of sterling worth in other respects, but stark mad upon the question of witchcraft, communicated his mania to all classes of the nation. His contemporary and disciple, Boguet, showed how that France swarmed with witches and wizards. 'They increase and multiply on the land,' said he, 'even as do the caterpillars in our gardens. Would that they were all got together in a heap, so that a single fire might burn them all at once.' Savoy, Flanders, the Jura Mountains, Lorraine, Béarn, Provence, and in almost all parts of France, the frightful hecatombs were seen ablaze. In the seventeenth century the witch-fever somewhat abated, though it burst out here and there, centralising itself chiefly in the convents of hysterical nuns. The terrible histories of the priests Gaufridy and Urban Grandier are well known. In Germany, and particularly in its southern parts, witch-burning was still more frequent. In one small principality at least 242 persons were burnt between 1646 and 1651; and, *horribile dictu*, in the official records of these executions, we find that among those who suffered were children from one to six years of age! In 1657 the witch-judge, Nicholas Remy, boasted of having burnt 900 persons in fifteen years. It would even seem that it is to the proceedings against sorcery that Germany owes the introduction of torture as an ordinary mode of getting at the truth. Mr. Roskoff reproduces a catalogue of the executions of witches and wizards in the episcopal town of Würzburg, in Bavaria, up to the year 1629. In 1659 the number of those put to death for witchcraft amounted, in this diocese, to 900. In the neighbouring bishopric of Bamberg at least 600 were burnt. He enumerates thirty-one executions in all, not counting some regarded by the compilers of the catalogue as not important enough to mention. The number of victims at each execution varies from two to seven. Many are distinguished by such surnames as 'The Big Hunchback, The Sweetheart, The Bridge-keeper, The Old Pork-woman,' &c. Among them appear people of all sorts and conditions, actors, workmen, jugglers, town and village maidens, rich burghers, nobles, students, magistrates even, and a fair number of priests. Many are simply entered as 'a foreigner.' Here and there is added to the name of the condemned person his age and a short notice. Among the victims, for instance, of the twentieth execution figures 'Little Barbara, the prettiest girl in Würzburg;' 'a student who could speak all manner of languages, who was an excellent musician, *vocaliter et instrumentaliter;*' 'the master of the hospice, a very learned man.' We find, too, in this, gloomy account the cruel record of children burnt for witchcraft; here a little girl of about nine or ten years of age, with her baby sister, younger than herself (their mother was burnt a little while afterwards); here boys of ten or eleven; again, a young girl of fifteen; two children from the poorhouse; the little boy of a councillor. The pen falls from one's hand in recapitulating such monstrosities. Cannot those who would endow Catholicity with the dogma of papal infallibility hearken, before giving their vote, to the cries that rise before God, and which history re-echoes, of those poor innocent ones whom pontifical bulls threw into flames? The seventeenth century saw the rapid diminution of trials and tortures. In one of his good moments, Louis XIV. mitigated greatly the severity of this special legislation. For this he had to undergo the remonstrances of the Parliament of Rouen, which believed society would be ruined if those who dealt in sorcery were merely condemned to perpetual confinement. The truth is, that belief in witchcraft was so wide-spread, that from time to time even throughout the seventeenth century there were isolated executions. One of the latest and most notorious was that of Renata Saenger, superior of the convent of Unterzell, near Würzburg (1748). At Landshut, in Bavaria, in 1756, a young girl of thirteen years was convicted of impure intercourse with the Devil, and put to death. Seville in 1781, and Glaris in 1783, saw the last two known victims to this fatal superstition.'[23]

The Reformation swept away in Northern countries, for the upper classes, as many Christian saints and angels as priestcraft had previously turned to enemies for the lower. The poor and ignorant simply tried to evoke the same ideal spirit-guardians under the pagan forms legendarily associated with a golden age. Witchcraft was a pathetic appeal against a cruel present to a fair, however visionary, past. But Protestantism has brought on famine of another kind—famine of the heart. The saints of the Church have followed those of paganism; and although one result of the process has been a vast increase in enterprise, science, and wealth, man cannot live by these alone. Modern spiritualism, which so many treat with a superciliousness little creditable to a scientific age, is a cry of starved sentiment and affections left hopeless under faded heavens, as full of pathetic meaning as that which was wrung from serfs enticed into temples only to find them dens of thieves. Desolate hearts take up the burthen of desolate homes, and appeal to invisible powers for guidance; and for attestation of hopes which science has blighted, ere poetry, art, and philanthropy have changed these ashes into beauty. Because these so-called spirits, evoked by mediums out of morbid nerves, are really longed-for ideals, the darker features of witchcraft are not called about them. That fearful movement was a wronged Medea whose sorrows had made Hecate—to remember the dreadful phrase of Euripides—'the chosen assistant dwelling in the inmost recesses of her house.' Modern spiritualism is Rachel weeping for her children, not to be comforted if they are not. But the madness of the one is to be understood by the plaintive appeal of the other.

## NOTES

1 S. Cyp. ap. Muratori, Script. it. i. 295, 545. The Magicians used to call their mirrors after the name of this flower-devil—Fiorone. M. Maury, 'La Magie,' 435 n.

2 This whole subject is treated, and with ample references, in M. Maury's 'Magie,' p. 41, seq.

3 'La Sorcière.'

4 Dasent's 'Norse Tales,' Introd. ciii.

5 'Chips,' ii.

6 'Chester Plays,' 1600.

7 'Declaration of Popish Impostures,' 1603.

8 So Shakespere, 'The Devil damn thee black.'

9 In an account, 1568, we find:—'pay'd for iij li of heare ijs vjd.'

10 The Directions for the 'Castle of Good Perseverance,' say: '& he þt schal pley belyal, loke þt he have guñe powdr breññg in pypysīh's hands & ī h's ers & ī h's ars whãne he gothe to batayle.'

11 This notion was widespread. I have seen an ancient Russian picture in which the Devil is dancing before a priest who has become drowsy over his prayer-book. There was once a Moslem controversy as to whether it was fair for pilgrims to keep themselves awake for their prayers by chewing coffee-berries.

12 'Liber Revelationum de Insidiis et Versutiis Dæmonum adversus Homines.' See Reville's Review of Roskoff, 'The Devil,' p. 38.

13 See M. Maury's 'Magie,' p. 48.

14 The history has been well related by a little work by Dr. Albert Réville: 'Apollonius of Tyana, the Pagan Christ.' Chatto & Windus.

15 Sinistrari names Luther as one of eleven persons whom he enumerates as having been begotten by Incubi, 'Enfin, comme l'ecrit Codens, cité par Maluenda, ce damné Héré-siarque, qui a nom Martin Luther.'—'Démonialité,' 30.

16 Glanvil's 'Saducismus.'

17 King Lear, iii. 4. Asmodeus and Mohammed are, no doubt, corrupted in these names, which are given as those of devils in Harsenet's 'Declaration of Popish Impostures.'

18' A Discourse of Witchcraft. As it was acted in the Family of Mr. Edward Fairfax, of Fuystone, in the county of York, in the year 1621. Sibi parat malum, qui alteri parat.'

19 W. F. Poole, Librarian of Chicago, to whom I am indebted for a copy of Governor Thomas Hutchinson's account of 'The Witchcraft Delusion of 1692,' with his valuable notes on the same.

20 The delicacy with which these animals are alluded to rather than directly named indicates that they had not lost their formidable character in Elfdale so far as to be spoken of rashly.

21 Glanvil, 'Saducismus Triumphatus,' p. 170.

22 Porphyry, ap. Euseb. v. 12. The formula not preserved by Eusebius is supposed by M. Maury ('Magie,' 56) to be that contained in the 'Philosophumena,' attributed to Origen:—'Come, infernal, terrestrial, and celestial Bombo! goddess of highways, of cross-roads, thou who bearest the light, who travellest the night, enemy of the day, friend and companion of darkness; thou rejoicing in the baying of dogs and in shed blood, who wanderest amid shadows and over tombs; thou who desirest blood and bearest terrors to mortals,—Gorgo, Mormo, moon of a thousand forms, aid with a propitious eye our sacrifices!'

23 'The Devil,' &c., p. 51.

# Chapter XXV
## Faust and Mephistopheles

Mephisto and Mephitis — The Raven Book — Papal sorcery — Magic seals —
Mephistopheles as dog — George Sabellicus *alias* Faustus — The Faust myth —
Marlowe's Faust — Good and evil angels — El Magico Prodigioso — Cyprian and
Justina — Klinger's Faust — Satan's sermon — Goethe's Mephistopheles —
His German characters — Moral scepticism — Devil's gifts — Helena —
Redemption through Art — Defeat of Mephistopheles

**THE NAME MEPHISTOPHELES** has in it, I think, the priest's shudder at the fumes of the laboratory. Duntzer [1] finds that the original
form of the word was 'Mephostophiles,' and conjectures that it was
a bungling effort to put together three Greek words, to mean 'not
loving the light.' In this he has the support of Bayard Taylor, who also
thinks that it was so understood by Goethe. The transformation of
it was probably amid the dreaded gases with which the primitive
chemist surrounded himself. He who began by 'not loving the light'
became the familiar of men seeking light, and lover of their mephitic
gases. The ancient Romans had a mysterious divinity called Mephitis,
whose grove and temple were in the Esquiliæ, near a place it was
thought fatal to enter. She is thought to have been invoked against
the mephitic exhalations of the earth in the grove of Albunea. Sulphur
springs also were of old regarded as ebullitions from hell, and both
Schwarz and Roger Bacon particularly dealt in that kind of smell.
Considering how largely Asmodeus, as 'fine gentleman,' entered into
the composition of Mephistopheles, and how he flew from Nineveh
to Egypt (Tobit) to avoid a bad smell, it seems the irony of mythology

that he should turn up in Europe as a mephitic spirit.

Mephistopheles is the embodiment of all that has been said in preceding chapters of the ascetic's horror of nature and the pride of life, and of the mediæval priest's curse on all learning he could not monopolise. The Faust myth is merely his shadow cast on the earth, the tracery of his terrible power as the Church would have the people dread it. The early Raven Book at Dresden has the title:—' † † † D. J. Fausti † † † Dreifacher Höllen-Zwung und Magische (Geister-Commando) nebst den schwarzen Raaben. Romæ ad Arcanum Pontificatus unter Papst Alexander VI. gedruckt. Anno (Christi) MDI.' In proof of which claim there is a Preface purporting to be a proclamation signed by the said Pope and Cardinal Piccolomini concerning the secrets which the celebrated Dr. Faust had scattered throughout Germany, commanding *ut ad Arcanum Pontificatus mandentur et sicut pupilla oculi in archivio Nostro serventur et custodiantur, atque extra Valvas Vaticanas non imprimantur neque inde transportentur. Si vero quiscunque temere contra agere ausus fuerit,* DIVINAM *maledictionem latæ sententiæ ipso facto servatis Nobis Solis reservandis se incursurum sciat. Ita mandamus et constituemus Virtute Apostolicæ Ecclesiæ* JESU CHRISTI *sub pœna Excommunicationis ut supra. Anno secundo Vicariatus Nostri. Romæ Verbi incarnati Anno M.D.I.*

This is an impudent forgery, but it is an invention which, more than anything actually issued from Rome, indicates the popular understanding that the contention of the Church was not against the validity of magic arts, but against their exercise by persons not authorised by itself. It was, indeed, a tradition not combated by the priests, that various ecclesiastics had possessed such powers, even

Popes, as John XXII., Gregory VII., and Clement V. The first Sylvester was said to have a dragon at his command; John XXII. denounced his physicians and courtiers for necromancy; and the whispers connecting the Vatican with sorcery lasted long enough to attribute to the late Pius IX. a power of the evil eye. Such awful potencies the Church wished to be ascribed to itself alone. Faust is a legend invented to impress on the popular mind the fate of all who sought knowledge in unauthorised ways and for non-ecclesiastical ends.

In the Raven Book just mentioned, there are provisions for calling up spirits which, in their blending of christian with pagan formulas, oddly resemble the solemn proceedings sometimes affected by our spiritual mediums. The magician (*Magister*) had best be alone, but if others are present, their number must be odd; he should deliberate beforehand what business he wishes to transact with the spirits; he must observe God's commandment; trust the Almighty's help; continue his conjuration, though the spirits do not appear quickly, with unwavering faith; mark a circle on parchment with a dove's blood; within this circle write in Latin the names of the four quarters of heaven; write around it the Hebrew letters of God's name, and beneath it write *Sadan*; and standing in this circle he must repeat the ninety-first Psalm. In addition there are seals in red and black, various Hebrew, Greek, and Latin words, chiefly such as contain the letters Q, W, X, Y, Z,—*e.g.*, Yschyros, Theos, Zebaoth, Adonay. The specimen (Fig. 22), which I copied from the book in Dresden, is there called 'Sigillum Telschunhab.' The 'Black Raven' is pictured in the book, and explained as the form in which the angel Raphael taught Tobias to summon spirits. It is said also that the Magician must in certain cases write with blood of a fish (Tobit again) or bat on 'maiden-parchment,'—this being explained as the skin of a goat, but unpleasantly suggestive of a different origin.

*Fig. 22.—Seal from Raven Book*

In this book, poorly printed, and apparently on a private press, Mephistopheles is mentioned as one of the chief Princes of Hell. He is described as a youth, adept in all arts and services, who brings spirit-servants or familiars, and brings treasures from earth and sea with speed. In the Frankfort Faust Book (1587), Mephistopheles says, 'I am a spirit, and a flying spirit, potently ruling under the heavens.' In the oldest legends he appears as a dog, that, as we have seen, being the normal form of tutelary divinities, the symbol of the Scribe in Egypt, guard of Hades, and psychopomp of various mythologies. A dog appears following the family of Tobias. Manlius reports Melancthon as saying, 'He (Faust) had a dog with him, which was the Devil.' Johann Gast ('Sermones Conviviales') says he was present at a dinner at Basle given by Faust, and adds: 'He had also a dog and a horse with him, both of which, I believe, were devils, for they were able to do everything. Some persons told me that the dog frequently took the shape of a servant, and brought him food.' In the old legends this dog is named *Praestigiar*.[2]

As for the man Faust, he seems to have been personally the very figure which the Church required, and had the friar, in whose guise Mephistopheles appears, been his actual familiar, he could hardly have done more to bring learning into disgrace. Born at the latter part of the fifteenth century at Knittlingen, Wurtemberg, of poor parents, the bequest of an uncle enabled him to study medicine at Cracow University, and it seems plain that he devoted his learning and abilities to the work of deluding the public. That he made money by his 'mediumship,' one can only infer from the activity with which he went about Germany and advertised his 'powers.' It was at a time when high prices were paid for charms, philtres, mandrake mannikins; and the witchcraft excitement was not yet advanced enough to render dealing in such things perilous. It seems that the Catholic clergy made haste to use this impostor to point their moral against learning, and to identify him as first-fruit of the Reformation; while the Reformers, with equal zeal, hurled him back upon the papists as outcome of their idolatries. Melancthon calls him 'an abominable beast, a sewer of many devils.' The first mention of him is by Trithemius in a letter of August 20, 1507, who speaks of him as 'a pretender to magic' ('Magister Georgius Sabellicus, Faustus Junior'), whom he met at Gelnhaussen; and in another letter of the same year as at Kreuznach, Conrad Mudt, friend of Luther and Melancthon, mentions (Oct. 3, 1513) the visit to Erfurth of Georgius Faustus Hemitheus Hedebeyensis, 'a braggart and a fool who affects magic,' whom he had 'heard talking in a tavern,' and who had 'raised theologians against him.' In Vogel's Annals of Leipzig (1714), kept in Auerbach's Cellar, is recorded under date 1525 Dr. Johann Faust's visit to the Cellar. He appears therefore to have already had *aliases*. The first clear account of him is in the 'Index Sanitatis' of Dr. Philip Begardi (1539), who says: 'Since several years he has gone through all regions, provinces, and kingdoms, made his name known to everybody, and is highly renowned for his great skill, not alone in medicine, but also in chiromancy, necromancy, physiognomy, visions in crystal, and the like other arts. And also not only renowned, but written down and known as an experienced master. Himself admitted, nor denied that it was so, and that his name was Faustus, and called himself *philosophum philosophorum*. But how many have complained to me that they were deceived by him—verily a great number! But what matter?—*hin ist hin.*'

These latter words may mean that Faust had just died. He must have died about that time, and with little notice. The rapidity with which a mythology began to grow around him is worthy of more attention than the subject has received. In 1543 the protestant theologian Johann Gast has ('Sermones Convivialium') stories of his diabolical dog and horse, and of the Devil's taking him off, when his body turns itself five times face downward. In 1587 Philip Camerarius speaks of him as 'a well-known magician who lived in the time of our fathers.' April 18, 1587, two students of the University of Tübingen were imprisoned for writing a Comedy of Dr. Faustus: though it was not permitted to make light of the story, it was thought a very proper one to utilise for pious purposes, and in the autumn of the same year (1587) the original form of the legend was published by Spiess in Frankfort. It describes Faust as summoning the Devil at night, in a forest near Wittenberg. The evil spirit visits him on three occasions in his study, where on the third he gives his name as 'Mephosto-philes,' and the compact to serve him for twenty-four years for his soul is signed. When Faust pierces his hand, the blood flows into the form of the words *O homo fuge!* Mephistopheles first serves him as a monk, and brings him fine garments, wine, and food. Many of the luxuries are brought from the mansions of prelates, which shows the protestant bias of the book; which is also shown in the objection the Devil makes to Faust's marrying, because marriage is pleasing to God. Mephistopheles changes himself to a winged horse, on which Faust is borne through many countries, arriving at last at Rome. Faust passes three days, invisible, in the Vatican, which supplies the au-thor with another opportunity to display papal luxury, as well as the impotence of the Pope and his cardinals to exorcise the evil powers which take their food and goblets when they are about to feast. On his further aerial voyages Faust gets a glimpse of the garden of Eden; lives in state in the Sultan's palace in the form of Mohammed; and at length becomes a favourite in the Court of Charles V. at Innsbruck. Here he evokes Alexander the Great and his wife. In roaming about Germany, Faust diverts himself by swallowing a load of hay and horses, cutting off heads and replacing them, making flowers bloom at Christmas, drawing wine from a table, and calling Helen of Troy to appear to some students. Helen becomes his mistress; by her he has a son, Justus Faustus; but these disappear simultaneously with the dreadful end of Dr. Faustus, who after a midnight storm is found only in the fragments with which his room is strewn.

Several of these legends are modifications of those current

before Faust's time. The book had such an immense success that new volumes and versions on the same subject appeared not only in Germany but in other parts of Europe,—a rhymed version in England, 1588; a translation from the German in France, 1589; a Dutch translation, 1592; Christopher Marlowe's drama in 1604.

In Marlowe's 'Tragical History of Doctor Faustus,' the mass of legends of occult arts that had crystallised around a man thoroughly representative of them was treated with the dignity due to a subject amid whose moral and historic grandeur Faust is no longer the petty personality he really was. He is precisely the character which the Church had been creating for a thousand years, only suddenly changed from other-worldly to worldly desires and aims. What he seeks is what all the energy of civilisation seeks.

> EVIL ANGEL. Go forward, Faustus, in that famous art
> Wherein all Nature's treasure is contained:
> Be thou on earth as Jove is in the sky,
> Lord and commander of these elements.
>
> FAUST. How am I glutted with conceit of this!
> Shall I make spirits fetch me what I please,
> Resolve me of all ambiguities,
> Perform what desperate enterprise I will?
> I'll have them fly to India for gold,
> Ransack the ocean for orient pearl,
> And search all corners of the new-found world
> For pleasant fruits and princely delicates;
> I'll have them read me strange philosophy,
> And tell the secrets of all foreign kings;
> I'll have them wall all Germany with brass,
> And make swift Rhine circle fair Wertenberg;
> I'll have them fill the public schools with silk,
> Wherewith the students shall be bravely clad.

For this he is willing to pay his soul, which Theology has so long declared to be the price of mastering the world.

> This word damnation terrifies not him,
> For he confounds hell in Elysium:
> His ghost be with the old philosophers!

The 'Good Angel' warns him:

> O Faustus, lay that damned book aside,
> And gaze not on it, lest it tempt thy soul,
> And heap God's heavy wrath upon thy head!
> Read, read the Scriptures:—that is blasphemy.

So, dying away amid the thunders of the Reformation, were heard the echoes of the early christian voices which exulted in the eternal tortures of the Greek poets and philosophers: the anathemas on Roger Bacon, Socinus, Galileo; the outcries with which every great invention has been met. We need only retouch the above extracts here and there to make Faust's aspirations those of a saint. Let the gold be sought in New Jerusalem, the pearl in its gates, the fruits in paradise, the philosophy that of Athanasius, and no amount of selfish hunger and thirst for them would grieve any 'Good Angel' he had ever heard of.

The 'Good Angel' has not yet gained his wings who will tell him that all he seeks is included in the task of humanity, but warn him that the method by which he would gain it is just that by which he has been instructed to seek gold and jasper of the New Jerusalem,— not by fulfilling the conditions of them, but as the object of some favouritism. Every human being who ever sought to obtain benefit by prayers or praises that might win the good graces of a supposed bestower of benefits, instead of by working for them, is but the Faust of his side—be it supernal or infernal. Hocus-pocus and invocation, blood-compacts and sacraments,—they are all the same in origin; they are all mean attempts to obtain advantages beyond other people without serving up to them or deserving them. To Beelzebub Faust will 'build an altar and a church;' but he had probably never entered a church or knelt before an altar with any less selfishness.

A strong Nemesis follows Self to see that its bounds are not overpassed without retribution. Its satisfactions must be weighed in the balance with its renunciations. And the inflexible law applies to intellect and self-culture as much as to any other power of man. Mephistopheles is 'the kernel of the brute;' he is the intellect with mere canine hunger for knowledge because of the power it brings. Or, falling on another part of human nature, it is pride making itself abject for ostentation; or it is passion selling love for lust. *Re-enter Mephistopheles with Devils, who give crowns and rich apparel to Faustus, dance, and then depart.* To the man who has received his intellectual and moral liberty only to so spend it, Lucifer may well say, in Marlowe's words—

> Christ cannot save thy soul, for he is just:
> There's none but I have interest in the same.

Perhaps he might even better have suggested to Faust that his soul was not of sufficient significance to warrant much anxiety.

Something was gained when it was brought before the people in popular dramas of Faust how little the Devil cared for the cross which had so long been regarded as the all-sufficient weapon against him.[3] Faust and Mephistopheles flourish in the Vatican despite all the crosses raised to exorcise them. The confession of the cross which once meant martyrdom of the confessor had now come to mean martyrdom of the denier. Protestantism put its faith in Theology, Creeds, and Orthodoxy. But Calderon de la Barca blended the legend of Faust with the legendary temptation of St. Cyprian, and in 'El Magico Prodigioso' we have, in impressive contrast, the powerlessness of the evil powers over the heart of a pure woman, and its easy entrance into a mind fully furnished with the soundest sentiments of theology. St. Cyprian had been a worshipper of pagan deities [4] before his conversion, and even after this he had once saved himself while other christians were suffering martyrdom. It is possible that out of this may have grown the legend of his having called his earlier deities—theoretically changed to devils—to his aid; a trace of the legend being that magical 'Book of Cyprianus' mentioned in another chapter. In his tract 'De Gratia Dei' Cyprian says concerning his spiritual condition before conversion, 'I lay in darkness, and floating on the world's boisterous sea, with no resting-place for my feet, ignorant of my proper life, and estranged from truth and light.' Here is a metaphorical 'vasty deep' from which the centuries could hardly fail to conjure up spirits, one of them being the devil of Calderon's drama, who from a wrecked ship walks Christ-like over the boisterous sea to find Cyprian on the sea-shore. The drama opens with a scene which recalls the most perilous of St. Anthony's temptations. According to Athanasius, the Devil having utterly failed to conquer Anthony's virtue by charming images, came to him in his proper black and ugly shape, and, candidly confessing that he was the Devil, said he had been vanquished by the saint's extraordinary sanctity. Anthony prevailed against the spirit of pride thus awakened; but Calderon's Cyprian, though he does not similarly recognise the Devil, becomes complacent at the dialectical victory which the tempter concedes him. Cyprian having argued the existence and supremacy of God, the Devil says, 'How can I impugn so clear a consequence?' 'Do you regret my victory?' 'Who but regrets a check in rivalry of wit?' He leaves, and Cyprian says, 'I never met a more learned person.' The Devil is equally satisfied, knowing, no doubt, that gods worked out by the wits alone remain in their abode of abstraction and do not interfere with the world of sense. Calderon is artful enough to throw the trial of Cyprian back into his pagan period, but the mirror is no less true in reflecting for those who had eyes to see in it the weakness of theology.

'Enter the Devil as a fine gentleman,' is the first sign of the temptation in Calderon's drama—it is Asmodeus [5] again, and the 'pride of life' he first brings is the conceit of a clever theological victory. So sufficient is the doorway so made for all other pride to enter, that next time the devil needs no disguise, but has only to offer him a painless victory over nature and the world, including Justina, the object of his passion.

> Wouldst thou that I work
> A charm over this waste and savage wood,
> This Babylon of crags and aged trees,
> Filling its coverts with a horror
> Thrilling and strange?...
> I offer thee the fruit
> Of years of toil in recompense; whate'er
> Thy wildest dream presented to thy thought
> As object of desire, shall be thine. [6]

Justina knows less about the philosophical god of Cyprian, and more of the might of a chaste heart. To the Devil she says—

Thought is not in my power, but action is:
I will not move my foot to follow thee.

The Devil is compelled to say at last—

Woman, thou hast subdued me,
Only by not owning thyself subdued.

He is only able to bring a counterfeit of Justina to her lover.

Like Goethe's Mephistopheles, Cyprian's devil is unable to perform his exact engagements, and consequently does not win in the game. He enables Cyprian to move mountains and conquer beasts, until he boasts that he can excel his infernal teacher, but the Devil cannot bring Justina. She has told Cyprian that she will love him in death. Cyprian and she together abjure their paganism at Antioch, and meet in a cell just before their martyrdom. Over their bodies lying dead on the scaffold the Devil appears as a winged serpent, and says he is compelled to announce that they have both ascended to heaven. He descends into the earth.

What the story of Faust and Mephistopheles had become in the popular mind of Germany, when Goethe was raising it to be an immortal type of the conditions under which genius and art can alone fulfil their task, is well shown in the sensational tragedy written by his contemporary, the playwright Klinger. The following extract from Klinger's 'Faust' is not without a certain impressiveness.

'Night covered the earth with its raven wing. Faust stood before the awful spectacle of the body of his son suspended upon the gallows. Madness parched his brain, and he exclaimed in the wild tones of dispair:

'Satan, let me but bury this unfortunate being, and then you may take this life of mine, and I will descend into your infernal abode, where I shall no more behold men in the flesh. I have learned to know them, and I am disgusted with them, with their destiny, with the world, and with life. My good action has drawn down unutterable woe upon my head; I hope that my evil ones may have been productive of good. Thus should it be in the mad confusion of earth. Take me hence; I wish to become an inhabitant of thy dreary abode; I am tired of light, compared with which the darkness in the infernal regions must be the brightness of mid-day.'

But Satan replied: 'Hold! not so fast—Faust; once I told thee that thou alone shouldst be the arbiter of thy life, that thou alone shouldst have power to break the hour-glass of thy existence; thou hast done so, and the hour of my vengeance has come, the hour for which I have sighed so long. Here now do I tear from thee thy mighty wizard-wand, and chain thee within the narrow bounds which I draw around thee. Here shalt thou stand and listen to me, and tremble; I will draw forth the terrors of the dark past, and kill thee with slow despair.

'Thus will I exult over thee, and rejoice in my victory. Fool! thou hast said that thou hast learned to know man! Where? How and when? Hast thou ever considered his nature? Hast thou ever examined it, and separated from it its foreign elements? Hast thou distinguished between that which is offspring of the pure impulses of his heart, and that which flows from an imagination corrupted by art? Hast thou compared the wants and the vices of his nature with those which he owes to society and prevailing corruption? Hast thou observed him in his natural state, where each of his undisguised expressions mirrors forth his inmost soul? No—thou hast looked upon the mask that society wears, and hast mistaken it for the true lineaments of man; thou hast only become acquainted with men who have consecrated their condition, wealth, power, and talents to the service of corruption; who have sacrificed their pure nature to your Idol—Illusion. Thou didst at one time presume to show me the moral worth of man! and how didst thou set about it! By leading me upon the broad highways of vice, by bringing me to the courts of the mighty wholesale butchers of men, to that of the coward tyrant of France, of the Usurper in England! Why did we pass by the mansions of the good and the just? Was it for me, Satan, to whom thou hast chosen to become a mentor, to point them out to thee? No; thou wert led to the places thou didst haunt by the fame of princes, by thy pride, by thy longing after dissipation. And what hast thou seen there? The soul-seared tyrants of mankind, with their satellites, wicked women and mercenary priests, who make religion a tool by which to gain the object of their base passions.

'Hast thou ever deigned to cast a glance at the oppressed, who, sighing under his burden, consoles himself with the hope of an hereafter? Hast thou ever sought for the dwelling of the virtuous friend of humanity, for that of the noble sage, for that of the active and upright father of a family?

'But how would that have been possible? How couldst thou, the most corrupt of thy race, have discovered the pure one, since thou hadst not even the capacity to suspect his existence?

'Proudly didst thou pass by the cottages of the pure and humble, who live unacquainted with even the names of your artificial vices, who earn their bread in the sweat of their brow, and who rejoice at their last hour that they are permitted to exchange the mortal for the immortal. It is true, hadst thou entered their abode, thou mightst not have found thy foolish ideal of an heroic, extravagant virtue, which is only the fanciful creation of your vices and your pride; but thou wouldst have seen the man of a retiring modesty and noble resignation, who in his obscurity excels in virtue and true grandeur of soul your boasted heroes of field and cabinet. Thou sayest that thou knowest man! Dost thou know thyself? Nay, deeper yet will I enter into the secret places of thy heart, and fan with fierce blast the flames which thou hast kindled there for thee.

'Had I a thousand human tongues, and as many years to speak to thee, they would be all insufficient to develop the consequences of thy deeds and thy recklessness. The germ of wretchedness which thou hast sown will continue its growth through centuries yet to come; and future generations will curse thee as the author of their misery.

'Behold, then, daring and reckless man, the importance of actions that appear circumscribed to your mole vision! Who of you can say, Time will obliterate the trace of my existence! Thou who knowest not what beginning, what middle, and end are, hast dared to seize with a bold hand the chain of fate, and hast attempted to gnaw its links, notwithstanding that they were forged for eternity!

'But now will I withdraw the veil from before thy eyes, and

then—cast the spectre despair into thy soul.'

'Faust pressed his hands upon his face; the worm that never dieth gnawed already on his heart.'

The essence and sum of every devil are in the Mephistopheles of Goethe. He is culture.

> Culture, which smooth the whole world licks,
> Also unto the Devil sticks.

He represents the intelligence which has learned the difference between ideas and words, knows that two and two make four, and also how convenient may be the dexterity that can neatly write them out five.

> Of Metaphysics learn the use and beauty!
> See that you most profoundly gain
> What does not suit the human brain!
> A splendid word to serve, you'll find
> For what goes in—or won't go in—your mind.
>
> On words let your attention centre!
> Then through the safest gate you'll enter
> The temple halls of certainty.[7]

He knows, too, that the existing moment alone is of any advantage; that theory is grey and life ever green; that he only gathers real fruit who confides in himself. He is thus the perfectly evolved intellect of man, fully in possession of all its implements, these polished till they shine in all grace, subtlety, adequacy. Nature shows no symbol of such power more complete than the gemmed serpent with its exquisite adaptations,—freed from cumbersome prosaic feet, equal to the winged by its flexible spine, every tooth artistic.

From an ancient prison was this Ariel liberated by his Prospero, whose wand was the Reformation, a spirit finely touched to fine issues. But his wings cannot fly beyond the atmosphere. The ancient heaven has faded before the clearer eye, but the starry ideals have come nearer. The old hells have burnt out, but the animalism of man couches all the more freely on his path, having broken every chain of fear. Man still walks between the good and evil, on the hair-drawn bridge of his moral nature. His faculties seem adapted with equal precision to either side of his life, upper or under,—to Wisdom or Cunning, Self-respect or Self-conceit, Prudence or Selfishness, Lust or Love.

Such is the seeming situation, but is it the reality? Goethe's 'Faust' is the one clear answer which this question has received.

In one sense Mephistopheles may be called a German devil. The Christian soul of Germany was from the first a changeling. The ancient Nature-worship of that race might have had its normal de-velopment in the sciences, and alone with this intellectual evolution there must have been formed a related religion able to preserve so-cial order through the honour of man. But the native soul of Germany was cut out by the sword and replaced with a mongrel Hebrew-Latin soul. The metaphorical terrors of tropical countries,—the deadly worms, the burning and suffocating blasts and stenches, with which the mind of those dwelling near them could familiarise itself when met with in their scriptures, acquired exaggerated horrors when left to be pictured by the terrorised imagination of races ignorant of their origin. It is a long distance from Potsdam and Hyde Park to Zahara. Christianity therefore blighted nature in the north by apparitions more fearful than the southern world ever knew, and long after the pious there could sing and dance, puritanical glooms hung over the Christians of higher latitudes. When the progress of German culture began the work of dissipating these idle terrors, the severity of the reaction was proportioned to the intensity of the delusions. The long-famished faculties rushed almost madly into their beautiful world, but without the old reverence which had once knelt before its phenomena. That may remain with a few, but the cynicism of the noisiest will be reflected even upon the faces of the best. Goethe first had his attention drawn to Spinoza by a portrait of him on a tract, in which his really noble countenance was represented with a diabolical aspect. The orthodox had made it, but they could only have done so by the careers of Faust, Paracelsus, and their tribe. These too helped to conventionalise Voltaire into a Mephistopheles.[8]

Goethe was probably the first European man to carry out this scepticism to its full results. He was the first who recognised that the moral edifice based upon monastic theories must follow them; and he had in his own life already questioned the right of the so-called morality to its supreme if not tyrannous authority over man. Hereditary conscience, passing through this fierce crucible, lay levigable before Goethe, to be swept away into dust-hole or moulded into the image of reason. There remained around the animal nature of a free man only a thread which seemed as fine as that which held the monster Fenris. It was made only of the sentiment of love and that of honour. But as Fenris found the soft invisible thread stronger than chains, Faust proved the tremendous sanctions that surround the finer instincts of man.

Emancipated from grey theory, Faust rushes hungrily at the

golden fruit of life. The starved passions will have their satisfaction, at whatever cost to poor Gretchen. The fruit turns to ashes on his lips. The pleasure is not that of the thinking man, but of the accomplished poodle he has taken for his guide. To no moment in that intrigue can the suffrage of his whole nature say, 'Stay, thou art fair!' That is the pact—it is the distinctive keynote of Goethe's 'Faust.'

> Canst thou by falsehood or by flattery
> Make me one moment with myself at peace,
> Cheat me into tranquillity?—come then
> And welcome life's last day.
> Make me to the passing moment plead.
> Fly not, O stay, thou art so fair!
> Then will I gladly perish.

The pomp and power of the court, luxury and wealth, equally fail to make the scholar at peace with himself. They are symbolised in the paper money by which Mephistopheles replenished the imperial exchequer. The only allusion to the printing-press, whose inventor Fust had been somewhat associated with Faust, is to show its power turned to the work of distributing irredeemable promises.

At length one demand made by Faust makes Mephistopheles tremble. As a mere court amusement he would have him raise Helen of Troy. Reluctant that Faust should look upon the type of man's harmonious development, yet bound to obey, Mephistopheles sends him to THE MOTHERS,—the healthy primal instincts and ideals of man which expressed themselves in the fair forms of art. Corrupted by superstition of their own worshippers, cursed by christianity, they 'have a Hades of their own,' as Mephistopheles says, and he is unwilling to interfere with them. The image appears, and the sense of Beauty is awakened in Faust. But he is still a christian as to his method: his idea is that heaven must be taken by storm, by chance, wish, prayer, any means except patient fulfilment of the conditions by which it may be reached. Helen is flower of the history and culture of Greece; and so lightly Faust would pluck and wear it!

Helen having vanished as he tried to clasp her, Faust has learned his second lesson. When he next meets Helen it is not to seek intellectual beauty as, in Gretchen's case, he had sought the sensuous and sensual. He has fallen under a charm higher than that of either Church or Mephistopheles; the divorce of ages between flesh and spirit, the master-crime of superstition, from which all devils sprang, was over for him from the moment that he sees the soul embodied and body ensouled in the art-ideal of Greece.

The redemption of Faust through Art is the gospel of the nine-teenth century. This is her vesture which Helen leaves him when she vanishes, and which bears him as a cloud to the land he is to make beautiful. The purest Art—Greek Art—is an expression of Humanity: it can as little be turned to satisfy a self-culture unhumanised as to consist with a superstition which insults nature. When Faust can meet with Helen, and part without any more clutching, he is not hurled back to his Gothic study and mocking devil any more: he is borne away until he reaches the land where his thought and work are needed. Blindness falls on him—or what Theology deems such: for it is metaphorical—it means that he has descended from clouds to the world, and the actual earth has eclipsed a possible immortality.

The sphere of Earth is known enough to me;
The view beyond is barred immortality:
A fool who there his blinking eyes directeth,
And o'er his clouds of peers a place expecteth!
Firm let him stand and look around him well!
This World means something to the capable;
Why needs he through Eternity to wend?

The eye for a fictitious world lost, leaves the vision for reality clearer. In every hard chaotic object Faust can now detect a slumbering beauty. The swamps and pools of the unrestrained sea, the oppressed people, the barrenness and the flood, they are all paths to Helen—a nobler Helen than Greece knew. When he has changed one scene of Chaos into Order, and sees a free people tilling the happy earth, then, indeed, he has realised the travail of his manhood, and is satisfied. To a moment which Mephistopheles never brought him, he cries 'Stay, thou art fair!'

Mephistopheles now, as becomes a creation of the Theology of obtaining what is not earned, calls up infernal troops to seize Faust's soul, but the angels pelt them with roses. The roses sting them worse than flames. The roses which Faust has evoked from briars are his defence: they are symbols of man completing his nature by a self-culture which finds its satisfaction in making some outward desert rejoice and blossom like the rose.

**NOTES**

1 Scheible's 'Kloster,' 5, 116. Zauberbücher.
2 Bayard Taylor's 'Faust,' note 45. See also his Appendix I. for an excellent condensation of the Faust legend from the best German sources.
3 Tertull. ad Marcion, iii. 18. S. Ignatii Episc. et Martyr ad Phil. Ep. viii. 'The Prince of this world rejoices when any one denies the cross, for he knows the confession of the cross to be his ruin.'
4 See his 'Acta,' by Simeon Metaphrastus.
5 I have been much struck by the resemblance between the dumpy monkish dwarf, in the old wall-picture of Auerbach's Cellar, meant for Mephistopheles, and the portrait of Asmodeus in the early editions of 'Le Diable Boiteux.' But, as devils went in those days, they are good-looking enough.
6 Shelley's Translation.
7 Bayard Taylor's Translation. Scene iv.
8 See Lavater's Physiognomy, Plates xix. and xx., in which some artist has shown what variations can be made to order on an intellectual and benevolent face.

# Chapter XXVI
# The Wild Huntsman

The Wild Hunt — Euphemisms — Schimmelreiter — Odinwald — Pied Piper —
Lyeshy — Waldemar's Hunt — Palne Hunter — King Abel's Hunt — Lords of
Glorup — Le Grand Veneur — Robert le Diable — Arthur — Hugo — Herne —
Tregeagle — Der Freischütz — Elijah's chariot — Mahan Bali — Déhak — Nimrod
— Nimrod's defiance of Jehovah — His Tower — Robber Knights — The Devil in
Leipzig — Olaf hunting pagans — Hunting-horns — Raven — Boar — Hounds —
Horse — Dapplegrimm — Sleipnir — Horseflesh — The mare Chetiya —
Stags — St. Hubert — The White Lady — Myths of Mother Rose —
Wodan hunting St. Walpurga — Friar Eckhardt

**THE MOST IMPORTANT** remnant of the Odin myth is the universal legend of the Wild Huntsman. The following variants are given by Wuttke.[1] In Central and South Germany the Wild Hunt is commonly called Wütenden Heere, *i.e.*, Wodan's army or chase—called in the Middle Ages, Wuotanges Heer. The hunter, generally supposed to be abroad during the twelve nights after Christmas, is variously called Wand, Waul, Wodejäger, Helljäger, Nightjäger, Hackelberg, Hackel-berend (man in armour), Fro Gode, Banditterich, Jenner. The most common belief is that he is the spectre of a wicked lord or king who sacrilegiously enjoyed the chase on Sundays and other holy days, and who is condemned to expiate his sin by hunting till the day of doom. He wears a broad-brimmed hat; is followed by dogs and other animals, fiery, and often three-legged; and in his spectral train are the souls of unbaptized children, huntsmen who have trodden down grain, witches, and others—these being mounted on horses, goats, and cocks, and sometimes headless, or with their entrails dragging behind them. They rush with a fearful noise through the air, which resounds with the cracking of whips, neighing of horses, barking of dogs, and cries of ghostly huntsmen. The unlucky wight encountered is caught up into the air, where his neck is wrung, or he is dropped from a great height. In some regions, it is said, such must hunt until relieved, but are not slain. The huntsman is a Nemesis on poachers or trespassers in woods and forests. Sometimes the spectres have combats with each other over battlefields. Their track is marked with bits of horseflesh, human corpses, legs with shoes on. In some regions, it is said, the huntsmen carry battle-axes, and cut down all who come in their way. When the hunt is passing all dogs on earth become still and quiet. In most regions there is some haunted gorge, hill, or castle in which the train disappears.

In Thuringia, it is said that, when the fearful noises of the spectral hunt come very near, they change to ravishing music. In the same euphemistic spirit some of the prognostications it brings are not evil: generally, indeed, the apparition portends war, pestilence, and famine, but frequently it announces a fruitful year. If, in passing a house, one of the train dips his finger in the yeast, the staff of life will never be wanting in that house. Whoever sees the chase will live long, say the Bohemians; but he must not hail it, lest flesh and bones rain upon him.

In most regions, however, there is thought to be great danger in proximity to the hunt. The perils are guarded against by prostration on the earth face downward, praying meanwhile; by standing on a white cloth (Bertha's linen), or wrapping the same around the head; by putting the head between the spokes of a wheel; by placing palm leaves on a table. The hunt may be observed securely from the cross-roads, which it shuns, or by standing on a stump marked with three crosses—as is often done by woodcutters in South Germany.

Wodan also appears in the Schimmelreiter—headless rider on a white horse, in Swabia called Bachreiter or Junker Jäkele. This apparition sometimes drives a carriage drawn by four white (or black) horses, usually headless. He is the terrible forest spectre Hoimann, a giant in broad-brimmed hat, with moss and lichen for beard; he rides a headless white horse through the air, and his wailing cry, 'Hoi, hoi!' means that his reign is ended. He is the bugbear of children.

In the Odinwald are the *Riesenäule* and *Riesenaltar*, with mystic marks declaring them relics of a temple of Odin. Near Erbach is Castle Rodenstein, the very fortress of the Wild Jäger, to which he passes with his horrid train from the ruins of Schnellert. The village of Reichelsheim has on file the affidavits of the people who heard him just before the battles of Leipzig and Waterloo. Their theory is that if the Jäger returns swiftly to Schnellert all will go well for Germany; but if he tarry at Rodenstein 'tis an omen of evil. He was reported near Frankfort in 1832; but it is notable that no mention of him was made during the late Franco-German war.

A somewhat later and rationalised variant relates that the wild huntsman was Hackelberg, the Lord of Rodenstein, whose tomb—really a Druidical stone—is shown at the castle, and said to be guarded by hell-hounds. Hackelberg is of old his Brunswick name. It was the Hackelberg Hill that opened to receive the children, which the Pied Piper of Hamelin charmed away with his flute from that old town, because the corporation would not pay him what they had promised for ridding them of rats. It is easy to trace this Pied Piper, who has become so familiar through Mr. Robert Browning's charming poem, to the Odin of more blessed memory, who says in the Havamal, 'I know a song by which I soften and enchant my enemies, and render their weapons of no effect.'

This latter aspect of Odin, his command over vermin, connects him with the Slavonic Lyeshy, or forest-demon of the Russias. The ancient thunder-god of Russia, Perun, who rides in his storm-chariot through the sky, has in the more christianised districts dropped his mantle on Ilya (Elias); while in the greater number of Slavonic districts he has held his original physical characters so remarkably that it has been necessary to include him among demons. In Slavonian Folklore the familiar myth of the wild huntsman is distributed—Vladimir the Great fulfils one part of it by still holding high revel in the halls of Kief, but he is no huntsman; Perun courses noisily through the air, but he is rather benevolent than otherwise; the diabolical characteristics of the superstition have fallen to the evil huntsmen (Lyeshies), who keep the wild creatures as their flocks, the same as shepherds their herds, and whom every huntsman must propitiate. The Lyeshy is gigantic, wears a sheepskin, has one eye without eyebrow or eyelash, horns, feet of a goat, is covered with green hair, and his finger-nails are claws. He is special protector of the bears and wolves.

In Denmark the same myth appears as King Volmer's Hunt. Waldemar was so passionately fond of the chase that he said if the Lord would only let him hunt for ever near Gurre (his castle in the north of Seeland), he would not envy him his paradise. For this blasphemous wish he is condemned to hunt between Burre and Gurre for ever. His cavalcade is much like that already described. Volmer rides a snow-white charger, preceded by a pack of coal-black hounds, and he carries his head under his left arm. On St. John the women open gates for him. It is believed that he is allowed brief repose at one and another of his old seats, and it is said spectral servants are sometimes seen preparing the ruined castle at Vordingborg for him, or at Waldemar's Tower. A sceptical peasant resolved to pass the night in this tower. At midnight the King entered, and, thanking him for looking after his tower, gave him a gold piece which burned through his hand and fell to the ground as a coal. On the other hand, Waldemar sometimes makes peasants hold his dogs, and afterwards throws them coals which turn out to be gold pieces.

The Palnatoke or Palne Hunter appears mostly in the island of *Fuen*. Every New Year's night he supplies himself with three horse-shoes from some smithy, and the smith takes care that he may find them ready for use on his anvil, as he always leaves three gold pieces in their stead. If the shoes are not ready for him, he carries the anvil off. In one instance he left an anvil on the top of a church tower, and it caused the smith great trouble to get it down again.

King Abel was interred after his death in St. Peter's Church in Sleswig, but the fratricide could find no peace in his grave. His ghost walked about in the night and disturbed the monks in their devotions. The body was finally removed from the church, and sunk in a foul bog near Gottorp. To keep him down effectively, a pointed stake was drove through his body. The spot is still called Königsgrabe. Notwithstanding this, he appears seated on a coal-black charger, followed by a pack of black hounds with eyes and tongues of fire. The gates are heard slamming and opening, and the shrieks and yells are such that they appal the stoutest hearts.

At the ancient capital of Fuen, Odense, said to have been built by Odin, the myth has been reduced to a spectral Christmas-night equipage, which issues from St. Canute's Church and passes to the ancient manor-house of Glorup. It is a splendid carriage, drawn by six black horses with fiery tongues, and in it are seated the Lords of Glorup, famous for their cruelty to peasants, and now not able to rest in the church where they were interred. It is of evil omen to witness the spectacle: a man who watched for it was struck blind.

In France *Le Grand Veneur* bears various names; he is King Arthur, Saint Hubert, Hugo. His alleged appearances within historic times have been so strongly attested that various attempts have been made to give them rational explanations. Thus Charles VI. of France, when going to war in Bretagne, is said to have been met by such a spectre in the Forest of Mans, and became insane; he believed himself to have been the victim of sorcery, as did many of his subjects. It has been said that the King was met by a disguised emissary of the Duc de Bretagne. More particular accounts are given of the apparition of the Wild Huntsman to Henry IV. when he was hunting with the Comte de Soissons in the Forest of Fontainebleau, an event commemorated by 'La Croix du Grand Veneur.' According to Matthieu,[2] both the King and the Count heard the cries of the hunt, and when the Count went to discover their origin, the terrible dark figure stood forth and cried, 'You wish to see me, then behold!' This incident has been explained variously, as a project of assassination, or as the jest of two fellows who, in 1596, were amusing Paris by their skill in imitating all the sounds of a hunt. But such phantoms had too long hunted through the imagination of the French peasantry for any explanation to be required. Robert le Diable, wandering in Normandy till judgment-day, and King Arthur, at an early date domesticated in France as a spectral huntsman (the figure most popularly identified at the time with the phantom seen by Henry IV.), are sufficient explanations. The ruins of Arthur's Castle near Huelgoat, Finistère, were long believed to hide enormous treasures, guarded by demons, who appear sometimes as fiery lights (*ignes fatuui*), owls, buzzards, and ravens—one of the latter being the form in which Arthur comes from his happy Vale of Avallon, when he would vary its repose with a hunt.[3]

A sufficiently curious interchange of such superstitions is represented in the following extract from Surtees:—'Sir Anthon Bek, busshop of Dureme in the tyme of King Eduarde, the son of King Henry, was the maist prowd and masterfull busshop in all England, and it was com'only said that he was the prowdest lord of Christienty. It chaunced that emong other lewd persons, this sir Anthon entertained at his court one Hugh de Pountchardon, that for his evill deeds and manifold robberies had been driven out of the Inglische courte, and had come from the southe to seek a little bread, and to live by staylinge. And to this Hughe, whom also he imployed to good purpose in the warr of Scotland, the busshop gave the land of Thikley, since of him called Thikley-Puntchardon, and also made him his chiefe huntsman. And after, this blake Hughe died afore the busshop; and efter that the busshop chasid the wild hart in Galtres forest, and sodainly ther met with him Hugh de Pontchardon, that was afore deid, on a wythe horse; and the said Hughe loked earnestly on the busshop, and the busshop said unto him, 'Hughe, what makethe thee here?' and he spake never word, but lifte up his cloke, and then he showed sir Anton his ribbes set with bones, and nothing more; and none other of the varlets saw him but the busshop only; and y$^e$ said Hughe went his way, and sir Anton toke corage, and cheered the dogges; and shortly efter he was made Patriarque of Hierusalem, and he same nothing no moe; and this Hugh is him that the silly people in Galtres doe call *le Gros Veneur*, and he was seen twice efter that by simple folk, afore y$^{at}$ the forest was felled in the tyme of Henry, father of King Henry y$^{at}$ now ys.'

Upon this uncanny fellow fell the spectral mantle of Hugo Capet; elsewhere as is probable, worn by nocturnal protestant assemblies—Huguenots.

The legend of the Wild Huntsman tinges many old English stories. Herne, the Hunter, may be identified with him, and the demons, with ghostly and headless wish-hounds, who still hunt evil-doers over Dartmoor on stormy nights, are his relations. The withered look of horses grazing on Penzance Common was once explained by their being ridden by demons, and the fire-breathing horse has found its way by many weird routes to the service of the Exciseman in the 'Ingoldsby Legends,' or that of Earl Garrett, who rides round the Curragh of Kildare on a steed whose inch-thick silver shoes must wear as thin as a cat's ear, ere he fights the English and reigns over Ireland. The Teutonic myth appears very plainly in the story of Tregeagle. This man, traced to an old Cornish family, is said to have been one of the wickedest men that ever lived; but though he had disposed of his soul to the Devil, the evil one was baulked by the potency of St. Petroc. This, however, was on condition of Tregeagle's labouring at the impossible task of clearing the sand from Porthcurnow Cove, at which work he may still be heard groaning when wind and wave are high. Whenever he tries to snatch a moment's rest, the demon is at liberty to pursue him, and they may be heard on stormy nights in hot pursuit of the poor creature, whose bull-like roar passed into the Cornish proverb, 'to roar like Tregeagle.'

On a pleasant Sunday evening in July 1868, I witnessed 'Der Freischütz' in the newly-opened opera-house at Leipzig. Never else-where have I seen such completeness and splendour in the weird effects of the infernal scene in the Wolf's Glen. The 'White Lady' started forth at every step of Rodolph's descent to the glen, warning him back. Zamiel, instead of the fiery garb he once wore as Samaël, was arrayed in raiment black as night; and when the magic bullet was moulded, the stage swarmed with huge reptiles, fiery serpents crawled on the ground, a dragon-drawn chariot, with wheels of fire, driven by a skeleton, passed through the air; and the wild huntsman's chase, composed of animals real to the eye and uttering their dis-tinguishable cries, hurried past. The animals represented were the horse, hound, boar, stag, chamois, raven, bat, owl, and they rushed amid the wild blast of horns.

I could but marvel at the yet more strange and weird history of the human imagination through which had flitted, from the varied regions of a primitive world, the shapes combined in this apotheosis of diablerie. Probably if Elijah in his fire-chariot, preached about in the neighbouring church that morning, and this wild huntsman careering in the opera, had looked closely at each other and at their own history, they might have found a common ancestor in the mythical Mahan Bali of India, the king whose austerities raised in power till he excited the jealousy of the gods, until Vishnu crushed him with his heel into the infernal regions, where he still exercises sovereignty, and is permitted to issue forth for an annual career (at the Onam festival), as described in Southey's 'Curse of Kehama.' And they might probably both claim mythological relationship with Yami, lord of death, who, as Jami, began in Persia the career of all warriors that never died, but sometimes sleep till a magic horn shall awaken them, sometimes dwell, like Jami himself and King Arthur, in happy isles, and in other cases issue forth at certain periods for the chase or for war—like Odin and Waldemar—with an infernal train.

But how did these mighty princes and warriors become demon huntsmen?

In the Persian 'Desatir' it is related that the animals contested the superiority of man, the two orders of beings being represented by their respective sages, and the last animal to speak opposed the claim of his opponent that man attained elevation to the nature of angels, with the remark, 'In his putting to death of animals and similar acts man resembleth the beasts of prey, and not angels.'

The prophet of the world then said, 'We deem it sinful to kill harmless, but right to slay ravenous, animals. Were all ravenous animals to enter into a compact not to kill harmless animals, we would abstain from slaying them, and hold them dear as ourselves.'

Upon this the wolf made a treaty with the ram, and the lion became friend of the stag. No tyranny was left in the world, till man

(Dehak) broke the treaty and began to kill animals. In consequence of this, none observed the treaty except the harmless animals.[4]

This fable, from the Aryan side, may be regarded as showing the reason of the evil repute which gathered around the name of Dehak or Zohak. The eating of animal food was among our Aryan ancestors probably the provisional commissariat of a people migrating from their original *habitat*. The animals slain for food had all their original consecration, and even the ferocious were largely invested with awe. The woodcutters of Bengal invoke Kalrayu—an archer tiger-mounted—to protect them against the wild beasts he (a form of Siva) is supposed to exterminate; but while the exterminator of the most dangerous animals may, albeit without warrant in the Shastr, be respected in India, the huntsman is generally of evil repute. The gentle Krishna was said to have been slain by an arrow from the bow of Ungudu, a huntsman, who left the body to rot under a tree where it fell, the bones being the sacred relics for which the image of Jugernath at Orissa was constructed.[5]

It is not known at what period the notion of transmigration arose, but that must have made him appear cannibalistic who first hunted and devoured animals. Such was the Persian Zohak (or Dehak). His Babylonian form, Nimrod, represented also the character of Esau, as huntsman; that is, the primitive enemy of the farmer, and of the commerce in grains; the preserver of wildness, and consequently of all those primitive aboriginal idolatries which linger in the heaths (whence heathen) and country villages (whence pagans) long after they have passed away from the centres of civilisation. Hunting is essentially barbarous. The willingness of some huntsmen even now, when this serious occupation of an early period has become a sport, to sacrifice not only animal life to their pleasure, but also the interests of labour and agriculture, renders it very easy for us to understand the transformation of Nimrod into a demon. In the Hebrew and Arabian legends concerning Nimrod, that 'mighty hunter' is shown as related to the wild elements and their worshipper. When Abraham, having broken the images of his father, was brought by Terah before Nimrod, the King said, 'Let us worship the fire!'

> 'Rather the water that quenches the fire,' said Abraham.
> 'Well, the water.'
> 'Rather the cloud that carries the water.'
> 'Well, the cloud.'
> 'Rather the wind that scatters the cloud.'
> 'Well, the wind.'
> 'Rather man, for he withstands the wind.'
> 'Thou art a babbler,' said Nimrod. 'I worship the fire and will cast thee into it.'

When Abraham was cast into the fiery furnace by Nimrod, and on the seventh day after was found sitting amid the roses of a garden, the mighty hunter—hater of gardens—resolved on a daring hunt for Abraham's God himself. He built a tower five thousand cubits high, but finding heaven still far away, he attached a car to two half-starved eagles, and by holding meat above them they flew upward, until Nimrod heard a voice saying, 'Godless man, whither goest thou?' The audacious man shot an arrow in the direction of the voice; the arrow returned to him stained with blood, and Nimrod believed that he had wounded Abraham's God.

He who hunted the universe was destroyed by one of the weakest of animated beings—a fly. In the aspiring fly which attacked

Nimrod's lip, and then nose, and finally devoured his brain, the Moslem and Hebrew doctors saw the fittest end of one whose adventurous spirit had not stopped to attack animals, man, Abraham, and Allah himself.

But though, in one sense, destroyed, Nimrod, say various myths, may be heard tumbling and groaning about the base of his tower of Babel, where the confusion of tongues took place; and it might be added, that they have, like the groan, a meaning irrespective of race or language. Dehak and Nimrod have had their brothers in every race, which has ever reached anything that may be called civilisation. It was the barbaric Baron and the Robber Knight of the Middle Ages, living by the hunt, who, before conversion, made for the Faithful Eckhardts of the Church the chief impediment; they might then strike down the monk, whose apparition has always been the legendary warning of the Demon's approach. When the Eckhardts had baptized these knights, they had already been transformed to the Devils which people the forests of Germany, France, and England with their terrible spectres. The wild fables of the East, telling of fell Demons coursing through the air, whispered to the people at one ear, and the equally wild deeds of the Robber Knights at the other. The Church had given the people one name for all such phantasms—Devil—and it was a name representative of the feelings of both priest and peasant, so long as the Robber Knights were their common enemy. Jesus had to be a good deal modified before he could become the model of this Teutonic Esau. It is after the tradition of his old relation to huntsmen that the Devil has been so especially connected in folklore with soldiers. In the 'Annals of Leipzig,' kept in Auerbach's Cellar, famous for the flight of Mephisto and Faust from its window on a wine-cask, I found two other instances in which the Devil was reported as having appeared in that town. In one case (1604), the fiend had tempted one Jeremy of Strasburg, a marksman, to commit suicide, but that not succeeding, had desired him to go with him to the neighbouring castle and enjoy some fruit. The marksman was saved by help of a Dean. In 1633, during a period of excessive cold and snow, the Devil induced a soldier to blaspheme. The marksman and the soldier were, indeed, the usual victims of the Wild Huntsmen's temptations; and it was for such that the unfailing magic bullets were moulded in return for their impawned souls.

How King Olaf—whose name lingers among us in 'Tooley Street,' so famous for its Three Tailors![6]—spread the Gospel through the North after his baptism in England is well known. Whatever other hunt may have been phantasmal, it was not Olaf's hunt of the heathen. To put a pan of live coals under the belly of one, to force an adder down the throat of another, to offer all men the alternatives of being baptized or burnt, were the arguments which this apostle applied with such energy that at last—but not until many brave martyrdoms—the chief people were convinced. Olaf encountered Odin as if he had been a living foe, and what is more, believed in the genuine existence of his former God. Once, as Olaf and his friends believed, Odin appeared to this devastator of his altars as a one-eyed man in broad-brimmed hat, delighting the King in his hours of relaxation with that enchanting conversation for which he was so famous. But he (Odin) tried secretly to induce the cook to prepare for his royal master some fine meat which he had poisoned. But Olaf said, 'Odin shall not deceive us,' and ordered the tempting viand to be thrown away. Odin was god of the barbarian Junkers, and the people rejoiced that he was driven into holes and corners; his rites remained mainly among huntsmen, and had to be kept very secret. In the *Gulathings Lagen* of Norway it is ordered: 'Let the king and bishop, with all possible care, search after those who exercise pagan rites, who use magic arts, who adore the genii of particular places, of tombs, or rivers, and who, after the manner of devils in travelling, are transported from place to place through the air.'

Under such very actual curses as these, the once sacred animals of Odin, and all the associations of the hunt, were diabolised. Even the hunting-horn was regarded as having something præternatural about it. The howling blast when Odin consulteth Mimir's head[7] was heard again in the Pied Piper's flute, and passed southward to blend its note with the horn of Roland at Roncesvalles,—which brought help from distances beyond the reach of any honest horn, and even with the pipe of Pan.

That the Edda described Odin as mounted on a mysterious horse, as cherishing two wolves for pets, having a roasted boar for the daily *pièce de résistance* of his table, and with a raven on either shoulder, whispering to him the secret affairs of the earth, was enough to settle the reputation of those animals in the creed of christian priests. The Raven was, indeed, from of old endowed with the holy awfulness of the christian dove, in the Norse Mythology. To this day no Swede will kill a raven. The superstition concerning it was strong enough to transmit even to Voltaire an involuntary shudder at its croak. Odin was believed to have given the Raven the colour of the night that it might the better spy out the deeds of darkness. Its 'natural theology' is, no doubt, given correctly by Robert Browning's Caliban, who, when his speculations are interrupted by a thunderstorm, supposes his soliloquy has been conveyed by the raven he sees flying to his god Setebos. In many parts of Germany ravens are believed to hold souls of the damned. If a raven's heart be secured it procures an unerring shot.

From an early date the Boar became an ensign of the prowess of the gods, by which its head passed to be the device of so many barbaric clans and ancient families in the Northern world. In Vedic Mythology we find Indra taking the shape of a Wild Boar, also killing a demon Boar, and giving Tritas the strength by which a similar monster is slain.[8] According to another fable, while Brahma and Vishnu are quarrelling as to which is the first-born, Siva interferes and cries, 'I am the first-born; nevertheless I will recognise as my superior him who is able to see the summit of my head or the sole of my feet.' Vishnu, transforming himself to a Boar, pierced the ground, penetrated to the infernal regions, and then saw the feet of Siva, who on his return saluted him as first-born of the gods. De Gubernatis regards this fable as making the Boar emblem of the hidden Moon.[9] He is hunted by the Sun. He guards the treasure of the demons which Indra gains by slaying him. In Sicilian story, Zafarana, by throwing three hog's bristles on embers, renews her husband's youth. In Esthonian legend, a prince, by eating pork, acquires the faculty of understanding the language of birds,—which may mean leading on the spring with its songs of birds. But whether these particular interpretations be true or not, there is no doubt that the Boar, at an early period, became emblematic of the wild forces of nature, and from being hunted by King Odin on earth passed to be his favourite food in Valhalla, and a prominent figure in his spectral hunt.

Enough has already been said of the Dog in several chapters of this work to render it but natural that this animal should take his place in any diabolical train. It was not as a 'hell-hound,' or descendant of the guardians of Orcus, that he entered the spectral procession of Odin, but as man's first animal assistant in the work of obtaining a living from nature. It is the faithful friend of man who is demoralised in Waldemar's Lystig, the spectre-hound of Peel Castle, the Manthe Doog of the Isle of Man, the sky-dogs (Cwn wybir or aunwy) of Wales, and Roscommon dog of Ireland.

Of the Goat, the Dog, and some other diabolised animals, enough has been said in previous pages. The nocturnal animals would be as naturally caught up into the Wild Huntsman's train as belated peasants. But it is necessary to dwell a little on the relations of the Horse to this Wild Hunt. It was the Horse that made the primitive king among men.

'The Horse,' says Dasent, 'was a sacred animal among the Teutonic tribes from the first moment of their appearance in history; and Tacitus has related how, in the shade of those woods and groves which served them for temples, white horses were fed at the public cost, whose backs no mortal crossed, whose neighings and snortings were carefully watched as auguries and omens, and who were thought to be conscious of divine mysteries. In Persia, too, the classical reader will remember how the neighing of a horse decided the choice for the crown. Here in England, at any rate, we have only to think of Hengist and Horsa, the twin heroes of the Anglo-Saxon migration—as the legend ran—heroes whose name meant *horse*, and of the Vale of the White Horse, in Berks, where the sacred form still gleams along the down, to be reminded of the sacredness of the horse to our forefathers. The Eddas are filled with the names of famous horses, and the Sagas contain many stories of good steeds, in whom their owners trusted and believed as sacred to this or that particular god. Such a horse is Dapplegrimm in the Norse tales, who saves his master out of all his perils, and brings him to all fortune, and is another example of that mysterious connection with the higher powers which animals in all ages have been supposed to possess.'

It was believed that no warrior could approach Valhalla except on horseback, and the steed was generally buried with his master. The Scandinavian knight was accustomed to swear 'by the shoulder of a horse and the edge of a sword.' Odin (the god) was believed to have always near him the eight-legged horse Sleipnir, whose sire was the wonderful Svaldilfari, who by night drew the enormous stones for the fortress defending Valhalla from the frost-giants. On Sleipnir the deity rode to the realm of Hela, when he evoked the spirit of the deceased prophetess, Vala, with Runic incantations, to learn Baldur's fate. This is the theme of the Veytamsvida, paraphrased by Gray in his ode beginning—

> Up rose the king of men with speed,
> And saddled straight his coal-black steed

The steed, however, was not black, but grey. Sleipnir was the foal of a magically-created mare. The demon-mare (Mara) holds a prominent place in Scandinavian superstition, besetting sleepers.

In the Ynglinga Saga, Vanland awakes from sleep, crying, 'Mara is treading on me!' His men hasten to help him, but when they take hold of his head Mara treads on his legs, and when they hold his legs she tramples on his head; and so, says Thiodolf—

> Trampled to death, to Skyta's shore
> The corpse his faithful followers bore;
> And there they burnt, with heavy hearts,
> The good chief, killed by witchcraft's arts.

All this is, of course, the origin of the common superstition of the nightmare. The horse-shoe used against witches is from the same region. We may learn here also the reason why hippophagy has been so long unknown among us. Odin's boar has left his head on our Christmas tables, but Olaf managed to rob us of the horse-flesh once eaten in honour of that god. In the eleventh century he proclaimed the eating of horse-flesh a test of paganism, as baptism was of Christianity, and punished it with death, except in Iceland, where it was permitted by an express stipulation on their embracing Christianity. To these facts it may be added that originally the horse's head was lifted, as the horse-shoe is now, for a charm against witches. When Wittekind fought twenty years against Charlemagne, the ensign borne by his Saxon followers was a horse's head raised on a pole. A white horse on a yellow ground is to-day the Hanoverian banner, its origin being undoubtedly Odinistic.

The christian edict against the eating of horse-flesh had probably a stronger motive than sentimental opposition to paganism. A Roman emperor had held the stirrup for a christian pontiff to mount, and something of the same kind occurred in the North. The Horse, which had been a fire-breathing devil under Odin, became a steed of the Sun under the baptized noble and the bishop. Henceforth we read of coal-black and snow-white horses, as these are mounted in the interest of the old religion or the new.

It is very curious to observe how far and wide has gone religious competition for possession of that living tower of strength— the Horse. In ancient Ceylon we find the Buddhist immigrants winning over the steed on which the aborigines were fortified. It was a white horse, of course, that became their symbol of triumph. The old record says—

'A certain yakkhini (demoness) named Chetiya, having the form and countenance of a mare, dwelt near the marsh of Tumbariungona. A certain person in the prince's (Pandukabhayo) retinue having seen this beautiful (creature), white with red legs, announced the circumstance to the prince. The prince set out with a rope to secure her. She seeing him approach from behind, losing her presence of mind from fear, under the influence of his imposing appearance, fled without (being able to exert the power she possessed of) rendering herself invisible. He gave chase to the fugitive. She, persevering in her flight, made the circuit of the marsh seven times. She made three more circuits of the marsh, and then plunged into the river at the Kachchhaka ferry. He did the same, and (in the river) seized her by the tail, and (at the same time grasped) the leaf of a palmira tree which the stream was carrying down. By his supernatural good fortune this (leaf) became an enormous sword. Exclaiming, 'I put thee to death!' he flourished the sword over her. 'Lord!' replied she to him, 'subduing this kingdom for thee, I will confer it on thee: spare me my life.' Seizing her by the throat, and with the point of the sword boring her nostril, he secured her with his rope: she (instantly) became tractable. Conducting her to the Dhumarakkho mountain, he obtained a great accession of warlike power by making her his battle-steed.'[10] The wonderful victories won by the prince, aided by this magical mare, are related, and the tale ends with his setting up 'within the royal palace itself the mare-faced yakkhini,' and providing for her annually 'demon offerings.'

Equally ambiguous with the Horse in this zoologic diablerie is the Stag. In the Heraklean legends we find that hero's son, Telephon, nursed by a hind in the woods; and on the other hand, his third 'labour' was the capture of Artemis' gold-antlered stag, which brought on him her wrath (it being 'her majesty's favourite stag'). We have again the story of Actæon pursuing the stag too far and suffering the fate he had prepared for it; and a reminiscence of it in the 'Pentamerone,' when the demon Huoreo allures Canneloro into the wood by taking the form of a beautiful hind. These complex legends are reflected in Northern folklore also. Count Otto I. of Altmark, while out hunting, slept under an oak and dreamed that he was furiously attacked by a stag, which disappeared when he called on the name of God. The Count built a monastery, which still stands, with the oak's stump built into its altar. On the other hand, beside the altar of a neighbouring church hang two large horns of a stag said to have brought a lost child home on its back. Thus in the old town of Steindal meet these contrary characters of the mystical stag, of which it is not difficult to see that the evil one results from its misfortune in being at once the huntsman's victim and scapegoat.[11]

In the legend of St. Hubert we have the sign of Christ—risen from his tomb among the rich Christians to share for a little the crucifixion of their first missionaries in the North—to the huntsmen of Europe. Hubert pursues the stag till it turns to face him, and behold, between its antlers, the cross! It is a fable conceived in the spirit of him who said to fishermen, 'Come with me and I will make you fishers of men.' The effect was much the same in both cases. Hubert kneels before the stag, and becomes a saint, as the fishermen left their nets and became apostles. But, as the proverb says, when the saint's day is over, farewell the saint. The fishermen's successors caught men with iron hooks in their jaws; the successors of Hubert hunted men and women so lustily that they never paused long enough to see whether there might not be a cross on their forehead also.

It was something, however, that the cross which Constantine could only see in the sky could be seen by any eye on the forehead of a harmless animal; and this not only because it marked the rising in christian hearts of pity for the animals, but because what was done to the flying stag was done to the peasant who could not fly, and more terribly. The vision of Hubert came straight from the pagan heart of Western and Northern Europe. In the Bible, from Genesis to Apocalypse, no word is found clearly inculcating any duty to the animals. So little, indeed, could the christians interpret the beautiful tales of folklore concerning kindly beasts, out of which came the legend of Hubert, that Hubert was made patron of huntsmen; and while, by a popular development, Wodan was degraded to a devil, the baptized sportsman rescued his chief occupation by ascribing its most dashing legends to St. Martin and their inspiration to the Archangel Michael.

It is now necessary to consider the light which the German heart cast across the dark shadows of Wodan. This is to be discovered in the myth of the White Lady. We have already seen, in the confessions of the witches of Elfdale, in Sweden, that when they were gathering before their formidable Devil, a certain White Spirit warned them back. The children said she tried to keep them from entering the Devil's Church at Blockula. This may not be worth much as a 'confession,' but it sufficiently reports the theories prevailing in the popular mind of Elfdale at that time. It is not doubtful now that this White Lady and that Devil she opposed were, in pre-christian time, Wodan and his wife Frigga. The humble people who had gladly given up the terrible huntsman and warrior to be degraded into a Devil, and with him the barbaric Nimrods who worshipped him, did not agree to a similar surrender of their dear household goddess, known to them as Frigga, Holda, Bertha, Mother Rose,—under all her epithets the Madonna of the North, interceding between them and the hard king of Valhalla, ages before they ever heard of a jealous Jehovah and a tender interceding Mary.

Dr. Wuttke has collected many variants of the myths of Frigga, some of which bear witness to the efforts of the Church to degrade her also into a fiend. She is seen washing white clothes at fountains, milking cows, spinning flax with a distaff, or combing her flaxen hair. She was believed to be the divine ancestress of the human race; many of the oldest families claimed descent from her, and believed that this Ahnenfrauannounced to them good fortune, or, by her wailing, any misfortune coming to their families. She brought evil only to those who spoke evil of her. If any one shoots at her the ball enters his own heart. She appears to poor wandering folk, especially children, and guides them to spots where they find heaps of gold covered with the flower called 'Forget-me-not'—because her gentle voice is heard requesting, as the only compensation, that the flowers shall be replaced when the gold is removed. The primroses are sacred to her, and often are the keys (thence called 'key-blossoms') which unlock her treasures. The smallest tribute she repays,—even a pebble consecrated to her. Every child ascending the Burgeiser Alp places a stone on a certain heap of such, with the words, 'Here I offer to the wild maidens.' These are Bertha's kindly fairies. (When Frederika Bremer was with a picnic on the Hudson heights, which Washington Irving had peopled with the Spirits he had brought from the Rhine, she preferred to pour out her champagne as a libation to the 'good spirits' of Germany and America.) The beautiful White Lady wears a golden chain, and glittering keys at her belt; she appears at mid-day or in strong moonlight. In regions where priestly influence is strong she is said to be half-black, half-white, and to appear sometimes as a serpent. She often helps the weary farmer to stack his corn, and sorely-tasked Cinderellas in their toil.

In pre-christian time this amiable goddess—called oftenest Bertha (shining) and Mother Rose—was related to Wodan as the spring and summer to the storms of winter, in which the Wild Huntsman's procession no doubt originated. The Northman's experience of seed-time and harvest was expressed in the myth of this sweet Rose hidden through the winter's blight to rise again in summer.

This myth has many familiar variants, such as Aschenputtel and Sleeping Beauty; but it was more particularly connected with the later legends of the White Lady, as victim of the Wild Huntsman, by the stories of transformed princesses delivered by youths. Rescue of the enchanted princess is usually effected by three kisses, but she is compelled to appear before the deliverer in some hideous aspect—as toad or serpent; so that he is repelled or loses courage. This is the rose hid under the ugliness of winter.

When the storm-god Wodan was banished from nature altogether and identified with the imported, and naturally inconceivable, Satan, he was no more regarded as Frigga's rough lord, but as her remorseless foe. She was popularly revered as St. Walpurga, the original May Queen, and it was believed that happy and industrious children might sometimes see her on May-day with long flowing flaxen hair, fine shoes, distaff in hand, and a golden crown on her head. But for the nine nights after May-day she was relentlessly pursued by the Wild Huntsman and his mounted train. There is a picture by G. Watts of the hunted lady of Bocaccio's tale, now in the Cosmopolitan Club of London, which vividly reproduces the weird impressiveness of this myth. The White Lady tries to hide from her pursuer in standing corn, or gets herself bound up in a sheaf. The Wild Huntsman's wrath extends to all her retinue,—moss maidens of the wood, or Holtzweibeln. The same belief characterises Waldemar's hunt. It is a common legend in Denmark that King Volmer rode up to some peasants, busy at harvest on Sobjerg Hill, and, in reply to his question whether they had seen any game, one of the men said—'Something rustled just now in yonder standing corn.' The King rushed off, and presently a shot was heard. The King reappeared with a mermaid lying across his horse, and said as he passed, 'I have chased her a hundred years, and have her at last.' He then rode into the hill. In this way Frigga and her little people, hunted with the wild creatures, awakened sympathy for them.

The holy friar. Eckhardt (who may be taken as a myth and type of the Church *ad hoc*) gained his legendary fame by being supposed to go in advance of the Wild Huntsman and warn villagers of his approach; but as time went on and a compromise was effected between the hunting Barons and the Church, on the basis that the sports and cruelties should be paid for with indulgence-fees, Eckhardt had to turn his attention rather to the White Lady. She was declared a Wild Huntress, but the epithet slipped to other shoulders. The priests identified her ultimately with Freija, or Frau Venus; and Eckhardt was the holy hermit who warned young men against her sorceries in Venusberg and elsewhere. But Eckhardt never prevailed against the popular love of Mother Rose as he had against her pursuer; he only increased the attractions of 'Frau Venus' beyond her deserts. In the end it was as much as the Church could do to secure for Mary the mantle of her elder sister's sanctity. Even then the earlier faith was not eradicated. After the altars of Mary had fallen, Frigga had vitality enough to hold her own as the White Witch who broke the Dark One's spells. It was chiefly this helpful Mother-goddess to whom the wretched were appealing when they were burnt for witchcraft.

At Urselberg, Wurtemberg, there is a deep hole called the 'Nightmaidens' Retreat,' in which are piled the innumerable stones that have been cast therein by persons desiring good luck on journeys. These stones correspond to the bones of the 11,000 Virgins in St. Ursula's Church at Cologne. The White Lady was sainted under her name of Ursel (the glowing one), otherwise Horsel. Horselberg, near Eisenach, became her haunt as Venus, the temptress of Tannhaüsers; Urselberg became her retreat as the good fairy mother; but the attractions of herself and her moss-maidens, which the Church wished to borrow, were taken on a long voyage to Rome, and there transmuted to St. Ursula and her 11,000 Virgins. These Saints of Cologne encountered their ancient mythical pursuers—the Wild Huntsman's train—in those barbarian Huns who are said to have slaughtered them all because they would not break their vows of chastity. The legend is but a variant of Wodan's hunt after the White Lady and her maidens. When it is remembered that before her transformation by Christianity Ursula was the Huntsman's own wife, Frigga, a quaint incident appears in the last meeting between the two. After Wodan had been transformed to the Devil, he is said to have made out the architectural plan for Cologne Cathedral, and offered it to the architect in return for a bond for his soul; but, having weakly allowed him to get possession of the document before the bond was signed, the architect drew from under his gown a bone of St. Ursula, from which the Devil fled in great terror. It was bone of his bone; but after so many mythological vicissitudes Wodan and his Horsel could hardly be expected to recognise each other at this chance meeting in Cologne.

## NOTES

1 'Der deutsche Volksaberglaube der Gegenwart.' Von Dr. Adolf Wuttke, Prof. der Theol. in Halle. Berlin: Verlag von Wiegand & Grieben. 1869.

2 'Histoire de France et des Choses Mémorables,' &c.

3 The universal myth of Sleepers,—christianised in the myth of St. John, and of the Seven whose slumber is traceable as far as Tours,—had a direct pagan development in Jami, Barbarossa, Arthur, and their many variants. It is the legend of the Castle of Sewing-shields in Northumberland, that King Arthur, his queen and court, remain there in a subterranean hall, entranced, until some one should first blow a bugle-horn near the entrance hall, and then with 'the sword of the stone' cut a garter placed there beside it. But none had ever heard where the entrance to this enchanted hall was, till a farmer, fifty years since, was sitting knitting on the ruins of the castle, and his clew fell and ran downwards through briars into a deep subterranean passage. He cleared the portal of its weeds and rubbish, and entering a vaulted passage, followed the clew. The floor was infested with toads and lizards; and bats flitted fearfully around him. At length his sinking courage was strengthened by a dim, distant light, which, as he advanced, grew gradually brighter, till all at once he entered a vast and vaulted hall, in the centre of which a fire, without fuel, from a broad crevice in the floor, blazed with a high and lambent flame, that showed all the carved walls and fretted roof, and the monarch and his queen and court reposing around in a theatre of thrones and costly couches. On the floor, beyond the fire, lay the faithful and deep-toned pack of thirty couple of hounds; and on a table before it the spell-dissolving horn, sword, and garter. The shepherd firmly grasped the sword, and as he drew it from its rusty scabbard the eyes of the monarch and his courtiers began to open, and they rose till they sat upright. He cut the garter, and as the sword was slowly sheathed the spell assumed its ancient power, and they all gradually sank to rest; but not before the monarch had lifted up his eyes and hands and exclaimed—
O woe betide that evil day
On which this witless wight was born,
Who drew the sword—the garter cut,
But never blew the bugle horn.
Terror brought on loss of memory, and the shepherd was unable to give any correct account of his adventure, or to find again the entrance to the enchanted hall.—Hodgson's 'Northumberland.'

4 This great discussion between the animals and sages is given in 'The Sacred Anthology' (London: Trübner & Co. New York: Henry Holt & Co.). It is a very ancient story, and was probably written down at the beginning of the christian era.

5 It is a strange proof of the ignorance concerning Hindu religion that Jugernath, raised in a sense for reprobation of cruelty to man and beast, should have been made by a missionary myth a Western proverb for human sacrifices!

6 St. Olaf = Stooley = Tooley.

7 High bloweth Heimdall
His horn aloft;
Odin consulteth
Mimir's head;
The old ash yet standing
Yggdrasill
To its summit is shaken,
And loose breaks the giant.—Voluspa.

8   'Rigveda,' x. 99.
9   'Zoolog. Myth.,' ii. 8, 10, &c.
10  'The Mahawanso.' Translated by the Hon. George Turnour, Ceylon, 1836, p. 69.
11  It was an ancient custom to offer a stag on the high altar of Durham Abbey, the sacrifice
    being accompanied with winding of horns, on Holy Rood Day, which suggests a form
    of propitiating the Wild Huntsman in the hunting season. On the Cheviot Hills there is a
    chasm called Hen Hole, 'in which there is frequently seen a snow egg at Midsummer, and
    it is related that a party of hunters, while chasing a roe, were beguiled into it by fairies,
    and could never again find their way out.'—Richardson's 'Borderer's Table-Book,' vi 400.
    The Bridled Devil of Durham Cathedral may be an allusion to the Wild Huntsman.

# Chapter XXVII

# Le Bon Diable

The Devil repainted — Satan a divine agent — St. Orain's heresy — Primitive universalism — Father Sinistrari — Salvation of demons — Mediæval sects — Aquinas — His prayer for Satan — Popular antipathies — The Devil's gratitude — Devil defending innocence — Devil against idle lords — The wicked ale-wife — Pious offenders punished — Anachronistic Devils — Devils turn to poems — Devil's good advice — Devil sticks to his word — His love of justice — Charlemagne and the Serpent — Merlin — His prison of Air — Mephistopheles in Heaven

**THE PHRASE WHICH** heads this chapter is a favourite one in France. It may have had a euphemistic origin, for the giants dreaded by primitive Europeans were too formidable to be lightly spoken of. But within most of the period concerning which we have definite knowledge such phrases would more generally have expressed the half-contemptuous pity with which these huge beings with weak intellects were regarded. The Devil imported with Christianity was made over, as we have seen, into the image of the Dummeteufel, or stupid good-natured giant, and he is represented in many legends which show him giving his gifts and services for payments of which he is constantly cheated. Le Bon Diable in France is somewhat of this character, and is often taken as the sign of tradesmen who wish to represent themselves as lavishing their goods recklessly for inadequate compensation. But the large accession of demons and devils from the East through Jewish and Moslem channels, of a character far from stupid, gave a new sense to that phrase and corresponding ones. There is no doubt that a very distinct reaction in favour of the Devil arose in Europe, and one expressive of very interesting facts and forces. The pleasant names given him by the masses would alone indicate this,—Monsieur De Scelestat, Lord Voland, Blümlin (floweret), Federspiel (gay-plumed), Maitre Bernard, Maitre Parsin (Parisian).

*The Devil is not so black as he's painted.* This proverb concerning the long-outlawed Evil One has a respectable antiquity, and the feeling underlying it has by no means been limited to the vulgar. Even the devout George Herbert wrote—

> We paint the Devil black, yet he
> Hath some good in him all agree.

Robert Burns naively appeals to Old Nick's better nature—

But fare ye weel, auld Nickie-ben!

> O wad ye tak a thought an' men'!
> Ye aiblins might—I dinna ken—
> Still ha'e a stake;
> I'm wae to think upon yon den,
> E'en for your sake!

It is hard to destroy the natural sentiments of the human heart. However much they may be overlaid by the transient exigencies of a creed, their indestructible nature is pretty certain to reveal itself. The most orthodox supporters of divine cruelty in their own theology will cry out against it in another. The saint who is quite satisfied that the everlasting torture of Satan or Judas is justice, will look upon the doom of Prometheus as a sign of heathen heartlessness; and the burning of one widow for a few moments on her husband's pyre will stimulate merciful missionary ardour among millions of christians whose creed passes the same poor victim to endless torture, and half the human race with her.

It is doubtful whether the general theological conception of the functions of Satan is consistent with the belief that he is in a state of suffering. As an agent of divine punishment he is a part of the divine government; and it is even probable that had it not been for the necessity of keeping up his office, theology itself would have found some means of releasing him and his subordinates from hell, and ultimately of restoring them to heaven and virtue.[1]

It is a legend of the island Iona that when St. Columba attempted to build a church there, the Devil—*i.e.*, the same Druid magicians who tried to prevent his landing there by tempests—threw down the stones as often as they were piled up. An oracle declared that the church could arise only after some holy man had been buried alive at the spot, and the saint's friend Orain offered himself for the purpose. After Orain had been buried, and the wall was rising securely, St. Columba was seized with a strong desire to look upon the face of his poor friend once more. The wall was pulled down, the body dug up; but instead of Orain being found dead, he sat up and told the assembled christians around him that he had been to the other world, and discovered that they were in error about various things,—especially about Hell, which really did not exist at all. Outraged by this heresy the christians immediately covered up Orain again in good earnest.

The resurrection of this primitive universalist of the seventh century, and his burial again, may be regarded as typifying a dream of the ultimate restoration of the universe to the divine sway which has often given signs of life through christian history, though many times buried. The germ of it is even in Paul's hope that at last 'God may be all in all' (1 Cor. xv. 28). In Luke x. 17, also, it was related that the seventy whom Jesus had sent out among the idol-worshipping Gentiles 'returned again with joy, saying, Lord, even the devils are subject unto us through thy name.' These ideas are recalled in various legends, such as that elsewhere related of the Satyr who came to St. Anthony to ask his prayers for the salvation of his demonic tribe. On the strength of Anthony's courteous treatment of that Satyr, the famous Consulteur of the Inquisition, Father Sinistrari (seventeenth century), rested much of his argument that demons were included in the atonement wrought by Christ and might attain final beatitude. The Father affirmed that this was implied in Christ's words, 'Other sheep I have which are not of this flock: them also I must bring, and they shall hear my voice; and there shall be one fold and one shepherd' [2] (John x. 16). That these words were generally supposed to refer to the inclusion of the Gentile world was not accepted by Sinistrari as impairing his argument, but the contrary. He maintained with great ingenuity that the salvation of the Gentiles logically includes the salvation of their inspiring demons, and that there would not be one fold if these aerial beings, whose existence all authorities attested, were excluded. He even intimates, though more timidly, that their father, Satan himself, as a participator in the sin of Adam and sharer of his curse, may be included in the general provision of the deity for the entire and absolute removal of the curse throughout nature.

Sinistrari's book was placed on the 'Index Expurgatorius' at Rome in 1709, 'donec corrigatur,' eight years after the author's death; it was republished, 'correctus,' 1753. But the fact that such sentiments had occupied many devout minds in the Church, and that they had reached the dignity of a consistent and scholarly statement in theology, was proved. The opinion grew out of deeper roots than New Testament phrases or the Anthony fables. The Church had been for ages engaged in the vast task of converting the Gentile world; in the course of that task it had succeeded only by successive surrenders of the impossible principles with which it had started. The Prince of this World had been baptized afresh with every European throne ascended by the Church. Asmodeus had triumphed in the sacramental inclusion of marriage; St. Francis d'Assisi, preaching to the animals, represented innumerable pious myths which had been impossible under the old belief in a universal curse resting upon nature. The evolution of this tendency may be traced through the entire history of the Church in such sects as the Paulicians, Cathari, Bogomiles, and others, who, though they again and again formulated anew the principle of an eternal Dualism, as often revealed some further stage in the progressive advance of the christianised mind towards a normal relation with nature. Thus the Cathari maintained that only those beings who were created by the evil principle would remain unrecovered; those who were created by God, but seduced by the Adversary, would be saved after sufficient expiation. The fallen angels, they believed, were passing through earthly, in some cases animal, bodies to the true Church and to heaven. Such views as these were not those of the learned, but of the dissenting sects, and they prepared ignorant minds in many countries for that revival of confidence in their banished deities which made the cult of Witchcraft.

St. Thomas Aquinas, the 'Angelical Doctor,' in his famous work

'Summa Theologiæ,' maintains that in the Resurrection the bodies of the redeemed will rise with all their senses and organs, including those of sex, active and refined. The authentic affirmation of that doctrine in the thirteenth century was of a significance far beyond the comprehension of the Church. Aquinas confused the lines between flesh and spirit, especially by admitting sex into heaven. The Devil could not be far behind. The true interpretation of his doctrine is to be found in the legend that Aquinas passed a night in prayer for the salvation and restoration of the Devil. This legend is the subject of a modern poem so fraught with the spirit of the mediæval heart, pining in its dogmatic prison, that I cannot forbear quoting it here:—

> All day Aquinas sat alone;
> Compressed he sat and spoke no word,
> As still as any man of stone,
> In streets where never voice is heard;
> With massive front and air antique
> He sat, did neither move or speak,
> For thought like his seemed words too weak.
>
> The shadows brown about him lay;
> From sunrise till the sun went out,
> Had sat alone that man of grey,
> That marble man, hard crampt by doubt;
> Some kingly problem had he found,
> Some new belief not wholly sound,
> Some hope that overleapt all bound.
>
> All day Aquinas sat alone,
> No answer to his question came,
> And now he rose with hollow groan,
> And eyes that seemed half love, half flame.
> On the bare floor he flung him down,
> Pale marble face, half smile, half frown,
> Brown shadow else, mid shadows brown.

'O God,' he said, 'it cannot be,
Thy Morning-star, with endless moan,
Should lift his fading orbs to thee,
And thou be happy on thy throne.
It were not kind, nay, Father, nay,
It were not just, O God, I say,
Pray for thy Lost One, Jesus, pray!

'How can thy kingdom ever come,
While the fair angels howl below?
All holy voices would be dumb,
All loving eyes would fill with woe,
To think the lordliest Peer of Heaven,
The starry leader of the Seven,
Would never, never, be forgiven.

'Pray for thy Lost One, Jesus, pray!
O Word that made thine angel speak!
Lord! let thy pitying tears have way;
Dear God! not man alone is weak.
What is created still must fall,
And fairest still we frailest call;
Will not Christ's blood avail for all?

'Pray for thy Lost One, Jesus, pray!
O Father! think upon thy child;
Turn from thy own bright world away,
And look upon that dungeon wild.
O God! O Jesus! see how dark
That den of woe! O Saviour! mark
How angels weep, how groan! Hark, hark!

'He will not, will not do it more,
Restore him to his throne again;
Oh, open wide that dismal door
Which presses on the souls in pain.
So men and angels all will say,
'Our God is good.' Oh, day by day,
Pray for thy Lost One, Jesus, pray!'

All night Aquinas knelt alone,
Alone with black and dreadful Night,
Until before his pleading moan
The darkness ebbed away in light.
Then rose the saint, and 'God,' said he,
'If darkness change to light with thee,
The Devil may yet an angel be.'[3]

While this might be the feeling of devout philosophers whose minds were beginning to form a conception of a Cosmos in which the idea of a perpetual empire of Evil could find no place, the humble and oppressed masses, as we have seen in the chapter on Witchcraft, were familiarising their minds with the powers and glories of a Satan in antagonism to the deities and saints of the Church. It was not a penitent devil supplicating for pardon whom they desired, but the veritable Prince of the World, to whom as well as to themselves their Christian oppressors were odious. They invested the Powers which the priests pronounced infernal with those humanly just and genial qualities that had been discarded by ecclesiastical ambition. The legends which must be interpreted in this sense are very numerous, and a few of the most characteristic must suffice us here. The habit of attributing every mishap to the Devil was rebuked in many legends. One of these related that when a party were driving over a rough road the waggon broke down and one of the company exclaimed, 'This is a bit of the Devil's work!' A gentleman present said, 'It is a bit of corporation work. I don't believe in saddling the Devil with all the bad roads and bad axles.' Some time after, when this second speaker was riding over the same road alone, an old gentleman in black met him, and having thanked him for his defence of the Devil, presented him with a casket of splendid jewels. Very numerous are legends of the Devil's apparition to assist poor architects and mechanics unable to complete their contracts, even carving beautiful church pillars and the like for them, and this sometimes without receiving any recompense. The Devil's apparition in defence of accused innocence is a well-known feature of European folklore. On one occasion a soldier, having stopped at a certain inn, confided to the innkeeper some money he had for safe-keeping, and when he was about to leave the innkeeper denied having received the deposit. The soldier battered down the door, and the neighbours of the innkeeper, a prominent man in the town, put him in prison, where he lay in prospect of suffering death for an attempted burglary. The poor soldier, being a stranger without means, was unable to obtain counsel to defend him. When the parties appeared before the magistrate, a smart young lawyer, with blue hat and white feathers, unknown in the town, volunteered to defend the soldier, and related the whole story with such effect that the innkeeper in his excitement cried, 'Devil take me if I have the money!' Instantly the smart lawyer spread his wings, and, seizing the innkeeper, disappeared with him through the roof of the court-room. The innkeeper's wife, struck with horror, restored the money. In an Altmark version of this story the Devil visits the prisoner during the previous night and asks for his soul as fee, but the soldier refuses, saying he had rather die. Despite this the Devil intervened. It was an old-time custom in Denmark for courts to sit with an open window, in order that the Devil might more easily fly away with the perjurer.

Always a democrat, the Devil is said in many stories to have interfered in favour of the peasant or serf against the noble. On one occasion he relieved a certain district of all its arrogant and idle noblemen by gathering them up in a sack and flying away with them; but unhappily, as he was passing over the town of Friesack, his sack came in collision with the church steeple, and through the hole so torn a large number of noble lords fell into the town—which thence derived its name—and there they remained to be patrons of the steeple and burthens on the people.

*Fig. 23.—The Wicked Ale-wife*

The Devil was universally regarded as a Nemesis on all publicans and ale-wives who adulterated the beer they dealt out to the people, or gave short measures. At Reetz, in Altmark, the legend of an ale-wife with whom he flew away is connected with a stone on which they are said to have rested, and the villagers see thereon prints of the Devil's hoof and the woman's feet. This was a favourite theme of old English legends. The accompanying Figure (23), one of the misereres in Ludlow parish church, Shropshire, represents the end of a wicked ale-wife. A devil on one side reads the long list of her shortcomings, and on the other side hell-mouth is receiving other sinners. A devil with bagpipe welcomes her arrival. She carries with her only her fraudulent measure and the fashionable head-dress paid for out of its wicked gains.

In a marionette performance which I witnessed at Tours, the accusations brought against the tradesmen who cheated the people were such as to make one wish that the services of some equally strict devil could be secured by the authorities of all cities, to detect adulterators and dealers in false weights and measures. The same retributive agency, in the popular interest, was ascribed to the Devil in his attitude towards misers. There being no law which could reach men whose hoarded wealth brought no good to themselves or others, such were deemed proper cases for the interposition of the Devil. There is a significant contrast between the legends favoured by the Church and those of popular origin. The former, made prominent in frescoes, often show how, at the weighing of souls, the sinner is saved by a saint or angel, or by some instance of service to the Church being placed in the scale against the otherwise heavier record of evil deeds. A characteristic legend is that which is the subject of the frescoes in the portico of St. Lorenzo Church at Rome (thirteenth century). St. Lawrence sees four devils passing his hermitage, and learns from them that they are going for the soul of Henry II. In the next scene, when the wicked Count is weighed, the scroll of his evil deeds far outweighs that of his good actions, until the Saint casts into the scale a chalice which the prince had once given to his church. For that one act Henry's soul ascends to paradise amid the mortification of the Devils. Though Charles Martel saved Europe from Saracen sway, he once utilised episcopal revenues for relief of the state; consequently a synod declares him damned, a saint sees him in hell, a sulphurous dragon issues from his grave. On the other hand, the popular idea of the fate of distinguished sinners may be found hid under misereres, where kings sometimes appear in Hell, and in the early picture-books which contained a half-christianised folklore.

It has been observed that the early nature-deities, reflecting the evil and good of nature, in part through the progress of human thought and ideality, and through new ethnical rivalries, were degraded into demons. They then represented the pains, obstructions, and fears in nature. We have seen that as these apparent external evils were vanquished or better understood, the demons passed to the inward nature, and represented a new series of pains, obstructions, and fears. But these, too, were in part vanquished, or better understood. Still more, they so changed their forms that the ancient demons-turned-devils were no longer sufficiently expressive to represent them. Thus we find that the Jews, mohammedans, and christians did not find their several special antagonists impressively represented by either Satan, Iblis, or Beelzebub. Each, therefore, personified its foe in accordance with later experiences—an Opponent called Armillus, Aldajjail, Antichrist (all meaning the same thing), in whom all other devils were merged.

As to their spirit; but as to their forms they shrank in size and importance, and did duty in small ways. We have seen how great dragons were engaged in frightening boys who fished on Sundays, or oppressive squires; how Satan presided over wine-casks, or was adapted to the punishment of profanity; how hosts of once tremendous fiends turned into the grotesque little forms which Callot, truly copying the popular notions around him, painted as motley imps disturbing monks at their prayers. Such diminutions of the devils correspond to a parallel process among the gods and goddesses, by which they were changed to 'little people' or fairies. In both cases the transformation is an expression of popular disbelief in their reality.

But revivals took place. The fact of evil is permanent; and whenever the old chains of fear, after long rusting, finally break, there follows an insurrection against the social and moral order which alarms the learned and the pious. These see again the instigations of evil powers, and it takes form in the imagination of a Dante, a Luther, a Milton. But when these new portraits of the Devil are painted, it is with so much contemporary colouring that they do not answer to the traditional devils preserved in folklore. Dante's Worm does not resemble the serpent of fable, nor does Milton's Satan answer to the feathered clown of Miracle Plays. Thus, behind the actual evils which beset any time, there stands an array of grand diabolical names, detached from present perils, on which the popular fancy may work without really involving any theory of Absolute Evil at all. Were starry Lucifer to be restored to his heavenly sphere, he would be one great brand plucked from the burning, but the burning might still go on. Theology itself had filled the world with other devils by diabolising all the gods and goddesses of rival religions, and the compassionate heart was thus left free to select such forms or fair names as preserved some remnant of ancient majesty around them, or some ray from their once divine halo, and pray or hope for their pardon and salvation. Fallen foes, no longer able to harm, can hardly fail to awaken pity and clemency.

With the picture of Dives and Lazarus presented elsewhere (vol. i. p. 281) may be instructively compared the accompanying scene of a rich man's death-bed (Fig. 24), taken from 'Ars Moriendi,' one of the early block-books. This picture is very remarkable from the suggestion it contains of an opposition between a devil on the dying man's right and the hideous dragon on his left. While the dragon holds up a scroll, bidding him think of his treasure (*Yntende thesauro*), the Devil suggests provision for his friends (*Provideas amicis*). This devil seems to be a representative of the rich man's relatives who stand near, and appears to be supported by his ugly superior, who points towards hell as the penalty of not making such provision as is suggested. There would appear to be in this picture a vague distinction between the mere bestial fiend who tempts, and the ugly but good-natured devil who punishes, and whom rich sinners cannot escape by bequests to churches.

One of the most notable signs of the appearance of 'the good Devil' was the universal belief that he invariably stuck to his word. In all European folklore there is no instance of his having broken a promise. In this respect his reputation stands far higher than that of the christians, seeing that it was a boast of the saints that, following

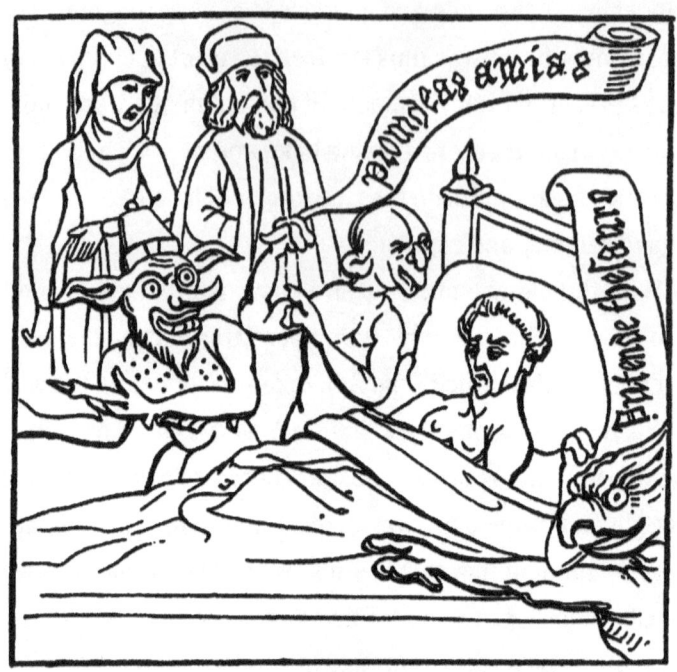

*Fig. 24.—A Mediæval Death-bed*

the example of their godhead, who outwitted Satan in the bargain for man's redemption, they were continually cheating the Devil by technical quibbles. There is a significant saying found among Prussian and Danish peasants, that you may obtain a thing by calling on Jesus, but if you would be sure of it you must call on the Devil! The two parties were judged by their representatives.

One of the earliest legendary compacts with the Devil was that made by St. Theophilus in the sixth century; when he became alarmed and penitent, the Virgin Mary managed to trick Satan out of the fatal bond. The 'Golden Legend' of Jacobus de Voragine tells why Satan was under the necessity of demanding in every case a bond signed with blood. 'The christians,' said Satan, 'are cheats; they make all sorts of promises so long as they want me, and then leave me in the lurch, and reconcile themselves with Christ so soon as, by my help, they have got what they want.'

Even apart from the consideration of possessing the soul, the ancient office of Satan as legal prosecutor of souls transmitted, to the latest forms into which he was modified, this character for justice. Many mediæval stories report his gratitude whenever he is treated with justice, though some of these are disguised by connection with other demonic forms. Such is the case with the following romance concerning Charlemagne.

When Charlemagne dwelt at Zurich, in the house commonly called 'Zum Loch,' he had a column erected to which a bell was attached by a rope. Any one that demanded justice could ring this bell when the king was at his meals. It happened one day that the bell sounded, but when the servants went to look no one was there. It continued ringing, so the Emperor commanded them to go again and find out the cause. They now remarked that an enormous serpent approached the rope and pulled it. Terrified, they brought the news to the Emperor, who immediately rose in order to administer justice to beast as well as man. After the reptile had respectfully inclined before the emperor, it led him to the banks of the river and showed him, sitting upon its nest and eggs, an enormous toad. Charlemagne having examined the case decided thus:—The toad was condemned to be burnt and justice shown to the serpent. The verdict was no sooner given than it was accomplished. A few days after the snake returned to court, bowed low to the King, crept upon the table, took the cover from a gold goblet standing there, dropped into it a precious stone, bowed again and crept away. On the spot where the serpent's nest had been, Charlemagne built a church called 'Wasserkelch.' The stone he gave to his much-loved spouse. This stone possessed the power of making the owner especially loved by the Emperor, so that when absent from his queen he mourned and longed for her. She, well aware that if it came into other hands the Emperor would soon forget her, put it under her tongue in the hour of death. The queen was buried with the stone, but Charlemagne could not separate himself from the body, so had it exhumed, and for eighteen years carried it about with him wherever he went. In the meantime, a courtier who had heard of the secret virtue of the stone, searched the corpse, and at last found the stone hidden under the tongue, and took it away and concealed it on his own person. Immediately the Emperor's love for his wife turned to the courtier, whom he now scarcely permitted out of his sight. At Cologne the courtier in a fit of anger threw the stone into a hot spring, and since then no one has succeeded in finding it. The love the Emperor had for the knight ceased, but he felt himself wonderfully attracted to the place where the stone lay hidden. On this spot he founded Aix-la-Chapelle, his subsequent favourite place of residence.

It is not wonderful that the tradition should arise at Aix, founded by the human hero of this romance, that the plan of its cathedral was supplied by the Devil; but it is characteristic there should be associated with this legend an example of how he who as a serpent was awarded justice by Charlemagne was cheated by the priests of

Aix. The Devil gave the design on condition that he was to have the first who entered the completed cathedral, and a wolf was goaded into the structure in fulfilment of the contract!

In the ancient myth and romaunt of 'Merlin' may be found the mediæval witness to the diabolised religion of Britain. The emasculated saints of the South-east could not satisfy the vigorous race in the North-west, and when its gods were outlawed as devils they brought the chief of them back, as it were, had him duly baptized and set about his old work in the form of Merlin! Here, side by side with the ascetic Jesus, brought by Gatien and Augustin, was a Northern Christ, son of an Arch-incubus, born of a Virgin, baptized in the shrunken Jordan of a font, performing miracles, summoning dragons to his aid, overcoming Death and Hell in his way, brought before his Pilate but confounding him, throning and dethroning kings, and leading forth, on the Day of Pentecost, an army whose knights are inspired by Guenever's kisses in place of flaming tongues. How Merlin 'went about doing good,' after the Northman's ideal of such work; how he saved the life of his unwedded mother by proving that her child (himself) was begotten by a devil without her knowledge; how, as a child, he exposed at once the pretension of the magistrate to high birth and the laxity of his lady and his parson; how he humiliated the priestly astrologers of Vortigern, and prophesied the destruction of that usurper just as it came to pass; how he served Uther during his seven years' reign, and by enabling him to assume the shape of the Duke of Cornwall and so enjoy the embraces of the Duchess Igerna, secured the birth of Arthur and hope of the Sangréal;[4] how he defended Arthur's legitimacy of birth and assisted him in causing illegitimate births; and how at last he was bound by his own spells, wielded by Vivien, in a prison of air where he now remains;—this was the great mediæval gospel of a baptized christian Antichrist which superseded the imported kingdom not of this world.

*Fig. 25.—From the 'Raree Show.'*

Merlin was the Good Devil, but baptism was a fatal Vivien-spell to him. He still dwells in all the air which is breathed by Anglo-Saxon men,—an ever-expanding prison! Whether the Briton is transplanted in America, India, or Africa, he still carries with him the Sermon on the

Mount as inspired by his baptized Prince of the Air, and his gospel of the day is, 'If thine enemy hunger, starve him; if he thirst, give him fire; if he hate you, heap melted lead on his head!' Such remains the soul of the greatest race, under the fatal spell of a creed that its barbarism needs only baptism to be made holiness and virtue.

In the reign of George II., when Lord Bute and a Princess of easy virtue were preying on England, and fanatical preachers were directing their donkeys to heaven beside the conflagration of John Bull's house, the eye of Hogarth at least (as is shown in our Figure 25, from his 'Raree Show') was able to see what the baptized Merlin had become in his realm of Air. The other worldly-Devil is serpent-legged Hypocrisy. The Nineteenth Century has replaced Merlin by Mephistopheles, the Devil who, despite a cloven foot, steps firmly on earth, and means the power that wit and culture can bring against the baptized giant Force. Him the gods fear not, even look upon with satisfaction. In the 'Prologue in Heaven,' of Goethe's 'Faust,' the Lord is even more gracious to Mephistopheles than the Jehovah of Job was to Satan. 'The like of thee have never moved my hate,' he says—

> Man's active nature, flagging, seeks too soon the level;
> Unqualified repose he learns to crave;
> Whence, willingly, the comrade him I gave,
> Who works, excites, and must create, as Devil.

This is but a more modern expression of the rabbinical fable, already noted, that when the first man was formed there were beside him two Spirits,—one on the right that remained quiescent, another on the left who ever moved restlessly up and down. When the first sin was committed, he of the left was changed to a devil. But he still meant the progressive, inquiring nature of man. 'The Spirit I, that evermore denies,' says the Mephistopheles of Goethe. How shall man learn truth if he know not the Spirit that denies? How shall he advance if he know not the Spirit of discontent? This restless spirit gains through his ignorance a cloven hoof,—a divided movement, sometimes right, sometimes wrong. From his selfishness it acquires a double tongue. But both hoof and serpent-tongue are beneath the evolutional power of experience; they shall be humanised to the foot that marches firmly on earth, and the tongue that speaks truth; and, the baptismal spell broken, Merlin shall descend, bringing to man's aid all his sharp-eyed dragons transformed to beautiful Arts.

---

NOTES

1   In the pre-petrified era of Theology this hope appears to have visited the minds of some, Origen for instance. But by many centuries of utilisation the Devil became so essential to the throne of Christianity that theologians were more ready to spare God from their system than Satan. 'Even the clever Madame de Staël,' said Goethe, 'was greatly scandalised that I kept the Devil in such good-humour. In the presence of God the Father, she insisted upon it, he ought to be more grim and spiteful. What will she say if she sees him promoted a step higher,—nay, perhaps, meets him in heaven?' Though, in another conversation with Falk, Goethe intimates that he had written a passage 'where the Devil himself receives grace and mercy from God,' the artistic theory of his poem could permit no nearer approach to this than those closing lines (Faust, II.) in which Mephistopheles reproaches the 'case-hardened Devil' and himself for their mismanagement. To the isolated, the not yet humanised, intellect sensuality is evil when senseless, and its hell is folly.

2   'Demonialite,' 60–62, &c. We may hope that this learned man, during his tenure of office under the Inquisition, had some mercy for the poor devils dragged before that tribunal.

3   'Reverberations.' By W. M. W. Call, M.A., Cambridge. Second Edition. Trübner & Co., 1876.

4   The Holy Grail was believed to have been fashioned from the largest of all diamonds, lost from the crown of Satan as he fell from Heaven. Guarded by angels until used at the Last Supper, it was ultimately secured by Arthur's knight, Percival, and—such is the irony of mythology—indirectly by the aid of Satan's own son, Merlin!

# Chapter XXVIII
## Animalism

'THE CHRISTIANS,' SAID Celsus, 'dream of some antagonist to God—a devil, whom they call Satanas, who thwarted God when he wished to benefit mankind. The Son of God suffered death from Satanas, but they tell us we are to defy him, and to bear the worst he can do; Satanas will come again and work miracles, and pretend to be God, but we are not to believe him. The Greeks tell of a war among the gods; army against army, one led by Saturn, and one by Ophincus; of challenges and battles; the vanquished falling into the ocean, the victors reigning in heaven. In the Mysteries we have the rebellion of the Titans, and the fables of Typhon, and Horus, and Osiris. The story of the Devil plotting against man is stranger than either of these. The Son of God is injured by the Devil, and charges us to fight against him at our peril. Why not punish the Devil instead of threatening poor wretches whom he deceives?'[1]

The christians comprehended as little as their critic that story they brought, stranger than all the legends of besieged deities, of a Devil plotting against man. Yet a little historic perspective makes the situation simple: the gods had taken refuge in man, therefore the attack was transferred to man.

Priestly legends might describe the gods as victorious over the Titans, the wild forces of nature, but the people, to their sorrow, knew better; the priests, in dealing with the people, showed that they also knew the victory to be on the other side. A careful writer remarks:—'When these (Greek) divinities are in any case appealed to with unusual seriousness, their nature-character reappears.... When Poseidon hesitates to defer to the positive commands of Zeus (Il. xix. 259), Iris reminds him that there are the Erinnyes to be reckoned with (Il. xv. 204), and he gives in at once.[2] The Erinnyes represent the steady supremacy of the laws and forces of nature over all personifications of them. Under uniform experience man had come to recognise his own moral autocracy in his world. He looked for incarnations, and it was a hope born of an atheistic view of external nature. This was the case not only with the evolution of Greek religion, but in that of every religion.

When man's hope was thus turned to rest upon man, he found that all the Titans had followed him. Ophincus (Ophion) had passed through Ophiomorphus to be a Man of Sin; and this not in one, but by corresponding forms in every line of religious development. The ferocities of outward nature appeared with all their force in man, and renewed their power with the fine armoury of his intelligence. He must here contend with tempests of passion, stony selfishness, and the whole animal creation nestling in heart and brain, prowling still, though on two feet. The theory of evolution is hardly a century old as science, but it is an ancient doctrine of Religion. The fables of Pilpay and Æsop represent an early recognition of 'survivals.' Recurrence to original types was recognised as a mystical phenomenon in legends of the bandit turned wolf, and other transformations. One of the oldest doctrines of Eschatology is represented in the accompanying picture (Fig. 26), from Thebes, of two dog-headed apes ferrying over to Hades a gluttonous soul that has been weighed before Osiris, and assigned his appropriate form.

Fig. 26.—A Soul's Doom (Wilkinson)

The devils of Lust are so innumerable that several volumes would be required to enumerate the legends and superstitions connected with them. But, fortunately for my reader and myself, these, more than any other class of phantoms, are very slight modifications of the same form. The innumerable phallic deities, the incubi and succubæ, are monotonous as the waves of the ocean, which might fairly typify the vast, restless, and stormy expanse of sexual nature to which they belong.

In 'The Golden Legend' there is a pleasant tale of a gentleman who, having fallen into poverty, went into solitude, and was there approached by a chevalier in black, mounted on a fine horse. This knight having inquired the reason of the other's sadness, promised him that, if he would return home, he would find at a certain place vast sums of gold; but this was on condition that he should bring his beautiful wife to that solitary spot in exactly a year's time. The gentleman, having lived in greater splendour than ever during the year, asked his wife to ride out with him on the appointed day. She was very pious, and having prayed to the Virgin, accompanied her husband to the spot. There the gentleman in black met them, but only to tremble. 'Perfidious man!' he cried, 'is it thus you repay my benefits? I asked you to bring your wife, and you have brought me the Mother of God, who will send me back to hell!' The Devil having vanished, the gentleman fell on his knees before the Virgin. He returned home to find his wife sleeping quietly.

Were we to follow this finely-mounted gentleman in black, we should be carried by no uncertain steps back to those sons of God who took unto themselves wives of the daughters of men, as told in Genesis; and if we followed the Virgin, we should, by less certain but yet probable steps, discover her prototype in Eve before her fall, virginal as she was meant to remain so far as man was concerned. In the chapters relating to the Eden myth and its personages, I have fully given my reasons for believing that the story of Eve, the natural childlessness of Sarah, and the immaculate conception by Mary, denote, as sea-rocks sometimes mark the former outline of a coast, a primitive theory of celibacy in connection with that of a divine or Holy Family. It need only be added here that this impossible ideal in its practical development was effectual in restraining the sexual passions of mankind. Although the reckless proclamation of the wild nature-gods (Elohim), 'Be fruitful and multiply,' has been accepted by christian bibliolators as the command of Jehovah, and philanthropists are even punished for suggesting means of withstanding the effects of nuptial licentiousness, yet they are farther from even the letter of the Bible than those protestant celibates, the American Shakers, who discard the sexual relation altogether. The theory of the Shakers that the functions of sex 'belong to a state of nature, and are inconsistent with a state of grace,' as one of their members in Ohio stated it to me, coincides closely with the rabbinical theory that Adam and Eve, by their sin, fell to the lowest of seven earthly spheres, and thus came within the influence of the incubi and succubæ, by their union with whom the world was filled with the demonic races, or Gentiles.

It is probable that the fencing-off of Eden, the founding of the Abrahamic household and family, and the command against adultery, were defined against that system of rape—or marriage by capture— which prevailed among the 'sons of Elohim,' who saw the 'daughters of men that they were fair,' and followed the law of their eyes. The older rabbins were careful to preserve the distinction between the *Bene Elohim* and the *Ischim*, and it ultimately amounted to that between Jews and Gentiles.

The suspicion of a devil lurking behind female beauty thus begins. The devils love beauty, and the beauties love admiration. These are perils in the constitution of the family. But there are other legends which report the frequency with which woman was an unwilling victim of the lustful Anakim or other powerful lords. Throughout the world are found legends of beautiful virgins sacrificed to powerful demons or deities. These are sometimes so realistic as to suggest the possibility that the fair captives of savage chieftains may indeed have been sometimes victims of their Ogre's voracity as well as his lust. At any rate, cruelty and lust are nearly related. The Blue Beard myth opens out horrible possibilities.

One of the best-known legends in Japan is that concerning the fiend Shudendozi, who derives his name from the two characteristics of possessing the face of a child and being a heavy drinker. The child-face is so emphasised in the stories that one may suspect either that his fair victims were enticed to his stronghold by his air of innocence, or else that there is some hint as to maternal longings in the fable.

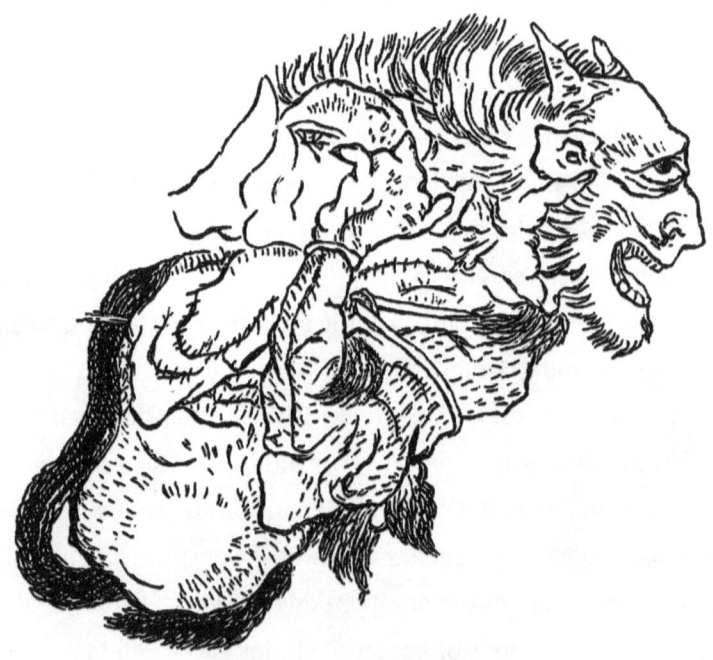

*Fig. 27.—Cruelty and Lust (Japanese)*

At the beginning of the eleventh century, when Ichijo II. was Emperor, lived the hero Yorimitsa. In those days the people of Kiyoto were troubled by an evil spirit which abode near the Rasho Gate. One night, when merry with his companions, Ichijo said, 'Who dare go and defy the demon of the Rasho Gate, and set up a token that he has been there?' 'That dare I,' answered Tsuma, who, having donned his mail, rode out in the bleak night to the Rasho Gate. Having written his name on the gate, returning, his horse shivers with fear, and a huge hand coming out of the gate seized the knight's helmet. He struggled in vain. He then cuts off the demon's arm, and the demon flies howling. Tsuma takes the demon's arm home, and locks it in a box. One night the demon, having the shape of Tsuma's aunt, came and said, 'I pray you show me the arm of the fiend.' 'I will show it to no man, and yet to thee will I show it,' replied he. When the box is opened a black cloud enshrouds the aunt, and the demon disappears with the arm. Thereafter he is more troublesome than ever. The demon carried off the fairest virgins of Kiyoto, ravished and ate them, no beauty being left in the city. The Emperor commands Yorimitsa to destroy him. The hero, with four trusty knights and a great captain, went to the hidden places of the mountains. They fell in with an old man, who invited them into his dwelling, and gave them wine to drink; and when they were going he presented them with wine. This old man was a mountain-god. As they proceeded they met a beautiful lady washing blood from garments in a valley, weeping bitterly. In reply to their inquiries she said the demon had carried her off and kept her to wash his clothes, meaning when weary of her to eat her. 'I pray your lordships to help me!' The six heroes bid her lead them to the ogre's cave. One hundred devils mounted guard before it. The woman first went in and told him they had come. The ogre called them in, meaning to eat them. Then they saw Shudendozi, a monster with the face of a little child. They offered him wine, which flew to his head: he becomes merry and sleeps, and his head is cut off. The head leaps up and tries to bite Yorimitsa, but he had on two helmets. When all the devils are slain, he brings the head of Shudendozi to the Emperor. In a similar story of the same country the lustful ogre by no means possesses Shudendozi's winning visage, as may be seen by the popular representation of him (Fig. 27), with a knight's hand grasping his throat.

A Singhalese demon of like class is Bahirawa, who takes his name from the hill of the same name, towering over Kandy, in which he is supposed to reside. The legend runs that the astrologers told a king whose queen was afflicted by successive miscarriages, that she would never be delivered of a healthy child unless a virgin was sacrificed annually on the top of this hill. This being done, several children were borne to him. When his queen was advanced in years the king discontinued this observance, and consequently many dis-eases fell upon the royal family and the city, after which the annual sacrifice was resumed, and continued until 1815, when the English occupied Kandy. The method of the sacrifice was to bind a young girl to a stake on the top of the hill with jungle-creepers. Beside her, on an altar, were placed boiled rice and flowers; incantations were uttered, and the girl left, to be generally found dead of fright in the morning. An old woman, who in early years had undergone this ordeal, survived, and her safety no doubt co-operated with English authority to diminish the popular fear of Bahirawa, but still few natives would be found courageous enough to ascend the hill at night.

One of the lustful demons of Ceylon is Calu Cumara, that is, the Black Prince. He is supposed to have seven different apparitions,—prince of fire, of flowers, of groves, of graves, of eye-ointments, of the smooth body, and of sexuality. The Saga says he was a Buddhist priest, who by exceeding asceticism and accumulated merits had gained the power to fly, but passion for a beautiful woman caused him to fall. By disappointment in the love for which he had parted with so much his heart was broken, and he became a demon. In this condition he is for ever tortured by the passion of lustful desire, the only satisfaction of which he can obtain being to afflict young and fair women with illness. He is a very dainty demon, and can be soothed if great care is taken in the offerings made to him, which consist of rice of finest quality, plantains, sugar-cane, oranges, cocoa-nuts, and cakes. He is of dark-blue complexion and his raiment black.

In Singhalese demonolatry there are seven female demons of lust, popularly called the Madana Yaksenyo. These sisters are— Cama (lust); Cini (fire); Mohanee (ignorance); Rutti (pleasure); Cala (maturity); Mal (flowers); Puspa (perfumes). They are the abettors of seduction, and are invoked in the preparation of philtres.[3]

'It were well,' said Jason to Medea, 'that the female race should not exist; then would there not have been any evil among men.'[4] The same sentiment is in Milton—

Oh why did God,
Creator wise, that peopled highest heaven
With spirits masculine, create at last
This novelty on earth, this fair defect
Of nature, and not fill the world at once
With men, as angels, without feminine? [5]

Many traditions preceded this ungallant creed, some of which
have been referred to in our chapters on Lilith and Eve. Corresponding to these are the stories related by Herodotus of the overthrow of
the kingdom of the Heraclidæ and freedom of the Greeks, through
the revenge of the Queen, 'the most beautiful of women,' upon her
husband Candaules for having contrived that Gyges should see her
naked. Candaules having been slain by Gyges at the instigation of the
Queen, and married her, the Fates decreed that their crime should
be punished on their fifth descendant. The overthrow was by Cyrus,
and it was associated with another woman, Mandane, daughter of
the tyrant Astyages, mother of Cyrus, who is thus, as the Madonna,
to bruise the head of the serpent who had crept into the Greek Paradise.[6] The Greeks of Pontus also ascribed the origin of the Scythian
race, the scourge of all nations, to a serpent-woman, who, having
stolen away the mares which Herakles had captured from Gergon,
refused to restore them except on condition of having children by
him. From the union of Herakles with this 'half virgin, half viper,'
sprang three sons, of whom the youngest was Scythes.

*Fig. 28.—JEALOUSY (Japanese)*

Not only are feminine seductiveness and liability to seduction represented in the legends of female demons and devils, but quite as much the jealousy of that sex. If the former were weaknesses which might overthrow kingdoms, the latter was a species of animalism which could devastate the home and society. Although jealousy is sometimes regarded as venial, if not indeed a sign of true love, it is an outcome of the animal nature. The Japanese have shown a true observation of nature in portraying their female Oni (devil) of jealousy (Fig. 28) with sharp erect horns and bristling hair. The raising 'of the ornamental plumes by many birds during their courtship,' mentioned by Mr. Darwin, is the more pleasing aspect of that emotion which, blending with fear and rage, puffs out the lizard's throat, ruffles the cock's neck, and raises the hair of the insane.[7]

An ancient legend mingles jealousy with the myth of Eden at every step. Rabbi Jarchi says that the serpent was jealous of Adam's connubial felicity, and a passage in Josephus shows that this was an ancient opinion. The jealousy of Adam's second wife felt by his first (Lilith) was by many said to be the cause of her conspiracy with the serpent. The most beautiful mediæval picture of her that I have seen was in an illuminated Bible in Strasburg, in which, with all her wealth of golden hair and her beauty, Lilith holds her mouth, with a small rosy apple in it, towards Adam. Eve seems to snatch it. Then there is an old story that when Eve had eaten the apple she saw the angel of death, and urged Adam to eat the fruit also, in order that he might not become a widower.

It is remarkable that there should have sprung up a legend that Satan made his second attack upon the race formed by Jehovah, and his plan for perpetuating it on earth by means of a flirtation with Noah's wife, and also by awakening her jealousy. The older legend concerning Noah's wife is that mentioned by Tabari, which merely states that she ridiculed the predictions of a deluge by her husband. So much might have been suggested by the silence of the Bible concerning her. The Moslem tradition that the Devil managed to get into the ark is also ancient. He caught hold of the ass's tail just as it was about to enter. The ass came on slowly, and Noah, becoming impatient, exclaimed, 'You cursed one, come in quick!' When Noah, seeing the Devil in the ark, asked by what right he was there, the other said, 'By your order; you said, "Accursed one, come in;" I am the accursed one!' This story, which seems contrived to show that one may not be such an ass as he looks, was superseded by the legend which represents Satan as having been brought into the ark concealed under Noria's (or Noraita's) dress.

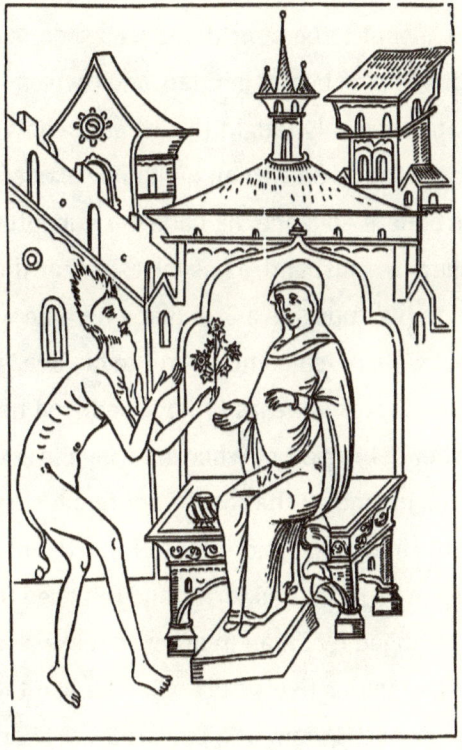

*Fig. 29.—Satan and Noraita*

The most remarkable legend of this kind is that found in the Eastern Church, and which is shown in various mediæval designs in Russia. Satan is shown, in an early sixteenth century picture belonging to Count Uvarof (Fig. 29), offering Noah's wife a bunch of *khmel* (hops) with which to brew *kvas* and make Noah drunk; for the story was that Noah did not tell his wife that a deluge was coming, knowing that she could not keep a secret. In the old version of the legend given by Buslaef, 'after apocryphal tradition used by heretics,' Satan always addresses Noah's wife as *Eve*, which indicates a theory. It was meant to be considered as a second edition of the attack on the divine plan begun in Eden, and revived in the temptation of Sara. Satan not only taught this new Eve how to make *kvas* but also *vodka* (brandy); and when he had awakened her jealousy about Noah's frequent absence, he bade her substitute the brandy for the beer when her husband, as usual, asked for the latter. When Noah was thus in his cups she asked him where he went, and why he kept late hours. He revealed his secret to his Eve, who disclosed it to Satan. The tempter appears to have seduced her from Noah, and persuaded her to be dilatory when entering the ark. When all the animals had gone in, and all the rest of her family, Eve said, 'I have forgotten my pots and pans,' and went to fetch them; next she said, 'I have forgotten my spoons and forks,' and returned for them. All of this had been arranged by Satan in order to make Noah curse; and he had just slipped under Eve's skirt when he had the satisfaction of hearing the intended Adam of a baptized world cry to his wife, 'Accursed one, come in!' Since Jehovah himself could not prevent the carrying out of a patriarch's curse, Satan was thus enabled to enter the ark, save himself from being drowned, and bring mischief into the human world once more.

This is substantially the same legend as that of the mediæval

Morality called 'Noah's Ark, or the Shipwright's Ancient Play or Dirge.' The Devil says to Noah's wife:—

> Yes, hold thee still le dame,
> And l shall tell thee how;
> l swear thee by my crooked snout,
> All that thy husband goes about
> ls little to thy profit.
> Yet shall l tell thee how
> Thou shalt meet all his will;
> Do as l shall bid thee now,
> Thou shalt meet every deal.
> Have here a drink full good
> That is made of a mightful main,
> Be he hath drunken a drink of this,
> No longer shall he learn:
> Believe, believe, my own dear dame,
> l may no longer bide;
> To ship when thou shalt sayre,
> l shall be by thy side.

There are some intimations in the Slavonic version which look as if it might have belonged to some Paulician or other half-gnostic theory that the temptation of Noraita (Eve ll.), and her alienation from her husband, were meant to prevent the repopulation of the Earth.[8]

The next attempt of the Devil, as agent of the Elohistic creation, to ruin the race of man, introduces us to another form of animalism which has had a large expression in Devil-lore. It is related in rabbinical mythology that when, as is recorded in Gen. ix. 20, Noah was planting a vineyard, the Devil (Asmodeus) came and proposed to join him in the work. This having been agreed to, this evil partner brought in succession a sheep, a lion, and a hog, and sacrificed them on the spot. The result was that the wine when drunk first gave the drinker the quality of a sheep, then that of a lion, and finally that of a hog.[9] It was by this means that Noah was reduced to swinish inebriation. There followed the curses on those around him, which, however drunken, were those of a father, and reproduced on the cleansed world all the dooms which had been pronounced in Eden.

If the date of this legend could be made early enough, it would appear to be a sort of revenge for this temptation of Noah to drunkenness that Talmudic fable shows Asmodeus brought under bondage to Solomon, and forced to work on the Temple, by means of wine. Asmodeus had dug for himself a well, and planted beside it a tree, so making for himself a pleasant spot for repose during his goings to and fro on earth. But Solomon's messenger Benaja managed to cover this with a tank which he filled with wine. Asmodeus, on his return, repeated to himself the proverb, 'Wine is a mocker, strong drink is raging, and whosoever is deceived thereby is not wise' (Prov. xx. 1); yet, being very thirsty, he drank, fell asleep, and when he awoke found himself loaded with chains.

However, after working for a time for Solomon, he discovered that king's weaknesses and played upon them. Solomon was so puffed up with a sense of his power that he accepted a challenge from his slave (Asmodeus) to show his superiority without the assistance of his magic ring, and without keeping his competitor in bonds. No sooner was Asmodeus free, and in possession of the ring, than he transported Solomon four hundred miles away, where he remained for a long time among the seductive beauties of the Courts of Naamah, Rahab, and other she-devils. Meanwhile the Devil, assuming the form of Solomon, sat on his throne, and became the darling of his Queen and concubines.

The Devil of Wine and strong drink generally has a wide representation in folklore. We find him in the bibulous Serpent of Japan, who first loses his eight heads metaphorically, and then literally from the first of Swords-men. The performances of Mephistopheles in Auerbach's Cellar are commemorated in its old frescoes, and its motto: 'Live, drink, carouse, remembering Faust and his punishment: it came slowly, but was in ample measure.' Thuringian legends relate that the Devil tries to stop the building of churches by casting down the stones, but this may be stopped by the builders promising to erect a winehouse in the same neighbourhood. An old English legend relates that a great man's cellar was haunted by devils who drank up his wine. On one occasion a barrel was marked with holy water, and the devil was found stuck fast on it.

Gluttony, both in eating and drinking, has had its many personifications. The characteristics of the Hunger demons are travestied in such devils as these, only the diabolical, as distinguished from the demonic element, appears in features of luxuriousness. The contrast between the starveling saints of the early Church and the well-fed friars of later times was a frequent subject of caricature, as in the accompanying example (Fig. 30) from the British Museum, fourteenth century (MS. Arundel), where a lean devil is satisfying himself through a fattened friar. One of the most significant features of the old legend of Faust is the persistence of the animal character in which Mephistopheles appears. He is an ugly dog—a fit emblem of the scholar's relapse into the canine temper which flies at the world as at a bone he means to gnaw. Faust does not like this genuine form, and bids the Devil change it. Mephistopheles then takes the form of a Franciscan friar; but 'the kernel of the brute' is in him still, and he at once loads Faust's table with luxuries and wines from the cellars of the Archbishop of Salzburg and other rich priests. The prelates are fond of their bone too. When Mephistopheles and Faust find their way into the Vatican, it is to witness carousals of the Pope and his Cardinals. They snatch from them their luxuries and wine-goblets as they are about to enjoy them. Against these invisible invaders the holy men bring their crucifixes and other powers of exorcism; and it is all snarling and growling—canine priest against puppy astrologer. Nor was it very different in the history of the long contention between the two for the big bone of Christendom.

*Fig. 30.—Monkish Gluttony*

The lust of Gold had its devils, and they were not different from other types of animalism. This was especially the case with such as represented money, extorted from the people to supply wealth to dissolute princes and prelates. The giants of Antwerp represent the power of the pagan monarchs who exacted tribute; but these were replaced by such guardians of tribute-money as the Satyr of our picture (Fig. 31), which Edward the Confessor saw seated on a barrel of Danegeld,

> Vit un déable saer desus
> Le tresor, noir et hidus.

There are many good fables in European folklore with regard to the miser's gold, and 'devil's money' generally, which exhibit a fine instinct. A man carries home a package of such gold, and on opening it there drop out, instead of money, paws and nails of cats, frogs, and bears—the latter being an almost personal allusion to the Exchange. A French miser's money-safe being opened, two frogs only were found. The Devil could not get any other soul than the gold, and the cold-blooded reptiles were left as a sign of the life that had been lived.

In the legends of the swarms of devils which beset St. Anthony we find them represented as genuine animals. Our Anglo-Saxon fathers, however, were quite unable to appreciate the severity of the conflict which man had to wage with the animal world in Southern countries and in earlier times. Nor had their reverence for nature and its forms been crushed out by the pessimist theory of the earth maintained by Christianity. Gradually the representation of the animal tempters was modified, and instead of real animal forms there were reported the bearded bestialities which surrounded St. Guthlac and St. Godric.

*Fig. 31.—Devil of a Danegeld Treasure (MS. Trin. Coll. Cantab. B. x. 2)*

The accompanying picture (Fig. 32) is a group from Breughel (1565), representing the devils called around St. James by a magician. These grotesque forms will repay study. If we should make a sketch of the same kind, only surrounding the saint with the real animal shapes most nearly resembling these nondescripts, it would cease to be a diabolical scene.

*Fig. 32.—St. James and Devils*

For beastliness is not a character of beasts; it is the arrest of man. It is not the picturesque donkey in the meadow that is ridiculous, but the donkey on two feet; not the bear of zoological gardens that is offensive morally, but the rough, who cannot always be caged; it is the two-legged calf, the snake pretending to be a man, the ape in evening dress, who ever made the problem of evil at all formidable. It was insoluble until men had discovered as Science that law of Evolution which the ancient world knew as Ethics.

A Hindu fable relates that the animals, in their migration, came to an abyss they could not cross, and that the gods made man as a bridge across it. Science and Reason confirm these ancient instincts of our race. Man is that bridge stretching between the animal and the ideal habitat by which, if the development be normal, all the passions pass upward into educated powers. Any pause or impediment on that bridge brings all the animals together to rend and tear the man who cannot convey them across the abyss. A very slight arrest may reveal to a man that he is a vehicle of intensified animalism.

The lust of the goat, the pride of the peacock, the wrath of the lion, beautiful in their appropriate forms, become, in the guise of a man uncontrolled by reason, the vices which used to be called possession, and really are insanities.

## NOTE

1 See Mr. J. A. Froude's article in 'Fraser's Magazine,' Feb. 1878, 'Origen and Celsus.'

2 Mr. W. W. Lloyd's 'Age of Pericles,' vol. ii. p. 202.

3 Journal of the Ceylon Branch of the R. A. S., 1865–6: Art. on 'Demonology and Witchcraft in Ceylon,' by Dundris de Silva Gooneratne Modliar.

4 Euripides, 'Medea,' 574.

5 'Paradise Lost,' x. 860.

6 Herodotus, 'Clio,' 7–14, 91.

7 'Expression of the Emotions.' By Charles Darwin. London: Murray, 1872. Chapter IV.

8 The giving of Eve's name to Noah's wife is not the only significant thing about this Russian tradition and its picture. Long-bearded devils are nowhere normal except in the representations by the Eastern Church of the monarch of Hell. By referring to p. 253 of this volume the reader will observe the influences which caused the infernal king to be represented as counterpart of the Deity. As this tradition about Noah's wife is suggestive of a Gnostic origin, it really looks as if the Devil in it were meant to act the part which the Gnostics ascribed to Jehovah himself (vol. ii. p. 207). The Devil is said in rabbinical legends to have seduced the wives of Noah's sons; this legend seems to show that his aim was to populate the post-diluvial world entirely with his own progeny, in this being an Ildabaoth, or degraded edition of Jehovah trying to establish his own family in the earth by the various means related in vol. i. chap. 8.

9 'Nischamath Chajim,' fol. 139, col. 2.

## Chapter XXIX
# Thoughts and Interpretations

I LATELY HEARD the story of a pious negro woman whose faith in hell was sorely tried by a sceptic who asked her how brimstone enough could be found to burn all the wicked people in the world. After taking some days for reflection, the old woman, when next challenged by the sceptic, replied, that she had concluded that 'every man took his own brimstone.' This humble saint was unconscious that her instinct had reached the finest thought of Milton, whose Satan says 'Myself am hell.' Marlowe's Mephistopheles also says, 'Where we are is hell.' And, far back as the year 633, the holy man Fursey, who believed himself to have been guided by an angel near the region of the damned, related a vision much like the view of the African woman. There were four fires—Falsehood, Covetousness, Discord, Injustice—which joined to form one great flame. When this drew near, Fursey, in fear, said, 'Lord, behold the fire draws near me.' The angel answered, 'That which you did not kindle shall not burn you.'

Such association of any principle of justice, even in form so crude, has become rare enough in Christendom to excite applause when it appears, though the applause has about it that infusion of the grotesque which one perceives when gallery-gods cheer the actor who heroically declares that a man ought not to strike a woman. When we go back to the atmosphere of Paganism we find that retribution had among them a real meaning. Nothing can be in more remarkable contrast than the disorderly characterless hell of Christendom, into which the murderer and the man who confuses the Persons of the Godhead alike burn everlastingly in most inappropriate fires, and the Hades of Egypt, Greece, and Rome, where every punishment bears relation to the offence, and is limited in duration to the degree of the offence.

'The Egyptians,' says Herodotus (ii. 123), 'were the first who asserted that the soul of man is immortal, and that when the body perishes it enters into some other animal, constantly springing into existence; and when it has passed through the different kinds of terrestrial, marine, and aerial beings, it again enters into the body of a man that is born, and that this revolution is made in three thousand years.' Probably Plato imported from Egypt his fancy of the return of one dead to relate the scenes of heaven and hell, Er the Armenian (Republic, x. 614) suggesting an evolution of Rhampsinitus (Herod. ii. 122), who descended to Hades alive, played dice with Ceres, and brought back gold. The vision of Er represents a terrible hell, indeed, but those punished were chiefly murderers and tyrants. They are punished tenfold for every wrong they had committed. But when this punishment is ended, each soul must return to the earth in such animal form as he or she might select. The animals, too, had their choice. Er saw that the choice was generally determined by the previous earthly life,—many becoming animals because of some spite derived from their experience. 'And not only did men pass into animals, but I must also mention that there were animals tame and wild who changed into one another, and into corresponding human natures, the good into the gentle, the evil into the savage, in all sorts of combinations.' Sly Plato! Such is his estimate of what men's selections of their paradises are worth!

Orpheus chose to be a swan, hating to be born of woman, because women murdered him; Ajax became a lion and Agamemnon an eagle, because they had suffered injustice from men; Atalanta would be an athlete, and the jester Thersites a monkey; and Odysseus went about to find the life of a private gentleman with nothing to do. If Plutarch's friend Thespesius had pondered well this irony of Plato, he would hardly have brought back from his visit to Hades the modification that demons were provided to assign the animal forms in which souls should be born again on earth. They could hardly have done for the wicked anything worse than Plato shows them doing for themselves. But the meaning of Plutarch is the same. Thespesius sees demons preparing the body of a viper for Nero to be born into, since it was said the young of that reptile destroy their mother at birth.

Among the Persians the idea of future rewards and punishments exceeds the exactness of the Koran—'Whoso hath done an atom of justice shall behold it, and whoso hath done an atom of injustice shall behold it.' The Persian Sufis will even subdivide the soul rather than that any good act should go down with the larger gross of wickedness. Sádi tells of a vision where a man was seen in hell, all except one foot, which was twined with flowers. With all his wickedness the man had with that foot shoved a bundle of hay within reach of a weary ox.

But while Persian poets—Sufis, ennobling the old name Sophist—preserved thus a good deal of the universalism of Parsaism, a Mohammedanism hard as the Scythians who brought it turned the heart of the people in that country to stone. In the Dresden Library there is an illuminated Persian MS., thought to be seven hundred years old, which has in it what may be regarded as a portrait of Ahriman and Iblis combined. He is red, has a heavy beard and moustache, and there is a long dragon's crest and mane on his head. He wears a green and blue skirt about his loins. His tongue rolls thirstily between his cruel teeth. He superintends a number of fish-like devils which float in a lake of fire, and swallow the damned. Above this scene are the glorified souls, including the Shah sitting cross-legged on his rug, who look down on the tortures beneath with evident satisfaction. Apparently this is the only amusement which relieves the *ennui* of their heaven.

If anything could make a rational man believe in a fiend-principle in the universe it would be the suggestion of such pictures, that men have existed who could conceive of happiness enjoyed in view of such tortures as these. This and some similar pictures in the East—for instance, that in the Temple of Horrors at Wuchang, China—are absolutely rayless so far as any touch of humanity is concerned. Are the Shah and his happy fellow-inspectors of tortures really fiends? In the light of our present intelligence they may seem so. Certainly no person of refined feeling could now expect to attain any heaven while others were in hell. But it *would* be possible, if persons could believe that many of those around them are not men and women at all, but fiends in human shape. These ferocious Hells are referable to a period when all who incurred the sentences of princes or priests were seen as mere masks of devils; they were only ascribed human flesh that they may suffer. The dogma of Hell was doomed from the moment that the damned were supposed to be really human.

Were those who killed the martyrs of heresy, for instance, to return to the world and look upon those whom they pierced, they could never recognise them. Were they to see the statues of Bruno, Huss, Cranmer, Servetus, the names and forms would not recall to them the persons they slew. They would be shocked if told that they had burned great men, and would surely answer, 'Men? We burned no men. The Devil came among us calling himself Huss, and we made short work with him; he reappeared under several *aliases*—Bruno, Servetus, Spinoza, Voltaire: sometimes we burned him, at other times managed to make him miserable, thank God! But we were not hurting real men, we were saving them.'

Around such ideas grew our yet uncivilised Codes of Law. In England, anno 1878, men are refused as jury-men if they will not say, 'So help me God!' on the ground that an atheist cannot have a conscience. Only let him really be without conscience, and call himself a christian when he is not, and courts receive the selfish liar with respect. The old clause of the death-sentence—'instigated thereto by the Devil'—has been dropped in the case of murderers, however; and that is some gain. Torture by fire of the worst murderer for one day would not be permitted in Christendom. Belief in hell-fire outlasts it for a little among the ignorant. But what shall be said of the educated who profess to believe it?

The Venerable Bede relates that, in the year 696, a Northumbrian gentleman, who had died in the beginning of the night, came to life and health in the morning, and gave an account of what he had seen overnight. He had witnessed the conventional tortures of the damned, but adds—'Being thus on all sides enclosed with enemies and darkness, and looking about on every side for assistance, there appeared to me, on the way that I came, as it were, the brightness of a star shining amidst the darkness, which increased by degrees,'—but we need not go on to the anti-climax of this vision.

This star rising above all such visions belongs to the vault of the human Love, and it is visible through all the Ages of Darkness. It cannot be quenched, and its fiery rays have burnt up mountains of iniquity.

'In the year 1322,' writes Flögel, after the 'Chronicon Sampetrinum Erfurtense,' 'there was a play shown at Eisenach, which had a tragical enough effect. Markgraf Friedrich of Misnia, Landgraf also of Thuringia, having brought his tedious warfare to a conclusion, and the country beginning now to revive under peace, his subjects were busy repaying themselves for the past distresses by all manner of diversions; to which end, apparently by the Sovereign's order, a dramatic representation of the *Ten Virgins* was schemed, and at Eisenach, in his presence, duly executed. This happened fifteen days after Easter, by indulgence of the Preaching Friars. In the 'Chronicon Sampetrinum' stands recorded that the play was enacted in the Bear Garden (*in horto ferarum*) by the Clergy and their Scholars. But now, when it came to pass that the Wise Virgins would give the foolish no oil, and these latter were shut out from the Bridegroom, they began to weep bitterly, and called on the Saints to intercede for them; who however, even with Mary at their head, could effect nothing from God; but the Foolish Virgins were all sentenced to damnation. Which things the Landgraf seeing and hearing, he fell into a doubt, and was very angry; and said 'What then is the Christian Faith, if God will not take pity on us for intercession of Mary and all the Saints?' In this anger he continued five days; and the learned men could hardly enlighten him to understand the Gospel. Thereupon he was struck with apoplexy, and became speechless and powerless; in which sad state he continued, bedrid, two years and seven months, and so died, being then fifty-five.'

In telling the story Carlyle remarks that these 'Ten Virgins at Eisenach are more fatal to warlike men than Æschylus' Furies at Athens were to weak women.' Even so, until great-hearted men rose up at Eisenach and elsewhere to begin the work destined to prove fatal alike to heartless Virgins and Furies. That star of a warrior's Compassion, hovering over the foolish Friars and their midnight Gospel, beams far. The story reminds me of an incident related of a mining district in California, where a rude theatre was erected, and a company gave, as their first performance, Othello. When the scene of Desdemona's suffocation approached, a stalwart miner leaped on the stage, and pulling out his six-shooter, said to the Moor, 'You damned nigger! if you touch that woman I'll blow the top of your head off!' A dozen roughs, clambering over the footlights, cried, 'Right Joe! we'll stand by you!' The manager met the emergency by crying, 'Don't shoot, boys! This play was wrote by Bill Shakespear; he's an old Californian, and it's all in fun!' Had this Moor proceeded to roast Desdemona in fire with any verisimilitude, it is doubtful if the manager could have saved him by an argument reminding the miners that such was the divine way with sinners in the region to which most of them were going. The top of that theologic hell's head is not very safe in these days when human nature is unchained with all its six-shooters, each liable to be touched off by fire from that Star revolving in the sphere of Compassion.

Day after day I gazed upon Michael Angelo's 'Last Judgment' in the Sistine Chapel. The artist was in his sixtieth year when Pope Clement VII. invited him to cover a wall sixty feet high and nearly as wide with a picture of the Day of Wrath. In seven years he had finished it. Clement was dead. Pope Paul IV. looked at it, and liked it not: all he could see was a vast number of naked figures; so he said it was not fit for the Sistine Chapel, and must be destroyed. One of Michael Angelo's pupils saved it by draping some of the figures. Time went on, and another Pope came who insisted on more drapery,—so the work was disfigured again. However, popular ridicule saved this from going very far, and so there remains the tremendous scene. But Popes and Cardinals always disliked it. The first impression I received from it was that of a complete representation of all the physical powers belonging to organised life; though the forms are human, every animal power is there, leaping, crouching, crawling,—every sinew, joint, muscle, portrayed in completest tension and action. Then the eye wanders from face to face, and every passion that ever crawled or prowled in jungle or swamp is pictured. The most unpleasant expressions seemed to me those of the martyrs. They came up from their graves, each bringing the instrument by which he had suffered, and offering it in witness against the poor wretches who came to be judged; and there was a look of self-righteous satisfaction on their faces as they witnessed the persecution of their persecutors. As for Christ, he was like a fury, with hand uplifted against the doomed, his hair wildly floating. The tortured people below are not in contrast with the blessed above; they who are in heaven look rather more stupid than the others, and rather pleased with the anguish they witness, but not more saintly. But gradually the eye, having wandered over the vast canvas, from the tortured Cardinal at the bottom up to the furious Judge,—alights on a face which, once seen, is never to be forgotten. Beautiful she is, that Mary beside the Judge, and more beautiful for the pain that is on her face. She has drawn her drapery to veil from her sight the anguish below; she has turned her face from the Judge,—does not see her son in him; she looks not upon the blessed,—for she, the gentle mother, is not in heaven; she cannot have joy in sight of misery. In that one face of pure womanly sympathy—that beauty transfigured in its compassionateness—the artist put his soul, his religion. Mary's face quenches all the painted flames. They are at once made impossible. The same universe could not produce both a hell and that horror of it. The furious Jesus is changed to a phantasm; he could never be born of such a mother.

If the Popes had only wished to hide the nakedness of their own dogmas they ought to have blotted out Mary's face; for as it now stands the rest of the forms are but shapes to show how all the wild forms and passions of human animalism gather as a frame round that which is their consummate flower,—the spirit of love enshrined in its perfect human expression.

So was it that Michael Angelo could not serve two masters. Popes might employ him, but he could not do the work they liked. 'The passive master lent his hand to the vast soul that o'er him planned.' He could not help it. The lover of beauty could not paint the Day of Wrath without setting above it that face like a star which shines through its unreality, burns up its ugliness, and leaves the picture a magnificent interpretation of the forms of nature and hopes of the world,—a cardinal hypocrite at the bottom, an ideal woman at the top.

Exhausted by the too-much glory of the visions of Paradise which he had seen, Dante came forth to the threshold opening on the world of human life, from which he had parted for a space, and there sank down. As he lay there angels caused lilies to grow beneath and around him, and myrtle to rise and intertwine for a bower over him, and their happy voices, wafted in low-toned hymns, brought soft sleep to his overwrought senses. Long had he slumbered before the light of familiar day stole once more into those deep eyes. The angels had departed. The poet awoke to find himself alone, and with a sigh he said to himself, 'It is, then, all but a dream.' As he arose he saw before him a man of noble mien and shining countenance, habited in an Eastern robe, who returned his gaze with an interest equal to his own. Quickly the eyes of Dante searched the ground beside the stranger to see if he were shadowless: convinced thus that he was true flesh and blood, the Florentine thus addressed him:—

'Pilgrim, for such thou seemest, may we meet in simple human brotherhood? If, as thy garb suggests, thou comest from afar, perchance the friendly greeting, even of one who in his native city is still himself a pilgrim, may not be unwelcome.

'Heart to heart be our kiss, my brother; yet must I journey without delay to those who watch and wait for wondrous tidings that I bear.

'Friend! I hear some meaning deeper than thy words. If 'twere but as satisfying natural curiosity, answer not; but if thou bearest a burden of tidings glad for all human-kind, speak! Who art thou? whence comest, and with what message freighted?

'Arda Viráf is the name I bear; from Persia have I come; but by what strange paths have reached this spot know I not, save that through splendours of worlds invisible to mortal sense I have journeyed, nor encountered human form till I found thee slumbering on this spot.

'Trebly then art thou my brother! I too have but now, as to my confused sense it seems, emerged from that vast journey. Thou clearest from me gathering doubts that those visions were illusive. Yet, as even things we really see are often overlaid by images that lurk in the eye, I pray thee tell me something thou hast seen, so that perchance we may part with mutual confirmation of our vision.

'That gladly will I do. When the Avesta had been destroyed, and the sages of Iran disagreed as to the true religion, they agreed that one should be chosen by lot to drink the sacred draught of Vishtasp, that he might pass to the invisible world and bring intelligence therefrom. On me the lot fell. Beside the fire that has never gone out, surrounded by holy women who chanted our hymns, I drank the three cups—Well Thought, Well Said, Well Done. Then as I slept there rose before me a high stairway of three steps; on the first was written, Well Thought; on the second,

Well Said; on the third, Well Done. By the first step I reached the realm where good thoughts are honoured: there were the thinkers whose starlike radiance ever increased. They offered no prayers, they chanted no liturgies. Above all was the sphere of the liberal. The next step brought me to the circle of great and truthful speakers: these walked in lofty splendour. The third step brought me to the heaven of good actions. I saw the souls of agriculturists surrounded by spirits of water and earth, trees and cattle. The artisans were seated on embellished thrones. Sublime were the seats of teachers, interceders, peace-makers; and the religious walked in light and joy with which none are satiated.

'Sawest thou the fairest of earth-born ladies—Beatrice?

'I saw indeed a lady most fair. In a pleasant grove lay the form of a man who had but then parted from earth. When he had awakened, he walked through the grove and there met him this most beautiful maiden. To her he said, 'Who art thou, so fair beyond all whom I have seen in the land of the living?' To him she replied, 'O youth, I am thy actions.' Can this be thy lady Beatrice?

'But sawest thou no hell? no dire punishments?

'Alas! sad scenes I witnessed, sufferers whose hell was that their darkness was amid the abodes of splendour. Amid all that glow one newly risen from earth walked shivering with cold, and there walked ever by his side a hideous hag. On her he turned and said, 'Who art thou, that ever movest beside me, thou that art monstrous beyond all that I have seen on earth?' To him she replied, 'Man, I am thy actions.'

'But who were those glorious ones thou sawest in Paradise?

'Some of their names I did indeed learn—Zoroaster, Socrates, Plato, Buddha, Confucius, Christ.

'What do I hear! knowest thou that none of these save that last holy one—whom methinks thou namest too lightly among men—were baptized? Those have these eyes sorrowfully beheld in pain through the mysterious justice of God.

'Thinkest thou, then, thy own compassion deeper than the mercy of Ormuzd? But, ah! now indeed I do remember. As I conversed with the sages I had named, they related to me this strange event. By guidance of one of their number, Virgil by name, there had come among them from the earth a most powerful magician. He bore the name of Dante. By mighty spells this being had cast them all into a sad circle which he called Limbo, over whose gate he wrote, though with eyes full of tears, 'All hope abandon, ye who enter here!' Thus were they in great sorrow and dismay. But, presently, as this strange Dante was about to pass on, so they related, he looked upon the face of one among them so pure and noble that though he had styled him 'pagan,' he could not bear to abandon him there. This was Cato of Utica. Him this Dante led to the door, and gave him liberty on condition that he would be warder of his unbaptized brethren, and by no means let any of them escape. No sooner, however, was this done than this magician beheld others who moved his reverence,—among them Trajan and Ripheus,—and overcome by an impulse of love, he opened a window in the side of Limbo, bidding them emerge into light. He then waved his christian wand to close up this aperture, and passed away, supposing that he had done so; but the limit of that magician's power had been reached, the window was but veiled, and after he had gone all these unbaptized ones passed out by that way, and reascended to the glory they had enjoyed before this Dante had brought his alien sorceries to bear upon them for a brief space.

'Can this be true? Is it indeed so that all the sages and poets of the world are now in equal rank whether or not they have been sealed as members of Christ?

'Brother, thy brow is overcast. What! can one so pure and high of nature as thou desire that the gentle Christ, whom I saw embracing the sages and prophets of other ages, should turn upon them with hatred and bind them in gloom and pain like this Dante?'

Thereupon, with a flood of tears, Dante fell at the feet of Arda Viráf, and kissed the hem of his skirt. 'Purer is thy vision, O pilgrim, than mine,' he said. 'I fear that I have but borne with me to the invisible world the small prejudices of my little Church, which hath taught me to limit the Love which I now see to be boundless. Thou who hast learned from thy Zoroaster that the meaning of God is the end of all evil, a universe climbing to its flower in joy, deign to

take the hand of thy servant and make him worthy to be thy friend,—
with thee henceforth to abandon the poor formulas which ignorance
substitutes for virtue, and ascend to the beautiful summits thou has
visited by the stairway of good thoughts, good words, good deeds.'

In 1745 Swedenborg was a student of Natural Philosophy in
London. In the April of that year his 'revelations' began amid the
smoke and toil of the great metropolis. 'I was hungry and ate with
great appetite. Towards the end of the meal I remarked a kind of
mist spread before my eyes, and I saw the floor of my room covered
with hideous reptiles, such as serpents, toads, and the like. I was
astonished, having all my wits about me, being perfectly conscious.
The darkness attained its height and then passed away. I now saw
a Man sitting in the corner of the chamber. As I had thought myself
alone, I was greatly frightened when he said to me, 'Eat not as much.'

In Swedenborg's Diary the incident is related more particularly. 'In the middle of the day, at dinner, an Angel spoke to me, and
told me not to eat too much at table. Whilst he was with me, there
plainly appeared to me a kind of vapour steaming from the pores of
my body. It was a most visible watery vapour, and fell downwards
to the ground upon the carpet, where it collected and turned into
divers vermin, which were gathered together under the table, and in
a moment went off with a pop or noise. A fiery light appeared within
them, and a sound was heard, pronouncing that all the vermin that
could possibly be generated by unseemly appetite were thus cast
out of my body, and burnt up, and that I was now cleansed from
them. Hence we may know what luxury and the like have for their

bosom contents.'

Continuing the first account Swedenborg said, 'The following night the same Man appeared to me again. I was this time not at all alarmed. The Man said, 'I am God, the Lord, the Creator, and Redeemer of the world. I have chosen thee to unfold to men the spiritual sense of the Holy Scripture. I will myself dictate to thee what thou shalt write.' The same night the world of spirits, hell and heaven, were convincingly opened to me, where I found many persons of my acquaintance of all conditions. From that day forth I gave up all worldly learning, and laboured only in spiritual things, according to what the Lord commanded me to write.'

He 'gave up all worldly learning,' shut his intellectual eyes, and sank under all the nightmares which his first vision saw burnt up as vermin. After his fiftieth year, says Emerson, he falls into jealousy of his intellect, makes war on it, and the violence is instantly avenged. But the portrait of the blinded mystic as drawn by the clear seer is too impressive an illustration to be omitted here.

'A vampyre sits in the seat of the prophet and turns with gloomy appetite to the images of pain. Indeed, a bird does not more readily weave its nest or a mole bore in the ground than this seer of the souls substructs a new hell and pit, each more abominable than the last, round every new crew of offenders. He was let down through a column that seemed of brass, but it was formed of angelic spirits, that he might descend safely amongst the unhappy, and witness the vastation of souls; and heard there, for a long continuance, their lamentations; he saw their tormentors, who increase and strain pangs to infinity; he saw the hell of the jugglers, the hell of the assassins, the hell of the lascivious; the hell of robbers, who kill and boil men; the infernal tun of the deceitful; the excrementitious hells; the hell of the revengful, whose faces resembled a round, broad cake, and their arms rotate like a wheel.... The universe, in his poem, suffers under a magnetic sleep, and only reflects the mind of the magnetiser.... Swedenborg and Behmon both failed by attaching themselves to the christian symbol, instead of to the moral sentiment, which carries innumerable christianities, humanities, divinities, in its bosom.... Another dogma, growing out of this pernicious theologic limitation, is this Inferno. Swedenborg has devils. Evil, according to old philosophers, is good in the making. That pure malignity can exist, is the extreme proposition of unbelief.... To what a painful perversion had Gothic theology arrived, that Swedenborg admitted no conversion for evil spirits! But the divine effort is never relaxed; the carrion in the sun will convert itself to grass and flowers; and man, though in brothels, or jails, or on gibbets, is on his way to all that is good and true.'

But even the Hell of Swedenborg is not free from the soft potency of our star. It is almost painful, indeed, to see its spiritual ray mingling with the fiery fever-shapes which Swedenborg meets on his way through the column of brass,—made, had he known it, not of angels but of savage scriptures. 'I gave up all worldly learning'—he says: but it did not give him up all at once. 'They (the damned) suffer ineffable torments; but it was permitted to relieve or console them with a certain degree of hope, so that they should not entirely despair. For they said they believed the torment would be eternal. They were relieved or consoled by saying that God Messiah is merciful, and that in His Word we read that 'the prisoners will be sent forth from the pit' (Zech. ix. 2). Swedenborg reports that God Messiah appeared to these spirits, and even embraced and kissed one who had been raised from 'the greatest torment.' He says, 'Punishment for the sake of punishment is the punishment of a devil,' and affirms that all punishment is 'to take away evils or to induce a faculty of doing good.' These utterances are in his Diary, and were written before he had got to the bottom of his Calvinistic column; but even in the 'Arcana Celestia' there is a gleam:—'Such is the equilibrium of all things in another life that evil punishes itself, and unless it were removed by punishments the evil spirits must necessarily be kept in some hell to eternity.'

*Reductio ad absurdum!* And yet Swedenborgians insist upon the dogma of everlasting punishments; to sustain which they appeal from Swedenborg half-sober to Swedenborg mentally drunk.

In the Library at Dresden there is a series of old pictures said to be Mexican, and which I was told had been purchased from a Jew in Vienna, containing devils mainly of serpent characters blended with those of humanity. One was a fantastic serpent with human head, sharp snoutish nose, many eyes, slight wings, and tongue lolling out. Another had a human head and reptilian tail. A third is human except for the double tongue darting out. A fourth has issuing from the back of his head a serpent whose large dragon head is swallowing a human embryo. Whatever tribe it was that originated these pictures must have had very strong impressions of the survival of the serpent in some men.

I was reminded of the picture of the serpent swallowing the human embryo while looking at the wall-pictures in Russian churches representing the conventional serpent with devils nestling at intervals along its body, as represented in our Figure (10). Professor Buslaef gave me the right archæology of this, no doubt, but the devils themselves, as I gazed, seemed to intimate another theory with their fair forms. They might have been winged angels but for their hair of flame and cruel hooks. They seemed to say, 'We were the ancient embryo-gods of the human imagination, but the serpent swallowed us. He swallowed us successively as one after another we availed ourselves of his cunning in our priesthoods; as we brought his cruel coils to crush those who dared to outgrow our cult; as we imitated his fang in the deadliness with which we bit the heel of every advancing thinker; as, when worsted in our struggle against reason, we took to the double tongue, praising with one fork the virtues which we poisoned with the other. Now we are degraded with him for ever, bound to him by these rings, labelled with the sins we have committed.'

It was by a true experience that the ancients so generally took nocturnal animals to be types of diabolism. Corresponding to them are the sleepless activities of morally unawakened men. The animal is a sleeping man. Its passions and instincts are acted out in what to rational man would be dreams. In dreams, especially when influenced by disease, a man may mentally relapse very far, and pass through kennels and styes, which are such even when somewhat decorated by shreds of the familiar human environment. The nocturnal form of intellect is cunning; the obscuration of religion is superstition; the dark shadow that falls on love turns it to lust. These wolves and bats, on which no ideal has dawned, do not prowl or flit through man in their natural forms: in the half-awake consciousness, whose starlight attends man amid his darkness, their misty outlines swell, and in the feverish unenlightened conscience they become phantasms of his animalism—werewolves, vampyres. The awakening of reason in any animal is through all the phases of cerebral and social evolution. A wise man said to his son who was afraid to enter the dark, 'Go on, child; you will never see anything worse than yourself.'

The hare-lip, which we sometimes see in the human face, is there an arrested development. Every lip is at some embryonic period a hare-lip. The development of man's visible part has gone on much longer than his intellectual and moral evolution, and abnormalities in it are rare in comparison with the number of survivals from the animal world in his temper, his faith, and his manners. Criminals are men living out their arrested moral developments. They who regard them as instigated by a devil are those whose arrest is mental. The eye of reason will deal with both all the more effectively, because with as little wrath as a surgeon feels towards the hare-lip he endeavours to humanise.

It is an impressive fact that the great and reverent mind of Spinoza, in pondering the problem of Evil and the theology which ascribed it to a Devil, was unconsciously led to anticipate by more than a century the first (modern) scientific suggestions of the principle of Evolution. In his early treatise, 'De Deo et Homine,' occurs this short but momentous chapter—

> 'DE DIABOLIS. If the Devil be an Entity contrary in all respects to God, having nothing of God in his nature, there can be nothing in common with God.
>
> 'Is he assumed to be a thinking Entity, as some will have it, who never wills and never does any good, and who sets himself in opposition to God on all occasions, he would assuredly be a very wretched being, and, could prayers do anything for him, his amendment were much to be implored.
>
> 'But let us ask whether so miserable an object could exist even for an instant; and, the question put, we see at once that it could not; for from the perfection of a thing proceeds its power of continuance: the more of the Essential and Divine a thing possesses, the more enduring it is. But how could the Devil, having no trace of perfection in him, exist at all? Add to this, that the stability or duration of a thinking thing depends entirely on its love of and union with God, and that the opposite of this state in every particular being presumed in the Devil, it is obviously impossible that there can be any such being.
>
> 'And then there is indeed no necessity to presume the existence of a Devil; for the causes of hate, envy, anger, and all such passions are readily enough to be discovered; and there is no occasion for resort to fiction to account for the evils they engender.'

In the course of his correspondence with the most learned men of his time, Spinoza was severely questioned concerning his views upon human wickedness, the disobedience of Adam, and so forth. He said—to abridge his answers—If there be any essential or positive evil in men, God is the author and continuer of that evil. But what is called evil in them is their degree of imperfection as compared with those more perfect. Adam, in the abstract, is a man eating an apple. That is not in itself an evil action. Acts condemned in man are often admired in animals,—as the jealousy of doves,—

and regarded as evidence of their perfection. Although man must restrain the forces of nature and direct them to his purposes, it is a superstition to suppose that God is angry against such forces. It is an error in man to identify his little inconveniences as obstacles to God. Let him withdraw himself from the consideration and nothing is found evil. Whatever exists, exists by reason of its perfection for its own ends,—which may or may not be those of men.

Spinoza's aphorism, 'From the perfection of a thing proceeds its power of continuance,' is the earliest modern statement of the doctrine now called 'survival of the fittest.' The notion of a Devil involves the solecism of a being surviving through its unfitness for survival.

Spinoza was Copernicus of the moral Cosmos. The great German who discovered to men that their little planet was not the one centre and single care of nature, led the human mind out of a closet and gave it a universe. But dogma still clung to the closet; where indeed each sect still remains, holding its little interest to be the aim of the solar system, and all outside it to be part of a countless host, marshalled by a Prince of Evil, whose eternal war is waged against that formidable pulpiteer whose sermon is sending dismay through pandemonium. But for rational men all that is ended, and its decline began when Spinoza warned men against looking at the moral universe from the pin-hole of their egotism. That closet-creation, whose laws were seen now acting now suspended to suit the affairs of men, disappeared, and man was led to adore the All.

It is a small thing that man can bruise the serpent's head, if its fang still carries its venom so deep in his reason as to blacken all nature with a sense of triumphant malevolence. To the eye of judicial man, instructed to decide every case without bribe of his own interest as a rival animal, the serpent's fang is one of the most perfect adaptations of means to ends in nature. Were a corresponding perfection in every human mind, the world would fulfil the mystical dream of the East, which gave one name to the serpents that bit them in the wilderness and seraphim singing round the eternal throne.

'Cursed be the Hebrew who shall either eat pork, or permit his son to be instructed in the learning of the Greeks.' So says the Talmud, with a voice transmitted from the 'kingdom of priests' (Exod. xix. 6). From the altar of 'unhewn stone' came the curse upon Art, and upon the race that represented culture raising its tool upon the rudeness of nature. That curse of the Talmud recoiled fearfully. The Jewish priesthood had their son in Peter with his vision of clean and unclean animals, and the command, 'Slay and eat!' Uninstructed is this heir of priestly Judaism 'in the learning of the Greeks,' consequently his way of converting Gentiles—the herd of swine, the *goyim*—is to convert them into christian protoplasm. 'Slay and eat,' became the cry of the elect, and their first victim was the paternal Jew who taught them that pork and Greek learning belonged to the same category.

But there was another Jewish nation not composed of priests. While the priestly kingdom is typified in Jonah announcing the destruction of Nineveh, who, because the great city still goes on, reproaches Jehovah, the nation of the poets has now its Jehovah II. who sees the humiliation of the tribal priesthood as a withered gourd compared with the arts, wealth, and human interests of a Gentile city. 'The Lord repented.' The first Gospel to the Gentiles is in that gentle thought for the uncircumcised Ninevites. But it was reached too late. When it gained expression in Christ welcoming Greeks, and seeing in stones possible 'children of Abraham;' in Paul acknowledging debt to barbarians and taking his texts from Greek altars or poets; the evolution of the ideal element in Hebrew religion had gained much. But historic combinations raised the judaisers to a throne, and all the narrowness of their priesthood was re-enacted as Christianity.

The column of brass in whose hollow centre the fine brain of Swedenborg was imprisoned is a fit similitude of the christian formula. The whole moral attitude of Christianity towards nature is represented in his first vision. The beginning of his spiritual career is announced by the evaporation of his animal nature in the form of vermin. The christian hell is present, and these animal parts are burnt up. Among those burnt-up powers of Swedenborg, one of the serpents must have been his intellect. 'From that day forth I gave up all worldly learning.'

Here we have the ideal christian caught up to his paradise even while his outward shape is visible. But what if we were all to become like that? Suppose all the animal powers and desires were to evaporate out of mankind and to be burnt up! Were that to occur to-day the effect on the morrow would be but faintly told in that which would be caused by sudden evaporations of steam from all the engines of the world. We may imagine a band of philanthropists, sorely disturbed by the number of accidents incidental to steam-locomotion, who should conspire to go at daybreak to all the engine-houses and stations in England, and, just as the engines were about to start for their work, should quench their fires, let off their steam, and break their works. That would be but a brief paralysis of the work of one country; but what would be the result if the animal nature of man and its desires, the works and trades that minister to the 'pomps and vanities,' all worldly aims and joys, should be burnt up in fires of fanaticism!

Yet to that fatal aim Christianity gave itself,—so contrary to that great heart in which was mirrored the beautiful world, its lilies and little children, and where love shed its beams on the just and the unjust! The organising principle of Christianity was that which crucified Jesus and took his tomb for corner-stone of a system modelled after what he hated. Its central purpose was to effect a divorce between the moral and the animal nature of man. One is called flesh and the other spirit; one was the child of God, the other the child of the Devil. It rent asunder that which was really one; its whole history, so long as it was in earnest, was the fanatical effort to keep asunder by violence those two halves ever seeking harmony; its history since its falsity was exposed has been the hypocrisy of professing in word what is impossible in deed.

Beside the christian vision of Swedenborg, in which the judaic priest's curse on swinish Greek learning found apotheosis, let us set the vision of a Jewish seer in whom the humanity that spared Nineveh found expression. The seer is Philo,—name rightly belonging to that pure mind in which the starry ideals of his Semitic race embraced the sensuous beauty which alone could give them life. Philo (Præm. et Pœnis, sec. 15–20) describes as the first joy of the redeemed earth the termination of the war between man and animal. That war will end, he says, 'when the wild beasts in the soul have been tamed. Then the most ferocious animals will submit to man; scorpions will lose their stings, and serpents their poison. And, in consequence of the suppression of that older war between man and beast, the war between man and man shall also end.'

Here we emerge from Swedenborg's brass column, we pass beyond Peter's sword called 'Slay-and-eat,' we leave behind the Talmud's curse on swine and learning: we rise to the clear vision of Hebrew prophecy which beheld lion and lamb lying down together, a child leading the wild forces subdued by culture.

'Why not God kill Debbil?' asked Man Friday. It is a question which not even Psychology has answered, why no Theology has yet suggested the death of the Devil in the past, or prophesied more than chains for him in the future. No doubt the need of a 'hangman's whip to haud the wretch in order' may partly account for it; but with this may have combined a cause of which it is pleasanter to think—Devils being animal passions in excess, even the ascetic recoils from their destruction, with an instinct like that which restrains rats from gnawing holes through the ship's bottom.

In Goethe's 'Faust' we read, *Doch das Antike find' ich zu lebendig.* It is a criticism on the nudity of the Greek forms that appear in the classical Walpurgis Night. But the authority is not good: it is Mephistopheles who is disgusted with sight of the human form, and he says they ought in modern fashion to be plastered over. His sentiments have prevailed at the Vatican, where the antique statues and the great pictures of Michael Angelo bear witness to the prurient prudery of the papal mind. 'Devils are our sins in perspective,' says George Herbert.

Herodotus (ii. 47) says, 'The Egyptians consider the pig to be an impure beast, and therefore if a man, in passing by a pig, should touch him only with his garments, he forthwith goes to the river and plunges in; and, in the next place, swineherds, although native Egyptians, are the only men who are not allowed to enter any of their temples.' The Egyptians, he says, do not sacrifice the goat; 'and, indeed, their painters and sculptors represent Pan with the face and legs of a goat, as the Grecians do; not that they imagine this to be his real form, for they think him like other gods; but why they represent him in this way I had rather not mention.' We need not feel the same prudery. The Egyptians rightly regarded the symbol of sexual desire, on whose healthy exercise the perpetuation of life depended, as a very different kind of animalism from that symbolised in the pig's love of refuse and garbage. Their association of the goat with Pan—the lusty vigour of nature—was the natural preface to the arts of Greece in which the wild forces were taught their first lesson—Temperance. Pan becomes musical. The vigour and vitality of human nature find in the full but not excessive proportions of Apollo, Aphrodite, Artemis, and others of the bright array, the harmony which Pan with his pipe preludes. The Greek statue is soul embodied and body ensouled.

Two men had I the happiness to know in my youth, into whose faces I looked up and saw the throne of Genius illumined by Purity. One of them, Ralph Waldo Emerson, wrote, 'If beauty, softness, and faith in female forms have their own influence, vices even, in a slight degree, are thought to improve the expression.' The other, Arthur Hugh Clough, wrote, 'What we all love is good touched up with evil.' Here are two brave flowers, of which one grew out of the thorny stem of Puritanism, the other from the monastic root of Oxford. The 'vices' which could improve the expression, even for the pure eyes of Emerson, are those which represent the struggle of human nature to exist in truth, albeit in misdirection and reaction, amid pious hypocrisies. The Oxonian scholar had seen enough of the conventionalised characterless 'good' to long for some sign of life and freedom, even though it must come as a touch of 'evil.' To the artist, nature is never seen in petrifaction; it is really as well as literally *a becoming*. The evil he sees is 'good in the making:' what others call vices are voices in the wilderness preparing the way of the highest.

'God and the Devil make the whole of Religion,' said Nicoli—speaking, perhaps, better than he knew. The culture of the world has shown that the sometime opposed realms of human interest, so personified, are equally essential. It is through this experience that the Devil has gained such ample vindication from the poets—as in Rapisardi's 'Lucifero,' a veritable 'bringer of Light,' and Cranch's 'Satan.' From the latter work ('Satan: A Libretto.' Boston: Roberts Brothers, 1874), which should be more widely known, I quote some lines. Satan says—

I symbolise the wild and deep
And unregenerated wastes of life,
Dark with transmitted tendencies of race
And blind mischance; all crude mistakes of will
And tendency unbalanced by due weight
Of favouring circumstance; all passion blown
By wandering winds; all surplusage of force
Piled up for use, but slipping from its base
Of law and order.

This is the very realm in which the poet and the artist find their pure-veined quarries, whence arise the forms transfigured in their vision.

To evoke Helena, Faust, as we have seen, must repair to the MOTHERS. But who may these be? They shine from Goethe's page in such opalescent tints one cannot transfix their sense. They seemed to me just now the primal conditions, by fulfilling which anything might be attained, without which, nothing. But now (yet perhaps the difference is not great) I see the Mothers to be the ancient healthy instincts and ideals of our race. These took shape in forms of art, whose evolution had been man's harmony with himself. Christianity, borrowing thunder of one god, hammer of another, shattered them— shattered our Mothers! And now learned travellers go about in many lands saying, 'Saw ye my beloved?' Amid cities ruined and buried we are trying to recover them, fitting limb to limb—so carefully! as if half-conscious that we are piecing together again the fragments of our own humanity.

'The Devil: *Does he Exist, and what does he Do?*' Such is the title of a recent work by Father Delaporte, Professor of Dogma in the Faculty of Bordeaux. He gives specific directions for exorcism of devils by means of holy water, the sign of the cross, and other charms. 'These measures,' says one of his American critics, 'may answer very well against the French Devil; but our American Beelzebub is a potentate that goeth not forth on any such hints.' Father Delaporte would hardly contend that the use of cross and holy water for a thousand years has been effectual in dislodging the European Beelzebub.

On the whole, I am inclined to prefer the method of the Africans of the Guinea Coast. They believe in a particularly hideous devil, but say that the only defence they require against him is a mirror. If any one will keep a mirror beside him, the Devil must see himself in it, and he at once rushes away in terror of his own ugliness.

No monster ever conjured up by imagination is more hideous than a rational being transformed to a beast. Just that is every human being who has brought his nobler powers down to be slaves of his animal nature. No eye could look upon that fearful sight unmoved. All man needs is a true mirror in which his own animalism may see itself. We cannot borrow for this purpose the arts of Greece, nor the fairy ideals of Germany, nor the emasculated saints of Christendom. These were but fragments of the man who has been created by combination of their powers, and their several ideals are broken bits that cannot reflect the whole being of man in its proportions or disproportions.

The higher nature of man, polished by culture of all his faculties, can alone be the faithful mirror before his lower. The clearness

of this mirror in the individual heart depends mainly on the civilisation and knowledge surrounding it. The discovered law turns once
plausible theories to falsehoods; a noble literature transmutes once
popular books to trash. When Art interprets the realities of nature,
when it shows how much beauty and purity our human nature is
capable of, it holds a mirror before all deformities. At a theatre in the
city of London, I witnessed the performance of an actor who, in the
course of his part, struck a child. He was complimented by a hurricane
of hisses from the crowded gallery. Had those 'gods' up there never
struck children? Possibly. Yet here each had a mirror before him and
recoiled from his worst self. A clergyman relates that, while looking at
pictures in the Bethnal Green Museum, he overheard a poor woman,
who had been gazing on a Madonna, say, 'If I had such a child as that
I believe I could be a good woman.' Who can say what even that one
glance at her life in the ideal reflector may be worth to that wanderer
amid the miseries and temptations of London!

It is not easy for those who have seen what is high and holy
to give their hearts to what is base and unholy. It is as natural for
human nature to love virtue as to love any other beauty. External
beauty is visible to all, and all desire it: the interior beauty is not
visible to superficial glances, but the admiration shown even for its
counterfeits shows how natural it is to admire virtue. But in order
that the charm of this moral beauty may be felt by human nature it
must be related to that nature—real. It must not be some childish
ideal which answers to no need of the man of to-day; not something
imported from a time and place where it had meaning and force to

others where it has none.

When dogmas surviving from the primitive world are brought to behold themselves in the mirror held up by Science, they cry out, 'That is not my face! You are caricaturing my beliefs!' This recoil of Superstition from its own ugliness is the victory of Religion. What priests bewail as disbelief is faith fleeing from its deformities. Ignorant devotion proves its need of Science by its terrors of the same, which are like those of the horse at first sight of its best friend, bearer of its burthens—the locomotive.

Religion, like every other high feature of human nature, has its animal counterpart. The animalised religion is superstition. It has various expressions,—the abjectness of one form, the ferocity of another, the cunning of a third. It is unconscious of anything higher than animalism. Its god is a very great animal preying on other animals, which are laid on his altars; or pleased when smaller animals give up their part of the earthly feast by starving their passions and senses. Under the growth of civilisation and intelligence that pious asceticism is revealed in its true form,—intensified animalism. The asceticism of one age becomes the self-indulgence of another. The two-footed animal having discovered that his god does not eat the meat left for him, eats it himself. Learning that he gets as much from his god by a wafer and a prayer, he offers these and retains the gifts, treasures, and pleasures so commuted,—these, however, being withdrawn from the direction of the higher nature by the fact of being obtained through the conditions of the lower, and dependent on their persistence. In process of time the forms and formulas of religion, detached from all reality—such as no conceivable monarch could desire—not only become senseless, but depend upon their senselessness for continuance. They refuse to come at all within the domain of reason or common-sense, and trust to mental torpor of the masses, force of habit in the aggregate, self-interest in the wealthy and powerful, bribes for thinkers and scholars.

Animalism disguised as a religion must render the human religion, able to raise passions into divine attributes of a perfect manhood, impossible so long as it continues. That a human religion can ever come by any process of evolution from a superstition which can only exist by ministry to the baser motives is a delusion. The only hope of society is that its independent minds may gain culture, and so surround this unextinct monster with mirrors that it may perish through shame at its manifold deformities. These are symbolised in the many-headed phantasm which is the subject of this work. Demon, Dragon, and Devil have long paralysed the finest powers of man, peopling nature with horrors, the heart with fears, and causing the religious sentiment itself to make actual in history the worst excesses it professed to combat in its imaginary adversaries. My largest hope is that from the dragon-guarded well where Truth is too much concealed she may emerge far enough to bring her mirror before these phantoms of fear, and with far-darting beams send them back to their caves in Chaos and ancient Night.

The battlements of the cloisters of Magdalen College, Oxford, are crowned with an array of figures representing virtues and vices, with carved allegories of teaching and learning. Under the Governor's window are the pelican feeding its young from its breast, and the lion, denoting the tenderness and the strength of a Master of youth. There follow the professions—the lawyer embracing his client, the physician with his bottle, the divine as Moses with his tables of the Law. Next are the slayers of Goliath and other mythical enemies. We come to more real, albeit monstrous, enemies; to Gluttony in ecclesiastical dress, with tongue lolling out; and low-browed Luxury without any vesture, with a wide-mouthed animal-eared face on its belly, the same tongue lolling out—as in our figures of Typhon and Kali. Drunkenness has three animal heads—one of a degraded humanity, another a sheep, the third a goose. Cruelty is a werewolf; a frog-faced Lamia represents its mixture with Lust; and other vices are represented by other monsters, chiefly dragons with griffin forms, until the last is reached—the Devil, who is just opposite the Governor's symbols across the quadrangle.

So was represented, some centuries ago, the conflict of Ormuzd and Ahriman, for the young soldiers who enlisted at Oxford for that struggle. A certain amount of fancy has entered into the execution of the figures; but, if this be carefully detached, the history which I have attempted to tell in these volumes may be generally traced in the Magdalen statues. Each represents some phase in the advance of the world, when, under new emergencies, earlier symbols were modified, recombined, and presently replaced by new shapes. It was found inadequate to keep the scholar throwing stones at the mummy of Goliath when by his side was living Gluttony in religious garb. The scriptural symbols are gradually mixed with those of Greek and German mythology, and by such contact with nature are able to generate forms, whose lolling tongues, wide mouths, and other expressions, represent with some realism the physiognomies of brutality let loose through admission to human shape and power.

It may be that, when they were set up, the young Oxonian passed shuddering these terrible forms, dreaded these werewolves and succubæ, and dreamed of going forth to impale dragons. But now the sculptures excite only laughter or curiosity, when they are not passed by without notice. Yet the old conflict between Light and Darkness has not ceased. The ancient forms of it pass away; they become grotesque. Such was necessarily the case where the excessive mythological and fanciful elements introduced at one period fall upon another period when they hide the meaning. Their obscurity, even for antiquarians, marks how far away from those cold battle-fields the struggle they symbolised has passed. But it ceases not. Some scholars who listen to the sweet vespers of Magdalen may think the conflict over; if so, even poor brother Moody may enter the true kingdom before them; for, when preaching in Baltimore last September, he said, 'Men are possessed of devils just as much now as they ever were. The devil of rum is as great as any that ever lived. Why cannot this one and all others be cast out? Because there is sin in the christian camp.'

The picture which closes this volume has been made for me by the artist Hennessey, to record an incident which occurred at the door of Nôtre Dame in Paris last summer. I had been examining an ugly devil there treading down human forms into hell; but a dear friend looked higher, and saw a bird brooding over its young on a nest supported by that same horrible head.

So, above the symbols of wrath in nature, Love still interweaves heavenly tints with the mystery of life; beside the horns of pain prepares melodies.

Even so, also, over the animalism which deforms man, rises the animal perfection which shames that; here ascending above the reign of violence by a feather's force, and securing to that little creature a tenderness that could best express the heart of a Christ, when it would gather humanity under his wings.

This same little scene at the cathedral door came before me again as I saw the Oxonian youth, with their morning-faces, passing so heedlessly those ancient sculptures at Magdalen. Over every happy heart the same old love was brooding, in each nestling faculties were trying to gain their wings. To what will they aspire, those students moving so light-hearted amid the dead dragons and satans of an extinct world? Do they think there are no more dragons to be slain? Know they that saying, 'He descended into hell;' and that, from Orpheus and Herakles to Mohammed and Swedenborg, this is the burthen felt by those who would be saviours of men?

It is not only loving birds that build their nests and rear their young over the horns of forgotten fears, but, alas! the Harpies too! These, which Dante saw nestling in still plants—once men who had wronged themselves—rear successors above the aspirations that have ended in 'nothing but leaves.' The sculptures of Magdalen are incomplete. There is a vacant side to the quadrangle, which, it is to be feared, awaits the truer teaching that would fill it up with the real dragons which no youth could heedlessly pass. Who can carve there the wrongs that await their powers of redress? Who can set before them, with all its baseness, the true emblem of pious fraud? When will they see in any stone mirror the real shape of a double-tongued Culture—one fork intoning litanies, another whispering contempt of them? The werewolves of scholarly selfishness, the Lamias of christian casuistry, the subtle intelligence that is fed by sages and heroes, but turns them to dust, nay, to venom, because it dares not be human, still crawls—these are yet to be revealed in all their horrors. Then will the old cry, Sursum Corda, sound over the ancient symbols whereon scholars waste their strength, by which they are conquered; and wings of courage shall bear them with their arrows of light to rescue from Superstition the holy places of Humanity.

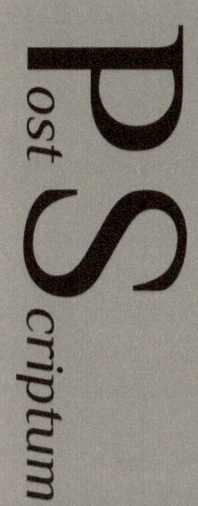

**PS**

*ost*
*criptum*

Conway,
a prolific
author and
abolitionist
radical

## About Moncure Daniel Conway

## VAMzzz Publishing

# Moncure Daniel Conway

Moncure Daniel Conway (Stafford County, March 17, 1832 – Paris, November 15, 1907) was an American writer, abolitionist, Methodist, Unitarian and Freethought minister. The historian John d'Entremont described him as *the most thoroughgoing white male radical produced by the antebellum South.* Conway descended from patriotic and patrician families of Virginia and Maryland. He spent most of the second half of his life abroad in England and France, and led freethinkers in London's South Place Chapel. He was a prolific author who published over 70 volumes. Many of his works concern social issues, and several focus on abolitionism, the availability of education for everyone, biographies and religious topics. *Solomon and Solomonic Literature* (1899), *Demonology and Devil Lore part 1 and 2* (1879) and *The Natural History of the Devil* (1859) deal with occult subjects, be it in a historical, analytical and philosophical direction.

Conway was born in Falmouth, Stafford County, Virginia, to parents descended from the First Families of Virginia. His father, Walter Peyton Conway was a wealthy slave-holding gentleman farmer, county judge and state representative. Conway's mother, Margaret Stone, was the granddaughter of Thomas Stone of Maryland (a signer of the Declaration of Independence). In addition to running the household, she also practiced homoeopathy, she had learned from her father. After attending the Fredericksburg Classical and Mathematical Academy, Conway followed his older brother to Methodist-affiliated Dickinson College in Carlisle, Pennsylvania, graduating in 1849. During his time at Dickinson, Conway helped to found the college's first student publication and came under the influence of Professor John McClintock, which caused him to embrace Methodism as well as an anti-slavery position. He first openly allied himself with abolitionists in July 1854 in the aftermath of the capture in Boston, of fugitive slave Anthony Burns. During the American Civil War (1861–1865), Conway accompanied thirty-one of his father's slaves, all of whom had escaped to Washington, D.C., on a harrowing train ride to freedom in southwestern Ohio. There he established what came to be known as the Conway Colony.

In June 1858, he married a feminist, Ellen Davis Dana, a well-schooled daughter of a prominent businessman, at the First Unitarian Church of Cincinnati, where he became minister in 1856. Ellen was also a fellow Unitarian and abolitionist. The couple had three sons (two of whom survived childhood) and a daughter during their long marriage, which ended with her death from cancer in 1898. In 1859 Conway abandoned Unitarianism for free thought, telling his ▶

'Conway married a feminist, Ellen Davis Dana, a well-schooled daughter of a prominent businessman.'

'Conway began to question the veracity of Biblical accounts of miracles, the divinity of Jesus, and the authority of the Bible.'

▶ congregation of the First Unitarian Church of Cincinnati, Ohio, that he no longer believed in miracles or Christ's divinity. A third of its members promptly left the church, but Conway's new "Free Church" survived. His liberal views were published in *Dial,* a short-lived literary and journalistic monthly (1860).

Conway moved to Cincinnati in 1862. There he was particularly impressed with several German intellectuals in the city, especially John B. Stallo and August Willich, the latter of whom sharpened Conway's perception of the problems faced by labour in the industrializing city. Under the influence of German free thinkers, Conway's theology moved further to the left as he studied David Frederich Strauss's *Das Leben Jesus* and began to question the veracity of Biblical accounts of miracles, the divinity of Jesus, and the authority of the Bible.

During the occupation before the devastating Battle of Fredericksburg, Conway also returned home to Falmouth in 1862, and learned that his family's house had been saved from demolition because of its connection with him, although it was commandeered for use as a hospital for injured soldiers. That year, Conway published another powerful plea for emancipation, *The Golden Hour.* After spending more and more time away from his church advancing the ▶

▶ abolitionist cause, and growing dissatisfied with the theological, liturgical, and social conservatism of mainstream Unitarianism, Conway left that denomination's ministry, after which he maintained an uneasy and uncertain relationship with Unitarianism in America and subsequently in England until he and Ellen made a clean break.

In 1863, while on a speaking tour in England, Conway's antislavery passion—not to mention his frustration with Lincoln's sometimes overly cautious approach to emancipation—brought him into trouble with his own government, when he attempted to bargain with the Confederate envoy to

*Conway, with family at their London home (circa 1890).*

Britain, James Murray Mason. Conway, who claimed falsely to speak for the abolition movement, offered to support disunion if the Confederates agreed to release their slaves. It was a proposal that did not come with the approval of the Lincoln administration, or anyone else for that matter. Confederates took pleasure in Conway's misstep, while abolitionists back home, most of whom had become thoroughgoing wartime nationalists, howled in protest. Conway, fearful of having his passport revoked, meekly apologized to U.S. secretary of state William H. Seward. In the meantime, Conway was being drafted to serve in the army of the Union (likely the work of a political foe) but paid someone to take his place.

Rather than go back to America, where Conway no longer felt welcome as a suspected traitor to his childhood Virginia friends and neighbours, Conway travelled to Italy. There he reunited with his wife and children in Venice before moving back to London. There in 1864 he became minister of the South Place Chapel (serving in 1864–65 and 1893–97) as well as leader of the then named South Place Religious Society in Finsbury, London. Women were allowed to preach at South Place Chapel; among them the famous theosophist Annie Besant, whom Mrs. Conway had befriended. After his son Emerson died in 1864, Conway abandoned theism. His thinking continued to move ▶

'Conway's antislavery passion—not to mention his frustration with Lincoln's sometimes overly cautious approach to emancipation—brought him into trouble with his own government.'

▶  from Emersonian transcendentalism toward a more humanistic Freethought. Conway continued writing and publishing, including articles in both British and American magazines. In 1868 Conway was one of four speakers at the first open public meeting in support of women's suffrage in Great Britain. His many literary and intellectual friends included Charles Dickens, Robert Browning, Thomas Carlyle, Charles Lyell, and Charles Darwin. He also served as a war correspondent during the Franco-Prussian War of 1870–71. Conway published biographies of Edmund Randolph, Nathaniel Hawthorne and Thomas Paine, as well as acted as the American agent for Robert Browning and the London literary agent for Walt Whitman, Mark Twain, Louisa May Alcott, and Elizabeth Cady Stanton. Conway attended the salon of radicals Peter and Clementia Taylor at Aubrey House in Campden Hill, West London. He also was a member of Clementia's "Pen and Pencil Club", at which young writers and artists read and exhibited their works. Conway even moved to Notting Hill to be near the Taylors at Aubrey House.

In the 1870s and 1880s Conway occasionally returned to the United States, where he reconciled with his Virginia family in 1875. In 1897 Conway and his now terminally-ill wife Ellen returned from London to New York City to fulfil Ellen's wish of dying on  ▶

*Ellen Dana Conway*

▶ American soil; she passed away on Christmas Day. Their son Dana also died that year. As the Spanish–American War approached, Conway turned toward pacifism and became estranged with his countrymen, moving to France to devote much of the remainder of his life to the peace movement and composition. However, he occasionally returned to Fredericksburg, which had come to admire his cultural accomplishments.

Conway also travelled to India, about which he wrote shortly before his death in his Parisian apartment on November 15, 1907. His body was ultimately returned to Westchester County, New York, for burial in the Kensico cemetery beside his wife Ellen, and their children (only his son Eustace survived both parents, dying in 1937). Conway Hall in Holborn, London is named in his honour. In 2004, Virginia Governor Mark R. Warner proclaimed Conway the only descendant of a Founding Father of the nation to physically lead slaves to freedom. Both Ohio and Virginia have erected historical markers in his honour, and Conway's childhood home was designated a U.S. and Virginia landmark. ■

# Other publications:

- *Free Schools in Virginia: A Plea for Education, Virtue and Thrift, vs. Ignorance, Vice and Poverty (1850)*
- *A Discourse on the Life and Character of the Hon. William Cranch, LL.D., Late Chief Justice of the District of Columbia (1855)*
- *The Old and the New: A Sermon Containing the History of the First Unitarian Church in Washington City (1855)*
- *Pharisaism and Fasting (1855)*
- *The True and the False in Prevalent Theories of Divine Dispensations (1855)*
- *The One Path; or, The Duties of North and South (1856)*
- *Spiritual Liberty (1856)*
- *Virtue vs. Defeat (1856)*
- *The Theater: A Discourse Delivered in the Unitarian Church (1857)*
- *Tracts for Today (1858)*
- *East and West: An Inaugural Discourse Delivered in the First Congregational Church, Cincinnati, O. (1859)*
- *The Natural History of the Devil (1859)*
- *Thomas Paine: A Celebration (1860)*
- *The Rejected Stone; or, Insurrection vs. Resurrection in America, by a Native of Virginia (1861)*
- *The Golden Hour (1862)*
- *Testimonies Concerning Slavery (1864)*
- *The Earthward Pilgrimage (1874)*
- *Mazzini: A Discourse Given at South Place Chapel, Finsbury (1872)*

'His many literary and intellectual friends included Charles Dickens, Robert Browning, Thomas Carlyle, Charles Lyell, and Charles Darwin.'

- *The Parting of the Ways: A Study on the Lives of Sterling and Maurice (1872)*
- *Republican Superstitions as Illustrated in the Political History of America (1872)*
- *In Memoriam: A Memorial Discourse in Honor of John Stuart Mill (1873)*
- *Consequences (1875)*
- *The First Love Again: A Discourse Delivered in the Church of the Redeemer, Cincinnati, Ohio, November 28, 1875, on the Occasion of the Reunion of the Two Societies, Which Had Divided Fifteen Years Previously, Chiefly on the Issue of Supernaturalism (1875)*
- *Intellectual Suicide (1875)*
- *Revivalism (1875)*
- *Human Sacrifices in England (1876)*
- *Christianity (1876)*
- *Our Cause and Its Claims upon Us: A Discourse Given at the Athenaeum, Camden Road, June 11th, 1876 (1876)*
- *The Religion of Children: A Discourse, with Readings and Meditation (1877)*
- *Alcestis in England: A Discourse Given at South Place Chapel (1877)*
- *Idols and Ideals, with an Essay on Christianity (1877)*
- *Unbelief: Its Nature, Cause, and Cure (1877)*
- *Entering Society: A Discourse by Moncure D. Conway, M.A., Delivered at South Place Chapel (1877)*
- *Atheism: A Spectre (1878)*
- *Liberty and Morality: A Discourse Given at South Place Chapel, Finsbury (1878)*
- *The Peril of War: A Discourse Delivered at*

*South Place Chapel, March 31st, 1878 (1878)*
- *Demonology and Devil-Lore (two volumes, 1879)*
- *The Criminal's Ascension: A Discourse Given March 2nd, 1879*
- *A Last Word, Spoken at the Athenaeum on the Closing of Our Services There, June 27th, 1880*
- *A Necklace of Stories (1880)*
- *What is the Religion of Humanity?: A Discourse at South Place Chapel, May 16th, 1880*
- *The Rising Generation: A Discourse before the South Place Society, June 27th, 1880*
- *Laureate Despair: A Discourse Given at South Place Chapel, December 11th, 1881*
- *Thomas Carlyle (1881)*
- *The Wandering Jew (1881)*
- *Travels in South Kensington, with Notes on Decorative Art and Architecture in England (1882)*
- *Emerson at Home and Abroad (1883)*
- *Lessons for the Day (two volumes, 1882, 1883).*
- *Emerson and His Views of Nature: An Address before the Royal Institution of Great Britain (1883)*
- *Farewell Discourses (1884)*
- *Pine and Palm (two volumes, 1887)*
- *Unitarianism and Its Grandchildren (1887)*
- *Omitted Chapters of History Disclosed in the Life and Papers of Edmund Randolph (1888)*
- *George Washington and Mount Vernon (1889)*

'Many of his works concern social issues, and several focus on abolitionism, the availability of education for everyone, biographies and religious topics.'

- *George Washington's Rules of Civility, Traced to Their Sources and Restored (1890)*
- *Life of Nathaniel Hawthorne (1890)*
- *Prisons of Air (1891)*
- *Barons of the Potomack and Rappahannock (1892)*
- *The Life of Thomas Paine (two volumes, 1892)*
- *Centenary History of the South Place Society (1894)*
- *Solomon and Solomonic Literature (1899)*
- *Thomas Paine et la Revolution dans les Deux Mondes (1900)*
- *Autobiography, Memories and Experiences of Moncure Daniel Conway, with Two Portraits (two volumes, 1904)*
- *My Pilgrimage to the Wise Men of the East (1906)*
- *Lessons for the Day (1907)*
- *Moncure D. Conway: Addresses and Reprints, 1850–1907 (1909)* ■

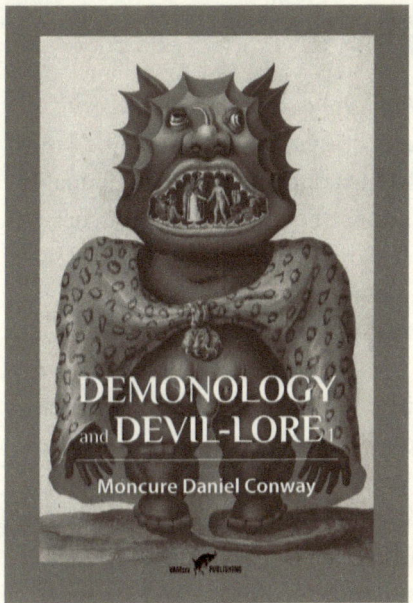

Recommended

*Demonology
and Devil-Lore
Volume 1*
Author:
Moncure Daniel Conway
490 pages, paperback
ISBN 978-94-92355-15-7

*Demonology and Devil Lore 1 & 2* were both published in 1897. Within the demonology scope, this rare and mostly forgotten, almost 1000 pages thick masterpiece, remains unsurpassed in quality and completeness. Even in the 21st century the works offer fascinating missing links for both the academic and student of occult traditions.

Author Moncure Daniel Conway divides Volume 1 in three parts and deals mainly with the evolution and thematic classification of ex-gods, demons and nature creatures. Part 1 offers information about the dawn of dualism, the political degradation of gods into demons due to theological animosity, and the difference between demon and devil. Part 2 examines the demonic realm, according to themes like hunger, heat, cold, the Elements, animals, darkness, dogs, storm, Walpurgis night, cats etc.. Part 3 is focussed extensively on the serpent, dragon, worm, the decline and generalization of demons, and we also encounter the werewolf and basilisk, among much more.

VAMzzz Publishing

# Paper books

*VAMzzz Publishing* is located in the very centre of old Amsterdam, in The Netherlands. Our publishing company creates high quality revised editions of five star occult, witchcraft, Gothic and esoteric classics, mostly written in the Fin de siècle-period and early 20th century.

As a publisher, we deeply respect the writer of any book we choose, so we join our forces (top level graphic design & thirty years of occult studies) to produce enchanting volumes which maximize the reading pleasure and inform, often with extra added information. In contrast to the current trend of digital screen addiction, we think, this variety of literature needs to be presented on paper. *No e-books, but real books!*

Apart from republications of valuable but forgotten books, we are also in the preparation of new publications on topics such as self-healing, magic, new astrology and more.

Previews of all books including a complete table of contents can be viewed on www.vamzzz.com. More books will be added to the list. *VAMzzz Publishing* strives to publish new volumes every month. Please visit our website regularly for the latest updates.

**VAMzzz Publishing**
P.O. Box 3340
1001 AC Amsterdam
The Netherlands
contactvamzzz@gmail.com
www.vamzzz.com

**Amazons** - *Two publications in one book -*
*I. The Amazons* by Guy Cadogan Rothery
*II. Religious Cults Associated With the Amazons*
    by Florence Mary Bennett
328 pages, Paperback, ISBN 9789492355089

Contents I: The Amazons of Antiquity – Amazons
in Far Asia – Modern Amazons of the Caucasus –
Amazons of Europe – Amazons of Africa – Amazons of
America – The Amazon Stones.
Contents II: The Amazons in Greek legend – The Great
Mother – Ephesian Artemis – Artemis Astrateia and
Apollo Amazonius – Ares.


**Ophiolatreia**
*Rites and Mysteries of Serpent Worship*
by Hargrave Jennings
186 pages, Paperback, ISBN 9789492355126

An account of the rites and mysteries connected with
the origin, rise and development of serpent worship in
various parts of the world, enriched with interesting
traditions, and a full description of the celebrated
serpent mounds & temples, the whole forming an
exposition of one of the phases of phallic, or sex
worship.


**Voodoos and Obeahs**
*Phases of West India Witchcraft*
by Joseph J. Williams
374 pages, Paperback, ISBN 9789492355119

This work goes into great depth concerning the New
World-African connection and is highly recommended if
you want a deep understanding of the dramatic historical
background of Haitian and Jamaican magic and witchcraft,
and the profound influence of imperialism, slavery and
racism on its development. Williams includes numerous
quotations from rare documents and books on the topic.

### Taboo, Magic, Spirits
*A study of primitive elements in Roman religion*
by Eli Edward Burriss
200 pages, Paperback, ISBN 9789492355034

In Ancient Rome Mana was the term used for a mysterious, magical medium, which could be helpful or harmful (Taboo). Just like the Chinese qi, it could empower the positive and the negative. Contents: Mana, Magic and Animism – Positive and Negative Mana (Taboo) – Miscellaneous Taboos – Magic Acts: The General Principles – Removing Evils by - Magic Acts – Incantation and Prayer– Naturalism and Animism.

### Chaldean Magic
*It's Origin and Development*
by François Lenormant
454 pages, Paperback, ISBN 9789492355027

The essentials of magic in Chaldea are presented inside a context of comparison or contrast to Egyptian, Median, Turanian, Finno-Tartarian and Akkadian magic, mythologies, religion and speech. Interesting is the Chaldean demonology, with its incubus, succubus, vampire, nightmare and many Elemental spirits, most of them coalesced with the primal powers of nature.

### Unicorn
*A mythological investigation*
by Robert Brown Jr.
124 pages, Paperback, ISBN 9789492355072

Brown Jr. believes the unicorn to be a lunar symbol, and draws on mythology from a wide range of sources all over the world to build his case. The author discusses the heraldic use of the unicorn, relates the creature to ancient goddesses like Astarte, Hecate en the Gorgon Medusa, and provides the reader with lost esoteric Moon-lore.

### Là-Bas
*A Journey into the Self*
by Joris-Karl Huysmans
378 pages, Paperback, ISBN 9789492355058

The plot of *Là-Bas* concerns the novelist Durtal, who is disgusted by the emptiness and vulgarity of the modern world. He seeks relief by turning to the study of the Middle Ages. Through his contacts in Paris, Durtal discovers that Satanism is not a thing of the past but alive and kicking in turn of the century France. The novel culminates with a description of a black mass.

### Devil-worship in France
*Or The Question of Lucifer*
by Arthur Edward Waite
240 pages, Paperback, ISBN 9789492355065

In *Devil-Worship in France,* Waite attempts to discern what is genuine from what is fake in the evidence of 19th century Satanism. To get the answers he spends a great deal of time investigating the French Masonic echelon, debunking a "conspiracy of falsehood" and determining what should be understood by Satanism and what not. Huysmans' diabolical novel *Là-Bas* (1891) inspired Waite to write this sceptical analysis.

### Testament of Solomon
*A First Century AD Grimoire*
76 pages, Paperback, ISBN 9789492355041

A first century AD grimoire, and therefore the oldest, and least known, of all grimoires (magical instruction books) in the occult tradition. The book describes health inflicting demons of zodiacal decans, summoned by King Solomon, and how he controlled them to use their forces to build his temple and more. Translated by F. C. Conybeare, appeared first in the *Jewish Quarterly Review* of October, 1898.

**Fairy Mythology** *(Volume 1)*
*Romance and Superstition of Various Countries 1*
by Thomas Keightley
404 pages, Paperback, ISBN 9789492355096

**Fairy Mythology** *(Volume 2)*
*Romance and Superstition of Various Countries 2*
by Thomas Keightley
404 pages, Paperback, ISBN 9789492355102

The term Fairy covers all kinds of nature spirits, not just the tiny sugar sweet creatures hovering around flowers. A unique and impressive book on this subject, published in a revised 2 volume-edition. No wiccan or pagan can afford to leave these books unopened. About Elves, Dwarfs, Kobolds, Trolls, Changelings, Meremaids, Nisses, Fairies, Brownies, Puck and other Elemental spirits all over the world.

**Etruscan Magic & Occult Remedies**
*(Two volumes in one book)*
by Charles Godfrey Leland
628 pages, Paperback, ISBN 9789492355003

Part One of the book offers complete and detailed insight in the Etruscan and Roman rooted pantheon of the Tuscan Streghe (witches). Part Two describes many of their spells, incantations, sorcery and several lost divination methods. Much information in this book, Leland received first hand from the Tuscan witches Maddalena and Marietta.

***Aradia***
*Gospel of the Witches*
by Charles Godfrey Leland
174 pages, Paperback, ISBN 9789492355010

This wonderful book describes the creation according to
Italian witch-lore. We also read about the witch-meeting
or sabbath (treguenda) and the book contains many
original magical recipes, like spells for love and good
fortune. Diana is further connected to the Moon and
the fairy world.